S0-FDH-601

# Life and Times in Nazi Germany

*Edited by Lisa Pine*

Bloomsbury Academic
An imprint of Bloomsbury Publishing Plc

B L O O M S B U R Y
LONDON · OXFORD · NEW YORK · NEW DELHI · SYDNEY

**Bloomsbury Academic**

An imprint of Bloomsbury Publishing Plc

| | |
|---|---|
| 50 Bedford Square | 1385 Broadway |
| London | New York |
| WC1B 3DP | NY 10018 |
| UK | USA |

**www.bloomsbury.com**

**BLOOMSBURY and the Diana logo are trademarks of Bloomsbury Publishing Plc**

First published 2016

© Lisa Pine and Contributors, 2016

All rights reserved. No part of this publication may be reproduced or transmitted in any form or by any means, electronic or mechanical, including photocopying, recording, or any information storage or retrieval system, without prior permission in writing from the publishers.

No responsibility for loss caused to any individual or organization acting on or refraining from action as a result of the material in this publication can be accepted by Bloomsbury or the authors.

**British Library Cataloguing-in-Publication Data**
A catalogue record for this book is available from the British Library.

ISBN: HB: 978-1-4742-1793-4
PB: 978-1-4742-1792-7
ePDF: 978-1-4742-1794-1
ePub: 978-1-4742-1795-8

**Library of Congress Cataloging-in-Publication Data**
A catalog record for this book is available from the Library of Congress.

Typeset by Integra Software Services Pvt. Ltd.
Printed and bound in India

# CONTENTS

# LIST OF ILLUSTRATIONS

# Chapter 9

# Chapter 10

# NOTES ON CONTRIBUTORS

**Joan L. Clinefelter** is Professor of History at the University of Northern Colorado, United States, where she teaches a wide variety of courses in European and German history. She is the author of *Artists for the Reich: Culture and Race from Weimar to Nazi Germany* (2005). While the Third Reich remains an abiding interest, her current research focuses on the Cold War radio station RIAS Berlin and its role in shaping a useable post-war German identity.

**Geoffrey Cocks** is Professor of History at Albion College in Michigan, United States. His research interests include Nazi Germany, the Second World War, the history of health and illness and the cinema of Stanley Kubrick. He is the author of *Psychotherapy in the Third Reich: The Goering Institute* (1985, 1997), *The Wolf at the Door: Stanley Kubrick, History, and the Holocaust* (2004) and *The State of Health: Illness in Nazi Germany* (2012).

**Irene Guenther** is Professor of Modern European and American History in The Honors College at the University of Houston, United States. Her book, *Nazi 'Chic'? Fashioning Women in the Third Reich* (2004), was awarded the Sierra Prize for 'Best History Book by a Female Historian' by the Western Association of Women Historians and the Millia Davenport Award for 'Best Book in Fashion History' by the Costume Society of America. Additionally, she is the recipient of several teaching excellence awards. She is the co-curator of *Postcards from the Trenches: Germans and Americans Visualize the Great War*, an exhibition commemorating the centennial of the First World War.

**David Imhoof** is Associate Professor of History at Susquehanna University in Pennsylvania, United States. His book, *Becoming a Nazi Town: Culture and Politics in Göttingen between the World Wars*, was published in 2013. He has also published on sports, film and sharpshooting in interwar Germany. A collection he is co-editing on the total work of art in modern Germany will appear in 2016. He serves as the Co-Director of the Music and Sound Studies Network for the German Studies Association and is co-editing a forthcoming edition of *Colloquia Germanica* on sound studies.

**Jonathan Lewy** holds a PhD from the Hebrew University of Jerusalem in Israel in 2011 and has written several articles and a book on drugs in Germany and the United States.

**Joe Perry** is Associate Professor of Modern German/European History at Georgia State University in Atlanta, United States. He is the author of *Christmas in Germany: A Cultural History* (2010). His scholarly interests focus on celebration and festivity, consumer culture, the mass media and identity construction. His current research projects explore the history of electronic dance music and the Berlin Love Parade and the emergence of television as a mass medium in post-war West Germany.

**Lisa Pine** is Reader in History at London South Bank University in the UK. Her research interests include the social history of Nazi Germany and the Holocaust. She is the author of *Education in Nazi Germany* (2010), *Hitler's 'National Community': Society and Culture in Nazi Germany* (2007) and *Nazi Family Policy, 1933–1945* (1997). She teaches courses on modern and contemporary history.

**Christopher J. Probst** teaches courses in modern European history, Nazi Germany and the Holocaust at Washington University in St. Louis and Maryville University (both in the United States). He is the author of *Demonizing the Jews: Luther and the Protestant Church in Nazi Germany* (2012). His research focuses on Protestant views of Jews and Judaism in twentieth-century Germany. In 2008, he was a Charles H. Revson Foundation Fellow at the Center for Advanced Holocaust Studies of the United States Holocaust Memorial Museum.

**Nancy Reagin** holds a PhD in History from Johns Hopkins University. She is currently Professor of History and chairs the Department of Women's and Gender Studies at Pace University in New York, the United States. She is the author of *Sweeping the German Nation: Domesticity and National Identity in Germany, 1870–1945* (2008) and *A German Women's Movement: Class and Gender in Hanover, 1880–1933* (1995) and has published numerous articles on modern German history, with a focus on women's history, nationalism and national identities and the development of European consumer cultures.

**Kristin Semmens** is Assistant Teaching Professor of Modern European and German History at the University of Victoria, Canada. She is the author of *Seeing Hitler's Germany: Tourism in the Third Reich* (2005). She has also written articles and given conference papers on German tourism history across the twentieth century, with a special focus on Berlin.

**Kevin P. Spicer, CSC** is the James J. Kenneally Distinguished Professor of History at Stonehill College, United States. He is the author of *Hitler's Priests: Catholic Clergy and National Socialism* (2008) and *Resisting the Third Reich: The Catholic Clergy in Hitler's Berlin* (2004) and the editor of *Antisemitism, Christian Ambivalence, and the Holocaust* (2007). He has also published articles in a variety of journals including *Church History, Historisches Jahrbuch* and *Holocaust and Genocide Studies*. Spicer is a board member of the Council of Centres on Jewish-Christian Relations (CCJR) and the co-editor of its journal *Studies in Christian-Jewish Relations*.

# ACKNOWLEDGEMENTS

I would like to thank my research assistant, Anthony Knight, for his help in identifying the contributors to this book. I am very grateful to Marek Jaros, the photograph archivist at the Wiener Library in London, for his assistance and advice in the selection of the cover image. My thanks are also due to Jason Crouthamel and Eric Kurlander for their insightful comments on the book proposal, which helped me to refine my first thoughts into the book this now is, and to Richard Overy and Jason Crouthamel (again) for their careful reading of the manuscript. I am extremely grateful for their thoughts and suggestions. I would especially like to thank Rhodri Mogford, our editor, for his enthusiasm for this project and for his help and encouragement from start to finish.

Lisa Pine

# GLOSSARY OF ABBREVIATIONS AND TERMS

| | |
|---|---|
| *Bekennende Kirche* | Confessing Church |
| *Blut und Boden* | blood and soil |
| *Bund deutscher Mädel* (BDM) | League of German Girls |
| *Deutsche Arbeitsfront* (DAF) | German Labour Front |
| *Deutschen Christen* | German Christians |
| *Deutsches Frauenwerk* (DFW) | German Women's Bureau |
| *Führer* | leader |
| *Gestapo* | secret state police |
| *Gleichschaltung* | coordination |
| *Heimat* | home, homeland |
| *Herrenvolk* | master race |
| *Hitler Jugend* (HJ) | Hitler Youth |
| *Kaiserreich* | Second Empire (1871–1918) |
| *Kirchenkampf* | church struggle |
| *Kraft durch Freude* (KdF) | Strength Through Joy |
| *Kriegsweihnachten* | War Christmas |
| *Kristallnacht* | Night of the Broken Glass |
| *Kulturkampf* | culture struggle |
| *Luftwaffe* | air force |
| NSDAP | National Socialist German Workers' Party |
| *NS-Frauenschaft* (NSF) | National Socialist Women's League |

| | |
|---|---|
| *NS-Lehrerbund* (NSLB) | National Socialist Teachers' League |
| *NS-Volkswohlfahrt* (NSV) | National Socialist People's Welfare |
| *Reichsnährstand* | Reich Food Corporation |
| *Schutzstaffeln* (SS) | Protection Squads (Nazi elite formation headed by Heinrich Himmler) |
| *Sicherheitsdienst* (SD) | Security Service |
| *Sturmabteilungen* (SA) | stormtroopers |
| *Tischkultur* | table culture |
| *Trachtenkleidung* | folk costume |
| *Trümmerfrau* | rubble woman |
| *Volk* | nation or people |
| *völkisch* | nationalist |
| *Volksgemeinschaft* | national community |
| *Volksgenossen* | national comrade |
| *Volksweihnachten* | People's Christmas |
| *Wehrmacht* | armed forces |
| *Winterhilfswerk* | Winter Relief Agency |

# Introduction

## *Lisa Pine*

The Nazi era has been the subject of a vast amount of historical research and debate. An examination of the impact of National Socialism upon German society sheds light on both the nature and impact of the Nazi dictatorship as a whole and the social setting in which its policies were executed. Yehuda Bauer has noted that 'National Socialist Germany was ruled by a criminal, murderous regime, and the day-to-day life of its citizens was coloured by this'.[1] Daily life – even the most trivial parts of it – took place within this context. The historiography of the Third Reich is vast, with studies of many different aspects of the politics of National Socialism, eugenics and racial hygiene, the war and the Holocaust, as well as the various Nazi organisations, to name but a few. Indeed, the social history of the Third Reich, the 'history of everyday life', has a large secondary literature. At first, some concerns were raised about this type of history and claims made that it was in danger of 'trivialising' the subject, but this is not the intention of historians working in this area – on the contrary, social history applies the use of different perspectives and themes in order to more fully understand the complex nature of life under National Socialism. The first major work on Nazi social history in English was Richard Grunberger's *A Social History of the Third Reich*, which covers a wide range of subjects including music and literature, Nazi speech and humour.[2] The historiography has grown extensively since then to include more detailed analyses of specific issues, such as class and gender.[3] There are also newer works on everyday life in the Third Reich.[4] In addition, the historiography of the Nazi era has burgeoned with the publication of many important monographs that deal with specific aspects of social and cultural life in Nazi Germany. The secondary literature on this subject continues to grow, as readers' interest and fascination in it remain undiminished.

This book adds significantly to this literature in a specific and particular way. It seeks to explore the variety and complexity of life in Nazi Germany through a compilation of thematic chapters that examine the extent to which a regime with totalitarian aims and ambitions succeeded in permeating different areas of social and cultural life in Germany. The individual chapters each deal with a different aspect of life in Germany in the Nazi era, assessing the extent of intervention of the Party and regime into them. They establish cases and areas of life in which the regime interposed itself heavily, as well as those in which National Socialism did not intrude and permeate as much. The authors illuminate aspects of life under Nazi rule that are less well known and examine the contradictions and paradoxes that characterised daily life in Nazi Germany. An analysis of how people lived their everyday lives extends our knowledge of the Nazi era and enhances our understanding of it.

Even at the outset, the response of the German population to the new National Socialist government in 1933 was mixed. Peter Fritzsche has commented on 'the sheer number of civilian well-wishers' who gathered to greet the newly appointed Chancellor, Adolf Hitler, on 30 January 1933, noting that 'nearly one million Berliners took part in this extraordinary demonstration of allegiance' to the NSDAP.[5] On 1 May 1933, the new government put on a May Day celebration in the German capital, complete with beer, sausages, an air show and fireworks – 'all the trappings of a fun-filled spring holiday' – although the day was designed to show a sense of national purpose and to tie German workers to the new state, as well as to provide family entertainment.[6] As the NSDAP took over the buildings of the German trade union organisations the next day and quickly suppressed what had been the largest trade union movement in Europe, the more coercive nature of the new state came to the fore, and as Fritzsche has noted, May Day and its aftermath clearly signalled 'both the genuine support and the sheer terror that composed public life in the Third Reich'.[7] The symbolic gestures of the National Socialist regime towards the German population were significant in creating and establishing the popular response towards it. However, it is a difficult picture to definitively recreate, because the popular response was so nuanced. While Fritzsche notes that 'there was considerable enthusiasm for the Nazi cause long after the seizure of power in January 1933', he also states that 'indifference to public events and withdrawal into private arenas characterised much of everyday life in Germany after 1933', suggesting that many Germans either were or became sceptical about the nature and intentions of the National Socialist state.[8] This ambivalence came to characterise the whole Nazi period, both during peacetime and throughout the wartime years. During the war, enlistment into military and labour services strengthened the role of Nazi institutions in daily life, yet at the same time, people became more critical of the Nazi Party and its policies, and even of Hitler himself, as the *Führer* (leader) myth began to falter, particularly after the Battle of Stalingrad.[9] Indeed, a variety of reasons accounted for dissent from Nazi norms, including as Jill Stephenson has noted, 'undiluted self-interest'.[10]

Much recent research on the social history of Nazi Germany has focused on the *Volksgemeinschaft* ('national community'). This was a concept that both featured in Nazi propaganda and influenced many aspects of everyday life. It was central to the Nazis' view of German society. Martina Steber and Bernhard Gotto note that: '*Volksgemeinschaft* was the Nazis' central social concept: it was within it, and via it, that visions of community in Nazi Germany were expressed, negotiated and put into practice.'[11] It was a promise, a utopia, a propaganda construction and an order – hence, it was a term that encompassed many things. It included the giving of donations to state-sponsored charity, in particular the *Winterhilfswerk* (Winter Relief Agency). It entailed communal activities, such as gathering to listen to Party radio broadcasts or involvement in a variety of Party activities. The ideal *Volksgemeinschaft* was a society in which class, religious and local loyalties disappeared in favour of the concept of the nation as a whole. Its members or *Volksgenossen* ('national comrades') had to behave in a particular way in order to belong. But again, the reality was not clear-cut. As Steber and Gotto note: 'there was immense pressure on citizens to conform, even if the loyalty created by such pressure had its limits'.[12]

Furthermore, the *Volksgemeinschaft* was used as a tool of repudiation, as much as it was one of integration. Certain sectors of German society were excluded from the *Volksgemeinschaft* on racial grounds (the Jews and the 'Gypsies'); others were precluded on account of their deviant sexual behaviour (homosexuals and prostitutes) and because they were considered to be either politically unreliable or 'asocial'. Those who failed to conform did not belong to the *Volksgemeinschaft*. And so, the *Volksgemeinschaft* was not only a propaganda construct, but also a project of social engineering. As such, it permeated the private lives of ordinary Germans throughout the duration of the Nazi era. While success, happiness and, in many cases, social advancement were promised to those who belonged to the *Volksgemeinschaft*, discrimination, persecution and ultimately destruction were the fate of those who did not belong to it. The *Volksgemeinschaft* was not, as Steber and Gotto note, 'a static condition', but a dynamic one.[13] Michael Wildt too argues that 'the *Volksgemeinschaft* is not to be analysed as a rigid social construct, but as the making of community, focusing on social practice instead of a societal status quo.'[14] It was a living community in which all members had their duties and obligations. During the war, the *Volksgemeinschaft* was presented increasingly as a 'community of struggle' or even, as defeat loomed in 1945, as a 'community of sacrifice' and a 'community of fate'.[15]

Wildt has shown how *Volksgenossen* could be involved in the realisation of the utopia of the *Volksgemeinschaft*. In serving the Nazi ideal – for example, as doctors sterilising the 'unfit', as policemen dealing with 'asocial elements', as local welfare officers or block wardens who supervised the German population – they became integrated and had a stake in Nazi society. Thus, their individualised self-empowerment through the concept of *Volksgemeinschaft* was not only about top-down power, but also about the participation of the population. Wildt argues that an immense pool of functionaries reflected this high degree of sharing in the Nazi social engineering project.[16] In addition, previously existing boundaries, particularly in regard to class, became blurred, and the promise of social advancement was appealing and attractive to many German workers. The regime's promises to *Volksgenossen* often fell short of real achievement, yet life was better than in the years immediately before the NSDAP came to power – sufficiently so that many Germans willingly bought into the idea of the *Volksgemeinschaft*. Yet, as Ian Kershaw notes, it is difficult to assess how far this entailed 'active commitment, as opposed to passive acceptance'.[17]

Another dimension to the dynamics of Nazi society was the concept of 'working towards the *Führer*'.[18] The power structure of the Third Reich lent itself to individuals undertaking initiatives within the Party and state administration for self-advancement or self-aggrandisement by anticipating and fulfilling Hitler's wishes. Much has been written about this in regard to the radicalisation of antisemitic policies, in particular. Yet it also impacted other aspects of social and political life and was related to the way in which opportunities offered by the new *Volksgemeinschaft* enticed citizens to behave in a particular type of way. Wildt notes too that 'the concept of the *Volksgemeinschaft* drew its political power not from a social reality achieved, but rather from its promise, and the mobilisation it inspired'.[19]

The relationship between consensus and terror in Nazi Germany was also important in determining people's thoughts and actions.[20] As Steber and Gotto note: 'consensus was inconceivable without terror, and terror without consensus.'[21] Participation in the *Volksgemeinschaft* brought its members pleasure and social enhancement and this factor needs to be taken into account alongside the aspects of terror and repression associated with the National Socialist government. As Wildt argues, the concept of *Volksgemeinschaft* entailed a 'diversity of behavioural strategies' among the German populace, exemplifying both 'joining in and turning away, willingness and reluctance' to conform to Nazi ideology and practice.[22] Detlef Schmiechen-Ackermann argues that the *Volksgemeinschaft* was 'produced daily in social interactions', with 'many motives and many different contexts'.[23]

The perspective of everyday experience adds an important dimension to our understanding of the Third Reich. Between 1933 and 1945, life was far from ordinary, and a deeper knowledge of the complexities of the structures of people's lives enables us to gain a comprehension of their actions. In studying this era, it is necessary to consider how everyday life was politicised by the regime and to examine the extent to which a clinging on to the non-political aspects of daily existence played a part in life under Nazi rule. As Schmiechen-Ackermann asserts: 'The social reality of life under the swastika was a complex balancing act.'[24] In examining the social practices of the *Volksgemeinschaft*, this book asks how people lived their everyday lives under the conditions of the Nazi dictatorship and offers a significant point of entry and enquiry into the subject for students and scholars in the field. The chapters of this book are divided into three sections. The first part on food and health contains chapters on food; alcohol, tobacco and drugs; and illness and health. The second part of the book on lifestyle comprises chapters on fashion; tourism; sports and clubs; and art. The third and final part of the book on religion is made up of chapters on Protestantism; Catholicism; and Christmas. The subjects have been selected to reflect on aspects of everyday life and activities that either have been little explored in the historical literature or have been the subject of specific academic monographs. Here, a comprehensive overview of each subject area is given so that a variety of topics can be considered together in a single volume that will allow readers a new lens with which to view daily life in Nazi Germany.

In a volume of this size, scope and nature, it has taken careful consideration, both in intellectual and practical terms, to select which topics to include and which to omit. This book does not by any means cover all aspects of everyday life. It does not delve into the subjects of working life and Nazi organisations, even though these both had a bearing on the experiences of the German population in the Third Reich. Moreover, it is not a book about the Nazi acquisition of empire and genocide – while the fate of the Jews and the experience of the Second World War find coverage within some of the chapters, they are not the primary sources of focus. Both the Holocaust and the history of the Second World War have been the subjects of numerous books. Nor too are the political and economic histories of the Third Reich central to this volume. This is a book about the everyday lives and ordinary experiences of Germans during the Third Reich. The Nazi regime had far-reaching goals – while it could not attain them all, it did achieve wide-ranging changes in a relatively short space of time, especially taking into consideration that half of that era was one of war.

The first part of the book opens with Nancy Reagin's chapter on food. Reagin shows how cooking, diet and the use of housekeeping resources during the Third Reich were shaped by the National Socialist agenda of economic autarky and military preparation. The goals of the Four Year Plan, followed by the demands of the war itself, drove both the conditions under which Germans kept house, as well as the propaganda directed at German housewives. Nazi endeavours to reshape German women's cooking and housekeeping built upon some widely shared values, but simultaneously, they contradicted other popular aspirations and housekeeping norms. Nazi leaders were especially wary of resurrecting consumers' memories of the First World War. They therefore promoted the creation of a variety of ersatz or substitute foods, to make up for the shortfalls. Food choices and cooking were the subject of intense propaganda as well, and the regime's interventions tried to persuade German women to adapt and comply with the constraints imposed by the Four Year Plan and to build support or understanding among German women and families for the shortages and extra labour required. Those foods available locally such as apples, potatoes and whole grains were presented as both healthier and more 'German' than luxury foods or imports. The Nazi regime launched ambitious campaigns to educate German housewives to make do with what was on offer in the market and to go to often surprising lengths to avoid any hint of waste.

Nazi propaganda was built upon the high value assigned to frugality among many sectors of the German population. But the push for 'German' foods and frugality sometimes contradicted popular notions of luxury and the *habitus* of the German bourgeoisie, which celebrated the value of some luxury foods like butter, and which cherished the notion of a Sunday 'roast' and other items that were central to German *Tischkultur* (table culture). In general, the regime was asking German women to embrace a more labour-intensive style of cooking and housekeeping, especially with regard to recycling and preserving foods and other resources. Such extreme frugality had always been common in working-class and lower middle-class families, but the Nazi government promoted it as a 'patriotic' duty for all housekeepers. The results did reshape German cooking and diet to a certain extent, but there was also evidence of widespread resistance to these measures and evasion of these restrictions. Reagin also notes the influence of the experience of food during the Nazi period upon Germans' post-war food choices and advertising. After 1950, West Germans increasingly embraced so-called 'international' dishes and 'labour-saving' frozen foods, products that were directly opposed to the choices and values regarding foods forced upon housewives during the Third Reich.

In Chapter 2, Jonathan Lewy examines a subject area that has been largely neglected by historians – namely, the history of alcohol, tobacco and drugs under National Socialism. The chapter demonstrates how the Nazis dealt with activities that we consider vices today. Although alcohol was popular in Germany, heavy drinking and the resulting diseases were frowned upon by the Nazi regime. In their policy towards alcohol, the Nazi authorities trod an uneasy path demarcated by an attempt to accommodate a thirsty public on one side and enforcing a biological imperative – as they saw it – on the other. Since the early nineteenth century, the 'drinking disease' was considered a hereditary disease. In the twentieth century, Nazi parlance turned the disease into a biological defect that had to be eradicated. Therefore, severe alcoholics were forcibly sterilised according to a law passed in July 1933. However, drinking did not stop in the Third Reich. High-ranking Nazi officials such as Martin Bormann and Reinhardt Heydrich were known drunkards. Beer remained a recognised essential in Bavaria during the war, and soldiers were given schnapps before special or difficult missions.

The Nazi policy towards tobacco was equally paradoxical. Certainly, tobacco use was considered a dangerous carcinogen and therefore was limited to adults. However, this did not keep the Nazi Party from using cigarette boxes for propaganda purposes or receiving the financial support of the tobacco magnate Philipp Reemtsma. Indeed, Hitler recognised the importance of tobacco to the autarkic German economy. The drug policy of the Third Reich is especially interesting, since to modern readers today, drug use might appear as the most serious vice of all. However, in Nazi Germany this was not the case. The few researchers who have referred to the question of drugs have assumed that the Nazis treated drug addicts as they did other 'asocials' and alcoholics, employing such measures as incarceration in concentration camps or sterilisation. Lewy's chapter shows that this view is erroneous. Far from persecuting drug addicts as they did other 'asocials', the Nazis tried to rehabilitate them and were even prepared to spend public money for that purpose. The National Socialist regime inherited its drug laws from the Weimar Republic. These laws had been imposed upon Germany under the terms of the Treaty of Versailles, and so, they did not reflect a natural evolution in German legislation. This caused odd legal mechanisms: drug possession without proper documentation was illegal, yet drug use itself remained legal. Following the traditions of the *Kaiserreich* (Second Empire, 1871–1918), drug use and drug addiction were not a crime and, in many cases, drug addicts bore no criminal liability for their actions. No special measures were taken against drug addicts; they were not considered 'asocials', and they were not persecuted in the same manner as alcoholics, the 'workshy', 'Gypsies' or Jews.

Following Lewy's exploration of alcohol, tobacco and drugs, in Chapter 3, Geoffrey Cocks examines the state of health in the Third Reich. He shows that while we know a great deal about the monstrous and murderous racism that was the *raison d'être* of the Third Reich and about the role of medicine, in particular, in effecting lethal Nazi racial policy, we know relatively little about health and illness in Nazi Germany. Experiences of illness and health under Hitler were an extension of the modern German past – the rapid development of a recently unified Germany into a modern industrial and commercial society, the First World War, economic disaster and political catastrophe. In addition, they were the outcome of the pervasive social, cultural and psychological dynamics of the demands, pleasures and needs of the German population.

The Nazi insistence on 'racial health' burdened the German population with demand, expectation and exploitation for work and war. Germans responded with a mixture of discipline, fanaticism, worry, physical and mental breakdown, as well as instances and degrees of agency on behalf of the self. More and more, life and experience in collapsing and collapsed Nazi Germany became both an individual and a general war of all against all in a frenzied landscape of battle and work, discipline and diversion, suffering and survival, fear and flight, pain and panic, injury, illness and death. The Third Reich in this way sustained in Germany the modern material, medical and commercial concern with health and illness. Cocks examines both the impact of Nazi health policy and practice, and the effects of well and ill selves acting within and around social, medical, political and discursive spaces. He illustrates the intersection of the lives of German people from all walks of life with inevitable but manipulable illness.

Beginning the second section of the book, in her chapter, Irene Guenther shows how during the Third Reich, female fashioning became the subject of intensive debate as well as contradiction. Instead of an agreed-upon plan of what German or Nazi fashion meant and a singular, consistently public image of the female, incongruities in the representation of fashion abounded. The result was that there was not one prevailing female image, but several. Examining the Third Reich through its clothing – the way in which the regime fashioned itself and German society – is revelatory. Clothing served as a means to visibly convey many of the notions elaborated by the Nazis' propaganda machine. It was employed to enhance the power and status of the regime, as well as to consolidate society and control behaviour. Additionally, clothing provided a tangible sign of inclusion into and exclusion from the *Volksgemeinschaft*. Clothing also served as a form of communication, as Germans silently inspected one another. What people wore or had to wear and how they fashioned themselves spoke volumes in Nazi Germany. The National Socialist regime defined ideals of national taste, including dress codes, to construct acceptable individual and collective identities. Inclusion into the *Volksgemeinschaft* could be attained by conformity to a contrived image that supported National Socialist ideology; similarly, 'otherness' was demonised and had its own appearance.

The Nazis utilised a variety of clothing directions, as they strove to consolidate and control the appearance, conduct, consumerism and attitudes of the German population. The Third Reich utilised *Trachtenkleidung* (folk costume) to illuminate Germany's cultural past and to promote its 'blood and soil' ideology. As *Trachtenkleidung* could not be bought, sold or worn by Jews, the fashion was a visible signifier of who did – and who did not – belong in the Third Reich. In addition, the Nazis promoted another sartorial image and dress code – the female uniform. This was a reflection of the Party's attraction to organisation and militarism. Similarly to *Trachtenkleidung*, the uniform also offered a visible sign of inclusion into the *Volksgemeinschaft*. It exuded power and enhanced the status of the regime; it projected symmetry; it signified order, accommodation and conformity; it reflected beliefs and value systems; and it shaped the attitudes of both the wearer and the observer. The Third Reich had a third fashion countenance, one that was intensely modern, supremely stylised and technologically advanced. It was this appearance that German fashion magazines depicted, fashion institutes promoted and German designers created for export fashion shows. Regardless of the *Trachtenkleidung* and uniform fashions that were created to support the regime and to consolidate society, magazines, newspapers and photographs of the time reveal that many urban German women wore the latest fashionable attire, much like style-conscious women in France and Britain. At various times, factions within the Nazi Party attempted to manipulate and redirect consumer culture so that it would better reflect the anti-modernist aspect of National Socialist ideology. Rarely, though, were they successful in doing so, since the modern, fashionable countenance served the Nazi state's agenda in a variety of ways. Guenther shows how fashion and clothing in the Third Reich were invested with manifold meanings and utilised or manipulated for multiple purposes.

In her chapter, Kristin Semmens examines developments in the tourism industry under National Socialism and their impact on life in Nazi Germany. The Nazi government took tourism seriously. Hitler professionalised the industry and passed laws that 'coordinated' it. Tourism officials gladly traded regional and local autonomy for what they had long wanted: state involvement and more streamlined practices, whether in advertising, statistics gathering or travel agency licensing. Moreover, after 1933, domestic and international visitors came in record numbers, and non-German experts praised the Nazi government's interventions. Semmens shows that the regime transformed the world in which tourism professionals worked, in ways that coincided with their own desires. Although conflict was never entirely absent, most within the industry agreed that the Nazis were good for tourism. Their intrusions were, for the most part, welcomed.

Semmens demonstrates that far-reaching changes naturally did not mean that every aspect of daily working life was instantly transformed for all tourism professionals. Although the regime stood poised to direct the most minute details (the font to be used in tourism advertising, for example), there were definite continuities between the Weimar era and the Third Reich: brochures selling towns and regions as holiday destinations were printed; the imposition of a spa tax was debated; national and international conferences were held; tourists' inquiries were addressed and so on. Many daily tasks and routines thus appeared normal. That normality, however, was in keeping with the NSDAP's overall goals for tourism. The Nazis transformed the tourism industry in far-reaching ways, which, for the most part, were grounded in consensus. The regime also had an impact on tourists themselves, in terms of their holiday practices, habits and experiences. The extent of its impact was dependent upon their travel destination, with places like the Black Forest remaining superficially untouched by Nazism, while Berlin was suffused with swastikas. Yet, here again, such different experiences occurred not in spite of, or in opposition to, Nazi control: they were deliberately fostered because they tallied with the regime's overall economic and ideological goals. Visitors praised the 'new' (and heavily Nazified) Berlin; they simultaneously extolled the 'timelessness' of other German destinations. In both instances, their responses met with the regime's approval.

Semmens's chapter revisits the debate about terror and consensus under National Socialism through the lens of tourism. Certainly, terror and coercion were not absent from this history: politically 'unreliable' Germans lost their jobs as the industry was 'coordinated'; some foreign tourists were victims of SA (*Sturmabteilungen* or stormtroopers) aggression in the violent early months of the Third Reich; Jewish Germans were increasingly excluded from all aspects of leisure travel. Yet, those measures too found favour within the industry or could be dismissed as exceptional. Even if they were opposed to some specific actions, most tourism professionals continued to support the regime's interventions generally. As was so often the case in the Third Reich, dissent and complicity – and often, outright support – coexisted. Life undoubtedly changed for both tourism professionals and their customers. For most, at least until the outbreak of war, it changed for the better. Semmens's evaluation of tourism concludes that despite the inescapable presence of the Nazi regime in people's lives, many Germans had no real desire to take a holiday from the Nazis.

In his chapter, David Imhoof examines the subject of sport in a specific local context in Göttingen, a town in Lower Saxony, in order to reflect on the impact of Nazism on sports. He discusses how sports developed in the Third Reich through evolutionary and revolutionary change and how larger structures – the state, the Nazi Party, sport organisations – shaped daily activities. Sports in the Third Reich allowed Germans to participate in the regime's ideological aims. But they also served as a refuge from political and economic tensions. Imhoof's chapter explains the ways in which Germans used sports to participate in the Third Reich. Indeed, sports reveal the complexity of the relationship of the Germans between leisure activities and the Nazi state. Germans used sports to empower and entertain themselves. Sometimes they used sports to hide from government officials or punish outsiders. Nazi leaders, for their part, celebrated the body, health and physical activity as an integral part of their racist, eugenic vision of the world.

The Nazi regime also created hierarchical organisations to direct all sporting activities. Imhoof's examination of these helps us to understand how Germans worked with the Nazi state in the highly personal, yet greatly politicised daily activity of sports. Ultimately, Imhoof argues, we can best understand the Nazi *Gleichschaltung* ('coordination') of sports as a process by which average Germans helped to create the sport culture of the Third Reich as much as they had it imposed upon them. This chapter describes a variety of sporting activities in which Germans engaged as participants and spectators. The history of sports in Göttingen during the Third Reich sheds light on how individuals, institutions and ideas functioned in Nazi Germany as a whole.

Next, Joan Clinefelter's chapter shows that the art produced between 1933 and 1945 served a vital function for the Nazi state. Clinefelter argues that the National Socialists used the visual arts to integrate Germans into the *Volksgemeinschaft*. By analysing Nazi policies, mass art exhibitions and the art market, her chapter demonstrates how Nazi culture excluded outsiders – Jews, Communists, Socialists and others – and embraced conservative art to win over the lower and middle classes, artists and the educated elites. The chapter begins by examining the development of cultural policy between 1933 and 1937. The Nazis pursued a dual strategy of exclusionary and inclusionary tactics. While modernists were attacked as inherently 'unGerman', conservative artists were hailed as the creators of an eternally pure German style. The Reich Chamber of Culture provided approved artists with national recognition and access to commissions, exhibitions and honours – simultaneously, it relegated modernist artists to the cultural periphery. Artists demonstrated their support for Nazi policy by organising local 'degenerate' art shows designed to defame modernist art and artists. Most often these shows were driven by professional rivalries and long-standing perceptions that the modernists had enjoyed an unfair competitive advantage during the Weimar Republic. Economic opportunism, as well as ideological support for National Socialism, drove many artists to ally with the Nazi state.

Clinefelter explores the integrative function of art in the Third Reich, with regard to educated elites and the middle and lower classes through a focus on mass exhibitions. The Degenerate Art Exhibition and the Great German Art Exhibition, held directly across the road from each other in Munich in 1937, offer the best illustrations of the role of art in forging the *Volksgemeinschaft*. While the Degenerate Art Exhibition vilified outsiders, the Great German Art Exhibition celebrated the Third Reich's artistic insiders. Held annually from 1937 to 1944, the Great German Art shows were the national venue for art that represented the will of the *Volk* (people or nation). Covered extensively in the press, radio and film, the Great German Art exhibitions enabled all classes in Germany to celebrate their cultural heritage, now recast within a Nazi framework. Clinefelter examines the art economy as yet another way to illustrate the role of art in integrating Germans into the *Volksgemeinschaft*. She shows how the Great German Art Exhibitions identified accepted artists, connected them with buyers and helped them to determine the prices that they could command for their works in galleries. The art market boomed as especially middle-class Germans sought to signal their membership of the *Volksgemeinschaft* by purchasing art approved by the regime. However, in the wartime years, art sales represented not only public approval, but also popular fears. After 1942, Germans increasingly purchased art as a hedge against inflation and the economic collapse that would surely follow defeat. The chapter ends with a consideration of the effects of the war on Nazi art and the inability of the Third Reich to create the kind of innovative outpouring of racialist excellence so hoped for by Hitler.

The final part of the book focuses on the subject of religion. The vast majority of the German population in 1933 was Christian – together Protestantism and Catholicism accounted for the religious beliefs of 96 per cent of the total population. Accordingly, this section contains a chapter each on Protestantism and Catholicism, with the final chapter of the book devoted to the subject of Christmas. In his chapter, Christopher Probst examines Protestantism in Nazi Germany. Protestants comprised 63 per cent of the German population during the Third Reich. Utilising church newsletters and newspapers, conference proceedings, internal church communications and published writings, Probst seeks to answer a number of important questions about German Protestant experiences and views during the Third Reich. He examines how Protestants responded towards the Nazi regime, and how the pressures and strictures of living in the Nazi state helped to fracture the Protestant Church into competing factions with distinct views on myriad issues. He explores how Protestants confronted the so-called 'Jewish Question'. The chapter begins with a description of the general context of the German Protestant Church as a state-supported institution, including the *Kirchenkampf* (church struggle) between the *Bekennende Kirche* (Confessing Church) on the one hand and the pro-Nazi *Deutschen Christen* (German Christians) on the other. The latter sought rapprochement with the Nazis, but their enthusiastic support for the regime often went unrequited. Probst analyses important themes addressed by Protestant pastors and theologians, including nationalism, antisemitism, the Lutheran doctrine of the 'two kingdoms' and the doctrine of the 'orders of creation', of which the *Volk* was most crucial. Many Protestant pastors and theologians wrote about the 'Jewish Question'. Most were keen to argue against 'racial' forms of antisemitism. Yet, most held traditional Christian anti-Judaic and/or antisemitic opinions. Nazi philologist Theodor Pauls's views illustrated one approach to such issues; Heidelberg pastor Hermann Maas's actions and ideas represented a starkly different outlook.

Pauls published a three-volume work titled *Luther und die Juden* (*Luther and the Jews*) in 1939, which was part of a long series of ostensibly scholarly works about 'positive Christianity'. Pauls offered the work as a 'gift' to the antisemitic and purportedly academic Institute for Research into and Elimination of Jewish Influence in German Church Life, which was dominated by the *Deutschen Christen*. In these volumes, Pauls wove together Martin Luther's 'two kingdoms' doctrine with ardent nationalism and antisemitism, lifting the most incendiary passages from Luther's anti-Judaic and antisemitic works and infusing them with Nazi racial conceptions. In contrast, Maas represented a philosemitic strand of Protestantism in Nazi Germany. He had joined the Society for Protection against Antisemitism in 1932. In 1933, he spent several months studying in Palestine. Maas co-founded the *Büro Grüber* (Grüber Office) together with Heinrich Grüber in 1938. Through this work and his ecumenical contacts abroad, Maas assisted in the emigration of many persecuted Jews and Jewish Christians. He accomplished all of this while serving as pastor of the Holy Spirit Church in Heidelberg from 1915 to 1943. As a result of his daring activities, he was harassed by the Gestapo and eventually had speaking, writing and professional restrictions imposed upon him. In 1943, church authorities forced him to resign his position at Heidelberg, under pressure from the regime, and later that year, he was transferred to France to endure work in a hard labour camp. Maas's actions and theological works, which exhibited sympathy for the Jewish victims of Nazism, represented an exception to the rule. Probst shows how Pauls's and

Maas's starkly disparate views about and actions towards the Jews served as windows to wider Protestant opinions about the German nation, the Nazi regime, Jews and Judaism during the Third Reich. They illustrate extreme poles on either side of the German Protestant divide, indicating the extent of different aspects of Protestant thought in German society under National Socialism.

In his chapter, Kevin Spicer shows how during the turbulent years of Hitler's rule, German Catholicism did not escape the evils of National Socialism unscathed. In 1933, when Hitler came to power, 33 per cent of the German population was Catholic. Ruthless state and party officials with unlimited power compelled both ordained and lay members of the Church to find their place among the loyal ranks of fellow German compatriots. Amid the flurry of events surrounding 1933, German Catholics had to make some hard choices, both personal and political. As an institution, the position of the Catholic Church towards National Socialism changed over time. Spicer identifies four main phases: 1930–1933, when German bishops publicly opposed National Socialism; 1933–1934, when German bishops jointly reversed their stance towards National Socialism while holding on to the illusion that they could work with the state; 1934–1939, when the state directly attacked the value system of the Catholic Church and purposefully worked to remove it from the life of the *Volksgemeinschaft*; and 1939–1945, when the state engaged in an annihilative war, carrying out the murder of the physically handicapped and the mentally ill, as well as the deportation and mass murder of German and European Jews, while simultaneously threatening the future existence of the Church.

Initially, the National Socialists' emphasis on nationalism and promise of economic renewal drew many Catholics to the movement. Catholics also feared being left out of the political process, labelled traitors by the new government and subjected to a second *Kulturkampf* (culture struggle) as in Bismarck's era. In March 1933, most Catholics including the German bishops believed in Hitler's promise that Christianity would serve as Germany's underlying foundation. A subsequent Concordat between Nazi Germany and the Vatican in July 1933 solidified the aspirations of such Catholic support. The murder of Erich Klausener, the Berlin Director of Catholic Action, during the Night of the Long Knives in June 1934, however, enabled the initial disillusionment with National Socialism to surface again. Subsequent encroachment on the freedom to operate of Catholic organisations, newspapers and publishing houses further complicated church–state relations.

Despite such tensions, the Catholic Church and National Socialism shared some traits in common. Both condemned the cultural excesses of the Weimar Republic and supported traditional gender roles and family life. Similarly, both spoke against the evils of modernity and attributed to Jews the cause of Germany's misfortunes. Yet, their forms of antisemitism – racial versus religious – differed significantly, though the Church's failure to consistently emphasise this point and end its anti-Jewish teaching made it challenging for Catholics to differentiate between the two. Still, in the proclamation of the Christian faith, many Catholic bishops and priests made statements that government officials labelled as 'political resistance', even though most churchmen rejected such characterisations. For their part, churchmen regularly insisted that they had to act solely to protect the interests of their Church and to secure pastoral freedom. Underlying the problem was that the Catholic Church institutionally rejected Judaism. The Catholic Church did not formally make a shift in this historical reality until 1965 when the Vatican issued *Nostra Aetate*, which called for recognition of Judaism and the rejection of all forms of antisemitism. Nevertheless, as Spicer shows, in the Third Reich, there were unique individuals who saw the evils of National Socialism and, in highly motivated ways, followed the Gospel command to 'love thy neighbour', even at the expense of their own survival.

In the final chapter of the book, Joe Perry examines the subject of Christmas under National Socialism. The Nazification of Germany's favourite holiday took many forms, on numerous levels. Building on historical notions in place since the mid-nineteenth century, Nazi functionaries cast Christmas as a celebration of the German *Volk* that had deep roots in the solstice worship of pre-Christian Germanic tribes. Traditional symbols and rituals, including decorations, family observances, carol singing, annual Christmas markets and particularly the Christmas tree, were stripped of their Christian content and were reworked to insert Nazi ideology into popular festivity. Nazi propagandists and functionaries worked hard to construct a Christmas that would celebrate the *Volksgemeinschaft* and its racial boundaries; an analysis of these efforts sheds a revealing light on the way National Socialism intervened in the everyday lives of German citizens and the conflict and consensus generated by this intrusion. This chapter offers fresh insight into the contradictory relationship between private life, political culture and identity production in Nazi Germany. The *NS-Volkswohlfahrt* (NSV or National Socialist People's Welfare) subsumed familiar forms of holiday charity-giving under the auspices of the *Winterhilfswerk* (WHW or Winter Relief Agency), one of the most popular Nazi institutions. Annual celebrations sponsored by National Socialist mass organisations, including the Hitler Youth, the National Socialist Women's League (NSF), the German Labour Front (DAF) and the *Wehrmacht* (armed forces), brought the values of the Nazi holiday to millions of Germans. A variety of Nazi propaganda institutions and publications championed reworked domestic festivities that exalted the family's place as the 'germ cell' of the nation in ways that emphasised the importance of women and mothers for building the national spirit of the German home.

Perry's chapter traces the Nazification of Christmas in chronological order across three main parts, beginning with initial attempts to shape a Nazi holiday around *völkisch* (nationalist) themes in the 1920s. It then explores the period between 1933 and 1939, when Nazi authorities eagerly used all the institutional muscle they could muster to popularise a highly ideologised *Volksweihnachten* ('People's Christmas'). The third section examines the attempts of the regime to celebrate *Kriegsweihnachten* ('War Christmas'), a resurrection of themes and ritual practices previously in place during the First World War. Throughout these sections, the chapter assesses the success of Nazi efforts to colonise Christmas. Though our knowledge of the people's response to 'People's Christmas' remains shrouded behind the highly controlled information politics of the dictatorial Nazi state, sources such as Security Service reports on the general mood and opinion and internal institutional records offer some insight into the popularity of the Nazi holiday. Perry shows that the Nazi orchestration of Christmas proceeded piecemeal and engendered conflict as well as conformity; attempts to dechristianise holiday observances were particularly unpopular. Nevertheless, on balance, it seems that Nazified rituals and traditions successfully appropriated and displaced public festivities and made real inroads into private celebrations. The reinvention of Christmas as a National Socialist holiday was an effective means of remaking social solidarity and national identification, not least because participation in Nazi observances offered German citizens real material and symbolic rewards, including a privileged place in an exclusionary racial state.

Together, these contributions offer readers an opportunity to rethink their ideas about everyday life in Nazi Germany and to examine the impact of the Nazi state on German people's lives. The Third Reich was indeed a brutal dictatorship, but within this context, people still had to continue their daily existences in a way that they were able to or chose to do. An analysis of these discrete aspects of life under National Socialism, within the broad themes of food and health, lifestyle and religion enables us to understand more about the nature of the Nazi state and illuminates the relationship of the German population to the Nazi government and its responses to Nazi ideologies and policies.

This book examines popular responses to the Nazi regime and establishes where it permeated people's lives and where it did not. For example, we know that fear and terror underpinned life in Nazi Germany, but recent research has shown that the real influence of the Gestapo (the secret state police) was perhaps much more limited than had been previously accepted.[25] Denunciations, on which the Gestapo relied, were often based on revenge, resentment or personal jealousy, rather than on wholehearted acceptance of Nazism and Nazi ideology. Tim Kirk has also commented on the complex relationship between the Nazi government and its citizens. He shows that the German *Volksgemeinschaft* was 'managed by a mixture of promise and exhortation, discipline and threat'.[26] The promotion and creation of the *Volksgemeinschaft*, as Fritzsche notes, 'offered particular social rewards' and had considerable appeal to the German population.[27] Fritzsche shows how: 'over the course of the twelve-year Reich, more and

more Germans came to play active and generally congenial parts in the
Nazi revolution and then subsequently came to accept the uncompromising
terms of Nazi racism.'[28] While the Nazi regime failed to achieve its goal to
rebuild, reshape and harmonise German society, it did enjoy considerable
popular consensus throughout much of the period. The pervasiveness of
the regime and its institutions were not clear-cut. In many cases, it appears
that people went along with the components of National Socialism that
they liked or that benefited them, not necessarily consenting to the regime
entirely. Jill Stephenson has used the phrase 'à la carte Nazis' to describe this
phenomenon and has noted that even Party members 'did not necessarily
swallow Nazi ideology whole'.[29] Many Germans were willing to subscribe
to certain aspects of Nazism but were disinclined to change their behaviour
and habits entirely in line with Nazi ideology.

Thus, the Nazi Party could not claim the complete allegiance of the
German population. While it attained a degree of consent, in particular,
through its sponsorship of entertainment and leisure, it did not succeed in
winning over the total control that it desired. Fritzsche notes that the regime
offered 'unprecedented opportunities for social mobility' and that 'the
promise and possibility of a renovated social sphere' created considerable
appeal for the Nazi movement.[30] Yet, as Stephenson contends, 'expecting the
mass of the people to accept Nazi priorities wholeheartedly and to reorientate
their working, social and family lives to accord with them was to court
disappointment' for the Nazi leadership.[31] Various forms of opposition to
and dissent from the ideas and ideals of Nazism, or even in comprehension
of them, all signified the failure of the regime to achieve total control of the
German populace. The Nazi regime, despite its terror apparatus and vast
propaganda machine, did not succeed in persuading the German people into
compliance with its ideology entirely. There were people who did manage to
maintain their own values or sense of morality during the Nazi era. There
were significant distinctions between what people thought, said and did,
and so, a complex picture emerges. In the confines of a dictatorial regime,
thoughts, words and actions did not always easily converge. It is these
discrepancies, and the spheres of daily life that the regime did not succeed in
penetrating, which this book seeks to explore.

# Notes

1    Y. Bauer, 'Overall Explanations, German Society and the Jews or: Thoughts
     about Context', in D. Bankier (ed.), *Probing the Depths of German
     Antisemitism: German Society and the Persecution of the Jews, 1933–1941*
     (New York, 2000), p. 16.

2    R. Grunberger, *A Social History of the Third Reich* (London, 1971).

3    T. Mason, *Social Policy in the Third Reich: The Working Class and the
     'National Community'* (Oxford, 1993); T. Mason, *Nazism, Fascism and the*

*Working Class: Essays by Tim Mason* (Cambridge, 1995); T. Mason, 'Women in Germany, 1925–1940: Family, Welfare and Work. Part I', *History Workshop Journal* 1 (1976), pp. 74–113; T. Mason, 'Women in Germany, 1925–1940: Family, Welfare and Work. Part II (Conclusion)', *History Workshop Journal* 2 (1976), pp. 5–32; J. Stephenson, *Women in Nazi Society* (London, 1975); J. Stephenson, *The Nazi Organisation of Women* (London, 1981).

4   R. Bessel, *Life in the Third Reich* (Oxford, 1987); D. Peukert, *Inside Nazi Germany: Conformity, Opposition and Resistance in Everyday Life* (London, 1987); D. Crew (ed.), *Nazism and German Society* (London, 1994); P. Ayçoberry, *The Social History of the Third Reich, 1933–1945* (New York, 1999); L. Pine, *Hitler's 'National Community': Society and Culture in Nazi Germany* (London, 2007).

5   P. Fritzsche, *Germans into Nazis* (Cambridge, MA and London, 1998), pp. 141–142.

6   Ibid., p. 217.

7   Ibid., p. 218.

8   Ibid., pp. 220–221.

9   I. Kershaw, *The 'Hitler Myth': Image and Reality in the Third Reich* (Oxford, 1989).

10  J. Stephenson, *Hitler's Home Front: Württemberg under the Nazis* (London, 2006), p. 359.

11  M. Steber and B. Gotto, '*Volksgemeinschaft*: Writing the Social History of the Nazi Regime', in M. Steber and B. Gotto (eds), *Visions of Community in Nazi Germany: Social Engineering and Private Lives* (Oxford, 2014), p. 2.

12  Ibid., p. 19.

13  Ibid., p. 7.

14  M. Wildt, '*Volksgemeinschaft*: A Modern Perspective on National Socialist Society', in Steber and Gotto (eds), *Visions of Community in Nazi Germany*, p. 55.

15  Steber and Gotto, '*Volksgemeinschaft*', p. 5.

16  See M. Wildt, *Hitler's Volksgemeinschaft and the Dynamics of Racial Exclusion: Violence Against Jews in Provincial Germany, 1919–1939* (London, 2012).

17  I. Kershaw, '*Volksgemeinschaft*: Potential and Limitations of the Concept', in Steber and Gotto (eds), *Visions of Community in Nazi Germany*, p. 38.

18  On this, see A. McElligott and T. Kirk (eds), *Working Towards the Führer* (Manchester, 2003).

19  Wildt, '*Volksgemeinschaft*', p. 49.

20  On this, see R. Gellately, *Backing Hitler: Consent and Coercion in Nazi Germany* (Oxford, 2011).

21  Steber and Gotto, '*Volksgemeinschaft*', p. 16.

22  Wildt, '*Volksgemeinschaft*', p. 55.

23  D. Schmiechen-Ackermann, 'Social Control and the Making of the *Volksgemeinschaft*', in Steber and Gotto (eds), *Visions of Community in Nazi Germany*, p. 252.

24   Ibid., p. 253.

25   On this, see K. Mallmann and G. Paul, 'Omniscient, Omnipotent, Omnipresent? Gestapo, Society and Resistance', in Crew (ed.), *Nazism and German Society*, pp. 166–96. See also R. Gellately, *The Gestapo and German Society: Enforcing Racial Policy, 1933–1945* (Oxford, 1990).

26   T. Kirk, *Nazi Germany* (Basingstoke, 2007), p. 221.

27   Fritzsche, *Germans into Nazis*, p. 229.

28   Ibid., p. 230.

29   Stephenson, *Hitler's Home Front*, p. 350.

30   Fritzsche, *Germans into Nazis*, p. 228.

31   Stephenson, *Hitler's Home Front*, p. 350.

# Select bibliography

Ayçoberry, P., *The Social History of the Third Reich, 1933–1945* (New York, 1999).

Bessel, R., *Life in the Third Reich* (Oxford, 1987).

Crew, D. (ed.), *Nazism and German Society* (London, 1994).

Fritzsche, P., *Germans into Nazis* (Cambridge, MA and London, 1998).

Kershaw, I., *The 'Hitler Myth': Image and Reality in the Third Reich* (Oxford, 1989).

McElligott, A. and Kirk, T. (eds), *Working Towards the Führer* (Manchester, 2003).

Pine, L., *Hitler's 'National Community': Society and Culture in Nazi Germany* (London, 2007).

Steber, M. and Gotto, B. (eds), *Visions of Community in Nazi Germany: Social Engineering and Private Lives* (Oxford, 2014).

Stephenson, J., *Hitler's Home Front: Württemberg under the Nazis* (London, 2006).

Wildt, M., *Hitler's Volksgemeinschaft and the Dynamics of Racial Exclusion: Violence against Jews in Provincial Germany, 1919–1939* (London, 2012).

# PART ONE

# Food and Health

# 1

# *Tischkultur*: Food Choices, Cooking and Diet in Nazi Germany

## *Nancy Reagin*

Throughout history, cooking and diet have represented an amalgam of both private and public tastes. The choices made in each household regarding what foodstuffs to purchase, how to store and prepare them, and what and when each person should eat have been driven (in part) by personal preferences and values. The meals that resulted have been shaped by each cook's training and talents, by the amount of time available in each household to devote to food preparation and (often) by the need to cater to the varying desires of the household 'audience' (usually family members) who consumed these meals. At the same time, each household's diet has been shaped by broader trends affecting the region or nation as a whole, such as changes in agricultural production and the technologies of food storage; popular beliefs regarding which foods are necessary, healthy or 'appropriate' for a given socio-economic group; the relative prices of various foodstuffs; and state policies, which have drastically influenced the availability of foods for private consumption.

'Guns will make us strong, but butter will only make us fat', claimed Hermann Goering. The Nazi authorities cared very much – to a degree of micromanagement seldom attempted by any regime, before or since – what went into Germans' stomachs. The Nazi era therefore offers an example of how state policies could intervene and reshape ordinary Germans' diets to a high degree, although the results of this intervention varied considerably, depending upon an individual's location, age, 'racial' classification, profession or workplace and familial status. It also highlights the peculiar, circumscribed position of consumers in an autarkic economy, along with the possibilities of and limits to forms of resistance available to ordinary German consumers, who persistently sought *die gute Butter* (the 'good butter' or 'the real thing' with regard to consumer goods).[1]

# The politics of consumption

Although Hitler himself was a vegetarian and a teetotaller, his regime's concern with ordinary Germans' diets was not driven primarily by considerations of health. Instead, Nazi policies regarding the production and distribution of foodstuffs were intended to align the diets of ordinary consumers with the needs of Germany's war preparations and (after 1939) to support the demands made on the German economy by the armed forces. At the same time, however, Nazi leaders clearly sought to avoid a repetition of the circumstances of the First World War. Indeed, they had no intention of recreating the factors that had led to Germany's defeat in that war, at least as they recalled this history. Nazi leaders were erroneously convinced that Germany had lost the First World War because resource-starved, hungry civilians were 'seduced' by revolutionaries and had 'stabbed the army in the back', leading to popular uprisings and subsequent military defeat. To avoid any future civilian uprisings, Nazi leaders were insistent throughout the 1930s and the early war years that ordinary 'Aryan' Germans should not be asked to sacrifice too much, although they might be asked to postpone some sorts of consumption in order to support rearmament.[2]

Nazi consumption policies thus reflected several goals, which were often in conflict with each other. The leadership tried to balance and manage these goals carefully, but the polycentric nature of the Nazi bureaucracy meant that there were many cross-cutting policies pushed by different agencies, which sometimes produced surprising results. Some of their goals were crucial to the establishment of the Nazis' political legitimacy and support from the majority of the German population: the pursuit of rapid economic recovery; ending the widespread hunger and misery of the Depression; ensuring modest gains in consumption; and above all, the reduction of unemployment levels. The 'battle' against high levels of unemployment was the one achievement – above all others – that ensured popular support for the new regime. Employment underwrote the guarantee of a 'decent' standard of living for the bulk of the population; this both legitimised the Nazi regime and was seen as crucial to ensuring military success.

But the drive to prepare for war in general, and the Four Year Plan, in particular, necessarily led to economic policies that often worked against civilian consumers' interests. Germany's economic planners worked towards an autarkic or self-sufficient German economy during the 1930s, so that Germany's reliance on imported raw materials and foodstuffs would never again become the weakness that it had proven in the First World War. Imports of non-essential consumer goods were often restricted, and war-related industries usually had first call on those raw materials that were imported. At the same time, policy makers encouraged the production of synthetic products that would replace imports along with substitutes for common (and often coveted) foodstuffs like butter and pork.

In order to restrain 'excessive' consumer demand and thus reduce the need of consumer industries for raw materials, the regime adopted a policy of *Lohnstopp* (wage freezes) in many industries and simultaneously increased the tax burden on ordinary Germans, so that consumers would have less discretionary income. Government policies that slowed the growth of consumer demand were working against considerable social headwinds, however. Germany's economy recovered quickly after 1933; the rapid increase in employment combined with pent-up consumer demand – which had been suppressed during the Depression – while Germany's population grew 7 per cent between 1933 and 1939.[3]

All of these factors hindered (although they did not stop) Nazi officials' attempts to restrain both imports and domestic consumption. Overall, consumption levels of many key foodstuffs and consumer goods grew during the 1930s in absolute terms, although they did not grow as sharply as Germany's overall GNP, which boomed under the stimulus of the 'military Keynesianism' of the rearmament programme. Although the German GNP grew dramatically during the mid to late 1930s, the increase in private consumption did not keep pace, and although it increased in absolute terms, private consumption therefore declined as a share of the nation's total GNP from 71 per cent in 1928 to 59 per cent by 1938.[4]

By 1935, the conflict between rising consumer demand and the drive to prepare for war was becoming more difficult to manage. The German economy was now essentially at a state of full employment, and the end of unemployment meant that pent-up consumer demand was now increasingly felt. At the same time, war-preparedness measures and growth in heavy industries meant that Germany was running out of imported raw materials, and Germany's gold and foreign currency reserves were by now depleted. In order to continue to rearm while not restricting consumption too much, Hitler announced the implementation of a Four Year Plan in 1936.[5]

After the Four Year Plan was introduced, armaments production became the chief determinant of economic policy. The Plan emphasised rapid rearmament, an increase in the production of militarily important raw materials and general war preparation. Eventually, the Plan 'encroached on all the major areas of economic policy-making...by 1938 [Hermann] Goering was "economic dictator" in all but name', with control over agriculture, labour, trade and prices.[6]

Yet, Germany's leaders still felt the need to secure popular support by allowing some growth in consumption, along with many of the features of a modern consumer culture, which included a broad selection of American imports – Coca-Cola established its first bottling plants in Germany during the 1930s – and the dissemination of key consumer goods (such as through the radio, which could distribute both entertainment and propaganda).[7] Hartmut Berghoff has astutely described the cumulative effect of the regime's consumer policies as leading to the 'enticement and deprivation' of consumers, as government economic policies combined the suppression of consumption in some areas with widespread distribution of key goods such as radios in selected high-profile areas and the promise of future consumption in others (e.g. the Volkswagen, promised but never mass-produced before 1945).[8]

## The Four Year Plan at home: autarkic shopping and cooking

Although the Nazi regime allowed an increase in consumption in some areas (and promised more, in the future), the demands of rapid militarisation drove the restraint or redirection of consumption in many other sectors, particularly in foodstuffs, textiles and other household goods. It was in the household – in the unpredictable, erratic shortages of meats, fats, imported foods, fabrics and toys, as well as through the introduction of inferior ersatz products – that ordinary Germans first felt the pinch of the Four Year Plan. And housewives, who managed their families' budgets and purchased most consumer goods, were among the first to see the impact of Germany's rearmament. Since their job was, in fact, to mediate between their families' desires and the reality of what was available in local shops, housewives also became the targets of intensive Nazi propaganda (Figure 1.1).

Some of the propaganda message dated back to the First World War, although the scale of Nazi attempts to influence ordinary domestic choices was new. The problem facing Nazi planners (as with their predecessors in the First World War) was that Germany could not be made self-sufficient when it came to food supplies. The population size had outstripped the ability of German agriculture to feed the nation without imports during the late nineteenth century; this was particularly true for supplies of grain, fats and meats. The best that any German government could hope to accomplish was to reduce Germans' reliance on food imports. Even reductions in imports could only be achieved if Germans switched to a more 'home-grown' diet: whole grain, dark bread; potatoes; lowered consumption of meat and fats (since Germany lacked enough fodder to be self-sufficient in meat and butter production); and indigenous fruits and vegetables such as cabbages and apples, in place of imports like oranges and bananas. Many of the basic outlines of the autarkic diet promoted under the Four Year Plan were

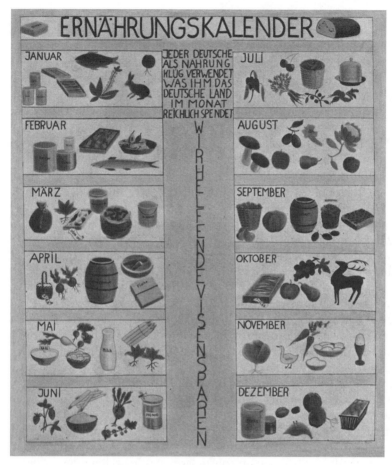

FIGURE 1.1 *Nutritional calendar from the Four Year Plan period (WL14392). Courtesy of the Wiener Library, London.*

thus already well established in older women's minds even before 1933, since these foodstuffs had been promoted in propaganda during the First World War. Indeed, the Nazi emphasis on whole grain bread was certain to remind many consumers of the darker bread containing whole grains and potato flour, referred to as *Kriegsbrot* ('wartime bread') during the First World War.[9] Nazi propagandists thus had to tread lightly, to avoid evoking consumers' memories of wartime deprivation and hunger; instead, the Four Year Plan promoted these foods as 'healthier' and as supporting Germany's drive for self-sufficiency.

The regime's goal was to adjust consumer demand to fit supply, within the framework of a partially autarkic economy, in which the armed forces had first call on resources. In effect, the leaders of the Nazi women's organisations were attempting to overcome the centrifugal effects of region, class and custom, by advocating unified, autarkic patterns of consumption and household management. But in trying to reach and change housewives' attitudes and workloads, Nazi bureaucrats ultimately confronted the reality that mass consumption contained both centralising and centrifugal impulses. The Nazi leadership could not completely overcome the segmentation inherent in mass markets and consumption patterns, which were divided along fault lines of class, gender, region and even locality.

The *Deutsches Frauenwerk, Abteilung Volkswirtschaft-Hauswirtschaft* (German Women's Bureau Section for Home Economics) was the chief organisation responsible for reaching female consumers, although (as in every area of Nazi policy) there were other Party and state agencies involved as well. After 1936, the work of all of these agencies was coordinated, and their propaganda was overseen by the *Reichsausschuss für Volkswirtschaftliche Aufklärung* (National Committee for Popular Economic Enlightenment).[10]

In order to reach every German housewife, the Nazi organisations embraced a variety of vehicles and techniques. Propaganda and housekeeping tips supporting the Four Year Plan were featured in the Women's Bureau's own house organ the *Deutsche Hauswirtschaft* and in the *NS Frauenwarte*. Recipes and weekly menu plans were distributed in the form of millions of flyers, postcards and brochures; tucked into female workers' pay envelopes; featured on the *Schwarze Brett* (a common bulletin board) in factories and workplaces; promoted on weekly radio broadcasts; and published in local newspapers. The Nazi women's organisations mounted hundreds of public exhibitions and cooking demonstrations in every region and produced slideshows, cinema newsreels and radio programmes to advocate particular patterns of consumption and housekeeping. The Section for Home Economics set up its own chain of 148 advice centres for housewives, which focused largely on advising women on consumer issues: recycling; the proper use of ersatz products; preserving foods; promoting dark breads and other foods featured in the 'home-grown diet' such as quark, fish instead of meat, jam in place of butter or margarine; and increased consumption of potatoes.

Their publications were generously funded by the *Reichsausschuss für Volkswirtschaftliche Aufklärung*, and Nazi women's groups produced staggering numbers of flyers and other publications. Between 1936 and 1940, for example, the *Reichsnährstand* (Reich Food Corporation), the Nazi agency that regulated and oversaw the production and distribution of agricultural products, distributed almost nine million copies of pamphlets, which touted quark, a featured Four Year Plan product. This agency also circulated eight million brochures on how to make preserves or jams, and five million copies of recipes designed to make the humble potato more attractive. The Women's Bureau even produced a board game for girls as part of this campaign, *Wettlauf mit dem Verderb* (compete against waste) while the *Reichsnährstand* gave away eighteen million *Kampf dem Verderb* (fight against waste) postcards, for women to use in their private correspondence.[11]

Such propaganda expanded upon widespread attitudes towards housekeeping and thrift already present among the German bourgeoisie and attempted to popularise and manipulate these established patterns of housekeeping and consumption. But in other areas, such as the promotion of new ersatz products, or the *Eintopf* ('One Pot') campaign, Nazi women's leaders were attempting to change or disrupt deeply entrenched customs and attitudes in private households. Their efforts to 'reform' German women's housekeeping and consumption were also shaped by the larger political and cultural meanings assigned within Nazi Germany to housewives' private choices regarding shopping and household management. In effect, Nazi women's leaders selected themes that had long been present in German discussions of consumption and housekeeping (e.g. the value of thrift or the virtues of 'natural' foods) and incorporated them into a vision of autarkic housekeeping, which served the needs of the Four Year Plan, and clearly linked private purchasing decisions to the needs of the national economy, as defined by the regime.

The Nazi women's organisations attempted to influence the most ordinary sorts of household decisions. The housewife's management of the household entailed a constant series of smaller or larger choices regarding consumption and the allocation of her time and labour. Such decisions, in turn, shaped the housewife's shopping list. Should she purchase canned fruits and vegetables or put them up herself in season? Should she serve a labour-saving (and traditional, in many social groups) 'cold' evening dinner of *belegtes* (bread topped with spreads, meat or cheese) or cook the second 'warm' meal of the day? Should she draw up a weekly *Küchenzettel* (menu plan) and keep household account books, which might enable her to track expenditures more closely and stay within a budget, but which also entailed more work? As in other sectors of production under the Four Year Plan, the regime's approach to housework stressed an intensification of labour.

Potatoes were a favourite topic in this regard; even here, Nazi home economics advisors found a way to make more work for housewives, in their attempts to both avoid waste and transform the humble root vegetable into dishes that could compete with now scarce luxury foods. Germans needed no encouragement to eat potatoes, of course, but cold, unappetising, leftover bits of potatoes were framed as a serious recurring problem for the Home Economics Section: not a scrap was to go to waste. The Nazi women's groups generated hundreds of recipe tips, offering housewives recipes (often entailing much more work than the original menu that had created the leftovers) to enable them to recycle and use up those cold remnants. One recipe, offered as a 'holiday treat' for the Christmas season, urged the housewife to assemble a heap of leftover cold potato bits or mashed potatoes and to knead them into a sort of dough before piping them into small snail-shaped rolls, before deep-frying them.[12] The peels were not to be wasted either; housewives were admonished to soak potato peels overnight in water before straining the mash, which they could then use in place of shop-bought starch for ironing shirts.[13]

The promotion of quark and fish to replace butter and meat exemplified the 'reforms' urged by Nazi propaganda. Quark was a favoured product for several reasons. It was made from the sour milk left over in the process of butter production, something that had previously often gone to animals, and it could be used as a spread for bread, in place of butter, margarine or *Schmalz* (fat), all of which were in short supply by the late 1930s. It also contained protein. The Nazi women's organisations mounted an extensive effort to increase the consumption of quark: circulating *Kostproben* (samples); offering public cooking demonstrations and special cooking courses centred on quark; trying to persuade local merchants to stock the product; and distributing millions of quark recipes. The shortage of butter and margarine no doubt aided their attempts to persuade housewives; consumption of quark rose dramatically in the 1930s and has remained a common food in the German diet until today.[14]

Conservatives had promoted fish during the Weimar period, to aid the German fishing industry. Under the Four Year Plan, however, fish was suggested as a substitute for the now sometimes scarce pork cutlet or sausage; by the late 1930s, a lack of fodder resulted in periodic shortages of pork and beef. Herring, in particular, was promoted, since it could be more easily preserved. The regime subsidised the fishing industry and fish preservation and distribution systems at every level, encouraging investments in fish-processing ships, new rail schedules to distribute fresh fish even to inland communities and new technologies to flash-freeze fish fillets.[15] The Home Economics Section offered tens of thousands of public demonstrations of fish cookery and short-term fish cooking courses under the Four Year Plan: almost 7,800 such courses (each lasting a few hours or days, usually with eighteen to twenty participants) took place in 1938. Reports sent to the Home Economics Section from provincial chapters consistently claimed that fish cooking courses (along with other cookery courses) were among their most popular offerings, while other campaigns apparently met with little response. After such courses, local Nazi women's leaders asserted that local fish sales usually rose, and indeed, nationally, fish consumption rose almost 50 per cent between 1934 and 1938.[16]

The Nazi women's organisations also attempted to alter housewives' attitudes and shopping lists in other respects, urging housewives to work harder, in order to conserve resources. A 'Letter from a Reader' published in the NS *Frauenwarte* in 1936 presented the 'model' diet and housekeeping strategy in a nostalgic invocation of the author's childhood in a large civil servant's family. 'In a well-managed household, absolutely nothing must be wasted', she admonished, recalling her own mother's impressive, tedious and labour-intensive efforts at economising. Every bit of worn or shabby clothing was cut down and re-sewn to create new clothes for smaller children; not a scrap of fabric was wasted. Water that had been used for boiling vegetables was never thrown out, but rather, it was recycled and used as stock for cooking other dishes the next day. The author's mother raised small animals and kept a garden, which supplied most of her family's diet; and she put up or canned enormous quantities of produce in season, to provide food throughout the winter.[17]

This sort of idealised bourgeois household economy could have been taken directly from the nineteenth-century advice manuals, but the larger context of such thrift was now quite different. Working harder, as well as scrimping and saving, a housewife could enable the entire family to 'get ahead' in life. In the traditional context, a housewife was making a martyr of herself for her own loved ones, who were not to feel the pinch. But under the Four Year Plan, the Women's Bureau's proposed 'thrift' served an entirely different purpose. Now, housewives were being organised 'from above', for the benefit of the Nazi state. They were to serve as agents of the state within the household, disciplining their families' eating habits and consumption patterns to meet the shifting needs of the Plan. Women were asked to sacrifice not in order to meet their own families' needs and strategies, but in order to meet the goals of the state. And the entire family would feel the pinch: housewives were being asked to 'sell' their families on the Nazi Sunday *Eintopf* ('One Pot') dinner instead of a roast and to persuade their husbands to accept herring in place of a pork cutlet, as well as quark in place of butter.

The Home Economics Section tried to influence the smallest daily habits and increased women's workloads. Women were told to teach their children never to put butter or jam on a plate but always to spread it directly onto a slice of bread, so that none was 'wasted' on the plate.[18] Provincial chapters of the Women's Bureau organised travelling exhibitions that reached the smaller towns, which included displays on 'A Full Rubbish Bin: How it Should and Should Not be'. Another exhibit to promote the 'German apple' featured a recipe for making a cheap drink out of leftover apple peels (which were generated in the process of baking, but which were not to be thrown out).[19]

In addition, members of the Hitler Youth (HJ) were sent door to door under the Four Year Plan to collect bones, buttons, old fabric and metal scraps, to be used for war preparation. The League of German Girls (BDM) was similarly employed to gather fallen fruits, wild herbs and old records. Plants such as rose hips, dandelions, nettles and wild mustard – which both housewives and girls' groups were urged to collect in forests or meadows and preserve – were referred to as 'wild vegetables'. Starting in 1938, girls were also asked to clean the combed-out hair from their families' hairbrushes and combs and to deliver the hair to local hairdressers, where it was collected and passed on for the production of military goods that required felt.[20] These strategies to replace imported products and to stretch food supplies had been used during the First World War, and their revival inevitably awakened consumers' fears and mistrust.

The German Women's Bureau and the Nazi propaganda machine urged housewives to get by on as little as possible, in order to suppress consumer demand. Their goal was to extract the private household, as much as possible, from the cash nexus, to encourage economic self-sufficiency and household autarky. A prime focus of the cooking courses and printed material put out by the Party comprised of instructions on how to can, put up and preserve foods and jams. Foods preserved at home were a key part of the ideal German diet during this period. Food preservation had long been the norm in rural areas and small towns, of course, where consumers had their own plots and gardens to supply produce: since it was their 'own' food, they would not want to waste any that they did not eat in season. But Nazi policy makers wanted to persuade *all* housewives, even those in big cities (who might not have sufficient storage space or possess the equipment required for canning) to invest a great deal of labour every summer and autumn, putting up produce that was seasonally available in urban markets.

And yet, the autarkic household was not merely to make as few demands on the broader economy as a whole; it was also engaged in an intricate, ever-changing minuet with agricultural and industrial production. The regime was trying to persuade German housewives to make ongoing adjustments to their *Küchenzettel* (weekly menu) and to constantly fine-tune their shopping lists and menus to reflect products that were available that month. In magazines, newspapers and on the *Schwarze Brett* in many workplaces, women were given lists each month of products that were currently abundant and those which were in shorter supply and urged to adjust their purchasing patterns and diets accordingly. If the grain crop had been better one year, they were to eat more *Vollkorn* (whole grain) bread; if the potato crop was larger the next, they were to switch to potato recipes. One season there might be an abundance of leeks (which had to be purchased and correctly preserved); the next autumn, an excess of apples, which housewives were urged to put up.

The regime strongly encouraged the use of ersatz products. If butter and *Schmaltz* (fat) were not available, then housewives were to substitute jam and sugar for fats: 'An Zucker sparen grundverkehrt, der Koerper braucht ihn, Zucker naehrt', housewives were told.[21] Thus, the regime was trying to adjust demand, instead of supply, in order to keep prices constant and to steer around shortages of more popular goods. This approach required housewives and their families to sometimes give up favourite family or regional dishes and to regularly experiment with new foods and products. The Nazi women's groups were thus struggling (with mixed success) against deeply entrenched tastes and habits, and a note of exasperation was often present, as in a *Deutsche Hauswirtschaft* article which exclaimed that 'it would be very desirable, if housewives would not always fall back upon the old favourites, but would rather also learn how to make tasty dishes out of other cuts of meat. When the asparagus crop comes in, people want to eat cutlets and *Schnitzel* [with asparagus], and prices immediately rise for these cuts.'[22]

Instead, housewives were urged to substitute the Sunday *Eintopf* meal, a stew or goulash, on the first Sunday of each month between October and March, for the pork or beef roast or chicken customary in more affluent households. The money that housewives saved was to be donated to the *Winterhilfswerk* (Winter Relief Agency). The 'One Pot Sunday' thus pursued a key goal of Nazi food policies – reducing meat and fats consumption – while promoting a feeling of *Volksgemeinschaft* (national community), since the *Winterhilfswerk* only gave help to the 'Aryan' deserving poor. 'One Pot Sunday' was heavily promoted and fairly successful; restaurants and other public or communal kitchens were also expected to observe the rule.[23]

The language and imagery used to describe the ideal domestic cuisine during the Nazi period were thus drawn from many sources. One root was the language of traditional bourgeois domestic thrift. Thus, some writers called for housewives to return to keeping the traditional German *Fettopf* (a container, in which women stored fat which had run off from cooking, blended with beef lard, kidney fat, etc.) to use as a source of fats in place of margarine or shortening. 'We have let many such German [housekeeping] customs fall by the wayside', one concluded, 'and adopted American [labour-saving] styles of work; away with these!'[24] More often, Women's Bureau writers used a language of efficiency and order to describe their approach to housekeeping and consumption. Germany was engaged in a 'production battle' in order to achieve 'nutritional liberty'. To reach this goal, the regime was practising 'the guidance of consumer demand', which was to take place within the framework of a new, regulated 'market order'. Housewives might well come up against 'temporary shortages' of favourite products, but 'a clever housewife will adjust her menu plan according to the surpluses and shortages of the current market'. The regime asserted that the rational use of leftovers helped a housewife's budget, her family's health and the Four Year Plan.[25]

A good *Küchenzettel* was not only adapted to the fluctuations in the 'market order', it was 'closer to nature' as well. Nazi women's groups argued that consumers not only needed to adapt to the Plan's ongoing surpluses and shortages, but also that they needed to go back to 'natural, seasonal' rhythms of consumption. City women had to learn that they could no longer demand fresh eggs at Christmastime (when hens did not naturally lay them), for example. As the 1936 annual report for the Westphalian Home Economics Section claimed:

The boundless imports of the postwar period seduced our housewives into making demands on the German market no longer connected to the soil, as in earlier times … Fresh strawberries in winter were now simply seen as a delicacy … [we must] bring the city woman back to a way of thinking that is bound to German soil and nature.[26]

To eat 'naturally' was healthier, too, as Nazi women writers constantly reminded housewives. The excessive consumption of meat and fats was a distressing symptom of modern civilisation; a diet based on whole grains and vegetables was considered to be much better nutritionally. And it was even more 'Aryan'; it was sometimes asserted. Staff members who worked in regional advice centres for housewives were taught that 'all [ancient] Aryans, possessing the surer instincts of primitive man, chose whole grains as the main source of nutrition dictated to us by Nature... [mass production] led us onto a false [dietary] path. But now modern nutrition again recognises the vitamin content and value of *Vollkornbrot*'.[27]

To eat bread 'dry', with no spreads or toppings at all, would have been the best possible outcome for the needs of the Four Year Plan; some German Women's Bureau slogans tried to push even this choice as a 'healthy' one, arguing that 'eating dry bread puts colour in your cheeks!'[28] Catchy as this slogan was – it rhymes in German – the Women's Bureau probably did not expect many consumers to embrace the idea, which ran directly against long-established dietary norms. The emphasis on health and nature accorded well with other aspects of Nazi public health policy, however.[29] But although the diet being promoted by the Women's Bureau was indeed 'healthier' (in some respects, in ways that the Nazis could not then have known), the food choices discussed here were primarily promoted not in order to improve consumers' health, but in order to meet the needs of an autarkic economy.[30]

## The limits of persuasion

Although 'home economics' programmes and the ubiquitous and abundant recipes distributed by Nazi women's organisations cajoled and exhorted housewives, many still refused to adopt a model diet that sometimes tended towards veganism. Sources offer many glimpses of consumers who – although they might be compelled to follow some of the Women's Bureau's suggestions because they could afford or obtain nothing better – often voiced reluctance, resistance, fear about what these consumption patterns portended (since they were reminded of the First World War), or simply a stubborn insistence on doing things as they had always done them.

Housewives in some areas clearly resisted the suggestion that they try dishes that might be common in other German regions: such as the 'flour dishes', barley or milk soups. Switching to any of these would help to reduce meat and fat consumption. Noodle dishes were traditional in the western and southern German states but provoked resistance in areas like East Prussia, leading the announcer on one 1939 radio broadcast to comment with annoyance that: 'It is wrong to say that such dishes [based on flour] don't "fill us up". We do not eat, in order to fill our stomachs until the next meal, but rather, in order to provide our bodies with the necessary nutrients. The so-called "flour dishes" do this very well, and if they don't "stick to the ribs", then this is no deficit, but rather proof of the fact that they are easily digested.'

Many Germans obviously disagreed: demand for all foodstuffs, including those which the regime hoped consumers would turn away from, grew steadily in the pre-war years, and meeting consumer demand through a sufficient increase in imports would have caused bottlenecks in arms production. In order to reduce reliance on grain imports, the regime prohibited farmers from devoting acreage to fodder crops. This policy, exacerbated by poor harvests in 1935 and 1936, drove up the shortfall in meat production; chronic shortages of butter and cream began around the same time, although supplies varied by region.[31] Consumers could switch to margarine (which was still easy to obtain before the war began), but margarine and other alternative fats were universally considered to be inferior to butter. Margarine was not seen as a wholesome, natural product, like butter, since it was made out of imported materials like whale blubber or coconut oil.[32] By late 1938, the regime had prohibited the production and distribution of cream and related high-fat dairy products, and once the war began, only low-fat milk was available.[33]

Other attempts to change women's habits – to get them to keep account books, do more canning or putting up, or get by without margarine – also seem to have met with resistance. As one 1936 report on a meeting of Westphalian Home Economics Section advisors noted:

> We must learn to do without that, which is currently not available in the market, and take that, which the market currently delivers. Here, it is urgent that we educate women quickly and persuasively. There is enough food available for all; there are simply a few temporary shortages of pork and butter. Unfortunately, during the last few months, more and more hoarding has been going on, which is making matters worse.[34]

Similarly, a report from a Women's Bureau leader in Gelsenkirchen admitted that permanent changes in women's housekeeping were very difficult to effect: 'My impression is that when one speaks to housewives about housekeeping matters – it doesn't matter, what the exact topic is – then they are all interested, even enthusiastic; they ask questions, and participate [in the programme]. But once they get back home, then the majority of women show themselves to be *very conservative* and simply cannot change how they do things.'[35]

The monthly reports from Women's Bureau workers in a variety of localities regularly repeated complaints from housewives about rising prices for food and shortages of pork and fats. Many women, especially those who were more affluent, did not want to switch to a diet of herring and boiled potatoes, which were traditionally the diet of the working poor. Home Economics Section leaders sometimes recognised this fact and often attempted to persuade bourgeois housewives to alter their choices *within* the category of 'luxury' foods, switching from imported (or unobtainable) pork cuts to locally farmed chicken for Sunday dinners, for example. But bourgeois husbands were probably the demographic group most accustomed to enjoying their 'favourites'. And in some instances, there was no 'luxury' substitute for a product, which was a staple on upper middle-class tables, such as butter. Margarine and substitute fat products were regarded as 'inferior'.

Some women, from both the working class and the middle class, resisted the idea of cooking the 'warm' evening dinner that most of the proposed menus promoted. The more common pattern (in many regions, but not all) was a warm midday meal, and then bread with some sort of spread or sausage for dinner, a custom that the Women's Bureau repeatedly criticised, with little success. The shortages of such *belegte* meant that housewives would have to do additional work for dinner, cooking 'warm' evening meals of potato or noodle dishes. Some were reluctant to do so.[36]

It was not surprising, therefore, that local Women's Bureau reporters sometimes wrote that working-class or lower middle-class women in their audiences found the propaganda offered to them condescending, because they already knew how to be thrifty and were spending as little as possible, already. Indeed, some of the advice offered to them insulted the intelligence of any experienced housewife.[37] At another meeting in the locality Buer, Westphalia in 1936, Nazi women activists showed a film on *Kampf dem Verderb*, which evoked similar protests. While the film was being shown, 'voices were raised in the [darkened] auditorium that asked "What! Are we in elementary school here? Any child knows that!" etc. These were not pampered ladies who said this; completely ordinary women enthusiastically joined in criticising the film.'[38] Thus, for women from poorer households, the advice of the Women's Bureau was often perceived as superfluous; for bourgeois housewives, it was often downright unwelcome.

By the late 1930s, Berliners had invented mocking nicknames for the regime's most favoured and heavily promoted products and ersatz products: peeled boiled potatoes (a favourite dish in suggested menus) were called 'Four Year Plan nuggets'; the ersatz coffee offered to consumers was derided as 'nigger sweat' [sic]; while the bluish skimmed milk that the Women's Bureau touted as 'healthy' was dismissed as 'cadaver juice'.[39] Consumers had other options available to them besides the exercise of bitter wit. Unlike urban housewives, who generally had to rely on what the local markets offered, rural housewives usually had their own gardens and small livestock (or farmed with their families) and thus had much more control over the ingredients available for their menus. Farming families often sought to evade the price controls and guidelines regarding what to plant, issued by Nazi planners. When the government prohibited using rye grain as animal fodder and lowered the prices set for rye grain between 1935 and 1938, for example, farmers near Celle dramatically increased the amount of barley they planted, since there were fewer regulations regarding barley.[40]

Indeed, farmers could sell food directly to urban consumers, who sometimes took trains out to their city's hinterland in order to buy wine, potatoes or other foodstuffs directly (and illegally) from the producers. The farmers got better prices than those set by the Four Year Plan, and urban consumers were able to secure goods that were in short supply: local authorities often chose to look the other way. Like everyone else, Nazi officials recognised such strategies as a revival of consumer tactics from the First World War, and (as with so many of their policies) sought to preserve consumers' morale in order to shore up support for the regime's militarism. In addition, Nazi officials in rural areas, where 'under the counter' trade thrived, were themselves locals and embedded in the communities they were supposed to be overseeing.[41] Much of the trade was done by means of bartering and evaded the cash nexus entirely, which made the enforcement of regulations regarding agricultural products and their distribution even harder to enforce. Farming families were often happy to trade foodstuffs for other products brought by urban customers from the city, since they were busy with the harvest.

Hoarding ('hamstering') and bartering were strategies pursued by an increasing number of consumers by the late 1930s, and such black market strategies became more and more common during the war. In rural Württemberg, owners of tobacco shops found that they could only obtain tobacco from urban wholesalers if they offered ham, butter and eggs obtained from local farmers in exchange. In Ulm, the *Sicherheitsdienst* (Security Service) reported on a typical example of someone presumably preparing for direct trade with farmers on a large scale when they noted that a local housewife had 'boasted that she had 150 preserving jars at home, and intended to buy a further 150'.[42]

## Private agency, public kitchens

Housewives often persisted in their personal or regional preferences in private, as long as they could obtain the ingredients they needed by hook or by crook. Institutional kitchens – the 'mass feeding' kitchens run by the armed forces, the *Reichsarbeitsdienst* (National Labour Service), the *Winterhilfswerk*, workplace canteens, restaurants, pubs and cafes – could be compelled to fall into line more easily, although higher-end restaurants could circumvent some restrictions. The Nazi authorities issued monthly updates regarding categories of ingredients which such 'big kitchens' were expected to use more of, less of, or consume in the same quantities, depending on the current availability of domestic produce. Once the war began, ever larger numbers of Germans – drafted into the army, or compelled to turn to institutional kitchens as food shortages became more acute in the later stages of the war – ate in the 'mass feeding institutions' instead of at home and thus were compelled to switch to a 'home grown' diet, which supported the war effort and, after 1942, increasingly reflected its privations. The number of 'mass kitchens' serving Germans outside of the armed forces rose from 2,700 in 1939 to 17,500 in 1943, and the number of people fed in them rose from 800,000 to almost 5 million annually.[43]

Restaurants, taverns and cafes did good business until the last two years of the war, even though they, too, generally had to conform to rationing guidelines. A 1943 menu from Berlin's famous Haus Vaterland (a pleasure palace that contained a complex of restaurants and cafes) shows the impact of rationing, along with the limits of such constraints. Originally developed by a Jewish family of restaurateurs, the owners had been forced to sell out to competitors for a low price. The Haus Vaterland menu offered unrationed portions of potatoes and vegetables, but many items like rolls had to be paid for with a combination of ration coupons and cash; as at other restaurants, whole grain rolls and bread were compulsory. Pancakes with fruit compote were on offer, but customers had to supply ration coupons worth 100 grammes of whole wheat bread, along with a ration coupon for 10 grammes of fat. More luxurious foods might escape such controls, however, since their ingredients (while more expensive) were not rationed. For example, the menu also offered a more costly 'fine dish' of crabmeat and mussels in white wine sauce, which required only a coupon for 10 grammes of fat.[44] At top-end restaurants, affluent customers could choose from a range of unrationed dishes, including lobster, oysters, champagne, and exotic fish and fowl. Most restaurants, dance halls and other places of amusement had to close following the declaration of total war after the German defeat at Stalingrad in 1943, however.[45]

The less glamorous 'mass kitchens' and the need to feed an army of millions led the regime to sponsor research and innovations in new food storage technologies during the late 1930s, in order to preserve and store mass quantities of foodstuffs, after a wartime blockade began. Once again, this policy was driven by memories of the First World War: Britain's blockade had led to the slow starvation of first civilians and then the armed forces, which Nazi leaders blamed for the uprisings that had allegedly resulted in the 'stab in the back' of Germany's military and her subsequent defeat. By improving and expanding food storage technologies, the Nazi leadership hoped that Germany could remain self-sufficient for longer in their war.[46]

The technologies and infrastructure required to freeze or dehydrate foods therefore received substantial investments under the Four Year Plan. Dehydrated foods were often less tasty than canned foods, but they were favoured because they did not require the use of metal and because production costs were lower than for canning. For the armed forces, dehydrated foods were also lighter and easier to transport. Thus, dehydrated foods 'became the army's favoured conservation method...the army was proud to dry everything', particularly potatoes and vegetables.[47] Since the decline in meat supplies made protein a concern, the army also sponsored the mass production of vegetarian soy burgers. Production of soy burgers and other soy-based foods increased from 10 tonnes per year to 600,000 tonnes per year by 1945.[48]

Nazi planners also favoured frozen foods. The research required to maintain the 'cooling chain' for frozen goods, along with packaging and storage techniques, was undertaken during the 1930s and expanded once the war began. The regime sponsored the construction of flatbed trailers and fish-processing ships, so that the armed forces could be supplied with carton-packed frozen fish fillets. The Nazis set up factories in Norway to freeze fish, and in the Netherlands, to freeze foods expropriated from France and Italy. 'By 1940, a quarter of the army's meat consumption came from frozen sources.'[49] All of these developments laid the foundation for a 'boom' in the deep-freezing industry in post-war Germany.

Even soy burgers and frozen fish could not completely fill the protein gaps caused by the war, however. After 1939, shortages of meat became worse, leading to the further proliferation of rumours and complaints among ordinary consumers. A 1940 memorandum sent from the Berlin office to all provincial Women's Bureau offices urged them to contradict popular stories that dog meat was now being introduced into the ground meats sold in shops.[50]

# Rationed diets

In some respects, the proclamation of war in September 1939 made the work of the Nazi women's organisations easier. They no longer had to admonish, urge or cajole housewives to eat less butter and more oats or to replace pork with fish. The rationing controls imposed at the start of the war did a lot of this work for them, by banning or limiting forms of consumption that the regime had been trying to discourage. The complex system of wartime rationing tried to fine-tune Germans' diets according to the amount of work they did, how old they were, their familial status and 'racial' designation: by 1945, there were 16 categories of 'ration receivers', including those who did night labour, 'heavy' or 'heaviest' physical labour, long work shifts, the so-called 'normal consumer' (a default level for adults), pregnant or nursing mothers, the ill or the aged. A racial hierarchy was layered on top of this system, with reduced rations given to the racially 'undesirable', along with rationing by age categories for those aged 0–6 years or 6–18 years. Rations were even set for dogs, which were graded by the regime according to their social utility.[51]

The early rations announced in August 1939 gave the 'normal consumer' the following foodstuffs per week: 700 grammes meat; 350 grammes fats; 280 grammes sugar; 110 grammes jam; 63 grammes coffee; and 60 grammes daily of milk products. Bread rations were initially set at 2.4 kilogrammes per week.[52] Gradually, other goods came under rationing, too; at the beginning of the war, rations for 'normal consumers' were supposed to total about 2,400 calories per day. Savvy consumers had been alerted by the pre-war propaganda to stock up on supplies and many households continued to preserve fruits and vegetables.[53]

By 1940, however, food prices were rising, and the supply of many products – including eggs, milk and fats – was uneven and erratic. One confidential study estimated that the total cost of food per household had gone up 14 per cent among working-class families since the late 1930s, while the consumption of fats and protein in such households had declined by 20 per cent and 6 per cent, respectively. Queuing for food had become standard, which reminded both Nazi officials and consumers of the long lines common during the First World War. Civilian rations were gradually but steadily reduced over the next three years. Weekly meat rations had been cut almost 50 per cent for 'normal consumers' by the summer of 1941, compared to the start of the war, and shortages of potatoes and fresh produce (even in the summer) began to appear in the cities. In September 1941, Goering ordered that all occupied areas had to be squeezed and stripped of resources as much as possible, to avoid further reductions in rations within Germany, but even so, rations issued to civilians declined steadily thereafter.[54]

By 1944 (after which date official record keeping became erratic) the war had certainly had an impact on ordinary civilian Germans' diets, forcing most people to switch to plant foods from animal foods, and to use substitutes for many products, such as coffee. Compensating for foodstuffs that were no longer available in quantity, the per capita German consumption of vegetables almost doubled between 1939 and 1944, as did the consumption of potatoes. During the same period, official rations for meat for 'normal consumers' fell from 26 kilogrammes per year to 8 kilogrammes, while fat consumption declined from 14 kilogrammes per year to 5.6 kilogrammes. Overall, rations never reached the lows they had during the First World War, however, even for meat and fats. This success was due in part to the Nazis' much better organised systems of rationing and distribution, along with their relentless plundering of the nations they occupied.[55]

Rations for German civilians were underwritten by the German armed forces' so-called Hunger Plan, which called for feeding German troops in the occupied areas of the Soviet Union by taking foodstuffs from the local population, although Nazi planners realised that this would lead to the death of millions from starvation. Confiscating the grain stocks of Ukraine, in particular, to feed the German army reduced the demands for foodstuffs placed on the German domestic economy. Soviet prisoners of war and Jewish communities in Eastern Europe became the main victims of the Hunger Plan, since Nazi authorities could easily cut off their food supplies, and millions died of hunger or hunger-related causes as a result of this policy.[56] Plunder and prior planning, with regard to frozen or dehydrated foods, meant that German troops received fairly good rations until the final two years of the war. Troops, even those stationed at home, were allowed 150 grammes of fat per day, far more than the 105 grammes per day allowed to even those civilians who were doing the heaviest forms of physical labour. Soldiers' rations allowed for 300 per cent as much meat consumption per week in 1941 as that allocated to civilians and 250 per cent as much bread per person. And this did not even include the plundered foodstuffs that the troops often obtained: soldiers stationed in France and western Europe, in particular, were able to loot or purchase many luxuries – coffee, butter, wine, cognac or champagne – and send them back home.

Like butter, coffee was a particularly coveted luxury item in these 'care packages'. By definition, it was an imported good, and thus supplies had been limited since the beginning of the Four Year Plan, and a brisk black market for coffee had emerged well before 1939. Roasted grain beverages were generally used as ersatz coffee by those who could not afford black-market prices. Coffee from occupied nations sent home by soldiers therefore came as a real windfall for many German civilians. Customs officials were told not to check the contents of the packages sent home by soldiers. As Ursula Heinzelmann notes, 'in fact, western Europe contributed more food to wartime Germany than the occupied Soviet Union, with vast amounts of meat and grain imported from France, Holland and Denmark. Denmark provided Germany with about a month's worth of butter, pork and beef a year' until the last two years of the war.[57]

Germans in rural areas ate better than urban dwellers, since many could grow their own foods, and many city people went to the countryside regularly to buy dairy products and vegetables or fruit. In the cities, civilians kept rabbits or chickens in their back gardens or on balconies; rabbits were often referred to as *Balkonschweine* ('balcony pigs'). Black markets and bartering grew steadily; by the end of the war, they were almost the only means for many civilians to obtain food at all. At the same time, the upper levels of Party leadership were notoriously corrupt, particularly when it came to food provisions. Ordinary Germans could see that some groups were prioritised or obtained access by 'the back door'; such Germans were often sarcastically referred to as 'butter racial comrades', compared to the more ordinary 'margarine racial comrades', nomenclatures that once again reflected the emotional and psychological values associated with butter.[58]

The food situation for German Jews and others deemed 'inferior' in the Nazi racial state had been much worse from the start and had become truly dire by 1942. By September 1942, Jews living in Germany were denied any rations at all for meat, eggs or milk; the extra rations of honey and jam normally allocated to children were denied to Jewish children. 'Jews were frequently prohibited from buying specific produce: rice, sugar, oranges, pastries, fresh vegetables, frozen food, almonds, nuts, even salt herrings, eggs, cheese and condensed milk … [in 1942] it was decreed that even non-rationed food was to be sold only to Jews after everyone else's needs had been satisfied.'[59] The Nazi authorities clearly saw the rations for Jewish Germans as a 'temporary' problem, however, since by this time deportations of German Jews to the camps in Poland were well underway.

The fact that the German army's frontlines were being pushed back towards Germany's own borders during the last two years of the war steadily reduced the amount of arable land that Germany could draw foods from. The more the army's rations had to be supplied by Germany itself – rather than by the occupied nations – the greater the pressure on civilian rations.

By late 1944, the flood of refugees pouring into western Germany, combined with the impact of bombing and the steady advance of the Allied armies, resulted in the breakdown of the transportation system, which caused the food distribution and rationing systems to suffer accordingly. In the winter of 1944–1945, the official rations for 'normal consumers' sank to 1,671 calories per day, but this assumed that supplies were even available.[60] By April 1945, large parts of the economy had simply ceased to function, and each household had to find its own way to procure enough food to survive.

# Conclusion

On balance, the strategies pursued by Nazi leaders in regard to consumers and the diets of ordinary Germans were largely successful. Certainly, Nazi leaders never faced a repeat of that (imagined) history – the civilian 'stab in the back' – that haunted them from the previous world war. Until the last few months of the war, civilian food supplies for average 'Aryan' Germans never reached the desperate straits that had been common during the last two years of the First World War, and the Nazi leadership never had to deal with any serious unrest or organised protests from German consumers.

In the process of pursuing their military goals, Nazi organisations mounted far-reaching campaigns that relied on every possible mode of propaganda and education, along with investments in new food processing and storage technologies, in an attempt to reach deep into ordinary Germans' housekeeping and dietary decisions. The success of these efforts varied considerably, depending on an individual household's location and other factors. Rural households had the resources to resist many official interventions, and could rely on their own farms or gardens – and barter with urban customers – to maintain a less restricted pre-war diet more successfully than most urban dwellers. German Jews or others who were seen as 'socially undesirable' in the racial state were the worst off: their diets were restricted even before the war began, and by 1942, those still outside the camps struggled to obtain enough calories simply to stay alive. Well-connected households, on the other hand, or those after 1940 who had a family member stationed in occupied western Europe, could still obtain luxury goods throughout the first few years of the war, and the Party elite ate well up to the very end.

Overall, however, the ability of the Nazi regime to influence Germans' consumption patterns was significant even before the war began. The combination of Nazi policy makers' enticement and deprivation, coercion and exhortation, ultimately succeeded in dampening the growth of household consumption throughout the 1930s and at redirecting demand to areas favoured by the regime. The autarkic diet so strongly promoted by the Women's Bureau did in fact gain ground under the Four Year Plan. German families increased their consumption of dark breads and potatoes somewhat, while cutting back on the amount of wheat flour and white bread that they ate. The amount of dietary fats consumed dropped by as much as 20 per cent even before the war began, and the amount of meat consumed per capita rose only slightly in spite of Germany's economic recovery, while the consumption of such 'favoured' foods as fish, oats, jam and quark grew substantially.[61]

The regime attempted to make housewives and their families feel empowered (and reconciled to women's increased workloads) by constantly stressing their importance to the Four Year Plan and the national economy. The leader of the National Socialist Women's League, Gertrud Scholtz-Klink, repeatedly invoked women's 'cooking spoons' as weapons that could benefit the nation. By economising, one Women's Bureau expert wrote, women made possible the construction of new western fortifications, which gave Germany more leverage in foreign diplomacy.[62]

The housekeeping and consumption strategies urged on German women during the late 1930s attributed power to them by arguing that women could reconcile the conflict between choosing 'guns or butter'. Guns were prioritised: but although families could not eat their fill of butter, they could at least enjoy a sufficiency of jams made by 'mother'. Nazi leaders hoped that access to cheaper, but palatable substitutes would defuse consumers' resistance to or criticisms of the privations imposed by the Four Year Plan. But many housewives apparently were not persuaded of their 'national importance' and stubbornly insisted on focusing on the needs of their own households.

Those who ate at 'big kitchens' run by the army, workplaces or other organisations were more or less compelled to fall in line with the 'new' diet, however. Where individual households might resist the guidelines of the Four Year Plan, and the rationing imposed after 1939, larger kitchens run by organisations could not. As supplies became more erratic after the war began, and many Germans were either in the armed forces or in other organisations that took them away from home, millions began to get their meals in canteens or messes run by the armed forces, factories or Nazi mass organisations. A regime that relentlessly celebrated the value of German domesticity had thus taken many Germans away from home cooking, and those who remained at home found that their traditional diet was often disrupted. The increase in the number of Germans fed in mass institutions was also furthered by and supported by the regime's interest in developing new food technologies, especially dehydration and frozen foods. Investment in frozen food technologies during this period laid the groundwork for a boom in frozen foods after the war.

Under the Four Year Plan, deeply rooted habits of domesticity – an emphasis on thrift, for example, and praise for a housewife's hard work and self-sacrifice – were strategically exploited by Nazi organisations in order to support a larger agenda that directly undermined consumers' choices, autonomy and standard of living. Nonetheless, looking back from the

FIGURE 1.2 *A family mealtime (WL3070). Courtesy of the Wiener Library, London.*

1950s, German consumers generally remembered the pre-war years as a 'good' period. Compared to the high unemployment and lean years of the Depression that preceded Nazi rule, and the disruptions and privations that characterised life in the last years of the war and the 'rubble years' that followed, the mid and late 1930s often seemed like a 'good' time in most Germans' memories: during these years, employment was high and most families' tables were set with enough to eat (Figure 1.2).

But Nazi propaganda and the push to a 'home grown' diet resulted in very real restrictions on consumers. These restrictions, in turn, formed only a prelude to the more drastic impact on many Germans' diets that the failure of the Third Reich produced between 1943 and 1948. Nazi policies thus had an influence that could be seen for decades, both in later generations' ideas about what constituted a 'natural, healthy' diet (e.g. whole grain bread and locally grown foods), but also in West Germany's 1950s *Fresswelle*, where enormously increased quantities of butter, cream, meats and refined carbohydrates, along with an increasing preference for 'international' foods – all items that were in short supply during the Nazi period – could once again be seen on most German tables, partly as a reaction to the restricted Nazi diet and the limitations created by the war and its immediate aftermath.

# Notes

1    The expression *die gute Butter* was commonly used during the Nazi period. Butter was one of the first foodstuffs to be in short supply under the Four Year Plan and one of the most desirable; its absence or attainability carried considerable symbolic value. See U. Heinzelmann, *Beyond Bratwurst: A History of Food in Germany* (London, 2014), p. 261.

2    See T. Mason, *Sozialpolitik im Dritten Reich: Arbeiterklasse und Volksgemeinschaft* (Opladen, 1977); H. Berghoff, 'Enticement and Deprivation: The Regulation of Consumption in Pre-war Nazi Germany', in M. Daunton and M. Hilton (eds), *The Politics of Consumption. Material Culture and Citizenship in Europe and America* (New York, 2001), pp. 165–184. See also R. Overy, *The Nazi Economic Recovery, 1932–1938*, 2nd ed. (Cambridge, 1996).

3    G. Corni and H. Gies, *Brot – Butter – Kanonen. Die Ernährungswirtschaft in Deutschland unter der Diktatur Hitlers* (Berlin, 1997), pp. 315, 359.

4    Overy, *The Nazi Economic Recovery*, pp. 261–264. See also Berghoff, 'Enticement and Deprivation', pp. 183–184.

5    Berghoff, 'Enticement and Deprivation'. See also R. Overy, *War and Economy in the Third Reich* (Cambridge, 1994), pp. 185–186.

6    Overy, *War and Economy in the Third Reich*.

7    See H. Thamer, *Verführung und Gewalt. Deutschland 1933–1945* (Berlin, 1986), pp. 511–520 and P. Betts, 'The Nierentisch Nemesis: Organic Design in West German Pop Culture', *German History* 19 (2001), pp. 196–197.

8    Berghoff, 'Enticement and Deprivation', p. 173; H. Berghoff, *Konsumpolitik. Die Regulierung des privaten Verbrauchs im 20. Jahrhundert* (Göttingen, 1999); H. Berghoff, 'Konsumgüterindustrie im Nationalsozialismus. Marketing im Spannungsfeld von Profit- und Regimeinteressen', *Archiv für Sozialgeschichte* 36 (1996), pp. 293–322; J. Wiesen, *Creating the Nazi Marketplace: Commerce and Consumption in the Third Reich* (New York, 2010); and P. Swett, *Selling Under the Swastika: Advertising and Commercial Culture in Nazi Germany* (Stanford, 2013).

9    See B. Davis, *Home Fires Burning* (Chapel Hill, 2000); A. Roerkohl, *Hungerblockade und Heimatfront* (Stuttgart, 1991) and Heinzelmann, *Beyond Bratwurst*.

10   K. Lacey, *Feminine Frequencies. Gender, German Radio, and the Public Sphere, 1923–1945* (Ann Arbor, 1996), p. 180.

11   M. Adelung, *Der 'Kampf dem Verderb' im Haushalt mit sparsamen Mittlen* (Ph.D. diss., Munich, 1940), p. 26.

12   See the recipe in *Deutsche Hauswirtschaft* 20 (1935), p. 123. See other examples in the Federal Archive in Berlin (hereafter, BA) NS 44/58, Anregungen für das Rundfunkprogramm in den Wintermonaten 1938/39.

13   For more on the intensification of housewives' work during the Nazi period, see N. Reagin, *Sweeping the German Nation: Domesticity and National Identity in Germany, 1870–1945* (New York, 2008), pp. 144–180.

14   The correspondence in housewives' organisation files indicates that many
     of their members were unfamiliar with quark, hence the need to distribute
     *Kostproben* (samples for tasting). Complaints that it was not well known
     nor widely carried in shops persisted into the 1930s; see BA NS 44/35,
     minutes of the schooling course for nutritional advisors, 20 September
     1937. The DFW claimed that quark consumption rose 60 per cent due to its
     efforts; see Adelung, *Kampf dem Verderb*, p. 48. The fact that earlier internal
     correspondence indicates that quark was unknown in many parts of Germany
     before the late 1930s, compared with its popularity today, supports the view
     that Nazi efforts did have some influence here.

15   H. Teuteberg, 'Cooling and Freezing Technologies in Twentieth Century
     Germany', in A. den Hartog (ed.), *Food Technology, Science and Marketing:
     European Diet in the Twentieth Century* (East Linton, 1995), p. 60.

16   For the national consumption levels of fish, see W. Hoffmann, *Das Wachstum
     der deutschen Wirtschaft seit der Mitte des 19. Jahrhunderts* (Berlin, 1965),
     p. 624, 632; however, H. Teuteberg, 'Der Verzehr von Nahrungsmitteln in
     Deutschland pro Kopf und Jahr seit Beginn der Industrialisierung (1850–
     1975)', *Archiv für Sozialgeschichte* 19 (1979), pp. 346–347, concludes that
     fish consumption rose only about one-third during roughly the same period.
     For the national figures of the German Women's Bureau regarding cooking
     courses, see BA NS 44/56, NSF and DFW 1938 *Jahresbericht*, pp. 43–46. For
     local reports on the success of cookery courses, see the State Archive of North
     Rhine-Westphalia (hereafter NWSM), NS-Frauenschaft Westfalen-Nord, No.
     340, Monatliche Tätigkeitsberichte des DFWs.

17   See the letter from a 'reader' in *NS Frauenwarte* 5 (1936/37), p. 130.

18   See NWSM NS-Frauenschaft Westfalen-Nord No. 133, Presse, 'Praktische
     Winke für die Hausfrau', 20 October 1936.

19   From descriptions of travelling exhibitions in Kreis Bielefeld in NWSM
     NS-Fruaenschaft Westfalen-Nord No. 60, Monatliche Tätigkeitsberichte der
     Abteilung Volkswirtschaft/Hauswirtschaft, 1935.

20   D. Reese, 'Bund Deutscher Mädel – Zur Geschichte der weiblichen deutschen
     Jugend im Dritten Reich', in Frauengruppe Faschismusforschung (ed.),
     *Mutterkreuz und Arbeitsbuch. Zur Geschichte der Frauen in der Weimarer
     Republik und im Nationalsozialismus* (Frankfurt, 1981), pp. 177–179.

21   Corni and Gies, *Brot – Butter*, p. 362. This slogan translates as: 'trying to
     reduce sugar [in the diet] is the wrong approach. The body needs sugar – it
     nourishes you!'

22   'Das "Ich" und "Wir" der Hausfrauen', *Deutsche Hausfrau* 19 (1934), p. 51.

23   See Heinzelmann, *Beyond Bratwurst*, pp. 259–260, and Corni and Gies, *Brot –
     Butter*, p. 358.

24   Flyer by Martha Voss-Zietz; copy in NWSM NS-Frauenschaft Westfalen-Nord,
     No. 231.

25   'Hausfrauen helfen den Vierjahresplan erfüllen', *Deutsche Hauswirtschaft* 23
     (1938), p. 195.

26   NWSM NS-Frauenschaft Westfalen-Nord, No. 378, 1936 Jahresbericht.

27  BA NS 44/7, minutes of an April 1939 schooling course for nutritional advisors; for similar arguments, see also Vorwerck, 'Hauswirtschaft in Selbstverwaltung', p. 30; BA NS 44/58, scripts for radio broadcasts for housewives from 1938, 'Gesunde Volksernährung'; and 'Über die deutsche Volksernährung', *Deutsche Hauswirtschaft* 21 (1936), p. 129, which concluded that 'the digestive process and biochemistry is different for each race'.

28  Corni and Gies, *Brot – Butter*, p. 355.

29  See R. Proctor, *The Nazi War on Cancer* (Princeton, 1999), especially pp. 120–172.

30  As Proctor notes, German medical experts strongly suspected at the time that a diet richer in fresh produce would help to reduce rates of stomach cancer, for example. The links between meat consumption and heart disease, or between whole grain fibre and colon cancer, for example, were not yet understood during the 1930s. Thus, in some respects, the Four Year Plan diet was only serendipitously 'healthy'.

31  Corni and Gies, *Brot – Butter*, pp. 329, 358–361.

32  For more on the connotations of butter versus margarine, see Reagin, *Sweeping the German Nation*, p. 97.

33  Heinzelmann, *Beyond Bratwurst*, p. 261.

34  NWSM NS-Frauenschaft Westfalen-Nord, No. 88, Protokolle of 1936 meeting of Gau Abteilungs-Leiterinnen.

35  NWSM NS-Frauenschaft Westfalen-Nord, No. 60, Monatsbericht for September 1935 from Kreis Gelsenkirchen.

36  In internal correspondence, DFW advisors repeatedly complained that in many regions, housewives just wanted to place *Wurst* or cold meats on the dinner table, rather than cooking a potato dish or *Milchsuppe* (which was unfamiliar to many German housewives). See for example the analysis of actual household account books in BA NS 44/45, Rundschreiben FW 96/37 (October, 1937).

37  See the recipes attached to some of the memoranda in BA NS 44, vol. 49, which recommend making jellies with only one part sugar to five parts fruit (with no pectin added), a recipe that any experienced cook would know could not work, since the amount of sugar would be insufficient in terms of getting the jam to solidify.

38  NWSM NS-Frauenschaft Westfalen-Nord, No. 378, October 1936 report for Gau division of Volkswirtschaft/Hauswirtschaft.

39  W. Bayles, *Postmarked Berlin* (London, 1942), p. 25. The translation is that of Bayles. The original saying in the first instance was undoubtedly *Negerschweiss*, which would be better translated as 'Negro sweat'.

40  Corni and Gies, *Brot – Butter*, p. 341.

41  See B. Kundrus, 'Greasing the Palm of the *Volksgemeinschaft*? Consumption under National Socialism', in M. Steber and B. Gotto (eds), *Visions of Community in Nazi Germany: Social Engineering and Private Lives* (New

York, 2014), pp. 157–170. See also J. Stephenson, 'Nazism, Modern War and Rural Society in Württemberg, 1939–45,' *Journal of Contemporary History* 32 (1997), pp. 343, 350.

42   Stephenson, 'Nazism, Modern War and Rural Society', p. 349.

43   Corni and Gies, *Brot – Butter*, pp. 357, 563.

44   Heinzelmann, *Beyond Bratwurst*, pp. 266–267.

45   Ibid., p. 274.

46   See U. Thoms, 'The Innovative Power of War: the Army, Food Sciences, and the Food Industry in Germany in the Twentieth Century', in I. Zweiniger-Bargielowska et al. (eds), *Food and War in Twentieth Century Europe* (Burlington, 2011), pp. 247–261; Teuteberg, 'Cooling and Freezing Technologies'. See also J. Drew, 'Die "Gleichschaltung im Stullenverzehr". Ernährungspsychologie im "Dritten Reich" – zwei Fundstücke', *Werkstatt Geschichte* 32 (2002), pp. 82–92.

47   Thoms, 'The Innovative Power of War', p. 252.

48   Ibid.

49   Ibid., p. 256, and also Teuteberg, 'Cooling and Freezing Technologies'.

50   See memo FW 147/40, dated 29 November 1940, in BA NS 44, vol. 49.

51   Corni and Gies, *Brot – Butter*, p. 555.

52   Ibid., p. 556.

53   Ibid., pp. 557–558.

54   Ibid, pp. 558–562 and Heinzelmann, *Beyond Bratwurst*, pp. 271–272.

55   Corni and Gies, *Brot – Butter*, p. 572.

56   See T. Snyder, *Bloodlands: Europe between Hitler and Stalin* (New York, 2010). See also A. Kay, *Exploitation, Resettlement, Mass Murder: Political and Economic Planning for German Occupation Policy in the Soviet Union, 1940–1941* (New York, 2006).

57   Heinzelmann, *Beyond Bratwurst*, pp. 272–273; see also Corni and Gies, *Brot – Butter*, p. 562. For an extended discussion of the plundering of occupied Europe by the Nazi forces, see G. Aly, *Hitler's Beneficiaries: Plunder, Racial War and the Nazi Welfare State* (New York, 2007).

58   Kundrus, 'Greasing the Palm of the *Volksgemeinschaft*', p. 161. For the widespread corruption among the Nazi leadership when it came to food distribution, see Corni and Gies, *Brot – Butter*, p. 569.

59   Heinzelmann, *Beyond Bratwurst*, pp. 274–275; see also Corni and Gies, *Brot – Butter*, p. 564.

60   Corni and Gies, *Brot – Butter*, p. 580.

61   Teuteberg, 'Verzehr von Nahrungsmitteln', pp. 346–347, concludes that consumption of fats fell by about 20 per cent per capita during these years; meat consumption rose very slightly, from 51.4 to 53.5 kilogrammes per capita; fish consumption rose as much as one-third; and rye bread and potato consumption increased modestly, while wheat bread consumption fell by almost 10 per cent. See also Thamer, *Verführung und Gewalt*, p. 489; Berghoff,

'Enticement and Deprivation', pp. 180–181 discusses the sporadic shortages of fats and the banning of heavy cream products in 1938. See also Corni and Gies, *Brot – Butter*, pp. 574–575.

62   See W. Herbert, 'Die Hausfrau spart!', *Hauswirtschaftliche Jahrbücher* 11 (1940), pp. 97–100, who concluded that because women's thrift made reductions in consumption possible, then 'resources … [can instead be used] to build western fortifications, which gives the *Führer* greater freedom in diplomatic negotiations'.

# Select bibliography

Berghoff, H., *Konsumpolitik. Die Regulierung des privaten Verbrauchs im 20. Jahrhundert* (Göttingen, 1999).

Berghoff, H., 'Enticement and Deprivation: The Regulation of Consumption in Pre-war Nazi Germany', in Daunton, M. and Hilton, M. (eds), *The Politics of Consumption. Material Culture and Citizenship in Europe and America* (New York, 2001), pp. 165–184.

Collingham, L., *The Taste of War: World War Two and the Battle for Food* (New York, 2012).

Corni, G. and Gies, H., *Brot – Butter – Kanonen. Die Ernährungswirtschaft in Deutschland unter der Diktatur Hitlers* (Berlin, 1997).

Heinzelmann, U., *Beyond Bratwurst: A History of Food in Germany* (London, 2014).

Proctor, R., *The Nazi War on Cancer* (Princeton, 1999).

Reagin, N., *Sweeping the German Nation: Domesticity and National Identity in Germany, 1870–1945* (New York, 2008).

Teuteberg, H., 'Cooling and Freezing Technologies in Twentieth Century Germany', in den Hartog, A. (ed.), *Food Technology, Science and Marketing: European Diet in the Twentieth Century* (East Linton, 1995), pp. 51–65.

Thoms, U., 'The Innovative Power of War: the Army, Food Sciences, and the Food Industry in Germany in the Twentieth Century', in Zweiniger-Bargielowska, I. et al. (eds), *Food and War in Twentieth Century Europe* (Burlington, 2011), pp. 247–261.

# 2

# Vice in the Third Reich? Alcohol, Tobacco and Drugs

## *Jonathan Lewy*

Countless volumes have been written on the Third Reich, yet its alcohol, drug and tobacco policies have been neglected. The few researchers who have referred to the question have assumed that the Nazis treated drug addicts as they did other anti-socials and alcoholics, employing such measures as incarceration in concentration camps or sterilisation. A close examination of the facts demonstrates that this view is erroneous. Whereas modern readers may consider the consumption of these substances – particularly of drugs – a vice, the Nazis did not necessarily agree. Far from being persecuted, drug addicts were treated well and at the expense of the public purse. This chapter explains why.

The daily lives of drinkers, smokers and drug addicts are difficult to trace. Few people referred to their habits in diaries unless they tried to quit. Oral history could have shed light on this topic, but no systematic interviews were ever conducted in Germany. Unless the habit was illegal, professionals or government officials wrote most of the texts either in scientific journals or in an attempt to influence public opinion. Some information on consumption can be gleaned from financial reports or from the struggles over trading revenues, thus portraying a fresh view of daily life in Nazi Germany; but the individual perspective is still lacking.

In many ways, the best thing that can happen to a historian is for the authorities to control a substance, because police reports and court proceedings provide a wealth of information that it would have been impossible to come by otherwise. Owing to the structure of the traditional legal process, it is easier to access legal portfolios than medical files. Attorneys are obliged to write organised dossiers to present their cases before judges, whereas doctors only write personal notes to remind themselves of their patients' ailments. The primary sources, therefore, have dictated the different approach to studying each substance. Yet the very fact that the police or a state attorney dealt with drug cases should not mislead the reader into thinking that the regime dealt with drug addicts more severely than alcoholics or smokers. Only a closer look reveals the nuances of how these vices were treated in the Third Reich. This chapter is divided into three main sections devoted to alcohol, tobacco and drugs respectively. Each section deals with topics including medicine, law, social usage and finally punishment.

# Alcohol

Alcohol was and has remained popular in Germany. In the nineteenth century, the alcohol industry – breweries and distilleries, wholesalers and retailers, restaurants and bars – played such an important economic role that the German government foundered in two attempts to restrict the sale of alcohol and its production in 1881 and in 1891. The bills for a *Trunksuchtgesetz* ('drinking disease law') failed to pass the Reichstag despite the support of the Kaiser and the support of the German temperance movements.[1]

Similarly to the United States, several competing temperance movements sought to limit alcohol consumption in Germany in the late nineteenth century, the most important of which were the Blue Cross, the Good Templars and the German League against the Abuse of Spirits. These organisations rarely found common ground and often fought each other instead of forming a united front. The first two were religious and therefore viewed drinking as a moral vice, whereas the latter claimed to be motivated by science. By the turn of the twentieth century, membership in all the organisations combined dwindled and none of them possessed much political clout. As a result, Germany stayed wet to the public's content.

Alcohol consumption rose and fell with the economy. German beer consumption reached 118 litres per capita in 1909, decreased to 102 litres in 1913 and fell to 39 litres when the First World War ended.[2] Once the economic situation improved after the war, consumption steadily rose until the crisis of 1930. After the Nazi takeover of power, alcohol consumption soared again. One estimate showed that 6.7 per cent of an individual's salary was spent on alcohol in 1935.[3] Other estimates were higher. According to a contemporary account, Germans spent 4 billion Reichsmarks on alcohol, or 9 per cent of the national income in 1933–1934.[4] In an attempt to curb this phenomenon, the *Arbeitsgemeinschaft für Rauschgiftbekämpfung* (Working Committee for Combating Drugs) in the Ministry of the Interior suggested a ban on the sale of spirits on paydays and a reduction in the number of shops where alcohol was sold.[5] None of these measures ever came to fruition and drinking in Germany was not restrained.

Instead of stopping drinking, the Nazis turned against the drinkers. Even before they came to power, on 31 March 1926 the Nazi daily newspaper, the *Völkischer Beobachter*, published an article that read: 'The struggle against alcohol, however, became an unquestionable and an undeniable moral national calling.'[6] Thus, the National Socialist German Workers' Party (NSDAP) positioned itself with the temperance movement early in its political struggle.

Some Nazis were even more radical. Dr Günther Hecht of the *Rassenpolitisches Amt der NSDAP* (Racial Political Office of the NSDAP) linked the dangers of drugs to the racial qualities of its users. He claimed that the lack of self-control of the 'oriental people' led to the ban on alcohol in Islam. Instead Arabs smoked hashish. The Mongols, in their quest for nirvana, took opium. Jews were alcohol-free but used cocaine or morphine to calm their nerves. Unlike the Orientals, the 'Aryan' race had no historical need for narcotics; its bane lay in alcohol, whose market was controlled by Jews. Alcohol was also a threat to youths and children who drank it, since the habit endangered family values and resulted in racial miscegenation and therefore, it had to be controlled.[7]

Hecht's connection of drug use with racial origin was common at the time. In the United States, it was believed that Chinese workers required opium, black dockworkers needed cocaine, Mexican journeymen could not do without the flower buds of the cannabis plant and Caucasians used morphine and whisky. Yet, despite this common belief, racism was not the grounds for the alcohol policy in the Third Reich. The measure taken against severe alcoholics in Nazi Germany was, indeed, severe – namely, sterilisation – but it was meant to purify the 'Aryan' race itself, rather than protecting it from other 'defiling' elements.

In the late nineteenth century, doctors and specialists all over the world had debated the forced and voluntary sterilisation of biologically deficient individuals. In Germany, unlike the United States and Scandinavia, they lacked the political backing to pass laws, thus sterilisation remained illegal in Germany in the nineteenth and early twentieth centuries.[8] In fact, before the summer of 1933, German eugenicists looked at their counterparts across the Atlantic with envy; whereas Germany prohibited the sterilisation of undesirables, no less than twenty-seven states in the United States allowed the procedure.[9] This jealousy was eventually assuaged upon the Nazi accession to power and the enactment of a sterilisation law in the summer of 1933.

The question of a sterilisation law was raised almost immediately after the Nazi takeover of power. The Fulda Bishops Conference objected to a draft of a law providing for the voluntary sterilisation of anti-socials in May 1933, adhering to the continual resistance of the Catholic Church to birth control. Even so, on 14 July 1933, in the same cabinet session that approved the Concordat with the Vatican, the German government approved the Law for the Prevention of Hereditarily Diseased Offspring, which was much more far-reaching than the earlier proposed bill. To avoid jeopardising the agreement with the Church, the publication of the decree was postponed to 25 July 1933 at the suggestion of the Vice Chancellor, Franz von Papen, who was a Catholic himself.[10]

The law fit the National Socialist scientific worldview like a glove, asserting that all diseases could be cured by scientific means, even if it came at the expense of the patients. The second section of the first paragraph of the law listed hereditary disease as: mental illness from birth; schizophrenia; manic depression; hereditary epilepsy; hereditary Huntington's chorea; hereditary blindness; hereditary deafness; and serious hereditary physical deformities. A separate section of the paragraph stated: 'Furthermore, whoever suffers from severe alcoholism, can be sterilised.'[11] Severe alcoholism was, therefore, lumped together with other hereditary diseases.

The law was not meant as a punitive measure but as a protective measure for the unborn. The authors of the law claimed it would reduce anti-social behaviour as well, since it was believed that biological defects had social repercussions, such as repetitive criminality.[12] If medical experience showed a high probability that an offspring would suffer from a hereditary disease, the potential parents were to be sterilised. Any state-employed physician was allowed to perform the procedure at a hospital, *Heil- und Pflegeanstalt* (sanatorium) or prison. The regional *Erbgesundheitsgericht* (Court for Hereditary Health), a *de facto* physicians' committee, evaluated each case and decided the fate of the 'patient'. Physicians in private practices were required to report anyone they suspected of having a hereditary disease to the regional authorities; failure to do so carried a fine of 150 Reichsmarks.[13]

No less than 1,700 such 'hereditary health courts' were created at the cost of 14 million Reichsmarks. In each court, two medical doctors and one jurist were present.[14] The goal was clear – to battle a biological defect, by preventing it from spreading from one generation to the next. As Hitler put it in *Mein Kampf*: 'Whoever is not bodily and spiritually healthy and worthy, shall not have the right to pass on the suffering in the body of his children.'[15]

The hereditary health courts were very eager to perform their duties, often deciding on cases without even interviewing the patients. In the end, some 350,000 individuals were victims of this policy, of which an unknown number were alcoholics.[16] Of the surviving records, alcoholism was a prominent reason for sterilisation in three separate internal reports conducted in 1934: 5 per cent of 6,052 men, 0.5 per cent of 6,032 women and 6.8 per cent of 325 men and women, respectively. In all, this encompassed about 327 sterilised alcoholics out of 12,400 victims.[17]

Why was alcoholism considered a hereditary disease? The answer went back to the medical understanding of alcoholism in Germany. Since the publication of C. von Brühl-Cramer's seminal book *Über die Trunksucht* in 1819, the German medical establishment recognised the hereditary nature of 'the drinking disease'. Although there were a few dissenters, the standard teaching in German speaking universities was that alcoholism (a term first coined in 1849 by the Swede, Magnus Huss) was hereditary, and that it could even skip a generation. Consequently, it was not surprising that men of medicine and science such as Dr Ernst Rüdin, Dr Arthur Gütt, Dr Leonardo Conti, Dr Gerhard Wagener and others wrote and supported the sterilisation law. In fact, they insisted on including severe alcoholics to the list of potential 'patients' who should be sterilised.

There were other voices in Germany calling for stricter measures against alcohol. In a 1935 speech at the *Deutscher Verein gegen den Alkoholismus* (German Union Against Alcoholism), Gerhart Feuerstein, the head of the Working Committee for Combating Drugs, stated that by April 1935, 1,364 'biologically defective' persons were sterilised in Hamburg, of which 561 (41 per cent) were severe alcoholics. Feuerstein insisted that the National Socialist state must protect its citizens against drugs as part of its many new medical undertakings. Drugs damaged the body and soul and accordingly cleansing the population of drugs should be part of the social hygiene programme of the state.[18]

Feuerstein used the term 'social hygiene' in his speech instead of racial hygiene despite the fact that only a biological programme existed. The use of the term may have been due to Feuerstein's confusion between 'biological' and 'social' hygiene, but it was more likely to have been due to his desire to broaden the biological programme into social spheres; that is to widen the extent of the law from severe alcoholism to drug addiction, and consequently to increase the importance of his own committee.

Feuerstein linked alcoholism with drug addiction, claiming that characteristics exhibited in one affliction existed in the other. He therefore labelled both alcohol and drugs *Rauschgiften* (euphoric poisons). He noted that *Rauschgift* users tended to produce many children costing the public excessive amounts of money. He questioned whether the various treatment sanatoria were effective because once a person succumbed to *Rauschgift*, the recovery rate was hopeless. With successful treatment unlikely, control became the only possible solution. The fact that alcohol was accessible to everyone made the eradication of alcoholism impossible; thus according to Feuerstein, the Third Reich had no choice but to ban alcohol. He stressed that education was the key to a successful campaign against *Rauschgiften*. The masses had to be taught about the dangers of alcohol and drugs before a potential addict would have the chance to touch the substances; the vice was to be prevented before it began.[19] Some education programmes were created, but the rest of Feuerstein's plans were never implemented.

The resulting policy in Nazi Germany probably appears strange to modern readers: on the one hand, the Nazis appeared lenient towards drug and alcohol use. Drugs were never put in the same category as alcohol, nor were drug addicts sterilised. Furthermore, the Nazis never dared to ban alcohol; on the other hand, they sterilised some drinkers, albeit discreetly.

On 28 September 1934, Dr Frey of the Health Department of the Berlin government chastised the local authorities for publishing the number of performed sterilisations. He reminded them that such information should be kept confidential.[20] By 1939, the sterilisation process had slowed down; only 5 per cent of all sterilisations occurred after that date, either due to lack of qualifying cases, internal changes within the hereditary health courts (in order to curb their enthusiasm, the make-up of the courts was changed), or the war.[21] For example, on 20 March 1940, the Health Office of Berlin-Steglitz reported to the Reich Main Health Office that due to the war effort and budgetary cutbacks, the local office was reducing its activities.[22]

The war seems to have changed the parameters of the struggle against severe alcoholism. In a report dated 9 February 1940, the *Sicherheitsdienst* (SD or Security Service) reviewed the fight against alcoholism in the *Wehrmacht*. It dealt with the possibility that new recruits who suffered from alcoholism would enter the military; consequently, a programme was developed to battle this danger. In addition, the SD also raised the possibility that alcoholics, who were barred from receiving wedding certificates according to the *Ehegesundheitsgesetz* (Marriage Health Law) of 1935, might try to enlist and get married as soldiers.[23] Thus, the fear of spreading the disease to offspring continued, since children were the most obvious implication of marriage.

Alcoholism as the defiler of discipline was also a major concern, as reflected in the criminal statistics of the SS courts in 1943. Out of 16,567 cases, 359 persons were convicted for drunkenness; one was jailed for a period between five to ten years. Four were sentenced to jail for up to five years, and the rest were sentenced for a period of less than a year. Only thirty-two of the convicted drunkards received light disciplinary penalties.[24]

The Nazi policy towards alcohol was pragmatic given the ideological worldview of the party. As was the case in the nineteenth century, the Nazi government refrained from banning alcohol; but the regime could not shake off its racial hygiene ideals. Thus, it sought to separate severe alcoholics from society as a whole to assure the creation of a perfect race. Since the problem was hereditary and therefore biological, the solution was physical and prevented by sterilisation. The next sections discuss whether the Nazis adopted similar policies towards tobacco and drugs, other substances that threatened the *Herrenvolk* (master race).

# Tobacco

About 149 cigarettes were smoked per person in the German Reich in 1913. No less than 489 cigarettes per capita were smoked in 1930, 503 cigarettes in 1933, 609 in 1937 and the numbers kept on rising.[25] After the First World War, cigarettes gained in popularity. This trend accounted for Nazi propaganda on cigarette packs, as well as rising medical and governmental concerns about tobacco.

In August 1929, the SA chief of staff Otto Wagener struck a deal with Arthur Dreßler, who founded a tobacco company in Dresden that produced Sturm cigarettes for SA men (other SA-friendly brands such as Trommler and Neue Front were also produced by Dreßler) (Figures 2.1 and 2.2). Originally, this was a sponsorship deal that was aimed to reduce Dreßler's advertisement costs by up to one Pfennig per pack. However, Dreßler's cash-flow problems forced Wagener to invest more money in the newly founded Sturm-Zigaretten-Fabrik Dreßler, and consequently the NSDAP found itself the proud owner of 49 per cent of the company in December 1929. Jacques Bettenhausen, a financier and publisher from Dresden, owned the other 51 per cent.

FIGURE 2.1 *Sturm cigarette advertisement (WL952).*
*Courtesy of the Wiener Library, London.*

**FIGURE 2.2** *Trommler cigarette advertisement (WL1192).Courtesy of the Wiener Library, London.*

The SA-cigarette deal proved to be extremely lucrative; within three years, Dreßler's cigarettes became one of the leading brands in Germany, benefitting the business, as well as the SA and the coffers of the Nazi Party. The SA leadership, including Ernst Röhm, Manfred von Killinger and Georg von Detten, received monthly stipends from Dreßler that paid for their staff, as well as luxury cars.[26] More importantly, the tobacco money enabled the SA to break free from the constraints of the Party, since this was not supervised by its treasurer.

In 1930, the stormtroopers were urged to smoke only Dreßler's cigarettes, and in exchange, they received coupons for buying equipment. Local SA units received rebates based on cigarettes sales. The next step in the tobacco bonanza was already in the making: the SA received an order to exert 'a little energy' in persuading bar owners from selling other brands. Not surprisingly, the exerted energy was often violent and criminal.[27] It was also a successful political tactic. Sturm cigarettes became so popular among the men that they served as an identification marker during the street fights of the SA in the early 1930s.[28]

Hitler's aversion to smoking and the Party's official line against 'big business' did not stop the Party from courting the tobacco industry.[29] On 20 July 1932, Philipp Reemtsma, the owner of the largest tobacco conglomerate in Germany responsible for the production of 60 per cent of the cigarettes in the country, had met Hitler. He sought permission to buy advertisement space in the *Völkischer Beobacher*, the NSDAP's daily newspaper. This meeting was a political and ideological sidestep for the Party, since it was the same Reemtsma the Nazis had accused of destroying the industry and the economy as a whole two and a half years earlier on the floor of the Reichstag.[30] However, the elections on 31 July 1932 threatened to leave the Party's treasury empty, and political flexibility was needed to replenish lost funds. Thus, the NSDAP was ready to follow the path of the SA and allowed Reemtsma's advertisements in its official daily newspaper.

For the Nazis, Reemtsma not only represented 'big business' which trampled the small business owners that the Nazis vowed to save, but also he sold a product that poisoned the 'racial purity' of the people. Reemtsma was certainly an ideological enemy and a financial competitor. Yet, money made friendship possible among enemies. Many Nazi voters were displeased with the visible connection of 'big German tobacco' with the Nazi Party; but the need for cash prevailed. In fact, cigarettes became so important to the financial health of the Party that until Sturm was removed by Reemtsma, the SA and the SS were on a collision course, as each Party element allied itself with a different competing tobacco corporation.[31]

Smoking was one habit that the fledgling SS used to distinguish itself from the larger SA. In 1927, members of the SS were ordered to stop smoking while at Party functions. The opposition to smoking was not necessarily ideological, but rather a way of maintaining an image of aloofness and discipline, thus contrasting the elite SS from the SA rabble.[32] The demand for discipline and exclusivity, however, did not stop the SS from getting its own cigarette deal in March 1932. This brought about fistfights in bars between the SS and the SA two years before the Night of Long Knives, as each party element tried to push forward its own brand of cigarettes.[33]

After the Night of Long Knives (30 June 1934), in which the SS murdered the SA leadership, Reemtsma took the opportunity to enter negotiations to either buy Sturm or end the SA cigarette endorsement. In response, the new SA leadership agreed to abandon Dreßler's brands for 250,000 Reichsmarks a year. The deal was struck, and soon afterwards Sturm, Trommler and Neue Front disappeared from the shelves. Reemtsma simply bought off his unwholesome competitor.[34]

The National Socialist attitude towards tobacco was ambivalent and changeable. Before 1933, the Party, the SA and the SS allied themselves with big tobacco companies. Propaganda was delivered on the covers of cigarette packs, yet the Nazi Party officially opposed smoking, using the famous slogan *Die deustche Frau raucht nicht!* ('The German woman does not smoke!'). Later on, as part of the year of health of 1939, the *Hitler Jugend* (Hitler Youth) came up with the slogan 'You have the Duty to be Healthy!' which aimed to discourage young people from smoking.

Hitler and the SA were willing to strike deals with Philip Reemtsma but scolded him nonetheless, sometimes in private and sometimes in public. In fact, Reemtsma even faced corruption charges in 1934 that were only dropped after Hermann Goering's intervention and after the promise of additional donations to the Party or to particular projects of the Party leadership.[35]

Upon the Nazi takeover of power, attempts were made to propel anti-smoking campaigns through official channels. One of these outlets was the *Reichsarbeitsgemeinschaft für Rauschgiftbekämpfung* (Reich Working Committee for Combating Drugs), which, as noted above, answered to the *Reichsausschuss für Volksgesundheitsdienst Hauptabteilung II – Gesundheitsführung beim Reichs- und Preuss. Ministerium des Innern* (Reich Committee for Public Health in the Ministry of the Interior). The goal of the working committee was to shape a coherent drug policy in Germany. It dealt with all manner of drugs and used the term 'euphoric poison addict' (*Rauschgiftsüchtiger*) to describe addicts, who were subcategorised according to the substance they used: alcohol, tobacco, morphine and other drugs.

Gerhart Feuerstein, the head of the working committee, focused on raising public opinion against nicotine and alcohol use and limiting them, but with few accomplishments. As with the case of alcohol, control measures against the tobacco companies were marginal at best. For example, the committee investigated Astra's claim of a 450 per cent increase in profit for its low nicotine cigarettes (or Lights), but nothing came of it.[36] In the end, the committee was so ineffective that it was dismissed at the end of 1940.

On 29 November 1940, a convention on youth and education sponsored by the *Reichsstelle gegen die Alkohol- und Tabakgefahren* (Reich Authority against the Dangers of Alcohol and Tobacco) of the Health Office, which had been created a year earlier, took place at the Ministry of the Interior. The main theme of the convention was the need to treat the tobacco and alcohol as

*Genussgifte* (drugs), when consumed by youths. Role models and educators were asked to avoid consuming tobacco and alcohol, in order to set an example to the younger generation. Other suggestions were to provide more information to schools on the dangers of tobacco and alcohol, to produce alcohol-free drinks for youths, to encourage 'drug-free' restaurants, where smoking and drinking were prohibited, to eliminate cigarette machines and to enforce strict measures on advertisements that stressed enjoyment from tobacco and alcohol.[37]

Few of these measures ever saw the light of day. Even role models failed to comply. The most famous case was that of one of Germany's leading aces, Adolf Galland, who insisted on installing a built-in lighter and ashtray in his fighter plane for his beloved cigars. His insignia was that of Mickey Mouse smoking a cigar, which attracted the wrath of his superiors, but in the end the ace had his way.

Aside from the remarkable similarity to measures taken by the United States in the twenty-first century against tobacco, few of these measures were actually adopted. The only successful programme was the propaganda against smoking. In fact, modern research suggests that there were fewer cases of lung cancer among German women of the Nazi generation than elsewhere in the developed world.[38]

Research on the damage caused by tobacco was also conducted in Nazi Germany. On 5 and 6 April 1941, State Secretary and the Reich Health Leader, Dr Leonardo Conti, convened the first scientific meeting for studying the dangers of tobacco in the city of Weimar. The meeting was opened with a telegram from the *Führer* and a gift of 100,000 Reichsmarks in grant money to the Institute for Tobacco Research at the Friedrich-Schiller University in Jena.

In his speech, Conti stated that most people underestimated the dangers of tobacco and smoking. He claimed that tobacco was such a dangerous poison that it should be fought against even more strenuously than alcohol. The next speaker, Prof. Karl Astel, the head of the Institute for Tobacco Research in Jena, stressed that women and children should avoid smoking at all costs. Dr H. Wintz, who claimed that tobacco particularly damaged females during puberty, pregnancy and after menopause, supported him. Wintz asserted that smoking in early life could result in sterilisation.[39]

Studies connecting tobacco to cancer had been published before the Nazi takeover of power, and research on tobacco continued to flourish during the Third Reich.[40] Dr Erwin Liek, one of Nazi Germany's leading doctors, often preached that cancer was a preventable disease, caused by human behaviour rather than by genetics. Food, smoking, promiscuous sex and other modern habits were the true culprits for the disease and as a result, it was the role of the new political order in Germany to limit smoking, in spite of the economic power of the tobacco industry.[41] However, the Nazi regime failed to ban smoking, perhaps because tobacco was not perceived as a biological threat, and the resulting cancer was behavioural rather than hereditary. Except for laws prohibiting the sale of tobacco to youths, no other law was passed banning or controlling tobacco use by adults. Severe tobacco addicts, if they were known to science at all, never suffered a sanction in the Third Reich.

On 1 November 1943, the German Ministry of Justice sent a communiqué to judges concerning the case of a 14-year-old-boy who was caught by a Hitler Youth leader with a lit cigarette in public. The boy's teacher testified that he had never had a worse student, or one with more disciplinary problems. Attempts to reform him, including the *Jugendarrest* (youth arrest), had failed.[42] The boy's mother claimed that he was uncontrollable. He had already received *Freizeitarrest* (detention) on eleven different occasions for smoking. In a pre-military camp, he had been sentenced to quarters for three weeks for smoking. The Juvenile Court finally sentenced the boy with three weeks in a juvenile prison.[43]

The legal ground for this punishment was the police Ordinance for the Protection of Youths (9 March 1940) signed by Heinrich Himmler. The ordinance included the following stipulations: Children under 18 were not to enter public areas after dark. Children under 18 required an adult escort to stay in a restaurant after 9.00 pm. Children under 16 needed an escort at all times. Children under 18 were barred from drinking spirits in restaurants. Children under 16 were not allowed to drink at all without an adult escort. Children under 18 were not allowed to smoke in public. The punishment for breaking the law was up to three weeks in prison and a 50 Reichsmark fine. The legal guardian of the child was liable for up to six weeks in prison and 160 Reichsmark fine for negligence.[44] In comparison, the price of a pack of Atika cigarettes was six pfennig. It was not surprising that the mother in the above-mentioned case declared that she could not control her son, or else she too would have been sent to prison.

Forbidding children from smoking was not a new Nazi idea. In 1924, the Jewish toxicologist, Lewis Lewin, had suggested a penalty of up to three months in jail or a fine for under-aged smoking.[45] In 1917, ordinances similar to the one signed by Himmler were promulgated in Mecklenburg-Schwerin, Mecklenburg-Strelitz, Bremen and the majority of Baden. Similar ordinances already existed in Sachsen-Meiningen and Alsace-Lorraine. The minimum age of prohibition varied from 16 to 18 depending on the jurisdiction.[46]

The First World War had loosened the discipline of children at home, of which one of the outcomes was smoking. Local governments tried to remedy the situation through legislation. A similar phenomenon appeared during the Second World War, as youth gangs roamed the empty streets of German cities. The Nazi government sought to restore discipline, thus extreme measures, such as laws banning jazz and smoking were introduced. However, the authorities refrained from imposing similar measures against adults, and the *Wehrmacht* continued supplying cigarettes to the troops as a morale booster.

Similarly to the Nazi policy towards alcohol, the regime's attitude towards tobacco was pragmatic. Smoking was understood as an evil that had to be stopped. It damaged the health of the individual and that of the *Volk*, but the Party had no qualms about taking Big Tobacco's money. After January 1933, when the Nazis were in a position to ban tobacco altogether, or at least control it significantly, they failed to do so. Banning tobacco would have been extremely unpopular, but more importantly, tobacco smoking was not hereditary. Even the cancer that it was purported to cause was behavioural in nature. As a result, and as was often the case elsewhere and later on in history, the ban was directed only against children, who could not resist.

# Drugs

Without a doubt, morphine was the drug of choice in Germany throughout the nineteenth and twentieth centuries. Other drugs were known in the country, especially since German pharmaceutical giants such as Bayer and Merck were the first to synthesise or manufacture many of the illicit drugs known, including morphine, cocaine, crystal meth and heroin.

German doctors were familiar with drugs and often prescribed them. They were also among the first to report on drug addiction in the late nineteenth century.[47] Eduard Levinstein, a Jewish doctor from Berlin, was the first to describe a condition he dubbed *Morphiumsucht* ('the morphine disease'), which was an almost modern description of the condition. His conclusion, which was adopted by the German medical establishment as a whole for the next 100 years, was that alcohol and drugs shared many characteristics, yet, they were different in nature. Namely, anyone who consumed drugs would eventually contract the disease, regardless of their racial, economic or social background.[48]

Even before the publication of Levinstein's formative book, German doctors had noted the complex relationship between wars and drugs. Later, these symptoms were dubbed addiction. Dr Heinrich Laehr, for example, noticed that soldiers who were treated with morphine injections in the wars of German unification (1864–1871) came to his clinic with the symptoms of a similar disease.[49] The association between drugs and wars continued. During the First World War and after, authors such as Walther Benjamin, Gottfried Benn, Hans Fallada (pen name Rudolf Ditzen), Ernst Jünger and others published their experiences of drugs whether as autobiographical essays or in poems and short stories. Yet, despite the prevalence of drugs use in literature, Germans lived in peace with drugs, and drug scares were very rare. German daily newspapers hardly ever echoed the American dread of blacks, Chinese or Mexicans on killing rampages while high on drugs, and probably as a result, the government remained passive. Aside from assuring the quality of manufactured drugs, the Reich's Health Office hardly controlled the drug trade in the country until the turn of the century.[50]

During the First World War, the government began implementing rudimentary controls over some drugs due to military use.[51] Morphine was favoured as a painkiller in field medicine, and cocaine was used for eye operations and for sinus infections. Consequently, the new set of drug laws that were passed in 1917–1918 governed the drug trade but did not ban drug use. In essence, the government wanted to license drug vendors and control them in order to protect its strategic drug stockpiles as part of the war effort.

After the First World War, Germany was forced to ratify the international treaties against drugs as part of the Treaty of Versailles, and so it entered the International Drug Control Regime unwillingly. The ratification brought about a new set of legislation in the country, which implemented stricter controls on drug sales and trade, yet, drug use always remained legal as long as an individual possessed a valid prescription. These prescriptions were never hard to come by, nor was it difficult to procure drugs on the black market since the authorities proved to be quite lethargic in enforcing the laws.

Drug use continued in the roaring days of the Weimar Republic, though probably it was not as prevalent as some film-makers portrayed Berlin in the 1920s.[52] In the 1930s, consumption remained steady and continued after the Nazi takeover of power. In 1942, *Kriminalkommissar* Erwin Kosmehl, the chief of the German drug police, estimated that there were just over 4,000 drug addicts listed in the card index of the criminal police for the entire Reich: 2,384 morphine addicts, 469 dicodid addicts, 465 cocaine addicts, 260 opium addicts, 254 eukadol addicts, 108 dolantin addicts and 84 pervitin addicts.[53] Physicians were the single largest group of addicts in Germany. Judge Beier of Berlin stated that it was easier for an addicted physician to prescribe narcotics to patients than for a non-addicted physician.[54] This was one reason that the control measures were focused on prescriptions.

It must be stated again: the German Opium Law of 1929, the criminal statute governing drugs, did not ban drug use. The criminal act was, in fact, the possession of drugs without a prescription. However, when the Nazis took over power, unwanted individuals, such as the 'work-shy' or 'repetitive offenders', were deemed anti-social. There was never a comprehensive list of what constituted anti-social behaviour, but usually those who were considered anti-social felt it severely even if their crime did not appear in the Penal Code. Today, drug use is often considered an anti-social behaviour in the United States and other countries, but did the Nazis share this view?

Criminologists often considered criminal behaviour an illness in the late nineteenth and early twentieth centuries. Others claimed it was a social or, in National Socialist terms, hereditary defect. As such, repetitive criminals were considered anti-social in the Third Reich and were normally sent to 'protective custody' in concentration camps.[55]

German law forbade unregistered drug trade; consequently, repetitive offences perpetrated by smugglers (be they drug users or not) may have been treated in the same manner as those of other habitual criminals. On 24

November 1933, the Law against Dangerous Habitual Criminals and the Measures of Protection and Correction were passed.[56] The law allowed the police to act against a morally delinquent criminal, in order to protect the general public from vices. In conjunction with the sterilisation law of 1933, these types of criminals could have been sterilised.[57] The list of criminals included rapists, paedophiles and others, but not drug addicts. Even though drug use entailed repetition, it must be remembered that drug use itself was not a crime in Germany.

Regardless of the legal status of drug use in Germany, the Measures of Protection and Correction allowed the courts to forcibly send drug addicts to rehabilitation programmes (a power that German courts had lacked up until then), but they were not sterilised, nor was their behaviour considered to be criminal. In June 1941, a bill covering the 'enemies of the community' was circulated among the various ministries.[58] The proposal codified the term anti-social and gave extreme enforcement authority to the police. This list included drug addicts, the work-shy and others, but it was rejected. A modified proposal was resubmitted on 19 March 1942 but was rejected again, this time hauling a strong opposition within the un-convened cabinet.[59] Hitler himself may have opposed the law because he believed that the German people would not stomach the new legislation.[60] As a result, drug users and drug addicts were not considered anti-socials officially.

Instead of labelling drugs addicts anti-socials or biologically defective like habitual criminals and severe alcoholics, the government sent them to rehabilitation programmes, believing that a cure could be found. Since drug addicts were not regarded as a biological hazard that would pollute the race, the regime handed them to the care of professionals. The judicial system, relying on physicians, oversaw the whole process and determined who should pay for the treatment and whether the patient, once released, should be treated in case of a relapse.

Treatment in Germany was simple. Usually after being caught breaking the prescription laws, addicts stood before a judge who ordered compulsory treatment in a sanatorium. In most cases, the health insurance carried the costs of the treatment, which normally lasted up to half a year. The treatment was harsh by modern standards, but not lethal. Patients were locked in secluded rooms while suffering from withdrawal symptoms and after a few weeks were released to join the general population of the sanatorium. After about six months without drugs, the patient was released from treatment and was subjected to occasional visits by the state attorney's office. If the investigators believed that the person in question had returned to drug use, he was sent again for treatment, this time without a court writ. This process often happened more than once and in some cases even occurred four or five times.

The approach to drug addiction was lax in the Third Reich, as long as the addicts were otherwise of impeccable 'Aryan' stock. Three examples offer a telling illustration of how addicts were viewed by, respectively, the Nazi leadership, Party functionaries and local officials.

The first involved the highest-ranking Nazi known to be a drug addict, Reichsmarschall Hermann Goering, the senior military officer in the Third Reich and Hitler's chosen successor. Goering was wounded in the failed Nazi coup in Munich in December 1923. After being smuggled out of Germany to the Austrian city of Innsbruck, he underwent an operation for which he was treated with morphine. He remained an addict ever since. In September 1925, he was hospitalised at the Langbro mental asylum in Sweden, where he ended up in the violent ward in a straightjacket after attacking a nurse for refusing to give him morphine. He was first released after three months, but soon he relapsed and was voluntarily hospitalised. A few months later, he was officially rehabilitated and released.[61]

After the Nazi takeover of power, Goering procured his record from Langbro and destroyed it. But he could not entirely erase his past, as word of his addiction leaked out in the 1930s, including to members of the foreign diplomatic corps.[62] Over the course of the decade, Goering underwent annual treatment by Dr Hubert Kahle, whose method of detoxification was to calm the nervous system by the administration of sleeping pills when withdrawal symptoms appeared. Goering underwent the treatment either in Kahle's clinic in Cologne or at his own mansion, where he later installed a sauna that was supposed to help him sweat out the drugs.[63]

Recent scholarship has called into question Goering's addiction, arguing that claims of his dependency on morphine are overblown: '[Goering's] addiction was not to narcotics but to the habit of taking pills. His physicians provided him with large numbers of harmless coloured pills, each containing a small quantity of paracodeine.'[64] Whether the pills Goering consumed all day were indeed harmless, however, remains open to question. Paracodeine is unquestionably a narcotic, as it is a synthetic derivative of codeine – one of the many alkaloids found in opium. And despite attempts to suggest otherwise, Goering was quite dependent on the pills. Paracodeine had been first synthesised and marketed in Germany in 1911, as an analgesic and cough suppressant.

Colonel Burton Andrus, the American commandant of the Luxembourg interrogation centre where Goering and other war criminals were held before being transferred to Nuremberg, reported that no less than 20,000 pills of paracodeine were found in Goering's suitcase. 'He has been in the habit of taking 20 pills per dose, two doses a day', Andrus stated.[65] Furthermore, Hitler's personal physician, Karl Brandt, informed his American captors that Goering consumed twenty times the normal daily dose of the drug.[66]

Despite being an open secret, Goering's drug addiction did not prevent him from maintaining a position of enormous power. In fact, his fall from grace was far more likely due to his incompetence on the battlefield than because of his drug habit. Hitler lost confidence in Goering because of a series of strategic losses, including the blunder at Dunkirk, defeat in the Battle of Britain and at Stalingrad.[67]

As the second-in-command in the Third Reich and appointed successor to Hitler, Goering clearly enjoyed a phenomenal amount of power that provided protection from the fate suffered by ordinary German drug addicts. Yet, the same soft approach to drug addiction is evident in examples taken from mid-level officials. One such example is Enno Lolling, a former staff doctor in the Imperial Navy and a practising physician in Neustrelitz, Mecklenburg. Lolling's drug addiction was made clear in a letter from the physicians association in Mecklenburg to the chief physician of the SS, presumably in response to an enquiry into Lolling's character during a purge of SS members in 1936:

> With reference to your query of 20 June 1936 we inform you that there is nothing objectionable against Herr Lolling MD, practicing physician at Neustrelitz-Strelitz [regarding his] professional, moral, collegial [behaviour] or political worldview. Yet we wish to note that Herr Dr. L. was a morphine addict[68] and required repeated rehabilitation. We are obliged to report this to you without being able to produce documentation. Consequently, we are requesting from you to treat the matter with extreme discretion and perhaps, if you think it necessary, ask Herr Dr. L. directly whether he is an addict.[69]

The chief physician of the SS, taking up the suggestion to contact Lolling directly, sent the Mecklenburg doctor the following query: 'I ask you for your word of honour as an SS man, whether you were a morphine addict or were addicted in any other way or [whether you] are [still addicted]. I await your honourable explanation by 30 July 1936.'[70] On that date, Lolling replied: 'I hereby hand over the insurance affidavit and declare on my word of honour as an SS [officer] that I have not taken morphine in any form since 1932 and have been completely free ever since and suffered no after effects. Further addictions were and are not present.'[71]

An addict's word of honour, no more, was enough to clear him from further investigation. Whether Lolling indeed remained clean is uncertain, particularly given that one of his colleagues later described him as a 'heavy drinker'.[72] What is clear is that Lolling's career was unaffected by his addiction. He became a physician in Dachau soon after his correspondence with the chief physician of the SS and was later promoted to chief physician at Sachsenhausen. He eventually rose to become chief physician at the Concentration Camps Inspectorate, putting him in charge of all doctors and medical staff at all SS concentration camps.

Such a soft treatment towards drug addicts was not limited to SS members. In the Third Reich, addiction was viewed as a disease like any other, and once it had been treated, the patient was usually declared healthy and allowed to resume work. The example of Dr W. Horn of Bad Kissingen is illustrative of this. The authorities identified Horn as an opiate addict in 1942, when he was convicted for falsifying prescriptions. He was fined 500 Reichsmarks, likely no more than one-third of his monthly income, and then submitted to treatment in a privately owned sanatorium in Bayreuth. Following treatment, Horn, like many addicts, relapsed. The local Health Office in Munich discovered that he had started taking opiates again and informed the local police. An investigation revealed that he had written falsified prescriptions for his patients in order to supply himself with drugs.

Horn admitted his guilt to the police and was subsequently convicted of breaking the Opium Law. The court fined the doctor 6,000 Reichsmarks and ordered him to pay for the costs of the trial, which amounted to 642.20 Reichsmarks. But beyond the financial penalty, Horn was neither hospitalised nor sent to jail.[73] And throughout the proceedings against him, Horn's medical licence was never revoked. Indeed, he continued to practise as a physician well after the end of the war.

The example of Dr Horn is perhaps the most illustrative of the three, in that it points to the sensitivity of the regime towards drug addicts. They generally came from the higher classes of German society. Physicians in particular were known to be susceptible to drug addiction, given their easy access to drugs. Rather than antagonise the politically important medical community, successive German governments attempted to gain the cooperation of physicians and pharmacists in the effort to control drug use.[74] Widely acknowledged drug addiction among another politically important constituency, veterans of the First World War, also contributed to the authorities' soft approach to drug control.

But given the overriding Nazi preoccupation with racial purity, the single most plausible explanation for why drug addicts were generally spared in the Third Reich is that drug addiction was not considered a hereditary disease. As such, it presented no danger to the master race and the potential for a cure remained, no matter how many times a patient relapsed.

Drug addiction itself was never considered a crime, nor was it grounds for forced treatment without a court order. Nor, for that matter, was drug use a known problem in German prisons, even those not operated by the iron-fisted SS. The Law against Dangerous Habitual Criminals did allow judges to order addicts into forced hospitalisation, but the sentence was not meant, at least *de jure*, as a castigatory measure. And unlike with cases of severe alcoholism, physicians were not required to report cases of drug addiction to hereditary health courts.[75]

While a multitude of factors shaped the Third Reich's atypically lenient handling of drug addicts, the underlying explanation surely lay in the long-held German view of drug addiction as a disease to which all are susceptible. For more than half a century, since Eduard Levinstein put his stamp on German drug treatment in the 1870s, it had been accepted wisdom that any individual who used drugs could fall prey to addiction, irrespective of class, state of mind or strength of will.

The German police was not completely inactive against drugs, but its activities were often marred with racism. Erwin Kosmehl connected Jews to the illicit drug trade in 1942. He asserted that Jews were often caught smuggling drugs and that international cooperation against the illicit drug trade acknowledged and dealt with this problem.[76] But the details of very few drug-related cases survived the war, and even fewer concerning drug smuggling. The League of Nations, for its part, never acknowledged the German claim for a 'Jewish Connection'.[77]

A single case of a Jew, out of twenty convictions, was found on drug-related matters in the German Foreign Ministry reports to the League of Nations in 1938.[78] A Yugoslav named Albert Meisel was caught on Christmas Eve 1937 smuggling 306 kg of raw opium into Austria. On 7 October 1938, a few months after the *Anschluss*, Meisel was convicted to ten months of hard labour. His partner in crime, a Swiss national named Franz Müller, was released.[79] The facts of the case are unknown, but the disparity in punishment between a Jew and a gentile is suggestive about the fairness of the trial in Nazi Germany. There were, however, gentiles who received heavier punishments than Meisel, such as Alfred Siedburg who was sentenced in Hamburg to three years in prison and a fine of 17,000 Reichsmarks for smuggling 160–180 kg of raw opium and 123 kg of morphine from Yugoslavia to Germany.[80]

Drug smuggling was not a problem in Germany. Aside from a few cases, and the constant police suspicion that the two-street Chinatown in Hamburg was a centre for drug smuggling and use, Germany was a drug producing state. It was the source, rather than the target of smugglers. There was no need to smuggle drugs into Germany, since they were not hard to come by. A doctor's prescription was sufficient to procure any drug at the pharmacy; therefore, the most significant drug crime was prescription falsification, rather than smuggling. Shortly after the First World War, Rudolf Ditzen wrote about his experience as a drug user. He met Wolfgang Parsenow, a discharged soldier who was treated with morphine for wounds suffered in combat. Upon his release, the soldier received a block of blank prescriptions of morphine, which the two shared.[81] As long as Parsenow's prescriptions were available, Ditzen was able to tap military stockpiles. But when his drug pipeline dried out, he turned to doctors, faking illnesses and pains to obtain morphine, or stealing their prescription pads to fill them on his own.[82]

Weimar Germany, in fact, proved to be a particularly good historical period for drug experimentations. No legal or ethical restrictions were imposed on drug research until well after the Second World War. For example, the attending physician at Heidelberg university hospital, Kurt Behringer, conducted experiments with hallucinogens on junior physicians at the institution. In his autobiography, psychiatrist Hans Bürger-Prinz recalled how, as a young assistant under Behringer, he was given mescaline while on duty, resulting in him hallucinating that his patients were squirming giant worms and the head nurse a skeleton.[83] Drug experiments on humans were relatively common. Some were carried out in an attempt to better understand the human organism, while others were aimed more at self-discovery. Some, like Walter Benjamin, arguably the best-known drug experimenter of that era, combined both motives, taking drugs under the guidance of Ernst Joël, Fritz Fränkel and Ernst Bloch.

Drug experiments on humans continued into the Third Reich. Probably, the best-known example was recorded during the Nuremberg Trials. The catalyst for the experiment was the death by poisoning of SS *Hauptscharführer* Köhler in Weimar. The police believed that the death might have resulted from the reaction of pervitin with another narcotic drug.[84] After the death, a conference took place in the Main Office of Reich Security; the Gestapo chief *Gruppenführer* Müller presided. *Gruppenführer* Nebe of the Reich Criminal Police was also present, as well as Professor Mrugowsky. The latter pointed out that pervitin was not a poison, and that it could be obtained without a prescription: 'One of the gentlemen present pointed out that in America experiments were carried out where up to 100 tablets of pervitin were administered and the effects were not fatal. But no one present could answer the question of whether a combination of pervitin and a soporific would be harmless, or whether it would lead to an increased reaction to any one direction. The latter appeared improbable to the experts.'[85] To settle the question, Müller ordered Dr Ding of the concentration camp in Buchenwald to conduct experiments on inmates. Three inmates volunteered after they were told the procedure was safe, and all three survived it.[86]

# Conclusion

This chapter has examined three vices known to modern readers – alcohol, tobacco and drugs. The first was dealt with harshly in its severe form in Nazi Germany. The second was tolerated but discouraged, and the third was tolerated and treated. Far from persecuting drug addicts as they did other anti-socials, the Nazis tried to rehabilitate them and were even prepared to spend public money for that purpose.

Smoking and drinking were common in Germany, even though the Nazi Party discouraged both activities. Hitler famously quit smoking as a young man and refrained from drinking (though he did partake on occasion). His staff, however, smoked and drank – just not in his presence. At times, the Nazis used Hitler's abstention as an ideal for the rest of the country, but they shied away from imposing strict controls, fearing public opinion. This is not to say that the Nazis had forgotten their political goals: cleansing the race from hereditary contaminants.

Since the early nineteenth century, the drinking disease was considered to be a hereditary disease. In the twentieth century, Nazi parlance turned the disease into a biological defect that had to be eradicated. Therefore, severe alcoholics were forcibly sterilised according to a law passed in 1933. But drinking did not stop in the Third Reich. Top officials such as Martin Bormann and Reinhardt Heydrich were known drunkards. Beer remained a recognised food essential in Bavaria during the war, and soldiers were given schnapps before special or difficult missions.

The Nazi policy towards tobacco was equally confusing. On the one hand, tobacco use was considered a dangerous carcinogen and therefore was limited to adults. In fact, the first age limit on smoking in history was imposed by Heinrich Himmler. However, this did not prevent the Nazi Party from using cigarette boxes for propaganda purposes or receiving the financial support of the tobacco magnate Philipp Reemtsma. In fact, Hitler himself recognised the importance of tobacco to the future autarkic German economy, even though he prided himself on quitting as a young man.

The drug policy of the Third Reich is the most interesting of the three, since to modern readers today, drug use might appear as the most serious vice of all. However, in Nazi Germany this was not the case. The Nazis allowed judges to force addicts into rehabilitation programmes. Drug addicts, unlike severe alcoholics were not considered a biological threat to the *Volk*, and therefore, they were given treatment.

# Notes

1   A. Heggen, *Alkohol und Bürgerliche Gesellschaft im 19. Jahrhundert* (Berlin, 1988), pp. 142–143; J. Roberts, *Drink, Temperance and the Working Class in Nineteenth-Century Germany* (Boston, MA, 1984), pp. 52–53.

2   M. Teich, 'The Industrialisation of Brewing in Germany (1800–1914)', in E. Aerts et al. (eds), *Production, Marketing and Consumption of Alcoholic Beverages since the Late Middle Ages* (Leuven, 1990), pp. 102–113.

3   W. Pieper (ed.), *Nazis on Speed: Drogen im 3. Reich* (Munich, vol. 1, 2002), pp. 42–44.

4   G. Feuerstein, *Rauschgiftbekämpfung – ein wichtiges Interessengebiet der Gemeindverwaltung* (Berlin, 1936), p. 8.

5   H. Boberach (ed.), *Meldungen aus dem Reich: Die geheimen Lageberichte des Sicherheitsdienst der SS 1938–1945* (Berlin, vol. 1, 1984), p. 273.

6   *Völkischer Beobachter*, 31 March 1926.

7   G. Hecht, 'Alkoholmissbrauch und Rassenpolitik', in *Bekämpfung der Alkohol- und Tabakgefahren: Bericht der 2. Reichstagung Volksgesundheit und Genussgifte* (Berlin, 1939), reprinted in Pieper (ed.), *Nazis on Speed*, vol. 1, pp. 178–186.

8   J. Noakes, 'Nazism and Eugenics: The Background to the Nazi Sterilisation Law of 14 July 1933', in R. Bullen et al. (eds), *Ideas into Politics* (London, 1984), pp. 75–94; R. Proctor, *Racial Hygiene* (Cambridge, MA, 1988), pp. 96–101.

9   F. Lenz, *Menschliche Auslese und Rassenhygiene*, in E. Baur, E. Fischer and F. Lenz (eds), *Grundriß der menschlichen Erblichkeitslehre und Rassenhygiene* (Munich, vol. 2, 1921), pp. 126–127.

10  G. Lewy, *The Catholic Church and Nazi Germany* (New York, 1964), pp. 258–259.

11  'Gesetz zur Verhütung erbkranken Nachwuchses', 14 July 1933, *Reichsgesetzblatt* I, p. 119. Revised on 4 February 1936 in *Reichsgesetzblatt* I, p. 529.

12  Proctor, *Racial Hygiene*, pp. 102–108.

13  'Gesetz zur Verhütung erbkranken Nachwuchses', 14 July 1933, *Reichsgesetzblatt* I, p. 119. Revised on 4 February 1936 in *Reichsgesetzblatt* I, p. 529.

14  Proctor, *Racial Hygiene*, pp. 102–104.

15  A. Hitler, *Mein Kampf*, quoted and translated in Proctor, *Racial Hygiene*, p. 95.

16  R. Winau, 'Sterilisation, Euthanasie, Selektion', in F. Kudlien (ed.), *Ärzte im Nationalsozialismus* (Cologne, 1985), pp. 197–207. Some claim that the number reached 400,000. See G. Bock, *Zwangssterilisation im Nationalsozialismus: Studien zur Rassenpolitik und Frauenpolitik* (Opladen, 1986), p. 230ff.

17  O. von Verschauer, *Erbpathologie: Ein Lehrbuch für Ärzte und Medizinstudierende* (Dresden, 1938 [1934]), p. 178, quoted in Proctor, *Racial Hygiene*, p. 108.

18  Feuerstein, *Rauschgiftbekämpfung*, pp. 3–11.

19  Ibid.

20  'Memorandum by Dr. Frey, 28 September 1934', LArch. Berlin B Rep. 012, No. 246.

21  Proctor, *Racial Hygiene*, pp. 114–117; Winau, 'Sterilisation, Euthanasie, Selektion', pp. 197–207.

22  'The health office of Berlin, Steglitz to *Hauptgesundheitsamt* Berlin, 20 March 1940', LArch. Berlin, B Rep. 012 Acc. 1641, No. 247.

23  'Gesetz zum Schutze der Erbgesundheit des deutschen Volkes (Ehegesundheitsgesetz)', 18 October 1935, *Reichsgesetzblatt* I, p. 1246; Boberach (ed.), *Meldungen aus dem Reich*, vol. 3, p. 744.

24  Der Reichsführer-SS und Chef der deutchen Polizei, *Kriminalistik des Hauptamtes SS-Gericht für das Jahr 1943*, vol. 2, found in LArch. Berlin, A Rep. 244 Acc. 1798, No. 2.

25  Pieper (ed.), *Nazis on Speed*, vol. 1, p. 45.

26  O. Wagener, *Hitler aus nächster Nähe. Aufzeichnungen eines Vertrauten 1929–1932* (Frankfurt, 1978 [1946]), pp. 60–62, p. 487n; H. Turner, Jr., *German Big Business and the Rise of Hitler* (New York, 1985), pp. 60–62.

27  Turner, *German Big Business and the Rise of Hitler*, p. 117.

28  Wagener, *Hitler aus nächster Nähe*, p. 62.

29  I. Kershaw, *Hitler 1889–1936: Hubris* (London, 1998), p. 348.

30  T. Grant, *Stormtroopers and the Crisis in the Nazi Movement* (London, 2004), pp. 109–112. Two local party-affiliated newspapers had already sought

Reemtsma's advertising money in July 1931, but their editors acted on their own, without discussing the matter with the *Führer*.

31　Grant, *Stormtroopers and the Crisis in the Nazi Movement*, p. 113.

32　Heinz Höhne, *The Order of the Death's Heads* (London, 1969), pp. 22, 25.

33　Turner, *German Big Business and the Rise of Hitler*, pp. 117, 392n; Grant, *Stormtroopers and the Crisis in the Nazi Movement*, pp. 113–119.

34　E. Lindner, *Die Reemtsmas: Geschichte einer deutschen Unternehmerfamilie* (Munich, 2008), pp. 131–133.

35　Ibid., pp. 114–123.

36　'Summary of the Stettin Conference, 10 October 1937', StA – München, Pol. Dir. 7582.

37　*Münchner Medizinische Wochenschrift* 88, no. 4 (24 January 1941), pp. 89–116. See also *Die 12 Forderungen gegen den Alkohol- und Tabakmissbrauch* published by the Central Office for the Health of the People of the NSDAP as part of the Reich Authority against alcohol misuse in the Ministry of Health in Pieper (ed.), *Nazis on Speed*, vol. 1, p. 256.

38　R. Proctor, *The Nazi War on Cancer* (Princeton, NJ, 1999), pp. 267–270.

39　*Münchner Medizinische Wochenschrift* 88, no. 27 (4 July 1941), pp. 745–772.

40　For a short list of studies, see Pieper (ed.), *Nazis on Speed*, vol. 1, pp. 254–260.

41　Proctor, *Nazi War on Cancer*, pp. 20–34.

42　According to 'Dienststrafverordnung für die Dauer des Krieges 20 May 1940', in *Reichsbefehl* 23/41k.

43　H. Boberach et al. (eds), *Richterbriefe: Dokumente zur Beeinflussung der deutschen Rechtsprechung 1942–1943* (Boppard a. R., 1975), pp. 204–205.

44　'Polizeiverordnung zum Schutze der Jugend vom 9 März 1940', in *Reichsgesetzblatt* I, p. 499.

45　L. Lewin, *Phantastica* (Cologne, 2002 [1924]), p. 412.

46　*Ärztliches Vereinsblatt für Deutschland* 44, no. 1138 (21 July 1917), p. 275.

47　The most important book on this topic is E. Levinstein, *Die Morphiumsucht: Eine Monographie nach eigenen Beobachtungen* (Berlin, 1877 [1883]). See also A. Erlenmeyer, *Die Morphiumsucht und ihre Behandlung* (Berlin, 1887 [1883]).

48　Levinstein, *Die Morphiumsucht*, pp. 1–7, pp. 10–11.

49　H. Laehr, 'Über Missbrauch mit Morphium-Injectionen', *Allgemeine Zeitschrift für Psychiatrie und psychisch-gerichtliche Medicin* 28, no. 3 (1872), pp. 349–352.

50　E. Hickel, 'Das Kaiserliche Gesundheitsamt and the Chemical Industry in Germany during the Second Empire: Partners or Adversaries?', in R. Porter and M. Teich (eds), *Drugs and Narcotics in History* (Cambridge, 1995), pp. 97–113.

51　'Verordnung, betreffend den Handel mit Opium und anderen Betäubungsmitteln', 22 March 1917 in *Reichsgesetzblatt*, p. 256; *Bekanntmachung des Preussischen Kriegsministeriums, betreffend*

*Beschlagnahme und Bestandserhebung von Cocablättern und Cocain*, 2 November 1918, No. 1/11 12, p. 2; 'Verordnung über den Verkehr mit Opium', 15 December 1918 in *Reichsgesetzblatt*, p. 1447.

52  A. Hoffmann, 'Von Morphiumpralinees und Opiumzigaretten: Zur beginnenden Problematisierung des Betäubungsmittelkonsums im Deutschland der 1920er Jahre', in B. Dollinger and H. Schmidt-Semisch (eds), *Sozialwissenchaftliche Suchtforschung* (Wiesbaden, 2007), pp. 251–276.

53  Kosmehl, *Der sicherheitspolizeiliche Einsatz bei der Bekämpfung der Betäubungsmittelsucht*, BArch. RD 19/30.

54  Ibid.

55  R. Gellately, *The Gestapo and German Society: Enforcing Racial Policy, 1933–1945* (Oxford, 1990).

56  'Gesetz gegen gefährliche Gewohnheitsverbrecher und über Massregeln der Sicherung und Besserung', 24 November 1933, *Reichsgesetzblatt* I, p. 995.

57  W. Becker, 'Paragraph 42k StGB. (Entmannung) in der Praxis', *Kriminalistik* 16, no. 6 (1942), pp. 63–65.

58  H. Friedlander, *The Origins of the Nazi Genocide: From Euthanasia to the Final Solution* (Chapel Hill, NC, 1995), p. 154; Gellately, *The Gestapo and German Society*, p. 196.

59  'Schreiben des Reichs- und Preussischen Innenministers Dr. Wilhelm Frick an den Reichsminister ohne Geschäftsbereich und Chef der Reichskanzlei Dr. Hans Heinrich Lammers mit Entwurf eines Gesetzes über die Behandlung Gemeinschaftsfremder mit Begründung' (Berlin, 24 June 1941) in W. Ayass (ed.), *'Gemeinschaftsfremde': Quellen zur Verfolgung von 'Asozialen', 1933–1945* (Koblenz, 1998), No. 114.

60  Friedlander, *The Origins of the Nazi Genocide*, p. 154.

61  R. Manvell and H. Fraenkel, *Hermann Goering* (London, 1962), pp. 38, 42–43, 385; B. Taylor, 'Hermann Goering and Josef Goebbels: Their Medical Casefiles (Part 1)', *Maryland State Medical Journal* 25, no. 11 (1976), pp. 35–47.

62  Manvell and Fraenkel, *Hermann Goering*, p. 142.

63  Ibid., p. 143.

64  R. Overy, *Goering* (London, 2000), p. 20.

65  B. Andrus, *The Infamous of Nuremberg* (London, 1969), pp. 30 and 48; A. Neave, *Nuremberg: A Personal Record of the Trial of the Major Nazi War Criminals in 1945–6* (London, 1978), p. 69; G. Gilbert, *Nuremberg Diary* (New York, 1961 [1947]), p. 17.

66  Manvell and Fraenkel, *Hermann Goering*, p. 315.

67  I. Kershaw, *Hitler, 1936–45: Nemesis* (London, 2000), pp. 296, 535, 620–621, 644–645.

68  In German: '*morphinsüchtig*'.

69  'Physician Chamber Mecklenburg-Lübeck to Reichsführer SS – the Reich Physician of the SS (Rostock, 21.7.36)', BArch. SSO Enno Lolling, 19 July 1888.

70  'The Reich Physician of the SS to SS-Scharführer Dr. Lolling (Berlin, 27 July 1936)', BArch. SSO Enno Lolling, 19 July 1888.

71  'Dr. Enno Lolling to the Reich Physician of the SS (Neustrelitz-Strelitz, 30 July 1936)', BArch. SSO Enno Lolling, 19 July 1888.

72  R. Lifton, *The Nazi Doctors: Medical Killing and the Psychology of Genocide* (New York, 1986), p. 198.

73  StA. München, Staanwa. Nr. 17670.

74  A. Linz, 'Behördliche Durchführung des Opiumgesetzes: Ziele und Ergebnisse', in G. Feuerstein (ed.), *Suchtgiftbekämpfung* (Berlin, 1944), pp. 24–32; 'Summary of the Stettin Conference, 10 October 1937', StA. München, Pol. Dir. 7582; E. Kosmehl, *Der sicherheitspolizeiliche Einsatz bei der Bekämpfung der Betäubungsmittelsucht*, BArch. RD 19/30.

75  A. Maehle, *Doctors, Honour and the Law: Medical Ethics in Imperial Germany* (New York, 2009), pp. 47–68.

76  E. Kosmehl, 'Der sicherheitspolizeiliche Einsatz bei der Bekämpfung der Betäubungsmittelsucht', a lecture given on 14 October 1942 in Berlin. A full copy of the lecture may be found in BArch. RD 19/30; an abridged version of the speech appears in G. Feuerstein's book recounting the conference, *Suchtgiftbekämpfung*, and is partially reproduced in Pieper (ed.), *Nazis on Speed*, vol. 1, pp. 196–203.

77  'League of Nations, Advisory Committee on Traffic in Opium and other Dangerous Drugs, Reports from Governments on the Illicit Traffic in 1938, 9 May 1938', NARA Acc# 170-74-005 box 119 file 1230–1.

78  Germany continued to report on its drug enforcement activities to the League of Nations until the end of 1939 even though it was not a member.

79  '*Reichskriminalpolizeiamt* to *Hauptamt* des RFSS, 23 January 1939', Pol. Arch. AA R 43.324.

80  '*Reichskriminalpolizeiamt* to *Hauptamt* des RFSS, 9 February 1939', Pol. Arch. AA R 43.324.

81  T. Crepon, *Leben und Tode des Hans Fallada* (Leipzig, 1992), pp. 101–103.

82  Ibid., p. 104.

83  H. Bürger-Prinz, *Ein Psychiater berichtet* (Hamburg, 1971), p. 70.

84  Nuremberg Military Tribunal 'Green' Series, 'The Medical Case; Military Tribunals No. I, Case 1', in *Trials of War Criminals Before the Nuremberg Military Tribunals under Control Council Law No. 10*, vol. 1, pp. 690–692.

85  Ibid.

86  Ibid.

# Select bibliography

Bock, G., *Zwangssterilisation im Nationalsozialismus: Studien zur Rassenpolitik und Frauenpolitik* (Opladen, 1986).

Friedlander, H., *The Origins of the Nazi Genocide: From Euthanasia to the Final Solution* (Chapel Hill, NC, 1995).

Gellately, R., *The Gestapo and German Society: Enforcing Racial Policy, 1933–1945* (Oxford, 1990).

Holzer, T., *Globalisierte Drogenpolitik: Die protestantische Ethik und die Geschichte des Drogenverbotes* (Berlin, 2002).

Lindner, E., *Die Reemtsmas: Geschichte einer deutschen Unternehmerfamilie* (Munich, 2008).

Noakes, J., 'Nazism and Eugenics: The Background to the Nazi Sterilisation Law of 14 July 1933', in Bullen, R. et al. (eds), *Ideas into Politics* (London, 1984), pp. 75–94.

Pieper, W. (ed.), *Nazis on Speed: Drogen im 3. Reich* (Munich, vols. 1–2, 2002).

Proctor, R., *Racial Hygiene* (Cambridge, MA, 1988).

Proctor, R., *The Nazi War on Cancer* (New Haven, CT, 1999).

Turner, Jr., H., *German Big Business and the Rise of Hitler* (New York, 1985).

Wachsmann, N., 'From Indefinite Confinement to Extermination: "Habitual Criminals" in the Third Reich', in Gellately, R. and Stolzfus, N. (eds), *Social Outsiders in Nazi Germany* (New Haven, CT, 2001), pp. 165–191.

# 3

# Illness in the State of Health

## *Geoffrey Cocks*

In 1924, Adolf Hitler stood before the People's Court in Munich on charges of treason. The defendant defiantly justified the 'Beer Hall Putsch' of the previous November by declaiming at length on his political aims and philosophy. He denigrated the state of Bavaria by referring admiringly to Prussia as the 'germ-cell of the [German] Empire'.[1] Such habitual recourse to biological metaphor was a reflection of the biological racism at the centre of Hitler's worldview. This racialist rhetoric was on even greater display in *Mein Kampf*, the autobiographical manifesto he wrote in prison later in 1924. Here, Hitler called the 'folkish state' he would establish 'a means to an end' by which the 'German national body' would recover from the degeneration that 'prattling quackery' had failed to diagnose and treat in the German Empire.[2] The Nazi state – in fact as well as fantasy – would be a State of Health in which racial selection, racial cultivation and racial extermination embodied a thoroughly monstrous 'medicalisation of politics'.[3] Hitler chose its symbol, the swastika (Sanskrit 'well-being'), to signify 'the mission of the fight for the victory of Aryan man', Aryans being, as Hitler had explained in a speech in Munich in 1920, an ancient 'race of giants and strength and health'.[4]

## Racial health under National Socialism

Hitler and Nazism were not *sui generis*; they were creatures of their time and place. And the time and place of the late modern era in Germany and

Europe was characterised as much as anything by growing social, medical, political and individual concern with the health of the body and mind. Germany in particular before 1933 was a highly politicised and medicalised setting for the experience of health and illness. European and German science and medicine in the late nineteenth and early twentieth centuries grew in effectiveness, authority and prestige. The organisation of public health was especially advanced in Germany before and after national unification in 1871. A social hygiene movement had great influence on government policies and programmes created to monitor, maintain and improve the health of the population. For socialists, this was a matter of public welfare and social equality. For many conservative physicians, it was a matter of strengthening the nation and preventing revolution from the left. Both socialists and conservatives also found powerful reinforcement from a eugenics movement that urged biological improvement of human populations and worried about 'degeneration' among humans as a result of improved medical care and public welfare. On the radical right, 'racial hygiene' located differences of 'superior' and 'inferior' 'races' as 'rooted in the body'.[5] In Germany, such nationalism and racism played an even larger role in matters of health and illness after the First World War. This was due not only to legions of physically and mentally disabled from the war and to post-war economic and political divisions and disruptions, but also to widespread concern for the revival of a defeated nation and the strengthening of its biological base.

The Great War of 1914–1918, the Great Influenza of 1918, the Great Inflation of 1923 and the Great Depression of 1929 were exceptionally problematic with regard to the German experience of health and illness. In turn, the demands and disasters of Hitler and Nazism in power intensified and multiplied threats to the physical and mental well-being – as well as to the very existence – of many millions of people. We know a great deal about the monstrous and murderous racism that was the *raison d'être* of the Third Reich. We know a great deal about the role of medicine in particular in effecting lethal Nazi racial policy. We know relatively little, however, about the experience of health and illness in Nazi Germany. This experience was historically important not only in terms of its place in the lives of millions of Germans between 1933 and 1945, but also because experiences with illness and health under Hitler were an extension of a recent German past of war, economic disaster and political catastrophe. They were an outgrowth too of the rapid development of a recently unified Germany into a modern, industrial and commercial society. And they were the outcome of pervasive social, cultural and psychological dynamics of the demands, pleasures and needs of a secular and material body, mind and self that formed a major and specific historical constituent of an ever more industrial, commercial and medical modern Western world.

The Nazi imposition of 'racial health' was itself an act of massive cultural cowardice in the face of the modern morbid, mortal and sexual body. Nazi insistence on such illusory racial health – not to mention its murderous application to Germany's 'racial enemies' – burdened Germans with demand, expectation and exploitation for work and war. Germans responded with a mixture of discipline, fanaticism, worry, physical and mental breakdown, and instances and degrees of agency on behalf of the self. The travails of body and mind under the demands of Nazism were also of such magnitude that Germans' concern with health and illness consumed space for empathy with the much greater sufferings of Jews and other Nazi outsiders who were excluded from the *Volksgemeinschaft* ('national community'). In the end, the racist Nazi *Volksgemeinschaft* fell victim to ongoing and aggravated dynamics privileging concern for increasingly endangered mind, body and self. More and more, life and experience in collapsing and collapsed Nazi Germany became an individual as well as a corporate war of all against all, in a frenzied landscape of battle and work, discipline and diversion, suffering and survival, fear and flight, pain and panic, injury, illness and death. In all of these terrible ways, the Third Reich sustained in Germany modern material, medical and commercial concern with health and illness.

The history of the experience of health and illness engages several important debates in the historiography of modern Germany and the Third Reich. It demonstrates that everyday life in Germany under Hitler was not a space apart from the demands and desires of the Nazi regime. The quotidian experience of health and illness often transpired within the private environments of the self as sanctuary from the state. But for historically structural reasons, this space could not help being only a temporary reprieve from ongoing occupational service to that state. This experience also documents that while the *Volksgemeinschaft* was an actual and appealing social reality for millions of Germans, it was also a site of individual and collective contestation between preceding and ongoing realities of modern industrial and commercial society. Nazism was itself also a violent extremity of aspects of modern industrialism, commercialism, nationalism and imperialism.[6] The noxious, irrational and racist strain of Hitler's antisemitism at the centre of his regime's fantasy of racial purity too was one culmination of a broader cultural crisis of masculinity and the body in the age of industrialisation, industrial warfare and medicalised anxiety about morbidity and mortality. Central to the history of society under Nazism, therefore, was that Germans acted and reacted not just as Germans, but as individuals of the modern era variably and by degree well and ill in body and mind. And they did so under conditions set by the Nazi regime that critically magnified the consciousness and consequences of health and illness in the modern age. The experience of health and illness, given its ubiquity and a modern urgency hypertrophied under the Nazis, offers a peculiarly rich and relevant means of understanding the significance of Nazi Germany as much more conduit than caesura in the modern history of Germany, Europe and the West.

# The body politic

What was the state of health in the State of Health? Here, we mean not just the incidence of acute, chronic or episodic illness and disease, but rather the experience of illness in terms of popular and official views, attitudes, discourses, representations and actions over time with regard to health and illness. The actions and outrages of Nazism in power were not merely the outcome of the imposition and embrace of a *Volksgemeinschaft*, but rather of a dynamic intersection of the fact and fantasy of such a community with a modern society inhabited by the material self. Hitler's state thus revived the dead metaphor of 'the body politic' in three ways. The first was the biologism of the Nazis' pseudoscientific lodestar Social Darwinism, which in the nineteenth century had resuscitated the ancient conception of government or state as an organic entity analogous to the human body. The second was the morbid, mortal and sexual body of each individual in the Third Reich that was the object of unprecedented political rhetoric, concern, supervision, intervention and thus also heightened self-concern and varied response. The third was the concept and context of the *Volksgemeinschaft* itself. These three bodies politic were intrinsically interlinked from 1933 to 1945, the first motivating and problematising the second, and the second empowering and inhibiting the third. There was thus a body politic of the modern self in Nazi Germany that complemented, sustained and sometimes – especially when the war was going badly – even obstructed the body politic of Hitler's state.

There is rich documentation for a history of health and illness between 1933 and 1945. Notable among these sources are the *Jahresgesundheitsberichte* (Annual Health Reports) prepared by Regional Medical Officers. Owing to the health problems throughout German society evident particularly since 1918, as well as to their own plans for racial purification, rearmament and war, the Nazi regime was even more concerned with the health of the German population than the preceding Imperial and Weimar governments. In 1935, the Nazis expanded the number of the many required narrative evaluations of health conditions added in 1923 to the annual tabulation of the incidence of disease. Most of the Medical Officers involved were hygienists and bacteriologists by training and therefore sympathetic to the new Nazi eugenic emphasis on the cultivation of individual health in service to the racial *Volksgemeinschaft* in place of a previous complementary emphasis on social reform and welfare. The Annual Health Reports provide comprehensive documentation of the objective conditions shaping and creating the subjective experience of health and illness in the Third Reich. There are also the many memoirs, diaries, letters and other first-person accounts that report directly on the experience of health and illness during Nazi Germany's six years of peace and six years of war. Novels written during and after the Third Reich also offer copious instances of and insights into the experience with health and illness under Hitler. Since matters of health and illness are universal among human beings, the experience of writers and novelists – not to mention their observations of others – is not unique to them as artists or intellectuals. The functions and dysfunctions of the body and the mind are fundamentally the same for those people who write or think for a living as they are for those who do not.

The Nazis inherited a comprehensive and efficient German state health-care system of some long standing. They inherited too a populace burdened with significant health challenges stemming from social conditions also aggravated by recent military, political and economic disasters, starting with pervasive malnutrition and illness during the First World War that culminated with the onset in 1918 of a worldwide influenza pandemic. During the first three months of 1933, Germany once again was in the grip of the flu. Heinrich Böll remembers falling ill with it at the end of January: 'On 30 January 1933, the 15-year-old is ill in bed with a severe case of flu ... public life was partially paralysed, many schools and government offices were closed at least locally and regionally.'[7] There were also more chronic health problems, however. Annual Health Reports from Erfurt for 1933 and 1934, for example, remarked on widespread neurasthenia among the many unemployed youth. Elsewhere, the same was true among war veterans and schoolchildren. Poor living conditions in towns and villages throughout Germany had been made worse by the Depression, while poor nutrition and overwork among rural men, women and children in particular lowered resistance to illness. Scabies and lice were common, while outbreaks of scarlet fever and diphtheria among children and rickets among infants were on the rise throughout the 1930s. In western Saxony, housing conditions in the rural district of Aschendorf-Hümmling were so bad that not only diphtheria, but also typhus and paratyphus were widespread. Medical officers in Thuringia reported a significant increase in deaths due to diphtheria each year from 1932 to 1934 and due to poor health generally among youth born between 1918 and 1922. Both civilian and military authorities as late as 1940 noted foot and teeth problems as well as 'general weakness' and underdevelopment as worryingly common among members of this age cohort.[8]

The Nazis strove to – and loudly claimed to – address these problems. They were committed to improving the health of the German 'race' for the purpose of economic recovery, which meant rearmament for a war of racial conquest. Workers were monitored and admonished to guard their health (Figure 3.1). Women's health was to be protected at home and at work in order to ensure their racial role as producers of healthy 'Aryan' offspring. Youth were organised into groups not just for purposes of supplemental political indoctrination outside of school, but also for physical training and cultivation of healthy habits. The result, predictably, was mixed. Hitler was fortunate that the bottom of the trough of the Great Depression was reached during 1932. Nazi propaganda, programmes and most Germans' enthusiasm for Hitler and the new *Volksgemeinschaft* also helped to raise levels of expectation and subjective and objective well-being. Some elements of Nazi health policy were even in line with 'progressive' health-care policies, such as the regime's concern with the threat posed by cancer and other diseases that led to a campaign against smoking, propaganda promoting clean food and water and programmes encouraging exercise and preventive medicine. These efforts were of course not progressive in aim, but rather part of a 'vast, hygienic experiment designed to bring about an exclusionist sanitary utopia ... [out of] fear of tiny but powerful agents corroding the German body'.[9]

In spite of all this Nazi activity – and because of it – one cannot speak of an improvement in health in Germany under National Socialism. Although

FIGURE 3.1 *Report every illness. Courtesy of Bundesarchiv-Bildarchiv Plak 033-017-099 Lehrmittelzentrale der Deutschen Arbeitsfront 1941/44 Jan Derk de Haan*

there was some amelioration in certain areas of health from 1932, between that year and 1937 mortality in most age groups, particularly among children, rose in contrast to declining death rates in Germany and Europe since 1919. This was due to cuts in spending on health in favour of funding Hitler's rearmament programme, the lack of animal proteins and fat from the curtailment of food imports, as well as price controls on agricultural products. It was also due to an increase in industrial accidents and injuries, the increasing consumption of alcohol and tobacco due to higher rates of employment and to unremitting persecution of 'racial enemies'. The Nazi emphasis on physical training and discipline for youth also had negative consequences on health. As in the schools, corporal punishment and even beatings were common in the Hitler Youth as a means of 'toughening' as well as punishment. In 1936, Reich Youth Leader Baldur von Schirach issued guidelines for 'toughening' young Germans, promising that parents could trust the Hitler Youth to make sure that damage to their children's health would be strenuously avoided. Still, in 1937, military officials in Munich complained that barefoot marches undertaken in any weather by the Hitler Youth were causing and aggravating serious foot conditions among draftees such as flat feet. An Annual Health Report from Mecklenburg for 1938 noted that adolescents seemed more nervous and that too much athletic activity was leading to heart problems, while among younger schoolchildren, heavy boots and packs used during marches could lead, among other things, to damaged feet.[10] The number of patients per doctor increased from 1933 to 1939 due to a fall in the unemployment rate and the Nazi policy of limiting the number of and access to doctors to combat what the regime saw as a plague of malingering. Payments to the State Sickness Funds and for disability pensions were reduced. Although the number of doctors and nurses increased, medical study was cut by two years, while from 1936 on an increasing number of doctors were conscripted into the armed forces or took up administrative positions in the Nazi system of medical monitoring and control of the population. There was a growing shortage of medical specialists, including many of the Jewish physicians who – feared above all by the Nazis as sexual predators on the bodies of 'Aryan' women – were by 1938 restricted to treating other Jews. Most non-Jewish doctors had rallied to the Nazi cause, some even before 1933, and for ideological as well as opportunistic reasons had supported the Nazi purge of their Jewish colleagues. One-third of all doctors in Germany belonged to the Nazi Physicians' League, and around 45 per cent, the highest percentage of any profession, belonged to the NSDAP. Doctors lost all professional autonomy in their subordination to the authority of the state when, in 1943, Hitler gave the state health administration power to compel doctors to provide information about their patients. Psychiatrists were recruited from 1933 on to supervise the forced sterilisation and then the wartime mass murder of mental patients.[11]

Most physicians thus served the Nazi state by ministering to a German populace upon whose physical and psychological capacities the regime depended in order to mobilise the nation for war. Many also served in the Nazi programme to root out those, mostly from the lower classes, suffering from 'hereditary illness'. But early on, the Nazis had to begin limiting the number of categories and cases subject to forced sterilisation. This was because both their own racism as well as economic and military necessity argued for making as many Germans as possible productive members of the *Volksgemeinschaft*. Doctors too, for professionally and patriotically opportunistic reasons, tended to emphasise their ability to treat and cure. There was also a great deal of public anxiety about the Law for the Protection of Hereditary Health, nervousness of which the Ministry of the Interior was itself anxiously aware. General unease was evident in the popular term for sterilisation, *Hitlerschnitt* ('Hitler cut'), from the word *Kaiserschnitt* (Caesarean section). Moreover, a number of Nazi Party members had since 1933 been caught up in the net cast by the law, many in the biliously baggy category of 'congenital feeble-mindedness'. It was for such reasons that the sterilisation programme ran out of steam after 1937. Physical disabilities – as well as alcoholism – were dropped entirely from the original list of hereditary conditions subject to the law, including clubfoot, a condition from which Propaganda Minister Joseph Goebbels suffered. The Nazis, while of course continuing to rely as necessary on propaganda and terror, simply could not afford to alienate, much less eliminate, millions of even less 'racially valuable' Germans upon whom they relied to fill the ranks of workers and soldiers.[12]

The invasive Nazi harping on health made Germans more anxious about illness. The regime's very insistence on individual fitness reinforced widespread and growing anxiety about the body and mind that had long been a feature of constructions and experiences of health and illness in modern Germany. And it occasioned individual and group recourse to manipulation of the system of health control progressively imposed by the regime. Part of the experience of health, illness, physicians and medicine was the omnipresent public, private and political discourse on these subjects in Nazi Germany. This constituted the face and picture of health and illness under a dictatorship that aggressively exploited the mass media of print, film and radio that were at its command. The Nazis habitually used health imagery to describe themselves and Germany.

Doctors and medicine therefore were popular subjects in the dictated literature and film of the Third Reich. At the same time, however, Goebbels understood that the medical profession was a sensitive subject, since it was a reminder of sickness and death. In 1939, he told a colleague that he did not want to see any more doctor films, although he would approve more as part of the war effort. Goebbels probably felt that the sudden and obvious absence of films about doctors would only reinforce concerns among the populace about the very issues of life and death that had made such films both popular and unsettling. The great historical medical melodrama *Paracelsus* (1943) was uniquely unsuccessful at the box office, most likely due to its premiere a month after the disastrous German defeat at Stalingrad. The key for the regime was to keep things heroic, but also light and airy when it came to doctors and medicine, focusing on the cure of illness and not its experience. Representative is the wounded soldier in the popular musical drama *Wunschkonzert* (1940) shown recuperating bravely and happily under the attentive and expert care of hospital staff. The many wartime novels about doctors were romantic tales of healing meant for a domestic female readership. Several of these novels were by women about women and displayed a modern and Nazi extension of the essentialised female as mother into the public realm of medical care. Betina Ewerbeck's *Angela Koldewey* (1939, 1942) concerns a physician with a malignant tumour who makes 'herself a subject for research on cancer'.[13] In Hilde Walde's *Die andere Maria* (1940), the daughter of a German apothecary works to combat pellagra among the impoverished of the Po Valley. Many of these titles were produced in a soldier's edition with tens of thousands of copies in print.[14]

Just as the regime obsessively used a discourse of health and illness in the promotion of its policies and in defence of its interests, popular discourse too used medical terminology and metaphor for its own experience, observation and commentary. One common strategy in addressing the contingency of living in a police state was that 'just to be on the safe side people were using the word illness for arrest'.[15] Even more common was popular comment on leading personages of the regime, who were in any case lionised in the Nazi press as virile leaders, but everyone knew were simply men who in many cases had significant medical issues. The Nazi leadership, heavily invested in the myth of the Nazi superman, strove to keep such realities hidden. In 1936, the daughter of Nazi diplomat Joachim von Ribbentrop was severely injured in an automobile accident. The regime made every effort to ensure that neither the German people nor the world knew that Ribbentrop, who was then Ambassador to Great Britain, might be distracted – or, a peculiarly sensitive issue for Nazis, 'weakened' – by worry over his daughter. Subsequently, there was another embarrassment to be pre-empted. In 1937, two Jewish newspapers in Vienna reported that Ribbentrop's daughter, whose head injuries had led to meningitis, had been sent to Amsterdam where her sight was saved in an operation by an émigré Jewish brain surgeon from Poland.

Within the Nazi government, illness was also used as a weapon of politics. In 1944, Minister of Armaments Albert Speer was incapacitated by exhaustion, depression and an inflammation of the knee. He was placed under the care of orthopaedist Karl Gebhardt in the SS Hospital at Hohenlychen. This arrangement was a source of concern for Speer, since Gebhardt's boss was Reichsführer-SS Heinrich Himmler, who was Speer's chief rival for control over Germany's military-industrial complex. Gebhardt apparently misdiagnosed his patient, which only increased Speer's anxiety about political intrigues against him as head of the Total War programme. Using his clout at Hitler's headquarters, Speer arranged to have another physician take over his care, and he recuperated in the Tyrol, although still officially under SS protection. Speer later reflected:

> In Hitler's Germany ... it was not advisable for a Minister to get ill. First of all, nobody believed it. Because if Hitler, who hated sacking people, did fire one of his higher officials, it was invariably attributed to 'ill health'. The paradoxical result was that if you were *really* ill, you had to pretend to be well in order to avoid rumours of impending dismissal.[16]

Germans would respond to the Nazi regimen of exhortation, work and worry through degrees and methods of agency and coping. This had already long been the case on the intimate quotidian ground of modern managed health and illness. While the modern era saw the growth of political and medical authority over the daily life of the individual, it also witnessed ongoing contestation between patient and doctor in an ever more medicalised society. This was particularly the case in Germany where there was a long tradition of state organisation of public health and medicine. The triumph of germ theory in the nineteenth century gave doctors the ability to diagnose and treat a wide range of diseases for the first time. But medicalisation also created greater social, official and scientific distance between physician and patient. And it added to the individual's right to health and responsibility for health. Industrialisation – followed by the first industrial war from 1914 to 1918 – increased daily dangers to body and mind. Miners in the Ruhr Valley faced some of the most hazardous working conditions in all of German industry. In addition to the high rate of injury, they faced the constant threat of rheumatism, influenza, laryngitis, anthracosis, silicosis, emphysema, trachoma and hookworm. Before 1918, there were no paid holidays for these workers, so sickness especially was sometimes resorted to as a way of getting time off work. Such opportunities were limited by colliery doctors, paid by the companies to keep men working, and so, workers were not paid for the first sick days off. That workers took these opportunities, though, is shown by the fact that the highest sickness rates in the mining industry occurred in the summer with sunny August as the most popular month for illness. Increasing competition among doctors before and after the First World War also meant that patients could shop around for doctors willing to sign them off as sick and thus eligible for Sickness Funds payments.[17]

The Nazis of course further stigmatised illness in terms of fitness, utility and collective identity and purpose. And they distrusted and politically immobilised a German working class that for so long had been represented by trade unions, Socialists and Communists. In the 1920s, moreover, both middle-class and working-class families had organised politically to press their demands for pensions and compensation as physically and mentally disabled victims of the war, as well as victims of work and the economy. Many physicians and psychiatrists were driven into the arms of the Nazis as a result of what they saw as a coordinated revolutionary challenge to the German nation and to the 'national body' they likewise saw as their professional and patriotic duty – and that of their patients – to protect and to cultivate. The Nazis exploited such sentiments to encourage among the 'respectable' middle-class Germans, wooed by the regime, what Claudia Koonz has called a 'Nazi conscience'. This was a combination of highly propagandised notions of the *Volksgemeinschaft*, with the autonomous modern self of material need and desire placed within a rapidly developing German post-liberal industrial, commercial and consumer society. Nazi racism was inherently flattering to individual members of the *Herrenvolk* ('master race') and allowed each 'Aryan' to internalise a version of the individual conscience characteristic of the modern self that – as 'personality' – was constantly fertilised by Nazi propaganda, as well as weeded out by Nazi terror.[18]

Germans, who had been acculturated and socialised into the modern conception, practice and rhetoric of the autonomous modern self, were often disposed by circumstance surrounding the well and ill body and mind in Nazi Germany to exercise what Alf Lüdtke has conceptualised as *Eigensinn*, that is a modern self that acts on the basis of attributes such as bodily autonomy, wilfulness, stubbornness and even prankishness. Especially when it came to Nazified consequences of the modern 'reign of a medical politics', individual actions often resided in the realm of 'antidiscipline' and 'the polytheism of scattered practices'.[19] While social discipline and the threat of sanction kept most Germans mainly pliable, obedient and enthusiastic about serving the Nazi state, the space of self and family was sometimes an active counterweight to the pressure of conformity to the norms of the *Volksgemeinschaft*. In the highly medicalised demand environment of Nazi Germany, health and illness were precisely the space most available for such individual agency.

Before the war, 'antidiscipline' was most apparent among less-trusted 'Aryans' such as the overlapping categories of women and workers. While the Nazi state provided insurance coverage for treatment of infertility in women, it was also the case that most of those forcibly sterilised were women from the lower classes, while abortions for all 'Aryans' were allowed on eugenic grounds only. Among women marked for sterilisation, there were instances of protest pregnancies. The SS estimated that 500,000 illegal abortions were performed in 1936 alone, while other Nazi authorities suspected many of the terminations of pregnancies in the Annual Health Reports were actually abortions. The Nazis had also made their first order of business the destruction of the Communist and Socialist parties and the trade unions. They reduced funding for health care and pensions. In 1936, an agent of the Social Democratic party in exile reported on a woman who, having lost her disability allowance for a finger lost to blood poisoning, disrupted a public meeting on pensions. The regime deployed legions of physicians and medical officials to exercise control over the workplace. However, labour shortages by 1937 meant declining work discipline through less fear of unemployment, especially now with more workers per family. This took the form of days off, reporting sick and being granted paid sick leave, strategies that became increasingly generalised among men and women across all social classes during the war. While officials sought to minimise this problem, they could not eliminate it. This was the case for two reasons. One was the rise in injuries and illness as a result of economic recovery. The second was that the Nazis needed these millions of German workers. Still, widespread incidence of coping only very rarely constituted instrumental much less intentional obstruction of Nazi aims. German workers, like women as a group, remained functionally loyal to the nation in peace and war. And coping itself provided respite from the demands of work essential to resumed effort and exertion as well as maintenance of a wage on which to live.[20]

From the very beginning of the Third Reich, much greater suffering from physical and nervous illness was experienced by the victims of Nazi racial policies. We have already mentioned forced sterilisation, but from 1933 on, the number of inmates in prisons and camps multiplied rapidly, abuse by guards increased and health conditions in these places were purposely allowed to deteriorate. Skin and venereal diseases were particularly rife. Corporal punishment, torture, execution and 'natural' death were commonplace. Persecution went on outside the prisons and camps as well, especially towards demonised and doomed German Jews. Victor Klemperer, a Jew married to a non-Jew, kept a diary in which there are frequent mentions of ill health as a result of material deprivation and minimal medical care. Klemperer had turned 52 in 1933, and he regularly complained of rheumatism and problems with his eyes, heart, bladder and stomach, as well as the suffering borne by his wife. Already on 3 April 1933, he noted that 'Eva's state of health suffers in the extreme from the German catastrophe'. The entry for 22 November noted: 'Dr Dressel examined my heart and blood pressure and once again found "everything in good condition". For how long? – a certain depression and resignation everywhere.' And much later, on 29 October 1937: 'Eva's health continues to be very poor, politics stagnating and gloomy, makes one want to throw up every day ...'.[21]

Anxiety about health was heightened among Germans in general by loud and lingering Nazi condemnation of the 'unfit' through which 'images of disability and ... illness constantly circulated'.[22] The Nazis' shrill and endlessly repeated insistence on health also mobilised guilt among the many Germans who had long internalised social and moral standards involving responsibilities of the individual to self, family, work, society and state. This calculus of suffering and service had the effect that Germans, as Christa Wolf later put it, 'raged against bodies' that were 'giving them signals: My head is splitting. I'm suffocating'.[23] The great tragedy is that the regime was able to exploit this newly complicated and mobilised cultural habitus in the construction of a Nazi conscience that in terms of one's health married duty to desire. Such habituation constituted an imposing amalgam of lubrication as well as inertia and friction in the gears of the Third Reich's social, economic and military machinery. For even though individual concern for the private self of body and mind compromised commitment to the *Volksgemeinschaft*, it created space to recuperate from the demands of the state so as to continue to meet those demands.

# The state of war

Most Germans were not enthusiastic about another war. Their lives, after all, had been shadowed and even shattered by considerable physical and mental travail ever since 1914. Recovery from the Depression and the psychological capital generated by the Nazi introit had contributed to an emphasis on private pleasures of the self rather than endurance of the pain now associated so strongly with the nation at war. And there was now also the new and horrible prospect of the mass bombing of cities from the air. So, in a crisis over the Tyrol in 1934, the Gestapo reported that already the country 'was in the grips of a veritable "war psychosis"... of fear'.[24] With German battlefield victories piling up in 1941, a Nazi official noted that the 'great mass of people waits for the end of the war with the same longing as the sick person looks for his recovery'. Unlike the First World War, the Germans did not on the whole suffer from malnutrition. Hitler's fear of another 'stab in the back' such as the one he and others blamed for Germany's defeat in 1918 led to widespread plunder of Nazi-occupied Europe for the sake of German stomachs and psyches. Real individual concerns about deprivation, illness, injury and death multiplied and sharpened under the blunt blows of this war. The first weeks of the war brought rationing of clothing as well as of food: per capita consumption fell 22 per cent between 1938 and 1941, by which time one Medical Officer reported increases in kidney and bladder inflammation as well as rheumatism among women from standing in line in shops for too long. The next year Reich Health Leader Leonardo Conti observed significant weight loss among the populace in Berlin, especially among youth; a year later in Dresden, Eva Klemperer noted 'how unhealthy the schoolchildren look'.[25] In addition to a critical shortage of insulin for diabetics and the general lack of fats in the diet, wartime shortages of food, vitamins, clothing and housing led to loss of weight and strength, underdevelopment in children and youth and decline in psychological well-being among people of all ages. Only infants and small children were thriving due to Nazi pro-natalism, while the elderly were consigned to neglect. Medical care was apportioned on the basis of productivity, with mothers, infants, soldiers and workers at the top and Jews, mental patients and slave labourers at the bottom.[26]

The result was increased incidence of illness while the availability of disinfectants and medicines became ever more problematic. Diseases such as tuberculosis, diphtheria, whooping cough and scarlet fever were increasingly common across Germany, and at Christmas in 1943, there was once again epidemic influenza. Adults began contracting and even dying from childhood illnesses such as diphtheria and scarlet fever, a sure sign of generally deteriorating health conditions. Test pilot Hanna Reitsch was hospitalised for three months in 1940 with scarlet fever, and the wife of an army general died of the disease in 1942. One U-boat had to return to port after an outbreak of diphtheria onboard following eight days in Germany. All of this was a function of the unprecedentedly swift reach across great distances of the effects of a modern war of mobility and the Nazi war of brutality. The report from Nördlingen in Bavaria for 1942 ascribed the rise in cases of diphtheria and tuberculosis among both children and adults to 'an increase in the virulence of the bacteria and a colossal rise in public vectors as a result of increased travel, evacuations and importation of workers'.[27] Typhus, especially feared by the Germans – and freighted with Nazi hysteria since it was endemic in the Slavic (and Jewish) East – was among the diseases brought into the Reich. Typhus imported via Eastern slave and forced labourers was contained to the labour camps, but the same was not true of cases among German soldiers home on leave. More generally, women were especially susceptible to stress and illness, reflected in many Annual Health Reports of exhaustion, nervousness, high blood pressure and ulcers among women in particular. This was because the conscription of men into the armed services forced more women into the civilian workplace and into the military as auxiliaries. Women had to bear a double burden of domestic labour and childcare, most often in the absence of a husband in the military, as well as the privations and dangers of total war. One neurologist reported the need for sedatives among his many female patients: a woman who worked both day and night as a tram conductor; another who agonised over signing anything that might get her husband in trouble; one whose son was missing in action; a fourth who had to run a grocery by herself and whose apartment had recently been damaged in an air raid. Women also endured rape, venereal disease and draconian wartime punishments for abortion.[28]

The war ramified the consumption and prescription of pharmaceutical drugs generally. This was a function of the commercial and even consumerist society Germany had become in the first decades of the twentieth century. Germany had the largest chemical and pharmaceutical industry in the world, and it marketed medicines and remedies aggressively at home and abroad (Figure 3.2). Moreover, the Nazis required medications to ensure a content and productive populace, as well as a ready and resilient army. Civilian demand for chemical relief from pain or anxiety increased during the war and was one major reason for the shortages that grew from chronic to acute by 1944. There were also conflicts carried over from peacetime between large pharmaceutical manufacturers and small apothecaries, with the latter facing strong competition from retail pharmacists, department stores and even grocery shops and beauty salons. Factories buying up pain medications and narcotics for their workers further aggravated shortages. The army had to set up its own manufacturing facilities for medicines to ensure supply. Chemists' shops remained important for the provision of prescription medicines, especially in smaller towns and as more drugs were placed under prescription in an attempt to reduce waste of wartime resources. Authorities recommended the use of natural alternatives, mostly to address the problem of supply, but in some cases also out of some Nazi ideological distrust of modern industrial medicine. On the demand side, there was a thriving black market in drugs. Individuals who sought chemical reinforcement and relief exploited the commercial instincts of private physicians and chemists. Such chemical coping too rendered quotidian concerns of millions of Germans with disorders and complaints of body and mind of service not only to individual needs, but also ongoing service to the Nazi state in peace and in war. In service to *Blitzkrieg*, drivers and fliers in the armed forces (like factory workers at home) were given the methamphetamine Pervitin to stay awake for long periods of time. Drugs were tested on concentration camp prisoners and large pharmaceutical companies opportunistically positioned themselves during the war for what would turn out to be the golden age of prescription drugs after 1945.[29]

FIGURE 3.2 *Protection against infection with formamint. Das Reich, 28 September 1941.*

The shortage of doctors on the home front, especially in rural areas, complicated the pervasive Nazi treating, monitoring, exhorting and disciplining of the population. The Nazis – fearful, among other things, of epidemics among Jewish slave labourers – were even constrained to consider and in a few instances effect exemption of Jewish doctors from deportation and extermination. Many of the doctors left over from conscription into the armed forces were too old or too inexperienced to serve either the regime or their patients effectively. The government feared that patients could 'fool' such doctors into providing certifications for absence from work, prescriptions for drugs, or even travel. Patients also often doubted the competency of their – now assigned and not chosen – physician, something about which soldiers on leave often complained. One bomber pilot wrote in his diary in 1941: 'Mother wrote me that she's been sick a lot. The doctor says it's anaemia. Old Dr. Kuhlmann is an idiot.'[30] The result was an increased need and tendency, where possible, to manipulate the creaking but still intrusive and dangerous Nazi system of medical 'care'. One state film bureaucrat complained that studio employees unwilling to work in Berlin were able to 'supply notes from prominent doctors ... so that it usually proves impossible to attribute [illness to] fear of bombs'.[31] In 1944, Marie Vassiltchikov recorded in her wartime diary that when she wanted to leave her job at the Foreign Ministry despite a ban on voluntary resignations, she opted once again for sickness as a strategy: 'The only solution, I conclude, is another illness.'[32] The SS inveighed darkly against the flu becoming a fashionable and – because of its ubiquity – manipulable disease that everyone just had to have instead of merely a manageable cold. Even foreign labourers sometimes tried to work the system. The SS Security Service reported complaints that Polish workers were given preference in seeing doctors because otherwise they would slack off at work. Polish and Russian female labourers used pregnancy (or making themselves sick) in order to be sent home, so from early 1943 on, their offspring were aborted, adopted, institutionalised or killed.[33]

The day-and-night strategic bombing offensive conducted by the British and the Americans had a devastating effect on the health of the German populace. The major causes of death (300,000) and injury in air raids were similar to those on the modern battlefield: blast, concussion, laceration, blunt force trauma, burns, suffocation, poisoning and inhalation of dust and smoke. The effect on mortality rates from disease was mixed, with increases in death from heart disease, pneumonia, influenza, suicide and old age all seemingly related to bombing. Long stays in air-raid shelters worsened the incidence of diphtheria among adults since mothers brought their ill children with them into the overcrowded shelters. Rheumatism and stress were also common afflictions arising from this daily and nightly environment. Medical officials worried about epidemics of colds, influenza, pneumonia, whooping cough and tuberculosis due to extended periods of time spent underground and to lowered resistance to illness generally. In 1942, the Air Ministry funded research into a vaccine for influenza; in 1944, the wife of Hitler's Chief of Operations Staff died from pneumonia contracted in an air-raid shelter. Disruption of transportation made doctor and hospital visits difficult, while propaganda against malingering discouraged people from seeking treatment for 'trivial' illnesses. There were shortages of clothing, bedding, disinfectants, drugs and housing accompanied by the spread of infectious diseases into the countryside and across the Reich by those bombed out of their homes in the cities. Children evacuated to the countryside, while safe from the bombs, suffered greatly from separation anxiety and other maladies.[34]

The German armed forces caused more harm than they suffered. Nevertheless, the scale and nature of the war they conducted meant that German soldiers did suffer in vast numbers. In addition to over 5 million dead, there were legions of the wounded, sick and disabled. Over the course of the conflict, around 55 per cent of all German soldiers required medical attention for illness. In 1943, the number of permanent losses to illness and injuries was 41,792. For tuberculosis, the annual figures ranged from 4,000 to 8,000; for blood disorders, the figure ranged from 3,500 to 4,000; and for digestive problems, the figure ranged from 3,000 to 5,000.[35] Illness increased from year to year because of the younger, older and sicker replacements flooding into service to replace those killed in action. As German manpower was stretched ever thinner, military aid stations and hospitals were compelled to send soldiers back into the field before they were fully fit. In order to prevent the spread of infection, special 'stomach battalions' were formed for soldiers suffering from dysentery. In spite of innoculations, typhus, cholera and dysentery were rife in the ranks, as was tuberculosis. Mental disorders too were widespread. Whereas hysteria was a result of the static nature of trench warfare during the First World War, the Second World War introduced headaches and stress due to the speed and change occasioned by a mechanised war of movement. An army study of September 1943 of those judged unfit for service over the preceding year recorded 11,000 soldiers as having been rejected or released due to mental illness; only in 1943 did permanent losses to illness and injuries begin to surpass nervous casualties by a wide margin. Military psychiatrists and psychotherapists fought over causes and cures. For example, army psychiatrists often prescribed death for 'congenital' homosexuality while psychotherapists in the *Luftwaffe* mandated treatment. The SS was constrained to emphasise that men discharged from the SS for 'abnormal personality development' were not suffering from an 'organic' mental illness that conceivably could make them subject to the T4 'euthanasia' programme that murdered more than 100,000 mental patients between 1939 and 1945.

The experience of illness in the German armed forces was of course highly medicalised. Doctors had both more and less authority in the military. They had more as the chief facilitators of the *Wehrmacht*'s insistence on repair for resumption of duty, but thereby less in terms of active responsibility for the welfare of the individual patient. Doctors and nurses, who were increasingly overworked and in ever shorter supply, ran the gamut in terms of soldiers' perception and experience. In 1943, U-boat 977 was assigned a surgeon claiming to be in poor health who was a gynaecologist by training. As in the civilian realm, officials worried that wily veteran soldiers could 'take advantage' or the many young, 'naïve' doctors being drafted into the armed forces. Some of the many often lethal experiments carried out on prisoners in concentration camps were apparently designed to determine how unwilling recruits made themselves sick in order to escape service or combat. The *Wehrmacht* also worried that reports in the press about new methods of treatment trumpeted by the Nazi regime as ongoing proof of German racial and scientific superiority made it harder for doctors who had to deal with the uncertainties of individual diagnoses under extreme circumstances. An irony of Hitler's war of conquest was that due to escalating Allied air raids, soldiers on leave for illness or injury had to face the growing danger of additional injury or even death at home.[36]

Heinrich Böll's experience with illness and doctors as a soldier was typical though peculiarly well-documented in over 900 very well-written letters home. His regular complaints included flu, diarrhoea, headaches, fever, weakness, pain and exhaustion. A young battalion doctor appeared unsympathetic, but Böll would 'try everything' to get recuperation leave. Böll feared a field hospital filled with mistrustful doctors vexed by overwork, but he was so bored by sentry duty that sometimes he reported sick in order to escape the barracks. From Catholic Cologne, he was out of sorts with army culture: 'it is a very sad story when one is sick among Prussians, especially with an illness [headache and eye trouble] that is not so easily classified... This continuous trooping to doctors is so painful to me that I should like to be able to say I am healthy.' A doctor in Paris sent him to a psychiatrist, and Böll worried that he would be taken for a malingerer. In the spring of 1943, Böll was in the Crimea and reported on a head wound, the sanctuary of a hospital for an operation and the hope that he would be put on a hospital train back to Germany. The best a sympathetic doctor could do was to send him to a recuperation company in Odessa, where Böll compared his lodgings to a jail and suffered from 'war sickness' and 'aid station sickness'. Only in March 1944 was he declared fit for service and sent on two weeks' home leave. By June, he was in Hungary suffering from shrapnel wounds in the back where a kindly doctor prescribed him pills for pain and fever. Böll ended up on a train that took him to a lice-ridden army hospital where he contracted trench fever; his headaches were relieved by bed rest and 'lots of drugs'. There, Böll reflected on the craziness of a war in which he had spent eight weeks in hospital and only three days in combat.[37]

The Nazis celebrated pain, injury and death as brave masculine sacrifices for nation and people. This ran up against painful realities rehearsed and embodied for Germans in the many badly disabled veterans from the First World War circulating in society after 1918. The regime censored references in soldiers' letters home to wounds and amputations. By 1943, the Nazis also tried to stir popular emotions through newsreels featuring heavily bandaged but vigorous wounded soldiers applauding speeches for Total War. To quell public anxiety, they also once again had to distinguish between 'hereditary' conditions subject to sterilisation or 'euthanasia' and disabilities suffered in the course of life. And they put disabled veterans to work, introducing a new term, *Kriegsversehrter*, for these men that conflated heroism with utility and cowardice with disability. In 1944, the Messerschmitt factory in Paris proudly announced that its disabled workers were adjusting in outstanding fashion to the new 72-hour week. The SS cooperated in a programme for the nascent German television network on the rehabilitation of amputees. There were, however, disagreements and competition among various civilian and military authorities and significant shortfalls in job training and placement. While prostheses since 1918 had allowed for degrees of 'symbolic remasculinisation', many of the disabled veterans were disappointed in their lot in life, and the regime had to worry about the effect of their bitterness on public morale. In September 1944, the Armaments Ministry complained that many disabled wanted desk jobs with a future, rather than the needed industrial labour jobs.[38]

Jews suffered more than anyone else under Nazism. The Jews' gruesome sufferings of body and mind were the direct outcome of certain Nazi obsessions with body, mind and 'race'. Hitler's antisemitic tirades in *Mein Kampf* were deployed in lecturing his military commanders in 1942:

> The discovery of the Jewish virus is one of the greatest revolutions to have taken place in the world. The Jew had been revealed! The same battle that Pasteur and Koch had to wage must be waged today by us. Countless diseases have their origin in one bacillus: the Jew! ... We shall regain our health only by eliminating the Jew.[39]

Hitler's paranoia regarding 'the Jew' reflected a crisis of masculinity in modern Europe. Industrial society was eroding the ideal of male superiority, while the war of 1914 had subjected men to helplessness and hysteria incompatible with the male self-image of strength and decisiveness. This crisis was particularly acute among Germans, many of whom had inherited the hypermasculinity of Prussian military culture. The most extreme reaction was among the men of the post-war *Freikorps* in which a number of future Nazi leaders served. For these nationalist para-military 'warriors', virulent compensatory fear and loathing of women transmogrified traditional antisemitism into 'the Jew' as the embodiment of everything that threatened the fantasy of the hard man of racial warfare. These irrational fears and obsessions were further aggravated by the more general modern medicalised concerns with morbidity and mortality. This meant that after 1933 growing preoccupation among Germans with the racial yet endangered modern self of material body and mind also excluded active or even passive empathy for Jews or others who did not belong to the *Volksgemeinschaft*. Such self-concern could even mobilise rage, abetted by Nazi propaganda and traditional antisemitism, against perpetually vilified 'others' out of resentment over one's own suffering of body and mind.[40]

Jews living in Germany during the war had little or no access to medical care. Air-raid shelters for 'privileged' Jews were so miserable that in Berlin, Elisabeth Freund had a doctor certify that she was too ill to go to the shelter. When deportations began in 1941, many German Jews killed themselves, most often with an overdose of the barbiturate Veronal or the phenobarbital Luminal. By 1944, an ill Victor Klemperer was considering suicide, but 'I do not have any Veronal, I have no courage, and I must try to survive the Third Reich, so that Eva's widow's pension is assured'.[41] The only official medical care for Jews in wartime Germany was the Jewish Hospital in Berlin, which in typically grotesque Nazi fashion had been set up to expedite selections for the death camps. It also served to isolate epidemic disease among malnourished and unhealthy Jews in Berlin and to assure segregation of medical care for Jews. As such, this medical space allowed for some agency and negotiation of illness among Jews in the nation's capital city. Until late 1942, the Nazis allowed some medical deferments from deportation to the East in order to camouflage the killing operations. The lie was that sick Jews could not 'work' upon being 'resettled', the same lie covering doctors and nurses on each transport. Those Jews hiding in Germany had no access to health care and simply suffered their illnesses. In the East, Jews suffered unimaginably – indeed, epidemics among Jews led to both the establishment and the dissolution of the ghettos, since the Nazi authorities worried about the spread of disease beyond the Jewish population. In the Łódź ghetto, 'pain was impossible to ignore, for the body was insistent: gums and nasal passages abscessing, tongues blistering, lungs filling, bones softening, bellies swelling, extremities aching. Their ailments and their pains staked an increasing claim to their consciousness and their very being'.[42] In the camps, victims of National Socialism got sick and worked, or got sick and died, or got sick and were gassed.

# Conclusion

Almost complete destruction of infrastructure came with German surrender in 1945. The occupying Allied armies and local public officials gradually rebuilt it. To the millions of casualties from the war were now added those suffering and dying from illness due to poor living and working conditions, as well as the ongoing disruption of medical and health services. The millions of refugees moving through occupied Germany exacerbated this situation. Outbreaks of tuberculosis, diphtheria and venereal diseases were common in both the cities and the countryside. Many wounded and disabled veterans continued to become addicted to drugs after the war, a problem that diminished but persisted during the 1950s. The looting of German field hospitals made painkillers and other drugs widely available. It was women, in any case, who comprised the majority of the population in the immediate post-war years. Their sufferings of body and mind were further compromised by the assumption of military authorities that women needed less calorific intake than men. Housework too under the conditions of scarcity and deprivation produced as much stress and illness as any 'real' job. Women also shared meagre rations with their children and husbands, which contributed to chronic exhaustion, weakening of the immune system and frequent illness. Germans after the war tended to emphasise such current and recent sufferings at the expense of acknowledgement of their complicity in the even greater sufferings of others. The bloody defeats at the front, the terrible air bombardments at home and the catastrophe of invasion and capitulation sharpened central modern and Nazi-inflected concerns with relief from suffering for the individual body, mind and self. Such late disasters of a lost war formed the most lasting, self-pitying and self-serving impressions upon post-war Germans in search of a usable past in which they were victims and not perpetrators. These memories would also form the basis for escape into a prosperous future of material security of which they would be the beneficiaries.[43]

In matters of health and illness, the history of the Third Reich demonstrates greater continuity than discontinuity with the course of modern German, Western and world history. Hitler's war finally and firmly elevated the needs of embodied subjectivity over dedication to the racial body, just as the Nazi version of a modern western commercial and medical culture of well-being competed with the fantasy and fact of *Volksgemeinschaft* before 1939. The health-care systems of both the German successor states of 1949 were largely continuous with developments in Germany from the 1880s through to the era of the two world wars. Physicians and pharmaceutical companies, as well as alternative medicine, continued to define individual experience of modern socialised, professionalised, commercialised and commodified health and illness. The social and cultural experiences of the material, morbid and mortal self in six years of Nazi peace, six years of Nazi war and twelve years of Nazi atrocity did not constitute the culmination of modern trends. They do, however, constitute important structural, experiential and discursive continuities in the history of Germany and the West before 1933 and after 1945.

# Notes

1   *The Hitler Trial before the People's Court in Munich*, trans. H. Francis Freniere et al. (Arlington, vol. 1, 1976), p. 186.

2   A. Hitler, *Mein Kampf*, trans. H. Ripperger (New York, 1939), pp. 201, 203, 453, 592, 594, 606.

3   P. Fritzsche, *Life and Death in the Third Reich* (Cambridge, MA, 2008), p. 51.

4   Quoted in B. Hamann, *Hitler's Vienna: A Dictator's Apprenticeship*, trans. T. Thornton (New York, 1999), p. 211; Hitler, *Mein Kampf*, p. 737.

5  E. Weitz, *A Century of Genocide: Utopias of Race and Nation* (Princeton, NJ, 2003), p. 24.

6  G. Eley, *Nazism as Fascism: Violence, Ideology, and the Ground of Consent in Germany 1930–1945* (London, 2013), pp. 13–48, 59–90, 210–214.

7  H. Böll, *What's to Become of the Boy? Or: Something to Do with Books*, trans. L. Vennewitz (New York, 1984), p. 8.

8  G. Cocks, *The State of Health: Illness in Nazi Germany* (Oxford, 2012), pp. 23–26, 63–65, 82–83.

9  R. Proctor, *The Nazi War on Cancer* (Princeton, NJ, 1999), p. 21; Cocks, *State of Health*, pp. 75, 78–81, 105–110.

10  Cocks, *State of Health*, pp. 75–76.

11  M. Kater, *Doctors under Hitler* (Chapel Hill, NC, 1989), pp. 12–88; R. Proctor, *Racial Hygiene: Medicine under the Nazis* (Cambridge, MA, 1988), pp. 95–114.

12  Cocks, *State of Health*, pp. 52–56, 85–91, 96, 109.

13  H. Boeschenstein, *The German Novel, 1939–1944* (Toronto, 1949), p. 33.

14  Ibid., pp. 34–36; Cocks, *State of Health*, pp. 81, 91–94, 242.

15  C. Beradt, *The Third Reich of Dreams*, trans. A. Gottwald (Chicago, IL, 1968), p. 48.

16  Quoted in G. Sereny, *Albert Speer: His Battle with Truth* (New York, 1995), p. 410, emphasis in original; Cocks, *State of Health*, pp. 98–99.

17  Cocks, *State of Health*, pp. 21–29.

18  Ibid., pp. 14, 29–32; C. Koonz, *The Nazi Conscience* (Cambridge, MA, 2003); M. Föllmer, *Individual and Modernity in Berlin: Self and Society from Weimar to the Wall* (Cambridge, 2013).

19  M. de Certeau, *The Practice of Everyday Life*, trans. S. Rendall (Berkeley, CA, 1984), p. 47, emphasis in original; Cocks, *State of Health*, pp. 12, 28.

20  Cocks, *State of Health*, pp. 108–110, 119, 135–136.

21  V. Klemperer, *I Will Bear Witness: A Diary of the Nazi Years, 1933–1941* (New York, 1998), pp. 11, 42, 240; Cocks, *State of Health*, pp. 65–66.

22  C. Poore, 'Who Belongs? Disability and the German Nation in Postwar Literature and Film', *German Studies Review* 26 (2003), p. 22.

23  C. Wolf, *Patterns of Childhood*, trans. U. Molinato and H. Rappolt (New York, 1980), p. 156.

24  Quoted in A. Tooze, *The Wages of Destruction: The Making and Breaking of the Nazi Economy* (New York, 2007), p. 68.

25  Klemperer, *Witness*, p. 316; Conti to Martin Bormann, 3 July 1942, T175, Roll 68, Frames 206–207, National Archives, Washington, DC.

26  W. Süss, *Der 'Volkskörper' im Krieg: Gesundheitspolitik, Gesundheitsverhältnisse und Krankenmord im nationalsozialistischen Deutschland* (Munich, 2003), pp. 32–40, 69; Cocks, *State of Health*, pp. 173–180.

27  Jahresgesundheitsbericht, Bayern/Nördlingen, 1942, Gesundheitsamt Nördlingen Nr. 115, Staatsarchiv Augsburg.

28 Cocks, *State of Health*, pp. 112, 121–125, 160–161, 182–184, 188–189, 215.

29 Ibid., pp. 138, 142, 193, 195.

30 G. Leske, *I Was a Nazi Flier*, ed. Curt Riess (New York, 1941), p. 67.

31 J. Fox, *Film Propaganda in Britain and Nazi Germany* (Oxford, 2007), p. 259.

32 M. Vassiltchikov, *Berlin Diaries, 1940–1945* (New York, 1987), p. 230.

33 Cocks, *State of Health*, pp. 193–195.

34 Ibid., pp. 199–201.

35 'Die DU-Entlassung', 27 September 1943, T78, Roll 188, Frames 9308–28, National Archives, Suitland, MD.

36 Cocks, *State of Health*, pp. 202–218.

37 H. Böll, *Briefe aus dem Krieg 1939–1945* (Cologne, 2001), vol. 1, pp. 50, 615, 618–621, 657–658, 673, 677; vol. 2, pp. 963, 969, 973–979, 995, 1001, 1007, 1011, 1018, 1064–1065, 1067–1068, 1071, 1073–1074, 1084, 1097, 1103–1108, 1116, 1118, 1121, 1123.

38 Cocks, *State of Health*, pp. 236–251.

39 W. Jochmann (ed.), *Adolf Hitler Monologe im Führerhauptquartier 1941–1944: Die Aufzeichnungen Heinrich Heims* (Hamburg, 1980), p. 293.

40 Cocks, *State of Health*, pp. 34–45, 104; Fritzsche, *Life and Death*, p. 89; Wolf, *Patterns of Childhood*, p. 156; J. Herf, *The Jewish Enemy: Nazi Propaganda During World War II and the Holocaust* (Cambridge, MA, 2010).

41 V. Klemperer, *I Will Bear Witness: A Diary of the Nazi Years, 1942–1945* (New York, 1999), pp. 103, 313.

42 G. Horwitz, *Ghettostadt: Łódź and the Making of a Nazi City* (Cambridge, MA, 2008), p. 258; Cocks, *State of Health*, pp. 164–165, 197–199, 210, 219–221, 225–235.

43 R. Moeller, *War Stories: The Search for a Usable Past in the Federal Republic of Germany* (Berkeley, CA, 2001); J. Reinisch, *The Perils of Peace: The Public Health Crisis in Occupied Germany* (Oxford, 2013); Cocks, *State of Health*, pp. 252, 265–266.

# Select bibliography

Böll, H., *Briefe aus dem Krieg 1939–1945* (Cologne, 2001).

Cocks, G., *The State of Health: Illness in Nazi Germany* (Oxford, 2012).

Fritzsche, P., *Life and Death in the Third Reich* (Cambridge, MA, 2008).

Kater, M., *Doctors under Hitler* (Chapel Hill, NC, 1989).

Klemperer, V., *I Will Bear Witness: A Diary of the Nazi Years* (New York, 1998, 1999).

Proctor, R., *Racial Hygiene: Medicine under the Nazis* (Cambridge, MA, 1988).

Proctor, R., *The Nazi War on Cancer* (Princeton, NJ, 1999).

Süss, W., *Der Volkskörper im Krieg: Gesundheitspolitik, Gesundheitsverhältnisse und Krankenmord im nationalsozialistischen Deutschland* (Munich, 2003).

United States Strategic Bombing Survey, *The Effect of Bombing on Health and Medical Care in Germany* (Washington, DC, Morale Division, 1947).

# PART TWO

# Lifestyle

# 4

# Fashioning Women in the Third Reich

## *Irene Guenther*

Historically, fashion and clothing in their particular contexts have been embedded with manifold meanings and have been utilised for multiple purposes. What people have been encouraged or required to wear, have chosen or refused to wear, how they have clothed themselves or have been clothed, and how a nation has imagined and fashioned its identity can tell us a great deal.[1] Examining the Third Reich through its clothing is revelatory. Clothing served as a means to visibly convey many of the notions put forward by the Nazis' propaganda machine. The Minister of Propaganda, Joseph Goebbels, understood all too well the potency of appearances. Clothing was used to support and implement Nazi gender ideology and antisemitism. Clothing was employed to enhance the power and status of the regime, as well as to consolidate society and manipulate behaviour. Additionally, clothes provided a tangible sign of inclusion in and exclusion from the *Volksgemeinschaft* ('national community'). Clothing also offered a form of communication as Germans silently inspected one another.[2] What one wore or was required to wear and how one fashioned oneself spoke volumes in Nazi Germany.

## The Weimar era

Already in the decade preceding the Third Reich, female fashion had become the subject of contentious debate. The French had long ridiculed German women for their bad taste and lack of fashion savvy, claiming that only French women were fashionable. Even so, by the mid-1920s, Berlin's fashion industry was noticeably outselling Paris in the areas of export and upscale *Konfektion* (ready-to-wear women's clothing). But with the Franco–German hostilities of the First World War a few years behind them, fashion-conscious German women wanted 'French' fashion, which was all the rage in the 1920s. They went to Paris to purchase whatever fashions they could afford. Of note, much of the ready-to-wear women's clothing that was sold in France was actually made in Germany and then exported to France, where the German label was removed and replaced with a French label. After all, French fashion sold. Although monetary profits and national pride were at stake, and the German fashion industry did what it could to educate female consumers on the true origins of their bought-in-Paris garments, most women refused to believe the story and continued to spend their money in France.[3]

German fashion designers, who revelled in the lively cultural scenes of Berlin and Paris, incorporated a plethora of modern influences into their work. Revues, cabarets, the latest dance craze, popular music, film stars, jazz, big city nightlife – designers drew from all of these trends to express in clothing the spirit of the time.[4] This caused conservative critics in Germany to rail ever more loudly against women's 'impudent use' of cosmetics and the latest female fashions, which they alternately described as 'Jewified', 'masculinised', 'French-dominated', 'degenerate' or 'poisonous'. Nasty commentaries claimed that French and French-inspired fashions were unhealthy, both morally and physically, and did not suit blonde-haired, blue-eyed, tall German women. Critics also denounced the dangerous American 'vamp' or Hollywood image that young German women were 'foolishly imitating' with penciled eyebrows, darkly-lined eyes, painted red mouths and provocative clothing. Short hair, shorter hemlines, trousers and cosmetics were causing the supposed moral decline of the German woman.[5]

Additionally, by the 1920s, Berlin's historic garment district – comprised of designers, at-home seamstresses and tailors, lace and button makers, textile weavers, middlemen and large-scale manufacturers – had become an acclaimed world centre of fashion. Highly exaggerating the percentage of Jews in the fashion industry, diatribes in pro-Nazi publications repeatedly railed against the 'crushing' Jewish presence, which was blamed for ruining economic opportunities for pure 'Aryan' Germans. Jews also were accused of conspiring to destroy feminine dignity by producing 'whorish' or 'masculinised' fashions. The Jews' over-representation in the industry, right-wing critics warned, had the power to contaminate fashions and, thereby, 'noble' German women. Jewish-designed 'dangerous fashion fads', which were likened to 'spiritual cocaine', had led to the increasingly immoral behaviour of women. This downward spiral in female appearance and conduct, critics argued, could be halted only with the creation of a 'unique German fashion'. Such reactionary, anti-Jewish and rabidly nationalistic messages were repeated on countless occasions and became ever more strident as the Great Depression enveloped Germany. By the time the Nazi Party came to power in 1933, the argument seemed clear. Only German-designed and German-manufactured clothes were good enough for German women. Racially appropriate clothing depended upon the elimination of French and, especially, Jewish influences from the German fashion industry.[6] Significantly, there was no consensus on what was meant by a 'unique German fashion' or what visible shape female fashioning would take in the Third Reich.

## Nazi proposals for female fashioning

In early May 1933, only a few months after the Nazis had come to power, the exclusive Berlin fashion salon Schulze-Bibernell held a private showing for two prominent Nazis – the Reich Stage Designer, Benno von Arent, and the Reich Youth Leader, Baldur von Schirach.[7] One of Germany's best fashion designers, Heinz Schulze, had chosen his loveliest models to present his sartorial creations to this small, but important audience. He had received a commission to design 'stylish dress uniforms' for the female leaders of the *Bund deutscher Mädel* (BDM or League of German Girls), the Nazi organisation for young girls and women. Midway through the showing, the Nazi Youth Leader curtly asked Schulze, 'Why aren't you showing me these designs on my girls?' The designer was bewildered. After all, his salon models had been named the most beautiful in all of Berlin. Schulze apologised and then replied, 'Herr Youth Leader, your girls surely cannot present [these dresses] like mine – they cannot walk.' The Youth Leader snapped back, 'Indeed, they should not walk, they should march – and in uniform!'[8] One of the proposals for fashioning women in the Third Reich was the uniform.

During the same week, the powerful Nazi Propaganda Minister Joseph Goebbels met with Bella Fromm, the social columnist for the *Vossische Zeitung*, to discuss a fashion show planned for the racetrack club in Berlin. Fromm, who was a German-Jew with prominent connections, had staged these shows for quite some time. Goebbels stated that he was pleased with her work but then ordered, 'From now on, I want the French fashion omitted. Have it replaced by German models.' Later that evening, Fromm wrote in her diary, 'I could not help but smiling. It was too wonderful to imagine – the racetrack, the elegant crowd. In place of our stylish models, however, the "Hitler Maidens" with Gretchen braids, flat heels, and clean-scrubbed faces! Black skirts down to the ankles … Neither rouge nor lipstick!'[9]

Why had Goebbels's demand for only German designs evoked such unfashionable visions in Fromm's imagination? Why did the absence of French fashions translate into a show of bad hairdos, drab colours, unbecoming outfits, unflattering shoes and unattractive models? It was because Nazi officials most often propagated that image, and because conservative cultural critics supported a return to 'traditional gender roles' and an anti-modern fashion that exemplified the Nazis' 'blood and soil' ideology: no cosmetics, only the 'natural' look; no international, trend-setting fads and styles; no tight, body-skimming clothes or 'manly' designs that might hinder fertility; and nothing that was racially inappropriate for the pure German woman. Instead, they envisioned a female fashion centred on tradition, practicality, conformity, community, motherhood, wide hips, domestic manufacture, German cultural history and National Socialism's ideologies and policies. Although Goebbels and his wife, Magda, purchased their extensive, elegant wardrobes from exclusive designer salons – some of which were owned by Jews – Goebbels publicly espoused the Nazi hardliners' anti-modernist views.[10] Unsoiled by foreign and commercial influences, the second proposal for female fashioning in the Third Reich was the historically rooted folk costume (*Tracht*) or dirndl dress.

The following month, in early June 1933, Hitler announced to Hela Strehl, a well-known German fashion editor, 'The Berlin women must become the best-dressed women in all of Europe. No more Paris models.'[11] A few days later, the *Deutsches Modeamt* (German Fashion Institute) was established with the backing of several government ministries.[12] Claiming that 'being well-clothed and tastefully dressed is as important to the German people as food and housing',[13] the fashion institute's mission was to 'create tasteful German fashion products'.[14] Freedom from the 'fashion dictatorship' of Paris was imperative in order to soothe the nation's inferiority complex. Designs were to 'reflect the nature and character of the German woman', but what that meant in terms of actual designs or clothing was left unclear.[15] Magda Goebbels was appointed the honorary president of the fashion institute. In a newspaper interview soon after her appointment, she unhesitatingly swept aside the proposed dirndl fashion and envisioned her role as follows: 'I hold it as my duty to appear as beautifully as I possibly can. In this respect, I will influence German women. They should be beautiful and elegant.... The German woman of the future should be stylish, beautiful and intelligent. The Gretchen type is finally conquered.'[16] Within days of her interview, the Propaganda Ministry issued a terse announcement, 'Frau Goebbels is in NO WAY connected with said Fashion Office.'[17] It was Goebbels himself who had ordered his wife to step down.[18]

The next fashioning proposal entailed 'purifying' Germany's clothing industry. While conservative critics had condemned both French and Jewish fashion influences throughout the 1920s, the Jews would become the main focus in this 'purification' effort. In actuality, the proposal had nothing to do with female image or fashion and everything to do with antisemitism, radical nationalism and economic considerations. Antisemitism – always present to a certain degree in the fashion industry – was quickly embraced and intensified by some individuals, while only slowly and reluctantly taken up by those who were dependent upon the many knowledgeable, talented and experienced German Jews who figured so prominently in the designing, producing and selling of fashion. Because this 'fashioning' proposal was the only one that was eventually heralded a complete, albeit protracted, success, we shall first turn our attention to the 'purification' or 'Aryanisation' of the German fashion world.

# 'Aryanisation'

On 1 April 1933, the government initiated a boycott of Jewish shops, offices and businesses. But because of widespread negative reactions and the many Germans who ignored the boycott, despite the uniformed SA men who stood at the entrance of Jewish-owned businesses, it was called off after one day. Even so, government officials let it be known that voluntary boycotts of Jewish businesses would be heartily welcomed. Only one month later, in May 1933, several long-time German clothing manufacturers and producers established the *Arbeitsgemeinschaft deutsch-arischer Fabrikanten der Bekleidungsindustrie* (Working Association of German-Aryan Manufacturers of the Clothing Industry), better known as Adefa. Its establishment did not come about because of any orders emanating from high within the Nazi state hierarchy. Rather, it was founded and comprised of persons working in the fashion industry: men who were motivated by personal opportunism, greed and their government's antisemitic agenda. Adefa's goal, which members confidently predicted would be easy to accomplish, was to purge 'the dangerously ubiquitous Jewish influence', to 'break the monopoly of the Jewish parasite' from all facets of the fashion industry. Only then could Germans reclaim the 'practically 100% Jewified clothing industry'.[19]

Despite such inflammatory language, the removal of Jews from all facets of the fashion world did not occur nearly as quickly as Adefa's leadership had hoped. A year after its establishment, the group was still pleading with German consumers and retailers to cooperate with its goals. And, even after Adefa's board members organised a major propaganda campaign in 1936, which included numerous fashion shows, photo spreads of Adefa-made fashions in magazines and shop windows sporting the Adefa symbol that assured shoppers the products within the shops were 'Aryan'-made, the group continued to run into resistance.[20] One year later, the director of Adefa complained, 'Numbers of irresponsible retailers are purchasing forty million German marks worth of clothing goods annually from Jewish wholesalers.' 'In fact,' he lamented, 'fourteen million Germans are being clothed by the Jew today.'[21]

Still by the spring of 1938, Adefa could not claim victory. To accompany its intensified purging efforts, the group's leadership came up with new designs and a new slogan, 'We can do it better!' The catchy motto aimed to convince a still ambivalent consumer public that 'Aryan' Germans were far more capable than German Jews of producing high-quality fashion.[22] A government secret morale report included the observation that 'Nazi

Party comrades and non-Party citizens alike continue to not shy away from making their purchases at Jewish establishments, sometimes even while in uniform'.[23] Five years after Adefa's establishment, its relentless propaganda and activities had been ineffective in convincing female shoppers to put the agenda of antisemitism before their own self-interest, at least when it came to their wardrobes.

Similarly, ties continued to exist between German and German Jewish manufacturers, retailers and suppliers in the clothing industry.[24] In fact, it was not until after the massive state-organised pogrom against German Jews in November 1938, known as *Kristallnacht*, that the removal of Jews from the German fashion world proceeded at a highly accelerated rate.[25] Trade and fashion schools were purged of any remaining board members or students who were not of 'Aryan' descent. Other measures included 'Aryanisation', a euphemism for the forcible transfer of Jewish businesses to non-Jewish ownership, and liquidations of Jewish-owned department stores, shops, designer salons and manufacturing plants. Occasionally, so-called 'friendly Aryanisations' were arranged, whereby Jewish owners signed over their enterprises to their 'Aryan' partners or coworkers in the hope that their businesses would continue after they had emigrated and that they could reclaim their positions once the Nazis were gone. Mostly, though, Jews whose establishments were 'Aryanised' had been coerced to sell at ridiculously reduced prices. Sometimes, they received no payment at all. Fervent Nazis, who had little or no experience in the industry, were often the eager recipients of 'Aryanised' Jewish fashion and fashion-related firms.[26]

Finally, on 15 August 1939, just two weeks before the German invasion of Poland and the onset of the Second World War, Adefa held its last meeting. The group's leadership ecstatically announced to a packed membership assembly that the Jews had been removed from every facet of the German fashion world. Through a combination of massive pressure, hate-filled propaganda, direct interventions, blacklists, denunciations, 'Aryanisation', liquidations and boycotts, all areas of clothing and textile manufacture were '*Judenrein*' – cleansed of Jews. Because of the Jews' century-old, integral role in establishing the German fashion world and ensuring its success through hard work, design talent, innovation, salesmanship and creativity, the purge had taken six full years, longer than any other economic sector in Nazi Germany.

The removal of the Jews from the fashion industry had a tragic effect on German culture and society. The famous Jewish design and *Konfektion* houses, which had been instrumental in garnering international acclaim for the fashion industry and had become an important aspect of the nation's cultural history, were either forcibly closed down or taken over by non-Jews and renamed. It was as though they had never existed. Additionally, the forced removal of Jewish designers, middlemen, salesmen and manufacturers equated to an incalculable, grievous human cost. Many of the Jews who were excluded from the fashion world were deported to Jewish ghettos. There, they worked endless hours under terrible conditions to produce uniforms for the German army. They also created clothing and other fashion products for visiting Nazi officials and their wives or for German businesses, which contracted cheap ghetto labour for huge profits. Others were sent to the SS-run slave labour camps, where their fashion design talents and tailoring skills kept them alive, but only for a while.

Institutionally, the fashion industry and its countless subset industries, which created the products German and foreign consumers purchased and with which they clothed and fashioned themselves in times past, had been both Nazified and 'Aryanised'.[27] But because many of the shops, salons and manufacturing facilities were taken over by people who had little or no experience, Germany's economically important and internationally renowned fashion industry quickly went downhill. And, even though the 'purification' goal had been fulfilled, removing German Jews from the fashion industry did nothing to alter the female fashions that Nazi hardliners had complained about for so long. With the onset of the Second World War only days after Adefa declared success, and concerns about wartime rationing and sufficient consumer goods uppermost in the minds of government officials, Germany still had no unique female fashion.

# The dirndl fashion proposal

What about the images most often proposed by Nazi hardliners – the female in dirndl dress or in uniform? The propaganda surrounding these two proposals advanced the 'natural look' and condemned cosmetics and other 'unhealthy vices', like smoking, as unfeminine and un-German. While the dirndl fashion looked to the past, promoting an image that illuminated the Nazis' emphasis on German cultural history and the pure values of traditional rural life, and the female uniform fashion spoke to the present, exemplifying the idea of conformity and community over individuality, both fashions signified a rejection of international trends, again, as un-German. Both proposals also supported and satisfied the Nazis' 'made-in-Germany' economic policy.

The farmer's wife, often labelled 'Mother Germany', was offered as one female ideal. Her natural looks, untouched by cosmetics, her physical strength and moral fortitude, her willingness to toil hard and to bear many children were glorified through countless exhibits, paintings, essays and photographs.[28] According to Nazi propaganda, the ideal farmer's wife should dress herself in traditional folk costume, *Trachtenkleidung*, which recalled a mythical, untarnished German past. Promoted as an expression of the 'German-Aryan character', the age-old dirndl was viewed as the most suitable example of 'racially pure' clothing, as a sartorial metaphor for pride in the German homeland and as symbol of the Nazis' anti-modernist *Blut und Boden* ('blood and soil') ideology (Figure 4.1). Moreover, it was hoped that the dirndl could act as an 'antidote' to 'French fashion poison' and serve as Germany's money-maker in the international fashion scene.[29] A fashion runway success could boost the German fashion industry, employment opportunities and the public's self-confidence, all of which had noticeably declined during the early years of the Great Depression.

FIGURE 4.1 *The historical folk costume (*Tracht *or* Dirndl*), resurrected during the Nazi years, visually conveyed the ideology of 'blood and soil' but was viewed by rural women as costly and highly impractical except for the occasional village celebration and was rejected outright by most urban women. Private collection of the author.*

Pamphlets, books, journal articles and lectures that promoted a 'return to *Tracht*' linked the image with fertility, traditional gender roles and 'true German values'. Such propaganda proliferated in the Third Reich.[30] Furthermore, the Nazis established an office whose sole purpose was to foment a '*Tracht* renewal movement' throughout the German Reich.[31] All of these measures espoused the virtue of *Trachtenkleidung* and the importance of its revival. Originally a folk costume with variations based on region, social class and other factors that had developed over the centuries, *Tracht* was to become women's national dress in Nazi Germany. And, importantly, *Tracht* would 'illuminate the National Socialist outlook of the wearer'.[32]

The folk costume, particularly the dirndl dress, quickly appeared in vast quantities and variations, as well as in all price ranges and could be found almost everywhere, from the smallest rural shops to the biggest urban department stores. *Tracht* also figured prominently near the beginning of Leni Riefenstahl's film *Triumph of the Will*, which documented the highly choreographed theatrics of the 1934 Reich Party Congress of the NSDAP held in Nuremburg. Additionally, at gatherings, folk festivals and Nazi-sponsored celebrations and parades, the folk costume became the required apparel. While such mass consumerism degraded *Tracht*'s weighty historical significance, the Nazis had succeeded in endowing it with political meaning. Moreover, because German Jews were not allowed to wear, manufacture or sell *Tracht*, this cultural-historical folk costume became a visible sartorial and economic signifier of inclusion in or exclusion from the *Volksgemeinschaft*.[33]

The problem with the *Tracht* campaign was that it gained little traction. Already years before the Nazis had come to power, most farm women had ceased to wear anything resembling the dirndl on a regular basis, due to its obvious impracticality and the difficult economic straits in which many rural families found themselves. Except for the rare special occasion or celebration, rural women had not regularly worn the traditional dirndl for decades. Most women living in cities rejected the dirndl as unfashionable.

Another problem was the campaign, initiated by the Ministry for Food and Agriculture, to get rural women to make their dirndls more 'authentic'. Translated into real terms, this meant that in an effort to decrease Germany's heavy reliance on wool and linen imports, rural women were told to grow fields of flax, enlarge their flocks of sheep, then spin the wool or linen threads, weave and dye the fabric and from this sew their dirndl dresses by hand, according to old German traditions. Community hand-weaving looms were set up in villages, and weaving schools were established in towns throughout rural Germany. However, poor attendance at these government-sponsored 'spinning evenings' indicated that neither farmers' wives nor young women had the time or the desire to weave, dye and sew their clothes after spending their days working on their farms.[34] The propaganda that accompanied the dirndl campaign also failed to convince urban women to wear the folk costume. Modernised variations of the dirndl dress occasionally appeared in fashion journals, but to no avail. Even the folk costume's supposed ability to 'deaccentuate big hips' fell on deaf ears.[35]

To the great disappointment of the pro-*Tracht* advocates, the majority of women living in large cities continued to clothe themselves according to the latest internationally popular styles pictured in German magazines like *Die neue Linie, Die Dame* and *Elegante Welt*. Magda Goebbels further hindered the campaign when she declared the dirndl dress to be 'horridly ugly and unstylish'.[36]

# The uniform proposal

The second female fashion image, which had the full support of Nazi officials, was the young German woman in uniform, a reflection of the Party's attraction to organisation, conformity and militarisation. The uniform exuded power and enhanced the status of the Nazi administration. It represented homogeneity, order and accommodation with the regime, as well as a rejection of international fashion trends. The uniform instilled beliefs and value systems and shaped the attitudes of both the wearer and the observer. It was touted as a way to erase social distinctions, which was one of the pledges made by the Nazis in their supposed quest to establish a classless *Volksgemeinschaft*. It served to suppress dissent, encourage obedience, squash individuality and depict affiliation with National Socialism. Furthermore, the uniform also functioned as a signifier of exclusion from the German *Volksgemeinschaft*. Jewish businesses were prohibited from producing or selling any symbols of the National Socialist movement, including swastikas, flags, pictures of Nazi leaders and uniforms. The purpose of the prohibition was to ensure that Jews would not 'defile' the Nazi movement or its members.[37] Yet, in direct contradiction to this, Jews were ordered to make uniforms, boots and epaulets for the *Wehrmacht* and the *Luftwaffe* after their deportation to eastern ghettos. And later, in the concentration camps, Jews worked as slave labourers to repair the uniforms and shoes of their oppressors.[38]

Organisations and their requisite uniforms quickly proliferated with the onset of the Third Reich.[39] For girls, young women, female youths in the labour service or women's auxiliary units established once the war began, each group had a distinct uniform or, minimally, different insignia, badges and armbands that specified rank and branch of service. Hair was to be kept neat and away from the face. Cosmetics were shunned as unnatural and unnecessary for these young women who glowed from health and love of country. Physical fitness was emphasised, largely so that these young women would eventually have many children and, in the meantime, would be 'fit' to serve their nation. No individual touches were allowed that might detract from the symbolic significance of the uniform, which sartorially expressed unity, conformity and community[40] (Figure 4.2).

FIGURE 4.2 *An assembly of* Bund Deutscher Mädel *(BDM) members. Organisational uniforms sartorially expressed unity, conformity, order, obedience and community. Private collection of the author.*

Many young girls were drawn to uniforms because they represented belonging to a group. And despite its rather steep price, which could be upwards of 60 Reichsmarks,[41] the uniform was promoted by the Nazi Party as a useful tool in dispelling class distinctions and conveying egalitarianism,[42] particularly once sewing patterns were produced for those who could not afford to buy their uniforms ready-made.[43] Both of these features were attractive to young women who previously had been excluded from organisations or peer groups due to a variety of factors. Moreover, the esteemed cords, braids and badges offered motivation to those members who wanted to move up the ranks of the BDM or some other group and attain positions of leadership and the power that presumably came along with such posts.[44]

Clothing females in uniforms, while fairly popular when the nation was at peace, became a political problem for the government once the conflict broadened throughout Europe, and more women were needed as war-essential auxiliaries. Uniforming large numbers of females and placing them in positions that had been traditionally designated as 'male only' obviously contradicted much of the government's gendered propaganda of the pre-war years. Another key concern was that the need for extensive female uniforms would make it undeniably visible to the home front that the war, being fought by males, was not going well.

In mid-1942, an edict of the Commander of the Armed Forces warned that the increased recruitment of German females into 'war essential positions should not continue to develop into a militarisation of women. The female soldier is not compatible with our Nazi conception of womanhood.'[45] Only months before, a directive from Hitler specified that uniforms should be provided solely for auxiliaries working in occupied territories. For those females stationed inside Germany: 'Suits are to be worn at work and, otherwise, civilian clothes are to be worn.' This would not only 'save textiles', the directive explained, but would also 'slow the stream' of uniformed women who 'now dominate the view at home'.[46] The important issue of morale was at stake, as was the Nazis' core gender doctrine of women as prolific mothers, not as military auxiliaries.

As the war continued and drastic textile shortages developed, some auxiliaries, who were only issued armbands indicating service affiliation, openly complained and privately resented that they were stuck wearing simple armbands while their sisters in the occupied territories were dressed from head to toe in official attire.[47] The Nazi government had only itself to blame for the problem. Since its inception eleven years before, the regime had been bedazzled by officialdom and had put it into practice wherever and whenever possible – in its legalese, its ceremonies, its hundreds of regulations, its proliferation of departments and ministries and in its outward appearance. By example and by force, it had pressed all things official onto its citizens, including uniforms. Women auxiliaries stationed inside as well as outside of the Reich wanted to look official as they risked their lives for their nation. In a letter addressed to top officials in the *Luftwaffe* and the *Reichsministerium der Luftfahrt*, the assertion was made that uniforms for females within Germany would solve the issue of 'social class differences' and would 'facilitate the maintenance of discipline' within the ranks of the women auxiliaries.[48] There were no suggestions, however, as to where the necessary fabric would come from. Government officials had earmarked the nation's dwindling textile supplies for the German armed forces, whose need for uniforms escalated as the war raged on. Officials also approved textiles, threads and clothing accessories for a Berlin-based fashion design organisation, the *Berliner Modelle Gesellschaft*, whose purpose was to produce top-of-the-line export fashions in order to bring Germany much-needed foreign currency.[49]

Despite their uniforms and their often dangerous assignments, female auxiliary personnel never received military status in any branches of the *Wehrmacht*. The ruse continued in the months following Hitler's 'total war edict' of 25 July 1944, after which the government ordered an official female *Wehrmacht* corps.[50] There was to be no militarisation of German women. Finally, in March 1945, with the Russian army closing in on Berlin, women between the ages of 25 and 35 entered the fighting front through the *Freikorps Adolf Hitler*. Trained in sabotage and terrorist acts, these 300 female volunteer partisan troops were given the same status and weapons as men. Even this hastily organised group had a coveted uniform, consisting of a camouflage suit with small red stripes and the words *Freikorps Adolf Hitler* on the sleeve.[51]

In the weeks following Germany's surrender, numbers of women on the home front were spotted wearing dirtied and torn uniform jackets that German soldiers, officers and state officials had hastily shed during their retreat. Textile and clothing shortages had been severe for the past two years, so women viewed the abandoned jackets as a godsend, although they rarely fit. In fact, so many women wore uniform jackets in the immediate post-war period that the four occupying powers prohibited any Nazi or German military uniform 'in its present colour' as civilian clothing, even if the garment had been altered. For women to keep their coveted jackets, they had to dye them a different colour before the 1 December 1945 deadline.[52]

# Modern fashion and beauty culture

Regardless of the relentless propaganda that accompanied the dirndl and uniform images, the Nazis had another countenance, one that was intensely modern, technologically advanced, supremely stylised and fashionably stylish. It was this appearance, tied to international trends, that German fashion magazines depicted, German fashion institutes like the *Frankfurter Modeamt* promoted and designers of the *Berliner Modelle Gesellschaft* created for export fashion shows in occupied countries. It was also the image according to which most German women, of all classes, tried to fashion themselves. Using patterns, buying ready-to-wear from department stores or ordering their fashions from salons, German women purchased similar cosmetics and wore the same fashions that were also popular in France, England and the United States (Figure 4.3).

Despite the Nazi hardliners' unfashionable proposals and the contrived 'German Gretchen in dirndl dress' image that beamed from innumerable posters, the wives of most Nazi officials persisted in fashioning themselves with make-up and designer apparel.[54] Out of the public's view, German female concentration guards indulged in hair dyes, permanents and cosmetics and demanded that Jewish prisoners sew them the latest styles.[55] Even the orders for clothing manufacture handed to Jews in the eastern European ghettos were not for dirndl dresses or other traditional attire. Hans Biebow, SS official and head of the German Ghetto Administration in the Łódź ghetto, knew that stylish fashions produced in the ghetto meant big orders from German businesses and large profits for the pockets of the Nazi government in Berlin.[56] Given the multitude of magazines and advertisements that pushed the latest in cosmetics, fashions and hair products, and the countless numbers of German women who bought such products, it was clear that Nazi officials who promoted 'the natural look' and the 'dirndl fashion' had been overruled. Instead, the overall policy adopted by Hitler – a mixture of

FIGURE 4.3 *High fashion designs by the* Frankfurter Modeamt *during the war years were 'for export only' while material shortages plagued the German home front. Private collection of Luise and Volker-Joachim Stern, Berlin.*

concession and outright approval – was fuelled by his desire to highlight the regime's modern aspects, to show a fashionable face abroad, to maintain a supportive female home front (especially as the war required more sacrifices) and to divert attention from the state's crimes.

Advertisements for deodorants, body powders, cosmetics, hair dyes and face creams abounded in the pages of women's magazines throughout the years of the Third Reich, as did hair removal products, breast-enhancing potions, face creams, tanning lotions, highlight shampoos and hair dyes.

Guidelines were published that illustrated the ideal eyebrows, lips, eyes and cheekbones women could attain through the careful application of make-up. Tips were offered on replicating the looks of Hollywood stars like Katherine Hepburn or Marlene Dietrich, who had left Germany for the United States in the early 1930s. Photographs in fashion journals depicted the newest clothing trends, while German fashion schools rejected the dirndl in favour of internationally popular designs.[57]

Even in the war years, advertisements for beauty products ran in most of the leading magazines. The only difference was inserted bylines consisting of 'delayed delivery', helpful hints on making the item last longer or claims that the product was so concentrated that only the smallest amount was needed.[58] Hair permanents and dyes remained available during most of the war. The initial ordinance banning permanents, imposed in January 1943 by decree of the Minister for the Economy, was not uniformly enforced, so women with money, time and connections went in search of hair salons where officials looked the other way.[59] Hitler's mistress, Eva Braun, got so upset when she heard of the proposed ban on permanents, along with a possible cosmetics production shutdown, that she rushed to Hitler with great indignation and demanded an explanation. Hitler backed off, and the decree was rescinded. On 1 April 1943, the German news agency, the *Deutsches Nachrichtenbüro*, announced that 'the production of permanent waves has been authorised again uniformly throughout the German Reich'. Hitler then asked his War Minister to avoid 'an outright ban' and instead to 'quietly stop production of hair dyes and other items necessary for beauty culture'.[60]

Eventually, permanents were absolutely prohibited because the chemicals were desperately needed for war production. However, hair salons remained open even into the war's fourth year for those who could still afford such luxuries. Afraid that he might lose women's support for the war effort, Goebbels refused to close beauty shops as late as March 1943.[61] In a discussion with Hitler about the total war measures that had been implemented thus far, the two men resolved that: 'During total war, war must not be conducted against women. Never has such a war been won by any government. Women constitute a tremendous power and as soon as you dare to touch their beauty parlours they are your enemies.'[62]

On the whole, fashion and fashion magazines conveyed an illusory status quo. They offered a make-believe world that seemed progressive, modern, international and largely apolitical. They also served as a smokescreen, a beautiful distraction, a diversionary tactic and a fantasy space into which to escape. Permitting women's fashion magazines to fill their pages with advertisements for cosmetics, photos of high fashion designs, pictures of glamorous models and film stars and 'how-to' guides on duplicating the newest trends in clothing and make-up, just as they had before the Nazis took power in 1933, created the illusion that nothing had really changed, not even in the world of fashion, with the onset of the Third Reich.

The distribution of upscale women's magazines continued until 1943, when production was stopped because of paper shortages and heavy bombing on the German home front. However, the Nazi propaganda magazine *Signal*, which was published in ten languages and distributed in all of the countries occupied by Germany, remained on news-stands throughout the war years. Every issue invariably included a lengthy section that featured stylish German women.[63] The magazine's highly posed photographs purposefully fabricated the deception that women on the home front were cheerful, well groomed and fashionably dressed even while bombs were dropping all around them.[64] At the same time, German high-fashion designs, manufactured only for export, paraded across the runways of occupied Europe as if there was no world war, no mass destruction and no genocide. All the while, women by the thousands were being deported to concentration camps, stripped of their clothing and identities, shaved, covered in formless and threadbare uniforms, beaten, starved and murdered.

# The war years

Clothing voucher cards were issued to all Germans on 14 November 1939. Only three weeks later, in a decree dated 7 December 1939, Jews were required to surrender any clothing cards in their possession.[65] As one Nazi official put it, 'a lesser race requires fewer clothes than a superior one'.[66] Announced on 1 September 1941, Jews in the German Reich above the age of six were required to add a piece of cloth to their worn and dwindling supply of clothing – a yellow star designating their Jewishness.[67] The ordinance took effect eighteen days later. Although much fanfare accompanied the Nazi Party's clothing collection drives in 1941, the confiscation of the Jews' winter clothes and furs was carried out in silence. Their possessions had to be handed in with all labels revealing maker and owner removed.[68] Mass deportations began in October 1941, but by that time Jews in eastern ghettos had been ordered to produce thousands of pieces of clothing, underwear and shoes each week as 'payment for their upkeep'. German enterprises and individuals with connections purchased those goods. At one time described as too 'poisonous', 'immoral' and 'degenerate' to design and manufacture fashions acceptable for the 'noble German woman', Jews in the ghettos were now feverishly sewing clothes for German shops, German consumers and the German army.[69]

In the women's concentration camp of Ravensbrück, the 30,000 to 50,000 inmates went weeks and months without washing and without sanitary towels, combs or changes of clothing. One pair of striped overalls or long shirt was provided, which was to last for three months. Towards the last year of the war, only bloodied soldiers' uniforms or used prisoners' clothing, infested with lice and fleas, were distributed to the inmates. Shoes consisted of wooden clogs or, far more likely, of rags. Socks and underwear were not provided. The more the Jews suffered, the larger the stockpile of their confiscated clothing grew in concentration camp warehouses.[70]

Back in Germany, the government took steps to maintain its fashionable countenance and its illusions of plenty throughout the war years, despite increasing scarcities. Faced with disastrous losses in the Soviet Union, almost daily bombing raids on the home front, and severe shortages in clothing, shoes, textiles, nappies and sanitary towels, Goebbels allowed magazines to continue publishing photographs of stylish fashions. Advertisements for consumer goods such as cosmetics, stockings, leather purses and upscale ready-to-wear clothing, all of which had long been unavailable, were regularly published. Only occasional bylines printed in tiny script, which stated that the product was not available for the duration of the war, gave a hint that something was amiss. But employing the phrase 'for the duration of the war' also offered wishful thinking. It encouraged dreams of future consumption possibilities; dreams that were temporarily out of the reach of the average female consumer, but would surely be obtainable in the better times that the regime promised would soon arrive. The phrase also implied victory and held out the hope that once the conflict had ended, life would return to a normal, recognisable, fashionable universe.

In 1944, Nazi officials agreed that female youth group leaders needed to be taught to dress with more elegance. When on trips outside of Germany, their appearance 'did not always reflect a high level of taste and style'. On 1 June 1944, five days before the Allied landings at Normandy, the Reich Ministry of the Economy granted an astounding allowance of 30,000 Reichsmarks to the state-supported *Deutsches Mode Institut* (German Fashion Institute), for its designers to create new outfits for 1,000 full-time BDM leaders.[71] Appearances – however deceptive – still meant everything to the regime.

Some of the time, such diversions and promises of plenty worked. But as the war began to take its toll on existing clothing supplies, large cracks developed in the government's propaganda image. The Nazis understood the importance of morale and the power of hope. Unwilling to risk losing the crucial support of women on the home front and fostering the false perception that German victory was close at hand, the Nazi government approved the continuation of hair permanents, beauty salons and fashion magazines filled with photos of desired consumer products far longer than was wise. It could not, however, magically produce piles of fabrics, clothing, shoes and stockings when there were none to be had. Sooner or later, that illusion would be unmasked.

Just six months after the war began, the economic staff of the city of Düsseldorf was forced to admit that 'the shoe issue [is beginning] to become a political question of the first order'.[72] In some areas of Germany, children stopped attending school because they had no shoes to wear.[73] The city of Dortmund became so desperate in its need to repair hundreds of shoes, since new ones could not be delivered, that officials gathered up used conveyor belts and old tyres with which to mend workers' shoes.[74]

Officials in numerous towns and cities reported mounting absenteeism due to lack of footwear, so instructions on making shoes by hand were distributed.[75] Goebbels wrote that 'the situation' was undermining home front support. Shortages in shoes, clothing, textiles and leather were becoming 'catastrophic', he noted in April 1941.[76] Women organised their own bartering centres in the hope of keeping their children in coats and socks. In Berlin, officials distributed leaflets to each family explaining that 'civilians could expect no new shoes unless extreme circumstances warranted a new pair'.[77] Individuals had to prove that they truly needed a new coat, and even then, coats were impossible to obtain. Synthetic fabrics, sometimes made with milk or potato pulp by-products, fell apart easily and smelled horribly upon getting wet.[78]

Security service morale reports overflowed with the complaints of hundreds of women, many of whom began openly criticising and disobeying Party regulations. Long simmering resentment held by women of the working class that upper-class women, and particularly the wives of the Nazi elite, had been exempted from wartime regulations, erupted with greater frequency as it became glaringly evident who had the right connections and money and who did not.[79] Luxury items were never rationed under the clothing card voucher plan instituted at the beginning of the war. For example, expensive shoes, those over 40 Reichsmarks, were points-free, as were hats. This 'luxury loophole' had evoked great bitterness among working-class Germans from the time the first clothing card was introduced in November 1939.[80]

Confronted with yet another request to donate to the state's clothing collection drive, a woman was overheard muttering: 'The government has taken my husband away from me, why should I have to give them his trousers as well.'[81] Another woman, who had lost her winter coat during a bombing raid, reworked her dead husband's uniform jacket – making it smaller and sewing flowers over the bullet holes so that it would provide her both comfort and warmth. When rumours circulated that women who owned more than three dresses would have their surplus clothing confiscated by the government, one woman threatened that if the authorities dared to take away what she had saved and mended over the years, she would 'spit on' the whole lot of them when they came to her home.[82] Soon after the disastrous defeat at Stalingrad, another security service morale report noted that the recent shutdown in mourning clothes coupons, just when they were needed most, had caused widespread criticism.[83]

As clothing supplies dwindled with each additional ration card, 'intolerable scenes' were reported at some of the rationing offices. By the end of 1943, women described their clothing cards and clothing patterns, five of which were crammed onto one thin piece of paper, as completely worthless. By that time, socks, underwear and woolen items, which were sorely needed with the weather so cold, were almost non-existent. In protest, some women donated their clothing ration cards to the state's paper recycling collections. Before long, the editor of one of the major Nazi newspapers saw through such gestures and asked if women were making fun of the collection drive by contributing something that was of no value to them.[84]

Tips for 'making do' and 'making new' proliferated as the state urged women to rework their old clothing into something fashionable. The total lack of any kind of sewing goods, from thread to elastic, belied the campaign's catchy mottos and prompted strident comments from women.[85] Women were also angered by the fact that magazines, all of which had been state-controlled for years, were still showing breathtaking fashions and shoes that were only available for export,[86] while they were piecing together some form of apparel for their families from worn tablecloths, horse blankets and curtains. Most of the clothing shops within Germany were empty; naked mannequins collected dust. As news spread that the Leipzig branch of the BDM had received 'thousands of metres of textiles for new dance costumes', while German mothers were having to 'make do' with no nappies, dilapidated shoes and underwear hand-knit from the threads of old burlap sacks, personal anger transformed into public demonstrations of outrage.[87]

This examination of female fashioning and the responses it evoked illuminates one of the core characteristics of Nazism, its perplexing mixture of normality and abhorrently cruel abnormality. While the government relied upon deviousness, seductive distractions, manufactured illusion and pure terror, there was a pervasive self-centredness, an indifference to the fate of those persons stamped 'undesirable', that also made Nazi Germany possible. Describing the notorious Buchenwald concentration camp, which housed both German political prisoners and Jews, Ruth Andreas-Friedrich noted in her diary, 'In Berlin, people are complaining that the coffee is giving out... When there's no tea at Buchenwald. No coffee. And no privy. At Buchenwald several hundred people died in seven days – clubbed, shot, harried to death. Freezing, shaved heads, standing at attention for fifteen hours.'[88] In the realm of female fashioning, blind and purposeful indifference surfaced repeatedly. The fact that German women felt fully justified to express their outrage about dwindling supplies of clothing or prohibitions on hair permanents, while concentration camp prisoners considered themselves fortunate if they had managed to secure a few rags to cover their feet, reveals the specific forms of privilege – symbolic as well as real – that defined membership in and exclusion from Hitler's *Volksgemeinschaft*.

# Conclusion

Two stories, both of which occurred as the Third Reich was crumbling to total defeat, serve to highlight the incongruities and failures of the Nazis' manifold attempts to fashion female appearance. While Berlin lay in rubble and the Soviet Army was almost outside the city gates, the designer fashion salon of Annemarie Heise received a last-minute request for an elegant dress. The 'rush order' was from Eva Braun, Hitler's beloved. As much of Berlin was in flames, the finished custom-made garment could not be delivered to Hitler's underground bunker, where he had been staying for months. A courier was sent from the bunker to make his way through the bombs in order to fetch the outfit. Instead of a dirndl dress, a female uniform, or a dress bought with wartime ration coupons, Eva Braun wore *haute couture* and Italian-made Ferragamo shoes for her marriage vows to and suicide pact with Hitler.[89]

In 1943, at Auschwitz, 23 young women were assigned to the 'sewing room' detail, located at the camp's *Stabsgebäude* where many of the SS female guards lived. This clothing design and tailoring studio was established at the insistence of the wife of Rudolf Höss, the feared commandant of Auschwitz. Frau Höss had been making personal use of free prisoner labour. Previously, an attic in the Höss villa had been transformed into a studio, where two Jewish female inmates designed and sewed clothing for the commandant's family. The materials usually came from 'Canada', the warehouse filled with the belongings of Jews who were sent directly to the gas chambers. Other inmates worked to supply the Höss family with luxury food items, as well as the finest leather shoes, silk lingerie and suits – almost all formerly owned by Jews. The commandant's house was filled with the finest furniture and overflowing cupboards and was surrounded by a 'flower paradise' that was tended by Auschwitz inmates. Frau Höss had everything and anything she wanted. At one point, she was heard to happily exclaim, '[H]ere I will live and die.' The Höss villa was located so close to the camp's 'torture room' that the inmates' screams occasionally disturbed the commandant during his afternoon nap.[90]

Because of mounting resentment and gossip by some camp employees about the Höss's prisoner-seamstresses, a design and tailoring studio was opened on the concentration camp's grounds.[91] Frau Höss hoped that this would stop the jealousy that had fuelled the criticism, as more people could take advantage of the Jewish inmates' slave labour and fashioning talents. The purpose of the Auschwitz clothing studio was to produce extensive and stylish wardrobes for the wives of SS officers and the camp's female SS guards. Altogether, there were usually some twenty prisoners who toiled in the workshop as designer-seamstresses. Each inmate had to produce two custom-made dresses per week. Every Saturday, exactly at noon, SS officials came to the studio to pick up their wives' or mistresses' fashions. Orders usually consisted of everyday clothes and lingerie, as well as exquisite cocktail dresses and evening gowns that were worn to Nazi Party celebrations and SS social events.

Sometimes, when the 'customers' were especially pleased with the clothes produced for them that week, the inmates were rewarded with an additional small piece of bread as part of their meagre food allocation. One female camp guard was so impressed with the fashions designed and sewn by the prisoners that she announced to them, 'When the war will be over [sic], I am going to open a large dressmaking studio with you in Berlin. I never knew that Jewesses could work, let alone, so beautifully.'[92] Surrounded by the unspeakable cruelty of Auschwitz, of which she was an official and integral part, the guard's words resound with inanity. Most of the female inmates, including those assigned to the design and tailoring studio, did not survive the genocide of the Third Reich. When Frau Höss was discovered after the war, hiding in an abandoned sugar factory, she was found amid astonishingly large amounts of the finest hand-tailored clothes and furs, all sewn or once owned by Auschwitz's dead.[93]

It was not Nazi regulations, the regime's failure to attain economic self-sufficiency or Adefa's 'Aryanisation' efforts that fashioned German women. Nor was it the relentless dirndl and uniform propaganda or the contentious fashion debates of the 1920s and 1930s that determined what women would or could wear, although all of these factored into what fashioning options were available. Moreover, the often contradictory directives issued by high-ranking Nazi officials including Hitler, who wanted to present a stylish nation to the rest of the world, keep the increasingly female home front happy and divert attention from the regime's crimes, resulted not in a 'unique German fashion', but in confusion, resentment towards the regime and class conflict.

Conformity is the *sine qua non* of dictatorships. Coerced conformity is usually linked to political and intellectual activities and behaviours, rather than to the sociocultural activity of appearance. Yet, in the Third Reich, female fashioning was political. Various fashions were designed in an attempt to direct women away from individuality and towards uniformity. Put another way, the regime tried to define ideals of national taste, including dress codes, to construct acceptable identities. Inclusion in the *Volksgemeinschaft* could be attained by conformity to a contrived image that supported various aspects of National Socialist ideology. Similarly, 'otherness' was demonised and had its own fashion.[94]

The uniform is the sartorial image that appears most often in photographs, films and documentaries of the Third Reich. Yet, as we have seen, the Nazis encouraged or allowed other fashions, alongside the mandated plethora of organisational uniforms, as they strove to consolidate and control the appearance, conduct, purchasing habits, gender roles and attitudes of German women. The Third Reich put several sartorial posters or images on display – the folk costume, the uniform or the latest 'modern' fashion tied to international trends.[95] Each was designed to support particular policies and goals of the regime. However, powerful officials like Hitler and Goebbels took an ambivalent approach comprised of coercion and consent when contending with the issue of female appearance, especially as women began voicing and acting upon their dissatisfaction. Expressions of discontent became increasingly widespread as the regime failed to provide adequate clothing provisions throughout the war years, while magazines depicted high-fashion exports and officials' wives, dressed like fashion models, excused themselves from mandatory war work. Such disaffection and even outright class conflict belied the Nazis' depiction of a harmonious, supportive *Volksgemeinschaft*.

Thus, the history of fashioning women in the Third Reich informs us about the ambiguous nature of Nazism at the intersection of gender, culture and politics. Fashion proved to be an unsuccessful tool in constructing the ideal female citizen. In fact, the Nazis' failed attempt to shape German womanhood, partially through the arenas of clothing and appearance, exposed the limits of state power in a highly visible manner. Most women were unwilling to refashion themselves solely for ideological, economic or political imperatives. Female fashioning proved to be intractable in that regard.[96] Thus, the government found itself largely unable to control, redefine or redirect female desires and tastes. Furthermore, the numerous contradictory fashion directives and ambivalent posturing of officials laid bare the state's fear of losing female support on the home front and a lucrative fashion market abroad.

This examination of female fashioning also reveals in telling ways how the Nazi government treated fashion differently from other cultural spheres, such as literature and art, where wholesale confiscations, stringent prohibitions and even bonfires or auctions of 'degenerate' works conveyed the state's firm resolve. In the area of women's fashion, equivocalness reigned. That irresolution, interwoven with antisemitism, militarism, rabid nationalism, failed attempts at economic autarky and the pervasive pretence that characterised Nazi Germany, shaped female fashioning at various times. For the most part, though, women consistently made their own clothing choices and styled their own appearances until home front shortages made that impossible. The result was that none of the officially prescribed female images and their concomitant fashions prevailed. In the end, it was the exigencies of total war and the state's genocidal crimes that peeled away Nazism's deceptively stylised countenance and fashioned the final female image of the Third Reich, the *Trümmerfrau* (rubble woman).

# Notes

1   V. Steele, *Paris Fashion: A Cultural History* (New York, 1998). Steele employs the lens of fashion to examine Paris culture through its fashions.

2   S. Newton, 'Fashions in Fashion History', *Times Literary Supplement* (21 March 1975), p. 305.

3   I. Guenther, *Nazi Chic: Fashioning Women in the Third Reich* (Oxford, 2004), pp. 24, 73, 80, 171.

4   M. Ganeva, *Women in Weimar Fashion: Discourses and Displays in German Culture* (Rochester, 2008).

5   For examples, see Frau Schünemann, 'Deutsche Kleidung für die deutsche Frau!', *Völkischer Beobachter* (9 July 1927); R. von Kropff, 'Von modischen und anderen Dingen', in E. Unverricht (ed.), *Unsere Zeit und wir: Das Buch*

*der deutschen Frau* (Gauting bei München, 1932, reprint 1933), pp. 441–446; and E. Semmelroth, 'Neue Wege zur deutschen Modegestaltung', *NS Frauen-Warte: Zeitschrift der NS Frauenschaft* (1 November 1933).

6    E. Salburg, 'Die Entsittlichung der Frau durch die jüdische Mode', *Völkischer Beobachter* (18 June 1927); 'Die Verjudung der Kunstseidenindustrie', *Völkischer Beobachter* (13 July 1928); 'Gegen die Misshandlung deutscher Frauen', *Völkischer Beobachter* (18 June 1927); H. Riecken, *Die Männertracht im neuen Deutschland* (Kassel, 1934), pp. 6–7; A. Gerlach, 'Klarheit in Modefragen', *Deutsche Allgemeine Zeitung* (23 July 1933); and A. Gerlach, 'Wie kleide ich mich deutsch, geschmackvoll und zweckmässig?', in E. Semmelroth and R. von Stieda (eds), *N.S. Frauenbuch* (Munich, 1934), pp. 230–235.

7    The Schulze-Bibernell salon was one of the most elegant, best-known Berlin fashion studios in the 1930s. After apprenticing in the high fashion department at Herrmann Gerson, and transforming exclusive designs into ready-to-wear fashions at Jutschenka's salon, Schulze opened a studio in 1934 in Berlin with Irmgard Bibernell, a former top model and fashion trendsetter. Within a short time, their clients included famous theatre and film stars, as well as the wives of top Nazi officials.

8    Benno von Arent, Reich Stage Designer, was appointed Reich Commissioner for German Fashion in 1942, although nothing tangible ever came of it. For von Arent, see the Bundesarchiv file BA R55/1032. This episode was told to the author during an oral interview conducted on 26 June 1995 with Gerd Hartung, fashion illustrator and journalist in Berlin; also recounted in M. Deicke-Mönninghoff, 'Und sie rauchten doch', *Zeitmagazin*, supplement to *Die Zeit*, no. 19 (6 May 1983), p. 36.

9    B. Fromm, *Blood and Banquets: A Berlin Social Diary* (New York, 1944), p. 111. Bella Fromm was Jewish and left Germany for the United States in 1938. Her diary has been the subject of some debate, since it was published six years after Fromm arrived in the United States and was possibly revised in part to accommodate the desires and interests of her American publisher and readers.

10   For just two examples of views regarding the 'correct' fashions for pure German women, see von Kropff, 'Von modischen und anderen Dingen', p. 441; and Gerlach, 'Klarheit in Modefragen'. There are literally hundreds of published views on the appropriate fashions for German women. For Goebbels's quote, see F. Taylor (ed.), *The Goebbels Diaries, 1939–1941* (New York, 1983), p. 249.

11   Fromm, *Blood and Banquets*, pp. 118–119.

12   Files on the German Fashion Institute or *Deutsches Modeamt*, later renamed the *Deutsches Mode-Institut*, are located mostly in the Bundesarchiv files BA R13 XIV/179, BA R3903/54 and BA R55/795, although there are pieces of information on the fashion institute scattered throughout other ministries' files. For the *Wirtschaftsgruppe Bekleidungsindustrie and the Wirtschaftsgruppe Textilindustrie*, see especially files in BA R3101/9157 and BA R3101/9158.

13   WSGB pamphlet entitled 'Die Bekleidungsindustrie: Aussichtreiches, vielseitiges Berufsfeld für junge Menschen', n.d.; and in BA R3903/54/1-4.

14 'Ein deutsches Mode-Amt', *Vossische Zeitung* (11 June 1933).

15 *Die Dame*, no. 22 (1933), p. 45.

16 'Frau Goebbels über die deutschen Frauen', *Vossische Zeitung*, 1st morning ed. (6 July 1933); and interview quoted in A. Ley, *Schulze-Varell, Architekt der Mode*, exhibition catalogue of the Münchner Stadtmuseum (Heidelberg: Edition Braus, 1991), pp. 10–12, ftn. 6.

17 Fromm, *Blood and Banquets*, p. 119, emphasis in the original.

18 Oral interview with Gerd Hartung, 26 June 1995.

19 Adefa was the acronym for *Arbeitsgemeinschaft deutscher Fabrikanten der Bekeidungsindustrie*, which was changed to *Arbeitsgemeinschaft deutsch-arischer Fabrikanten der Bekleidungsindustrie* on 7 September 1934. For the files of Adefa, including meeting notes, constitutions and letters, see BA 3101/8646. For the goals of Adefa, see also 'Im zweiten Jahrfünft', *Der Manufakturist*, no. 19/20 (19 May 1938); 'Die Geschichte der Adefa', *Völkischer Beobachter*, no. 11 (11 January 1934); 'Die "Adefa" in der deutschen Bekleidungsindustrie', *Völkischer Beobachter*, no. 123 (3 May 1934); and 'Juden aus der Bekleidungsindustrie ausgeschaltet', *D.A.K.*, no. 187 (18 August 1938).

20 'Die "Adefa" in der deutschen Bekleidungsindustrie', *Völkischer Beobachter*, no. 123 (3 May 1934); and 'Propaganda-Aktion arischer Bekleidungsfabrikanten', *Berliner Börsen-Zeitung*, no. 516 (2 February 1934).

21 BA NS 5 VI/16198, 16230 and BA R3101/8646. See also A. Barkai, *From Boycott to Annihilation: The Economic Struggle of German Jews, 1933–1943* (Hanover, 1989), especially pp. 125–126.

22 'Was will die "Adefa"', *Berliner Lokal-Anzeiger*, no. 53 (2 March 1938); 'Adefa im Vormarsch', *Völkischer Beobachter*, no. 61 (2 March 1938); 'Der Einzelhandel vor der Entscheidung', *Der Manufakturist*, no. 9/10 (10 March 1938); and 'Arisierung – ja oder nein?', *Die deutsche Volkswirtschaft*, no. 1 (1938). For intensified efforts to 'Aryanise' the clothing industry, see 'Adefa-Etikett im Fenster: Das Zeichen für "Ware aus arischer Hand"', *Textil-Zeitung*, no. 30 (4 February 1938), which also includes the public announcement regarding the required use of the Adefa symbol, both in shop windows and on items of clothing. For the new slogan and the 'Aryanisation' activities that Adefa inaugurated, see '"Wir können es besser!" Die Adefa, ein Vorbild zur Ausschaltung der jüdischen Wirtschaftsmacht', *W.P.D.*, no. 9 (12 January 1938); 'Der grosse Tag der Adefa', *Textil-Zeitung*, no. 11 (13 January 1938); 'Bernhard Köhler bestätigt die Adefa-These', *Textil-Zeitung*, no. 11 (13 January 1938); and 'Bernhard Köhler: Wir können es besser!', *Fränkische Tageszeitung* (14 January 1938).

23 BA R58/991, 'Bericht des SD, Abt. II 112'; also quoted in H. Genschel, *Die Verdrängung der Juden aus der Wirtschaft im Dritten Reich* (Göttingen, 1966), p. 123.

24 'Ware aus arischer Hand – Was will die Adefa?', *Völkischer Beobachter*, no. 61 (2 March 1938); 'Im zweiten Jahrfünft', *Der Manufakturist*, no. 19/20 (19 May 1938); O. Jung, 'Wirtschaftsfaktor Bekleidungsindustrie', *Die deutsche Volkswirtschaft*, no. 2 (1937), pp. 82–85; 'Ausbau der ADEFA-Organisation', *Berliner Tageblatt*, no. 134 (6 July 1938); 'Die Zukunft der Adefa', *Textil-*

*Zeitung*, no. 162 (8 July 1938); 'Grössere ADEFA vor erweiterten Aufgaben', *Der Manufakturist*, no. 27/28 (14 July 1938); and 'Deutsche Kleidung statt jüdischer Konfektion', *Arbeit und Wehr*, no. 26 (4th June issue, 1938): n.p.

25  Barkai, *From Boycott to Annihilation*, pp. 133–138; and J. Walk (ed.), *Das Sonderrecht für die Juden im NS-Staat: Eine Sammlung der gesetzlichen Massnahmen und Richtlinien – Inhalt und Bedeutung* (Heidelberg, 1981) for documents on the pogrom, as well as the 'Aryanisation' that followed the pogrom.

26  Guenther, *Nazi Chic*, pp. 136–142, 165, and ftns. 132–142 on pp. 373–374. See also U. Westphal, *Berliner Konfektion und Mode, 1836–1939. Die Zerstörung einer Tradition*, 2nd ed. (Berlin, 1992); F. Bajohr, *Arisierung in Hamburg. Die Verdrängung der jüdischer Unternehmer 1933–1945* (Hamburg, 1997); A. Barkai, *Vom Boykott zur 'Entjudung'. Der wirtschaftliche Existenzkampf der Juden im Dritten Reich 1933–1945* (Frankfurt, 1988), p. 111.

27  BA R3101/8646, 'Gedächtnis-Niederschrift der Auflösungs-Mitgliederversammlung' (15 August 1939). 'Die "Adefa" löst sich auf: Das Ziel erreicht,' *Völkischer Beobachter* (20 August 1939): 232. 'Die Selbstauflösung der Adefa,' *Frankfurter Zeitung* (23 August 1939). BA R3101/8646 for Adefa's 'Auflösung' notice und 'Satzungen der ADEFA-Stiftung'. For more on Adefa's activities, as well as the removal of Jews from all facets of the fashion industry, see Guenther, *Nazi Chic*, pp. 143–165.

28  G. Scholtz-Klink, *Verpflichtung und Aufgabe der Frau im national-sozialistischen Staat* (Berlin, 1936), p. 13; I. Wessel, *Mütter von Morgen* (Munich, 1936), p. 72; A. Koeppen, 'Die bäuerliche Frau in ihrer kulturellen Aufgabe', A. Sprengel, 'Die Bauersfrau als Berufstätige in der Landwirtschaft', and I. Suhn, 'Gelübde der Bäuerin', all in E. Semmelroth and R. von Stieda (eds), *N.S. Frauenbuch*, pp. 106–111, 98–105, 112; B. v. Arnim, 'Die Aufgaben der deutschen Landfrau', in Unverricht (ed.), *Unsere Zeit und wir: Das Buch der deutschen Frau* (Gauting bei München, 1932), pp. 413–416. See also issues of *Die deutsche Landfrau* (no. 28, 1935; no. 32, 1939; no. 26, 1941, cover page; no. 36, 1943).

29  H. M. Estl, 'Die Stadtfrau und das Trachtendirndl', *NS Frauen-Warte* 7, no. 1, p. 541; Dr. J. Künzig, 'Von Art und Leben deutscher Volkstrachten', in E. Semmelroth und R. von Stieda (eds), *N.S. Frauenbuch* (Munich, 1934), pp. 224–229; E. Retzlaff-Düsseldorf, *Deutsche Trachten* (Leipzig, 1937); 'Deutsche Tracht – Richtig Getragen', *Elegante Welt*, no. 11 (24 May 1940), pp. 4–6; and for the hope that it would become an international fashion trend, see 'In the beginning was the Dirndl', *Signal* (June/July 1940), pp. 41–43.

30  See especially the Nazi women's magazine *NS Frauen-Warte*, on whose front covers photographs or artistic depictions of farmer's wives often appeared, and *Die deutsche Landfrau*, which was directed at a rural audience. The second April 1935 issue of *Das Blatt der Hausfrau* features on its cover a painting of the ideal woman. For contemporary essays, see A. Koeppen, 'Das bäuerliche Frau in ihrer kulturellen Aufgabe', A. Sprengel, 'Die Bauersfrau als Berufstätige in der Landwirtschaft', and Suhn, 'Gelübde der Bäuerin', pp. 106–11, 98–105, 112; or Arnim, 'Die Aufgaben der deutschen Landfrau', pp. 413–416.

31 'Das bäuerliche Kleid: Aufgaben der Mittelstelle "Deutsche Tracht" in Innsbruck', *Das Reich* (16 March 1941); 'Deutsche Tracht – Richtig Getragen', *Elegante Welt*, no. 11 (24 May 1940), pp. 4–6.

32 S. Jacobeit, 'Die Wandlung vom "bäuerlichen Kleid" zur Kleidung von Klein- und Mittelbäuerinnen im faschistischen Deutschland, 1933 bis 1945', in Museum für Volkskunde (ed.), *Kleidung zwischen Tracht + Mode*, exhibition catalogue (Berlin, 1989), p. 148.

33 For a thorough analysis of the role of *Tracht* as cultural, political and racial signifier in the Third Reich, see Guenther, *Nazi Chic*, pp. 109–119.

34 For the *Tracht* campaign, see 'Das bäuerliche Kleid', *Das Reich* (16 March 1941); *Die deutsche Landfrau*, no. 28 (1935), no. 29 (1936), and no. 30 (1937); *Völkischer Beobachter* (2 February 1936); and *Nachrichtendienst*, vol. 8, no. 9 (September 1939), p. 389.

35 'In the beginning was the Dirndl', *Signal* (June/July 1940), p. 41.

36 'Frau Goebbels über die deutschen Frauen', *Vossische Zeitung*, 1st morning ed. (6 July 1933).

37 Genschel, *Die Verdrängung der Juden*, pp. 88, 90–91; and Barkai, *Vom Boykott zur Entjudung*, pp. 72–73, 119.

38 Guenther, *Nazi Chic*, pp. 255–259.

39 For a thorough English-translated compendium of documents and eyewitness accounts of German society during the Nazi period, see J. Noakes and G. Pridham (eds), *Nazism: A History in Documents and Eyewitness Accounts, 1919–1945*, 2 vols. (New York, vol. 1, 1983/84; vol. 2, 1988).

40 For uniform details and requirements of various female organisations, see Guenther, *Nazi Chic*, pp. 120–127.

41 N. Westenrieder, *'Deutsche Frauen und Mädchen!' Vom Alltagsleben 1933–1945* (Düsseldorf, 1984), pp. 66–67.

42 Von Schirach declared, 'All boys and girls are clad in our uniform so that no amount of money can embellish or enhance it. It is due in no small measure to these uniforms that Germany has acquired a new social order.' Quoted in H. Bleuel, *Sex and Society in Nazi Germany*, trans. J. Brownjohn (Philadelphia, 1973), p. 135.

43 Patterns in *Beyers Moden-Zeitung*.

44 For the most thorough scholarship on the BDM, see D. Reese, *Straff, aber nich stramm - herb, aber nicht derb. Zur Vergesellschaftung von Mädchen durch den Bund Deutscher Mädel im sozialkulturellen Vergleich zweier Milieus* (Weinheim, 1990).

45 From an Edict of the Oberkommando of the Wehrmacht, Keitel, of 22 June 1942 – 'Richtlinien des Oberkommandos der Wehrmacht. Fraueneinsatz im Bereich der Wehrmacht, insbesondere in den Gebieten ausserhalb der Reichsgrenze', BA NS 6/vorl. 338.

46 'Führernotiz. Uniformierung der im Reich eingesetzten weiblichen Hilfskräfte bei Heer, Marine, und Luftwaffe', reproduced in U. von Gersdorff, *Frauen im Kriegsdienst, 1914–1945* (Stuttgart, 1969), p. 356.

47 See Guenther, *Nazi Chic*, p. 129 for further details on the 'Führernotiz', as well as the problems it highlighted and complaints it evoked.

48 Letter to the Reichsminister der Luftfahrt and the Oberbefehlshaber der Luftwaffe (10 April 1943), in Gersdorff, *Frauen im Kriegsdienst*, pp. 390–391.

49 This fashion organisation was the Berliner Modelle GmbH. For more on the organisation, see Guenther, *Nazi Chic*, pp. 167–201.

50 The *Wehrmachthelferinnenkorps* was established on 29 November 1944 and was activated on 1 February 1945. 'Total mobilisation' had first been issued as a regulation on 27 January 1943 by Fritz Sauckel, the Plenipotentiary for Labour Deployment. Less than one month later, Goebbels proclaimed 'total war' in his speech at the Sportspalatz in Berlin on 18 February 1943. On 25 July 1944, only five days after the 20 July 1944 attempt on Hitler's life, he issued another edict for 'total war'.

51 G. Buxbaum, 'Asymmetrie symbolisiert einen kritischen Geist! – Zum Stellenwert von Mode, Uniform und Tracht im Nationalsozialismus', in O. Oberhuber (ed.), *Zeitgeist wider den Zeitgeist. Eine Sequenz aus Österreichs Verirrung* (Vienna, 1988), p. 187.

52 Occupation Military Government, *Weekly Information Bulletin*, Office of the Assistant Chief-of-Staff G-5 Division, USFET, Reports and Information Branch 8 (September 1945), p. 16.

53 See Guenther, *Nazi Chic*, pp. 91–141, for the self-fashioning of women in Nazi Germany.

54 Ibid., especially pp. 131–139, 266–267.

55 S. Milton, 'Women and the Holocaust: The Case of German and German-Jewish Women', in R. Bridenthal, A. Grossmann and M. Kaplan (eds), *When Biology Became Destiny: Women in Weimar and Nazi Germany* (New York, 1984), p. 309; and G. Schwarz, *Eine Frau an seiner Seite: Ehefrauen in der 'SS-Sippengemeinschaft'* (Hamburg, 1997). There are many other such descriptions in Holocaust survivors' memoirs.

56 L. Dobroszycki (ed.), *The Chronicle of the Lodz Ghetto 1941–1944*, trans. R. Lourie et al. (New Haven, 1984), with photos of the workshops. See also A. Adelson and R. Lapides (eds), *Lodz Ghetto: Inside a Community under Siege* (New York, 1989), with extensive information about the clothing and tailoring shops, as well as photographs of Nazi officials purchasing ties and other clothing items from the Jewish workshops. For the Warsaw Ghetto workshops, see U. Keller (ed.), *The Warsaw Ghetto in Photographs: 206 Views Made in 1941* (New York, 1984).

57 Guenther, *Nazi Chic*, pp. 104–106, 213–214, and accompanying footnotes that cite advertisements, 'how-to' columns, and essays in *Koralle, Silberspiegel, Die Dame, Elegante Welt, Moderne Welt, Das Blatt der Hausfrau, Beyers Mode für Alle, Die neue Linie, Sport im Bild, Die Mode* and *Das Magazin*.

58 Ibid., pp. 245–246 and accompanying footnotes that cite wartime magazine articles, photographs and advertisements.

59 J. Goebbels, *The Goebbels Diaries, 1942–1943*, trans., ed. and introduction by L. Lochner (Garden City, 1948), entry of 12 March 1943, p. 295.

60  The quote regarding permanents and cosmetics is from A. Speer, *Inside the Third Reich*, trans. R. and C. Winston (New York, 1981), p. 258. See also N. Gun, *Eva Braun: Hitler's Mistress* (New York, 1968), p. 212. For the ban on permanents and its inconsistent enforcement, see W. Boelcke (ed.), *The Secret Conferences of Dr. Goebbels*, trans. E. Osers (New York, 1970), entry for 12 March 1943 and editor's note, p. 341. For the *Deutsches Nachrichtenbüro* announcement that the ban on hair permanents had been rescinded, see H. Boberach (ed.), *Meldungen aus dem Reich, 1938–1945. Die geheimen Lageberichte des Sicherheitsdienstes der SS*, 17 vols. (Herrsching, 1984), vol. 13, no. 372 (1 April 1943), p. 5041; and W. Paul, *Der Heimatkrieg 1939 bis 1945* (Esslingen, 1980), pp. 42–43.

61  Goebbels, *The Goebbels Diaries, 1942–1943*, entry of 12 March 1943, p. 295.

62  Ibid., entry of 10 May 1943, p. 367.

63  S. Mayer (ed.), *Signal: Hitler's Wartime Picture Magazine* (New York, 1976). The magazine was published under the auspices of the *Wehrmacht*, but the Ministry of Propaganda was behind every article and photo essay.

64  For example, see 'They don't dream of capitulating', *Signal* (February 1945): n.p.

65  RWM [762/39 BWS; 783/39 BWA] RdErl. of 7 December 1939. For this and other clothing regulations pertaining to Jews, see also Walk (ed.), *Das Sonderrecht für die Juden im NS-Staat*. For the increasing restrictions on Jews and Jewish women's responses, see M. Kaplan, *Between Dignity and Despair: Jewish Life in Nazi Germany* (New York, 1998).

66  Robert Ley, excerpt from an article in *Der Angriff* (30 January 1940); quoted in H. Schwege (ed.), *Kennzeichen J: Bilder, Documente. Berichte zur Geschichte der Verbrechen des Hitlerfaschismus an den deutschen Juden 1933–1945* (Berlin, 1981), p. 382.

67  'Polizeiverordnung über die Kennzeichnung der Juden vom 1. September 1941', reproduced in ibid., pp. 177–178.

68  Walk (ed.), *Das Sonderrecht für die Juden im NS-Staat*, 'Gestapo Darmstadt [IV B 4 – Bo/kn] RdSchr. of 4 January 1942'; and ibid., 'RSHA [IV B 4 – 7/42] Erl. of 5 January 1942'.

69  Guenther, *Nazi Chic*, pp. 254–256.

70  Ibid., pp. 258–259; see also ftn. 525, pp. 430–431, which cites in-depth English and German primary and secondary sources on Ravensbrück.

71  BA R13 XIV/179, letters dated 27 April 1943, 8, 13 and 21 May 1943, and letter dated 1 June 1944.

72  'Übersicht über die wirtschaftliche Gesamtlage' (15 March 1940), Minister President Goering, Commissioner of the Four Year Plan, V.P. 4996 g; also quoted in M. Steinert, *Hitler's War and the Germans: Public Mood and Attitude during the Second World War*, trans. T. DeWitt (Athens: Ohio, 1977), p. 65.

73  Boberach (ed.), *Meldungen*, vol. 3, no. 45 (26 January 1940), p. 689; vol. 4, no. 88 (16 May 1940), p. 1147; vol. 6, no. 159 (3 February 1941), p. 1967; vol. 6, no. 173 (25 March 1941), p. 2147; and vol. 8, no. 245 (11 December 1941), pp. 3086–3088.

74  Boberach (ed.), *Meldungen*, vol. 4, no. 85 (6 May 1940), p. 1111.

75  Ibid., vol. 3, no. 43 (22 January 1940), p. 676; vol. 5, no. 129 (3 October 1940), p. 1642; vol. 6, no. 173 (25 March 1941), p. 2148; vol. 8, no. 245 (11 December 1941), pp. 3066–3068.

76  J. Goebbels, *Die Tagebücher von Joseph Goebbels: Sämtlicher Fragmente, 1923–1940*, 4 vols., ed. E. Fröhlich (Munich, 1987), vol. 4: 567 (4 April 1941), vol. 4: 653 (22 May 1941).

77  H. Smith, *Last Train from Berlin* (New York, 1943), p. 131.

78  For the policy of autarky, as it pertained to clothing, textiles and shoes, and its numerous failures, including soaring textile prices, see Guenther, *Nazi Chic*, pp. 232–242.

79  M. Wolff-Mönckeberg, *On the Other Side. To My Children: From Germany 1940–1945*, ed. and trans. R. Evans (London, 1979), pp. 29–31. For complaints about the behaviour of the Nazi elite, see Guenther, *Nazi Chic*, pp. 203–264, as well as ftns. 166, 171, 172, 173, pp. 407–408; and lengthy citations in ftn. 287, pp. 414–415.

80  Boberach (ed.), *Meldungen*, vol. 3, no. 2 (24 November 1939), p. 521.

81  L. Horstmann, *Nothing for Tears* (London, 1953), pp. 46–47.

82  National Archives, T-81, reel 6 (29 March 1943). See also E. Beck, *Under the Bombs: The German Home Front 1942–1945* (Lexington, 1986), p. 46.

83  For primary sources regarding mourning clothes cutbacks and subsequent numerous complaints, see Guenther, *Nazi Chic*, p. 409, ftns. 193–198.

84  Boberach (ed.), *Meldungen*, vol. 14 (30 August 1943), pp. 5695–5697, and vol. 15 (11 October 1943), p. 5873; M. Seydewitz, *Civil Life in Wartime Germany* (New York, 1945), p. 119.

85  For the innumerable tips published in women's magazines during the war years, see Guenther, *Nazi Chic*, pp. 218, 226–227, 242–247.

86  See especially the issues of *Die Mode* and *Signal*, 1941–1945.

87  Staatsarchiv Leipzig, 'SD-Inlandslagebericht' (24 June 1942); and R. Wagenführ, *Die deutsche Industrie im Kriege, 1939–1945*, 2nd ed. (Berlin, 1963), table 5 for 1943, pp. 174–176.

88  R. Andreas-Friedrich, *Berlin Underground, 1938–1945*, trans. Barrows Mussey (New York, 1947), p. 35.

89  Oral interview with Gerd Hartung (26 June 1995), who stated that the 'Heise dress' was well known among fashion insiders in Berlin after the war. See also Gun, *Eva Braun: Hitler's Mistress*, p. 279; and M. Deicke-Mönninghoff, 'Und sie rauchten doch', p. 40.

90  Description of Höss villa and Frau Höss's quote in Schwarz, *Eine Frau an seiner Seite*, p. 128.

91  This is referred to in some of the documents as the *Obere Nähstube* or 'upper sewing room'.

92  L. Shelley, ed. and trans., *Auschwitz – the Nazi Civilization. Twenty-Three Women Prisoners' Accounts. Auschwitz Camp Administration and SS Enterprises and Workshops* (Langham, 1992), pp. 213–228; SS guard quoted on pp. 216–217.

93   There are many accounts of inmates who were used as personal seamstresses, particularly those inmates who had been designers or high fashion seamstresses before being deported. For the Auschwitz designer-tailoring workshop, see Shelley (ed.), *Auschwitz – the Nazi Civilization*, pp. 213–228. For more on the Höss household, see Schwarz, *Eine Frau an seiner Seite*, pp. 135–142. For personal memoirs, see S. Bernstein, *The Seamstress: A Memoir of Survival* (New York, 1997); O. Lengyel, *Five Chimneys: A Woman Survivor's True Story of Auschwitz* (Chicago, 1995); and D. Ofer and L. Weitzman (eds), *Women in the Holocaust* (New Haven, 1998). For in-depth information on clothing production in the ghettos and camps, see Guenther, *Nazi Chic*, pp. 255–259.

94   Guenther, *Nazi Chic*, pp. 10–11.

95   E. Wilson, 'All the Rage,' in J. Gaines und C. Herzog (eds), *Fabrications: Costume and the Female Body* (New York, 1990), pp. 28–38, quote on p. 33.

96   C. Breward, *The Culture of Fashion: A New History of Fashionable Dress* (Manchester, 1995), p. 1. Breward argues: 'Criticism of clothing is taken more personally, suggesting a high correction between clothing and personal identity and values.' It is, therefore, more recalcitrant than other cultural domains to manipulation and control.

# Select bibliography

Barkai, A., *From Boycott to Annihilation: The Economic Struggle of German Jews, 1933–1943*, trans. W. Templer (Hanover, 1989).

Beck, E. R., *Under the Bombs: The German Home Front 1942–1945* (Lexington, 1986).

Breward, C., *The Culture of Fashion: A New History of Fashionable Dress* (Manchester, 1995).

Ganeva, M., *Women in Weimar Fashion: Discourses and Displays in German Culture* (Rochester, 2008).

Guenther, I., *Nazi Chic: Fashioning Women in the Third Reich* (Oxford, 2004).

Kaplan, M., *Between Dignity and Despair: Jewish Life in Nazi Germany* (New York, 1998).

Noakes, J. and Pridham, G. (eds), *Nazism: A History in Documents and Eyewitness Accounts, 1919–1945*. 2 vols. (New York, vol. 1, 1983/84; vol. 2, 1988).

Stephenson, J., *Women in Nazi Germany* (London, 2001).

Steele, V., *Paris Fashion: A Cultural History* (New York, 1988).

Westphal, U., *Berliner Konfektion und Mode, 1836–1939. Die Zerstörung einer Tradition*, 2nd ed. (Berlin, 1992).

# 5

# A Holiday from the Nazis? Everyday Tourism in the Third Reich

## *Kristin Semmens*

German tourism was in crisis during the Weimar Republic. The industry lacked effective, centralised guidance from the state. It suffered from a surfeit of local, regional and even national organisations, which overlapped and fought with one another. Travel agents vied with unqualified competitors for customers. Only the very rich could travel; German workers were excluded from seeing their own country. The economic catastrophes of hyperinflation and depression meant that tourism hosts suffered as fewer guests arrived. Yet, all this changed with the Nazi takeover in 1933. The new government took tourism seriously, both from an economic and an ideological standpoint. Tourism officials and travel agents gladly traded their autonomy for what they had long wanted: state involvement and more streamlined, professionalised practices. Moreover, domestic and international visitors soon came in record numbers. Businesses across Germany profited, not only from the upsurge in private, commercial tourists, but also from the state-subsidised *Kraft durch Freude* (KdF; Strength Through Joy) holiday programme for German workers. The Nazi regime transformed the world in which tourism professionals worked, tourists travelled and their hosts welcomed them.

Not surprisingly, official governmental publications applauded Hitler's transformation of German tourism, but so too did many others. Conflict was never entirely absent, but holidaymakers and many within the industry agreed: the Nazis were good for tourism. Crucially, much was allowed to continue 'as normal' in the touristic sphere after 1933. Day-to-day activities often looked much as they had before. Yet, since it was able to intervene into and direct even the most minute matters, the regime allowed and even fostered these continuities. They were part of its 'strategy of normalisation', whereby the appearance of normalcy actually enhanced the ability to control German society.[1] Normalcy was clearly a constructed concept: nothing was truly 'normal' under a racist, violent regime, but those seeming continuities in the touristic sphere were effective in solidifying Germans' support.

Historians of Germany, including those of the Third Reich, no longer consider tourism a 'fluffy' topic; most recognise how, ironically, the search for pleasure and relaxation can shed light on some of the most horrifying events of the past.[2] In keeping with this book's focus on everyday life under Hitler, this chapter examines some of the ordinary actors in the history of tourism: tourism officials, travel agents, commercial tourists, Strength Through Joy holidaymakers and hosts. Despite some surprising continuities in leisure travel well into the Second World War, it focuses on their daily experiences between 1933 and 1939. An investigation of tourism from an everyday perspective – examining what some did, felt, said and read, and what they praised and what they grumbled about – illuminates larger debates about coercion and consent in Nazi Germany. In brief, it challenges the recent (re)emphasis of 'the central role of exclusionary violence and political paranoia in the Nazi project'.[3] In the context of tourism, the regime's intrusions were often appreciated; manipulation and repression were less frequently required.

Admittedly, for most Germans under the swastika, holiday travel was not actually an *every* day experience. Only a small minority, less than 15 per cent, took an annual trip lasting more than five days between 1933 and 1945. Hitler indeed ultimately failed to make Germany into a nation of tourists taking lengthy holidays away from home.[4] But recent analyses of German tourism stressing that point ignore the innumerable short excursions and weekend trips taken in the Third Reich, surely still to be considered a form of tourism. More crucially, they overlook the millions for whom tourism *was* an everyday experience. This chapter examines Nazism's impact on at least a few of them.

# Tourism officials: welcoming coordination

The members of local, regional and state tourism bodies and the chairs, directors and committee heads of various societies, offices, associations and authorities were mostly men; very few women held such positions before or after 1933. For these men, the Nazi *Gleichschaltung* (coordination) of tourism had a major impact on their everyday working lives.[5] The process entailed an overhaul of the organisations responsible for leisure travel in Germany, while bringing them firmly into line with Nazi aims and ideals. In the case of tourism, *Gleichschaltung* was not superficial, subtle or gradual. It was relentless and thorough. Yet here, if terror and coercion played a decisive role, it was one that left few traces in the documents. Racially acceptable and politically reliable German tourism officials – the majority, it seems – praised the state for steering the industry fully, effectively and profitably. Elsewhere in Europe, others agreed. For them, greater state interest, support and centralisation in the touristic sphere would be a 'blessing'.[6]

As part of the coordination process, two separate tourism laws (one in 1933 and the other in 1936) streamlined the chain of command. At the top stood a Reich Tourism Association, housed within and ultimately controlled by the Ministry of Propaganda, but headed on a day-to-day basis by Hermann Esser, a Hitler disciple from the days of the Beer Hall Putsch. Orders travelled downward through state tourism organisations, responsible for distinct tourism regions, to newly created tourism communities and from there to the individual municipal societies, offices and administrations. This meant the dissolution of many pre-existing bodies or their amalgamation into new ones. Membership of certain organisations, along with the payment of dues and strict adherence to their statutes now dictated from the top, became mandatory. This same coordination process occurred within all other related branches of the economy, such as the catering and accommodation trades, and continued well into the Second World War.

The Nazi jackboot thus left its footprint everywhere, but it bears repeating that there was genuine support for the synchronisation of the tourism sector, based largely on comparisons with the Weimar era. Before 1933, there was a multitude of overlapping and sometimes hostile organisations at all levels. For example, at least ten different associations competed to promote tourism to the Black Forest, three different ones in the town of Titisee alone. Their members regularly failed to cooperate; some, one commentator remarked, carried on 'like enemies'.[7] Many officials had long called for an end to this chaotic fragmentation; few therefore complained, at least on paper, about the autonomy they lost in order to achieve this.

The 1933 *Gleichschaltung* legislation also mandated that 51 per cent of any executive committee had to belong to the NSDAP; all non-'Aryan' and politically suspect members were dismissed. Jewish members quickly disappeared. In Heiligenkirchen, south of Bielefeld, the Social Democratic representatives 'made their seats available' during an April 1933 tourism society meeting.[8] Michael Beutel, the Communist chairman of the Reichenbach Tourism Society in Saxony, was removed that summer.[9] This Nazification process meant a real loss of expertise. The new chair of the Rhineland Tourism Society, the recently appointed Nazi Mayor of Bonn, Ludwig Rickert, was a teacher, with no training in the field of tourism promotion. Other state tourism associations were also headed by high-ranking Party members with no background in the travel sector.[10] Yet, while the coordination of tourism organisations immediately affected some Germans' everyday lives, the sense gained from existent sources is that many key players remained in their positions. Were tourism officials predisposed to Nazism? Did they vote for the NSDAP during the Weimar Republic? It is impossible to know in most cases, and different regions suggest different conclusions. Resort towns in southern Bavaria and the Thuringian Forest showed above average support for the Nazi Party, but most tourism destinations in the Black Forest did not.[11] Individual cases reveal some approval of the NSDAP's racist platforms. As early as 1921, Herr Mülpfort in Wittenberg displayed an enormous swastika on the gables of the tourism office and campaigned to prevent Jews from visiting his town.[12]

For the remaining tourism officials, many everyday activities must have seemed familiar after 1933. They debated the merits of increasing the local spa tax. They arranged guided tours and excursions. They drew up budgets, hired poster illustrators, wrote brochure scripts and answered tourists' inquiries. Soon, however, the day-to-day routine began to look different for these men as the Nazi regime tightened its control over the industry. Decisions about which foreign magazine to advertise in were taken out of their hands. The Reich Tourism Association now dictated the acceptable font and sizes for brochures. Fines could be levied if statistics were not submitted punctually. No local visitors' newspaper could be published without written approval from Reich authorities.[13] Not every intrusion was welcomed, of course, and tourism officials protested and opposed certain measures.[14] Yet, as Ian Kershaw has argued, 'specific animosities were…perfectly compatible with wide-ranging consent to key facets of Nazi rule'.[15] Ultimately, then, many tourism officials easily overlooked their grievances and accepted the state's heavy-handed attempt at total control; not only were demands made long ago now being fulfilled, but also the economy improved quickly after 1933, and Germans were travelling again, further solidifying tourism officials' support for the Nazi government.

## Travel agents: reservations about the Reich?

Some tourism officials held their positions alongside their 'regular' jobs. For other Germans, such as travel agents, tourism was a full-time occupation. The number of travel agencies and their employees rose dramatically in Germany after 1918, but the Great Depression hit this growing profession hard.[16] Many agents must have looked for radical solutions to their economic woes. Did German travel agents vote for Hitler? It is impossible to say with certainty, and lower middle-class employees might have voted differently than did travel agency owners. Among the latter, there is evidence that some felt an affinity for the Nazi cause: in Vienna before the 1938 Anschluss, illegal Nazis used to gather at a German-owned travel agency, which displayed, instead of travel posters in its window, 'an enormous bust of Hitler' and a swastika flag.[17] Yet, even had they not voted for the NSDAP, the support of travel agents for the regime was boosted when Germany emerged so robustly from the Great Depression. More customers arrived to request brochures, book holiday packages, buy transportation tickets, reserve hotel rooms and arrange excursions. Much of this everyday activity looked familiar, but the Nazi regime had also thoroughly coordinated the travel arrangement sector, bringing many changes to the daily working lives of travel agents.[18] During the Weimar years, several travel agency associations had competed at the national level, something denounced by industry insiders. By 1935, the Nazis had replaced these with a single Reich Group for the Auxiliary Travel Industry to watch over the entire travel arranging sector. This meant unprecedented state intervention into the travel agency business. A decree of 1936 mandated that 51 per cent of all group tours organised by German travel agents take place within the German Reich, not beyond its borders. By 1937, the regime's authority over travel agents was extended further still with the Law for the Practice of Travel Arrangement.

The 1937 Law defined who was and was not permitted to work as a travel agent in Germany. It would, the tourism publications crowed, rid the industry of the supposedly 'unreliable', parasitic elements still at work within it. Finally, under Hitler, only qualified, trained professionals could make travel arrangements in Germany. This meant an end to 'unfair competition' from the so-called 'wild' or 'also' travel agencies, which were unregulated and often sold travel tickets alongside cigarettes and other products.[19] The Law contained no 'Aryan' Paragraph per se, but it could be used to oust Jewish travel agents or transgressors of other Nazi norms for failing to meet certain criteria. It is unclear if Carl Degener, a very successful Berlin travel agency owner, had such consequences in mind when he praised the law for facilitating the widely desired and long sought 'ruthless cleansing' of the industry.[20]

The Nazi regime was definitely poised to intervene in the daily activities of those who remained. Booking package tours to the Hitler hot spots like his former prison cell in Landsberg am Lech was acceptable; continuing to advertise the Soviet Union as a desirable destination was not (Figure 5.1).[21] Even while praising the regime's overall efforts to steer the industry, travel agents criticised specific limitations on their working lives: the regime's restrictions on sending group tours abroad were, for example, deeply unpopular. Their loudest complaints, however, involved what was ironically one of the Nazis' most loudly trumpeted successes, the Strength Through Joy (KdF) holidays.

FIGURE 5.1 *Hitler's former prison cell at Landsberg: a popular tourist attraction in the 1930s. Courtesy of Archiv Manfred Deiler, Landsberg, Germany.*

Propagandists claimed endlessly that commercial tourism and KdF travel stood 'shoulder to shoulder', but many travel agents called KdF an unfair competitor in the field of package tours, one which had stolen their former customers and against which, due to its low prices, they could not hope to contend. They resented providing information to Germans who then booked a less expensive holiday with KdF. In return, the regime chastised travel agents for their attitude and prohibited them from vying for business by lowering their prices to match those of KdF.[22] Travel agents still grumbled. Yet, despite these grievances, many did well under Hitler because, if they could afford it, Germans often preferred 'normal', non-KdF tours to the state-subsidised variety: 'A substantial number of middle-class customers were willing to pay 69 Reichsmark for a one-week holiday in the Bavarian Alps instead of 39 Reichsmark for a similar KdF trip in order to avoid the "hubbub" of organised mass camaraderie.'[23] Nevertheless, while generally well-disposed towards the regime's interventions in their livelihood, travel agents' complaints about the KdF continued until the war broke out, bringing KdF holidays to an end. After September 1939, however, there was a new competitor in the field of travel arrangements. Former soldier Hermann Wittrich had his own nickname for the German *Wehrmacht*: he called it the 'Hitler Travel Bureau'.[24]

# The 'normal' tourists

Examining tourism under Hitler from an everyday perspective must take the experiences of tourists themselves into consideration. Histories of tourism are sometimes criticised for not incorporating the voices of tourists sufficiently. Yet, sources on their lived realities can be difficult to come by. There are, of course, some memoirs, diaries and oral interviews that mention holiday plans and experiences. These offer fascinating individual impressions, but rarely are there a variety of references to the same destination during the same time period as to make any meaningful generalisations. Tourist literature can be helpful: guidebooks, brochures, posters, postcards and more. But this material may not ultimately give a sense of the tourists' 'tactical operations' – how they felt, what they thought or whether they actually visited the sites mentioned; such material does, however, suggest what many tourists were likely to have seen and done when they travelled in Nazi Germany.[25] Similarly, statistics about overnight stays and holiday duration tell nothing about tourists' desires, expectations and evaluations, although they do indicate basic facts about the 'ordinary' tourist. Putting those sources together, one can begin to imagine what everyday tourist experiences under Hitler were like (Figures 5.2, 5.3 and 5.4).

FIGURE 5.2 *Tourist brochure for Berlin, 1939. Private collection of the author.*

**FIGURE 5.3** *Tourist brochure for Munich and the Bavarian Alps, 1936. Private collection of the author.*

**FIGURE 5.4** *Tourist brochure for the Black Forest, 1937. Private collection of the author.*

The commercial tourists in the Third Reich – the regime referred to them as 'normal' tourists – were overwhelmingly German, making on average over 90 per cent of all recorded overnight stays between 1933 and 1939. Most of their holidays lasted less than five days: across Germany, the average length of stay was 4.5 days at any single location.[26] They tended to travel privately, as couples or with their families, but non-KdF group tours did also grow steadily more popular in the Third Reich. They travelled more in the summer months with the exception of stays at skiing resorts in the winter, and most trod a well-worn tourist trail, visiting established holiday destinations. Many parallels can be drawn between their experiences and those of international visitors to Hitler's Germany. Both groups read the same tourist material (albeit in translation), consulted the same maps, spoke to the same tour guides and booked the same hotels. As outsiders, foreigners naturally saw the Third Reich with different eyes, but the most significant difference in tourist experiences after 1933 was not necessarily between those of Germans and non-Germans but instead between destinations. In places such as Berlin, Munich and Nuremberg, travellers found themselves part of a distinct Nazi tourist culture, seeking out new attractions and reading tourist literature suffused by Nazism; elsewhere, whether in the Black Forest or the Bavarian Alps, they ventured through a surprisingly 'normal' landscape, where the swastika was often absent.[27] Regardless of the destination chosen, however, whether Nazi or 'normal', going away on holiday offered further proof that some kind of prosperous, ordinary life was finally possible again, something German tourists attributed to Hitler. Their holidays became part of the deceptively pleasurable side of life in the Third Reich.

Not only were more Germans travelling after 1933, international visitors multiplied as well. The official 260 per cent increase between 1932 and 1935 may have been an exaggeration, but there was a steady increase. In the summer of 1936, the Olympic year, 15 per cent of registered visitors came from abroad. American visits doubled between 1934 and 1937; Irish and British visits almost tripled.[28] Why did foreigners choose to holiday in Hitler's Germany? Some came because they had been to Germany before and loved its landscape or cities. But others were drawn again or for the first time by curiosity about what the Third Reich was like. One hotel owner in Bonn raved to an English guest: 'This is the best tourist season we have had in Germany for many years.... Curiosity as to whether we Germans have cloven hoofs is bringing people into our country.'[29] The Nazi regime also went to great lengths to entice visitors from abroad, desiring their custom both for the economic advantages they brought and the opportunity to assuage world opinion about its supposedly peaceful intentions: 'Come to Germany and see for yourself!', national advertisements declared. Foreigners enjoyed relatively inexpensive visa fees to enter the country, benefitted from favourable exchange rates and, critically, were offered major discounts on train travel not available to Germans.

The regime's efforts met with success. Bella Fromm, a Jewish German journalist, wrote in her diary: 'The foreigners are spoiled, pampered, flattered and beguiled.'[30] Their perceptions of Hitler's Germany have been the topic of several recent studies, but few of these visitors were the everyday pleasure travellers. They were authors, journalists, newspaper correspondents, diplomats, foreign statesmen and other invited guests, who had very different experiences than did the 'ordinary' visitor from abroad: while they often stayed longer, up to months at a time, and 'had access to Nazi officials well beyond the reach of tourists', they also had 'less opportunity to mix with the German people and experience every-day life'.[31] Thus, the problem with these collections of foreign guests' impressions, at least for this inquiry, is that they contain very little about the mechanics of everyday tourism. They might provide a hotel name but not the price for a room or a restaurant name without mentioning what was eaten. There are few references to what guidebooks they read, which souvenirs they bought or how many postcards they sent home. Still, even without those details, one can assume many international guests experienced Germany as 'an idyllic, verdant place full of law-abiding, cultured people', as travel features often described it.[32] Even the feted foreigners, though, could witness Nazi terror, and, on rare occasions, they became victims of violence themselves. *Time* magazine reported in August 1934 on 'Terrorised Tourists':

> All over the Fatherland last week tourists leaped to their feet at the sound of the Nazi anthem, raised their right arms as Nazi banners passed. They knew that five U. S. tourists who spoke no German had been beaten by Storm Troopers in quaint old Nuremberg for standing motionless and puzzled when ordered in German to salute.[33]

There were other such examples, but on the whole, foreigners' experiences as ordinary tourists in Hitler's Germany were positive, just as those of domestic travellers generally were, making both groups less aware of present and coming danger. Another group of holidaymakers, the KdF tourists, were similarly affected.

## 'Strength Through Joy' tourists

On 17 February 1934, trains left stations across Germany. They set off from Berlin, Dresden, Hannover and elsewhere, on their way to mountains in Upper Bavaria, the forests of Thuringia and beyond. Each 'special train' carried around 1,000 participants of the Strength Through Joy leisure time organisation. KdF had been created just months before, as a subsidiary to the German Labour Front, itself a replacement for the dissolved trade unions. KdF had three ideological aims: to solidify the support of the German working class, to strengthen the *Volksgemeinschaft* by minimising class conflict and to increase workers' productivity in preparation for war. This was to be achieved by raising workers' living standards; not by raising wages – the rearmament drive ruled out that option – but instead by breaking 'bourgeois privilege'. That meant, in practice, granting workers access to museum and theatre visits, adult education courses, attendance at sporting events and, most importantly, travel for pleasure. The latter was carried out under the auspices of the so-called 'gem' of KdF departments, the Office for Travel, Hiking and Holidays. By 1939, 43 million Germans had travelled with Strength Through Joy. KdF represented only, on average, around 10 per cent of all annual overnight stays in Germany, but in certain destinations, like Rothenburg ob der Tauber, almost 20 per cent of guests came via KdF.[34] Most KdF participants (known as KdF-lers) took only day trips or made weekend excursions, but a lucky minority went on overseas cruises aboard KdF's own purpose-built ocean liners to Norway or Portugal. The Office for Travel, Hiking and Holidays became Germany's biggest travel agency, one that could offer all inclusive group tours at prices vastly cheaper than any commercial offerings. The programme won significant support for the Nazi regime. Yet the KdF's spectacular democratisation of tourism, praised by Nazi commentators and foreign observers alike, was not all it seemed.

Who was the typical KdF-ler? Despite propaganda which shouted about the Nazis' success in sending all German workers on tour, the actual KdF-lers were more likely to be lower middle-class, white collar employees, especially on the overseas cruises where manual labourers were vastly underrepresented. They tended to come from cities and towns (KdF embraced few farmers), and they tended to be younger and often single; relatively few families travelled with children. Many KdF-lers had never travelled far for pleasure before.[35] How do we know what they experienced as tourists? Some memoirs and diaries, such as the uniquely extensive collections of Franz Göll, recall KdF holidays.[36] There are reports on the trips by the SS Security Service and accounts of holidaymakers' attitudes compiled by members of the Social Democratic Party in Exile (Sopade). KdF-lers' own letters of thanks and the songs and poems inspired by their holidays are shelved in archives. Recollections gained through interviews offer valuable insights.[37] There are also photographs. One shows a KdF group posed outside an inn in Glottertal in the Black Forest. On the back, the visitor from Schleswig-Holstein noted the 'good wine' he had enjoyed there.[38] Much of this evidence suggests overwhelmingly positive impressions of the KdF holidays.

However, historians also know what KdF participants did not like, and perhaps surprisingly, the best source for their complaints comes from official Nazi publications, which made explicit and enduring efforts to assuage them. KdF-lers grumbled about arriving in a fourth class train compartment. They had not stayed at a well-known tourism destination 'with a name' as they might have hoped: for them, the Black Forest town of Wolfach was a poor substitute for Baden-Baden.[39] They felt they received second-class treatment: they were served the KdF coffee, not the 'good sort', at a Bavarian pension; they ate a casserole in the Harz Mountains, not a fancier entrée; they were told that the wine was out of their price range by a snarly waitress in a Widmar restaurant.[40] Some KdF participants felt the holidays were overly regimented, with little time for individual pursuits. Sopade noted that holidaymakers were 'put off by the crowds'; American reporter William Shirer, who took part in several holidays at the express invitation of the regime, called life with KdF 'excruciatingly organised'.[41] At times, the KdF-lers also resented their wealthier compatriots who could afford the extras not included in the package price.[42] Others felt looked down upon by 'normal', commercial tourists. These everyday grievances did not go unheard. The Nazi regime made certain concessions, here as in so many other spheres, in order to bind the German population more closely to it. Such efforts to ensure customer satisfaction, openly discussed in newspapers, journals and speeches, reveal a dictatorship surprisingly sensitive to consumer demand. Ultimately, that willingness to fulfil specific desires worked to its own advantage: even those once critical were won over not only to the tourism programme, but also to the regime itself. Yet, more crucially, as numerous as critics of KdF might have been, many more of its holidaymakers appeared satisfied and appreciative of the new opportunities to travel, which made it, even for former Socialists, 'worth raising an arm now and then'.[43] The trips certainly created lasting memories for many Germans of the 'good times' under Hitler.[44]

# Hosting the tourists

The everyday experience of being a host to tourists also changed in Nazi Germany. While tourism studies scholars regularly investigate the rather clinical-sounding 'host populations' in their contemporary analyses of leisure travel, historians of German tourism have focused less explicitly on the attitudes of local residents to visitors and their interactions with them. A full picture of tourism in the Third Reich should include those experiences. The improvement in economic conditions after the desperation of the Depression led many Germans to support and applaud Hitler's regime; those Germans living in tourist destinations were no different. In places that were already established holiday locales, hotel and restaurant owners, tour guides, excursion company operators, souvenir makers and many more welcomed the upturn in visitor numbers. Elsewhere, villages and towns turned to tourism for the first time with the arrival of KdF holidaymakers. Especially in some of the country's poorer regions, KdF was seen as a means to economic salvation, one that certainly affected daily life. Allensbach, a town on Lake Constance, recorded 957 overnight stays in 1933; by 1937 that number soared to 25,000. Schongau, Bavaria, suddenly became a tourism 'stronghold', recording 16,000 overnight stays in 1935, up from 6,000 the year before.[45] The KdF programme was seen as a 'godsend' for many locals, like pension owner Josef Schauer in Oberammergau. Excluded by the local tourist office from accommodating Thomas Cook guests – his establishment was deemed unsuitable for foreigners – he opened his doors to KdF tourists instead.[46] Nazi propagandists regularly and rightly highlighted the value of tourism for entire local economies. Many businesses and resident craftsmen profited, recording better sales of everything from cameras to Carnival costumes to carved wooden KdF badges.[47]

Increased visitor numbers of any kind altered everyday life in destinations across Germany, but the arrival of the KdF-lers had unique effects on the daily rhythms of a village or town. KdF tourist culture differed most from its commercial counterpart through the extended and intimate contact between its holidaymakers and residents. Many residents, especially young adults, attended the greeting and farewell ceremonies, the dances, beer and *Heimat* evenings, folk concerts, performances and other daily get-togethers, all announced by local newspapers in advance and reported on afterwards. Some locals disliked being forced to provide entertainment and resented the mandatory hosting of endless social evenings. But others remembered these events fondly and appear to have genuinely enjoyed their experience as KdF hosts. In the Chiemgau region, some gladly gave up their own bedrooms to their guests, decorated their houses with flowers to welcome them and even moderated their Bavarian dialect so that their visitors could understand them better.[48] Real and enduring connections between hosts and guests were made, just as the Nazi regime had hoped: Leopold Schlosser from Wildenwart, Upper Bavaria, remembered a woman from Mannheim who stayed with his family and kept in touch for decades.[49]

There were times, however, when the KdF-lers strained the limits of supposedly innate German hospitality. Even in places where KdF tourism had saved local economies from destitution, there was anger at how little reimbursement hosts received per individual traveller. Compared to a 'normal' tourist, the KdF-ler paid less for the room and less for the meals and was exempt from the local spa tax. In Saxony, one local resident was adamant: 'It would be best', he maintained, 'if these people stayed at home.'[50] Even more vociferous complaints came from established, internationally known tourism locations like the spa town of Baden-Baden. The resistance to accommodating KdF holidaymakers in certain locations was so strong that ultimately the regime kowtowed, unwilling to jeopardise more profitable commercial tourism. Still, it was possible to go too far: one Bavarian innkeeper wrote 'Not visited by KdF tourists' in his prospectus in 1939. The brochure was banned and that proprietor was prohibited from receiving summer guests.[51]

The Nazi regime's control over German tourism could be unpopular with host communities in other ways. Some souvenir makers and sellers were dismayed by the regime's war against silliness (*Lächerlichkeit*) and kitsch. Only authentically German, tasteful products should serve as mementoes of a holiday. Cheap, mass-produced jokey objects were out of favour. Hand-crafted lace from the Erzgebirge, cuckoo clocks from the Black Forest and Bavarian dirndls were preferable items.[52] But those kitschy souvenirs were often profitable for local businesses, as were the allegedly tacky tourist practices of charging tourists to pose for photographs in front of artificial backdrops. Much to his chagrin, one photographer in the Drachenfels hills near Königswinter was forbidden from displaying a stone dragon at his stand along the path to the castle ruins, something visitors had previously paused – and paid – to capture on film.[53] While many applauded it, the Nazi regime's standardisation, regulation and professionalisation of the tourism industry could simultaneously have a negative impact on local hosts. Clamping down on the 'wild room' trade or 'wild tour guide' trade (like the 'wild travel agency' trade), part of more concerted efforts by the Nazis to outlaw under the table work, took away still needed sources of income.

Locals complained loudly about increased noise, travel congestion and litter brought by tourists. Many were even more dismayed by their behaviour. The KdF-lers were known to be especially problematic guests, ones who drank too much, disturbed the peace, dressed inappropriately and, so the joke went, generally lost too much 'strength through joy'. The KdF responded to grievances about its participants by publishing 'Ten Commandments' for them to follow during their holidays. The Bavarian town of Nesselwang posted similar rules of conduct for its KdF visitors.[54] Still, excessive alcohol consumption remained a cause for complaint. Loud singing during 'booze cruises' along the Rhine had been annoying local residents since the Weimar years, but attempts to crack down on this behaviour had little impact. A Sopade report from 1938 noted that the problem of 'truly disagreeable' KdF holidaymakers endured, describing 'an unbelievable amount of drunkenness and ribaldry'.[55] Some German communities under Hitler also viewed mass tourism as a threat to their heritage, their cultural identity and even their faith. Village old timers disapproved of the inauthentic folk performances put on to entertain the KdF-lers. In Oberammergau, one terrible performance by an outside dance troupe aroused the indignation of local spectators, who called it 'a scandal'.[56] Scheduling KdF day trips on religious holidays further aroused the hostility of Catholic residents, manifested in their refusal to say 'Heil Hitler', fly the swastika flag or attend the KdF farewell celebrations.[57] Such responses suggest a plurality of opinions of the Nazi tourism boom.

Greater visitor numbers meant potentially more serious dangers for hosts. More eyes and ears now watched and listened to what occurred in a hotel, in a pub or around a town. Since the Nazi regime and the Gestapo in particular relied heavily on denunciations, outsiders, with fewer ties and loyalties to a community, were, presumably, more threatening. Punishments could be far worse than being struck off the list of KdF accommodations, as was the case of one hotel owner on the Bavarian Schliersee after his parents were arrested.[58] Furthermore, registering guests with the police, a practice that had been the norm in the Weimar period and which carried on under Hitler, could bring unwelcome scrutiny into just who was staying with whom. For hosts who dared to welcome Jews after 1933, this could be particularly perilous.

# 'Jews not wanted here':
## antisemitism and tourism

The hostility and discrimination that Jewish tourists faced in Germany after 1933 has been well researched, but antisemitism also pervaded the everyday working lives of tourism professionals in ways that historians have yet to explore. The Nazi seizure of power and subsequent campaign of *Gleichschaltung* immediately forced Jews out of tourism societies, associations, authorities and offices, although estimating how many were affected is extremely difficult. Comparing pre- and post-1933 membership lists can suggest who left, but not always why. Still, the records can hint at the fates of some individuals. Heinrich Hirsch, a Jewish factory owner, was the long-serving and much-respected chairman of the local tourism society in Gross-Gerau (Hesse). His name no longer appeared in the meeting minutes by February 1933.[59] The Jewish businessman Nathan Marx, co-founder of the Eppingen Tourism Society, was soon ousted from its ranks.[60] The dismissal of Ludwig Landmann from his post as the Mayor of Frankfurt-am-Main ended his long-time role in the tourism society.[61]

Once the Jews were gone, how did antisemitism shape the everyday lives of those tourism officials still at work? They now had to subscribe to *Der Fremdenverkehr*, the official tourism journal, which regularly ranted about solving the 'Jewish Question' within the industry. Their correspondence often dealt with related matters. One official in the Thuringia State Tourism Association wrote to a travel agency newsletter to clear up potential 'misunderstandings' about the town of Judenbach: the town, he explained, 'had only its name in common with the non-Aryan race'.[62] Other tourism officials compiled and reported statistics on the numbers of Jews visiting their locale. The author of a report on the 1934 bathing season on Hiddensee, an island in the North Sea near Rügen, rejoiced that fewer Jews had visited that year than in 1933.[63] Yet, at the same time, at least in the early years of the Third Reich, those with vested interests in promoting tourism reassured Jews that they were still wanted in their communities. Their efforts spoke less to sympathy for Jews, of course, and more to their desire to protect and encourage economic growth. In June 1934, the spa administrators in Westerland, an upscale resort on the island of Sylt, wrote to say they 'would be happy to welcome' Dr Lindenheim, a Jewish doctor.[64] Tourism officials also worried aloud about the negative effects that antisemitic signs might have on the tourist trade along the Romantic Road and in the Garmisch-Partenkirchen region.[65] In 1934, the state tourism associations advised their members to pass along, in secret, the names of hotels and resorts that refused entry to Jews to local tourist offices and travel agencies, so that future Jewish travellers could be better served.[66]

Similarly, fearing the impact that they might have on a still struggling industry, tourism officials rarely incorporated explicit antisemitic language and imagery into their promotional material. When antisemitism did appear, its presence was not necessarily something new. There was continuity in the branding of certain tourist resorts as 'Jew free' long before 1933. The small town of Vitte on Hiddensee, for example, published a prospectus throughout the 1920s stating that Jews were not welcome there.[67] Of course, many other places became brand new 'Jew free' destinations after 1933 and later tourist publications went further in their overt racism. A brochure issued by the Nuremberg Tourism Association in 1939 declared: 'Healthy national and racial instincts…ensured Nuremberg's transformation into a stronghold of National Socialism, even before other cities had heard Adolf Hitler's call.'[68] In Rothenburg ob der Tauber, shops displayed postcards bearing images of the wooden plaques recently placed on the city's medieval gates, which incorporated sayings from the 1520s warning about greedy, dishonest Jews.[69] Generally, though, antisemitism shaped everyday tourist material less through the additions of racist language and imagery and more through absences and omissions. The 1936 edition of the Pharus map of Berlin had blank spaces where, only the year before, miniature depictions of synagogues had stood, indicating sights to be seen. During the Weimar years, Bühl, a small town in the Rhine Valley, sold postcards of the local synagogue, a practice that was quickly ended. In 1935, the Reich tourism newsletter admonished the Tourism Office in Trier, birthplace of Karl Marx, for still distributing a brochure that alluded to the house where the 'famous German Socialist' was born; it ordered the immediate destruction of such material.[70] Yet direct commands to add or get rid of specific touristic content were rare under Hitler. Such changes were usually made voluntarily, speaking to the mostly willing self-coordination of the industry as a whole. This degree of self-coordination was hardly a phenomenon unique to the tourism sector in the Third Reich. In order that the Nazi regime achieve the 'smooth functioning' of everyday life after 1933, something critical to its pursuit of longer-term political goals, it was not necessary for all Germans to support all Nazi ideas and every policy. Instead, it required that 'on a day-to-day basis…most people [would]…obey the law, try to stay out of trouble, and promote their own interests as best they could'.[71] Yet, not surprisingly, should self-coordination not proceed smoothly, the Nazi regime stood ever ready – and able – to intervene, forcing an acceptance of its own ideological agenda if necessary, especially concerning its hatred of Jews.

Antisemitism thus clearly impacted the everyday experiences of all German tourism professionals, including travel agents. When Hermann Esser said that the travel agency sector had to be pure, he meant not only free from unscrupulous agents but also, of course, from Jews. It is impossible to determine how many Jewish travel agents were at work in Germany before 1933 or carried on after. There was no outright ban on Jews working in the travel arrangement industry until July 1939, but earlier legislation was exploited to oust Jews as 'unfair' competitors. Some Jewish travel agents therefore lost their jobs, and as 'Aryans' distanced themselves and German

Jews travelled less, those still in business lost customers. Paradoxically, other Jewish travel agents were able to take advantage of new opportunities after 1933. One Jewish travel agency in Berlin, Traversum, opened a 'relaxation' (*Erholung*) department. It compiled a list of 400 Jewish-owned and 'Jewish-friendly' hotels for its clients and booked 1,500 holidays at these destinations in 1934.[72] Travel agents also took on new daily tasks under Hitler. As German and Austrian Jews tried to flee an increasingly difficult and frightening existence, lengthy queues of desperate people outside travel agencies became a common scene. Now, travel agents within ordered visas, booked tickets on ocean liners and made hotel reservations for hopeful emigrants. Technically, 'Aryan' travel agents were not supposed to assist Jews with their emigration plans, but this rule was flouted regularly. In continuing to offer these services, some 'Aryan' travel agents might have acted out of genuine sympathy to the emigrants' plight, but others recognised that there was money to be made from desperation. One Hapag-Lloyd agent took a 100 Reichsmark bribe to put a name on a waiting list for an already overfilled ship.[73] Jewish travel agents themselves were officially prohibited from practising their trade in 1939, with the exception of those working in Jewish agencies arranging emigration travel, an increasingly unlikely possibility by then. There was a joke about travel agencies told at the time: 'A Jew enters a Berlin travel agency. The travel agent sets a globe in front of him, spins it around, and says "Choose". After a short pause, the customer asks with a pained expression, "Do you have anything else?"'[74]

As the world held its doors closed to Jews trying to escape the Third Reich, a number of mysterious and morally ambiguous figures involved in travel arrangement emerged. There was, for example, Heinrich Schlie, owner of the Hanseatic Travel Agency in Berlin and a long-serving informant for the Security Service of the SS. He was involved in arranging ship tickets for emigrants and openly advertised those services to 'non-Aryan' clients. Accused of 'incorrectness' in Jewish matters, he was also imprisoned for currency infractions. Yet he was still consulted by the regime on arranging mass emigrations of German Jews, for example, to Ecuador in 1936. He later opened a second office in Vienna just down the road from Adolf Eichmann's Central Agency for Jewish Emigration, where, protected by Eichmann himself, he continued to make a 'lucrative business' out of Nazi hatred.[75] There was also Berthold Storfer, born a Jew but baptised a Catholic, who, although not a trained travel agent, became deeply enmeshed in making the arrangements to get Jews out of Austria. He also benefitted from extremely close connections with Eichmann's office. He was a controversial figure – some historians claim that he saved thousands by arranging their passage to Palestine, but others argue that he collaborated with the Nazi regime. He was murdered at Auschwitz in the autumn of 1944.[76]

The most disturbing connection between travel agencies and the Holocaust, however, is the surprisingly little-publicised role of the *Mitteleuropäisches Reisebüro* (Central European Travel Agency, or MER), now the *Deutsches*

*Reisebüro*, one of Germany's biggest travel agencies. Although it has long been known that MER handled the German railway bookings for the 'special trains' used for the mass deportations of Jews and transport of forced labourers, further details have only recently come to light that show how truly profitable this contract was.[77] MER employees sold blocks of tickets on trains to the East – in cattle cars when no passenger trains were available – at set prices, half fare for children under twelve and free for children under four. They issued return tickets only for the accompanying SS guards. Chillingly, MER staff simultaneously made travel arrangements for other customers, if not booking the 'normal' peacetime commercial holiday packages they once sold, then organising other forms of tourism at war. They used the same forms, stamped the same tickets and issued similar receipts. How much did these men and women know about what they were doing? How much did they care? Or, for MER travel agents, as for some German railway employees, was 'Auschwitz … only a train station'?[78] By contrast, there are more inspiring stories of travel agent courage under Nazi rule. In the occupied Czech lands, the national travel agency, Cedok, worked closely with Nicholas Winton, an English stockbroker, to bring 669 mostly Jewish children to Great Britain before the outbreak of the war.[79] Travel agents could claim they were merely doing their everyday jobs under the circumstances, but while Cedok employees were saving lives, MER was arranging journeys to hell.

In 1933, however, the Holocaust was not yet inevitable, and in the early years of the Third Reich, Jews continued to travel for pleasure in Germany. How did tourists themselves react to the antisemitism they encountered at their holiday destinations? For 'Aryan' Germans, a sign reading 'Jews not wanted' or a brochure advertising a hotel as 'Jew free' had become normal, something not worth commenting on, which might explain why so few did when they wrote their diary entries at the time or recounted their travel experiences after the war. Some non-Jewish foreigners were certainly shocked and dismayed at what they witnessed. One English woman was aghast to see a recently restored medieval plaque in Nuremberg, reading 'Shun the fox on the heath, and the Jew on the street'.[80] In her diary account of a visit to Germany in 1935, Virginia Woolf angrily recalled that she had merely stood by, and even raised her hand, alongside the cheering crowds of children awaiting Hermann Goering's arrival under banners proclaiming: 'The Jew is our enemy.'[81] Woolf's Jewish husband, Leonard, like other foreign Jews, could have chosen a different holiday destination that year. But what of German Jews who wanted to travel? Even if they could find places that would accept them, impoverished by unemployment and later limited by the regime's increasingly cruel transportation restrictions, many German Jews stayed put. But certainly not all did. Some chose to travel abroad in the earliest years of the Third Reich. In July 1935, the Gestapo reported that 90 per cent of travellers to Bornholm in Denmark were German Jews.[82] But as visa fees rose and exchange rates for foreign currency worsened, leaving the country – even for a short time – became much more difficult.

When German Jews did attempt to holiday in what was also their Fatherland, antisemitism potentially confronted them at every turn. Many individual hotels, guesthouses and entire resorts were known to be hostile to Jewish guests; some refused to accept them at all. Even in the Weimar years, the Central Association of German Citizens of the Jewish Faith had its own 'travel service' department to advise Jewish travellers on which destinations to avoid. By 1934, it focused on compiling information about where Jews were permitted, augmenting the efforts of some Jewish travel agents and individual Jewish communities to do the same.[83] If Jewish Germans did not do their research ahead of time and simply turned up at their chosen destination, they risked not finding anywhere to stay. One Jewish couple from Potsdam, who went to the Black Forest, found it 'hard to find a pension or hotel. Everywhere the first question concerned their religion, followed by remarks like: "We personally have nothing against Jews, but you must understand that we cannot take risks".'[84] Yet, this was certainly not the experience of all Jewish tourists before the autumn of 1938. During a driving trip through the country with his parents in late spring 1936, historian Peter Gay recalls seeing a sign proclaiming that the village of Hahn, near Frankfurt, was and remained 'free of Jews'. But this, 'astonishingly', was the 'only show of antisemitism' they had seen during their whirlwind tour.[85] Similarly, Frederick Weil, a wine exporter from Frankfurt, had mixed experiences as he and his wife travelled through the Reich in the summer of 1938 before they emigrated. Weil recalls easy conversations with female buyers in the Black Forest; some brought him farewell gifts. Things were very different in central Germany, where finding a hotel that would accept Jews was very difficult. He saw signs at the resort of Bad Harzburg saying 'Jews are forbidden to stay'. But at nearby Halberstadt, he was welcomed in the first hotel he tried. In Berlin, the Reich capital itself, Weil saw scarcely any antisemitic signs. In fact, Berlin hoteliers were surprised when he asked if he could stay there as a Jew.[86] Moreover, many of the internationally known spa towns, such as Baden-Baden and Bad Homburg vor der Höhe, did not impose the strict restrictions Jewish guests faced elsewhere; there, a superficial normality prevailed.[87]

Yet even at places where Jews were allowed to stay, antisemitism could naturally intrude. Anti-Jewish tracts might be discovered in the reading room; hostile remarks from other 'Aryan' guests might be overheard; open violence could erupt. In 1935, in Bad Tölz, local SA men smashed the windows of a hotel restaurant that served Jewish visitors.[88] As time went on, the Nazi regime placed increasing restrictions on Jewish tourists. Jacob Borut summarises the process:

As anti-Jewish pressure grew from below, the Interior Minister published a decree in 1937 that gave legal sanction to the many steps undertaken at local level to hinder Jewish presence in tourist facilities. From now on, Jews were not allowed to go to seaside and summer resorts (Seebäder and Sommerfrische), and were only allowed in spas (Heilbäder), only for medical purposes, and only when they could be accommodated in separate Jewish hotels and inns.... But this was not enough. The decree went on to forbid Jews to use all local facilities that were not directly used for medical purposes, such as gardens, sports facilities or restaurants and pubs.... The decree severely limited the possibilities of Jews to visit tourist facilities. In the whole of Bavaria, for example, only three places remained open to Jews.[89]

While numerous, the 'Aryan' hoteliers and innkeepers who delighted in such decrees – letting their racial hatred trump their own economic interests – were not representative of all tourism hosts. In the early years of the Third Reich, some locals at holiday resorts exhibited friendlier attitudes towards Jewish travellers. One pension owner in Ahlbeck, Pomerania, usually flew the swastika flag in front of her property, but when she had Jewish guests, she exchanged it for the Pomeranian flag, a very small but visible kindness.[90] As for Jewish hoteliers and innkeepers, they were obviously affected by both official and popular antisemitism after 1933. Listing their establishments in local visitor prospectuses was forbidden. They faced constant harassment, such as inspections and closures due to supposed sanitary violations. Their clientele dwindled as fewer Jews travelled, and most faced great pressure to 'Aryanise' their properties. Yet Jews still owned hotels and welcomed guests in private rooms until well into the Nazi years. The Hungarian Jew Bela Kaba-Kein, who ran the best hotel in Binz, Rügen, did so until it was sold to 'Aryans' in 1938.[91] Moreover, until later decrees prohibited it, these Jewish hosts accommodated 'Aryan' visitors as well. One official report on Bad Kissingen in 1936 estimated that, in Jewish owned establishments, 'Aryan' guests made up fully 15 per cent of the clientele.[92] One wonders what relations were like between hosts and guests in those places.

The increasing preference for Jewish-owned properties among German and foreign Jewish tourists – and later their necessity as other options disappeared – meant that some Jewish-owned hotels had good years under Hitler. The Hotel Strauss in Bad Brückenau, northern Bavaria, recorded 450 overnight stays by Jewish guests in June 1937, nearly double the number it had welcomed the year before.[93] Such everyday conditions sent the 'mixed signals' that Peter Gay describes so well in his memoir, blunting, at least for some Jewish hosts, the urgency of their situation. Yet sometimes the signals were very clear indeed. Those accused of flouting the regime's racist interdictions in the tourist sector faced real persecution and terror. In some cases, 'Aryans' bore the brunt of official censure. In Bad Wildungen in Hesse, a hotel owner who had violated the local rules with regard to when and where Jews could bathe 'was marched through the streets with a sign [reading] "I am a pig and have contact with Jews"'. More often, though, Jewish tourists were the victims, as in the case of a Nuremberg Jew visiting Bad Brückenau, 'who dared to drink from a public fountain at a time not allotted to Jews'. He 'had his *Kurkarte* [spa ticket] immediately revoked, and he was ordered to leave within 24 hours'.[94] By 1939, any semblance of 'normal', everyday pleasure travel had come to an end for Jewish Germans. A vicious and lengthy war soon eradicated it for all Germans.

# Conclusion: a holiday from politics?

Until the invasion of Poland, the history of German tourism under Hitler was one of broad consensus among those whom he favoured. Most tourism professionals, from tourism society chairmen to travel agents, greeted state coordination and control with enthusiasm. They gladly accepted their loss of autonomy, for the Nazis seemed to have fulfilled many of their long-standing career aspirations. They also upheld the Nazis' own view of tourism's political value: it was essential to uniting the country, increasing patriotism and overturning foreign 'misconceptions' about the new Germany. As the miseries of the Great Depression faded, their applause for Hitler grew louder still.

As for the tourists, domestic and foreign, most praised their travel experiences in Nazi Germany. Some enjoyed destinations seemingly unchanged under the dictatorship; others welcomed Nazism's distinct imprint on specific locations. Even foreigners tended to find the sites and symbols of fascism more fascinating than frightening. They generally admired the country's cleanliness, orderliness and apparent vitality and often departed with memories of a peace-loving and progressive country. For Germans themselves, including the newly minted mass holidaymakers, the KdF-lers, travel offered further opportunities to cement positive impressions of the achievements of their *Führer*. Especially for workers who had never travelled before, here was a tangible reminder that everyday life had improved. Host communities certainly welcomed the increased guest numbers: the accommodation trade watched the number of overnight stays rise, while local shops and businesses welcomed more customers through their doors.

Not all was acclaimed in the everyday world of German tourism after 1933: specific incursions by the Nazi regime were openly criticised. Travel agents resented new quota regulations on package tours. Souvenir sellers lamented new rules about kitsch. Holiday resorts grumbled about the changes wrought by an influx of KdF tourists. And not everything had visibly changed after 1933. The same people performed daily tasks that appeared familiar; visitors relaxed, read their guidebooks and saw the sights just as they always had. But these superficial continuities did not mean that the tourist sector was in some way untouched by Nazism. They were part of a façade of normalcy instrumentalised by the regime to further its control over tourism and German society as a whole. While behind that façade Jewish Germans and political enemies were brutally mistreated, most actors in this story fell willingly into line. Some closed their eyes to that persecution, silently accepting the expulsion of a colleague or the closure of another Jewish-owned travel agency; others actively supported the regime's antisemitism, inserting expressions of their hatred into tourist literature or explicitly praising laws reducing 'unfair competition' by 'parasites'.

The Nazi takeover profoundly shaped all Germans' everyday experiences of tourism, whether at work or on holiday. For some, those experiences opened their eyes to the true nature of a cruel and dangerous new regime. For many more, everyday practices led to increased support for Hitler or at least minimised overt resistance to him; in all cases, however, it was clear that the Nazi regime's impact on German tourism was palpable, widespread and – ultimately – inescapable. When Swiss journalist Annemarie Schwarzenbach visited Germany in 1937, she noted in her diary that it was impossible to take a 'holiday from politics' in the Third Reich.[95] But as an evaluation of tourism from an everyday perspective has revealed, many Germans had no real desire to take a holiday from the Nazis.

# Notes

1    F. Trommler, 'Between Normality and Resistance: Catastrophic Gradualism in Nazi Germany', *The Journal of Modern History* 64 (December 1992), p. 92.

2    J. Walton, 'Welcome to the *Journal of Tourism History*', *Journal of Tourism History* 1, no. 1 (2009), p. 1. See the range of titles within these notes.

3    E. Kurlander, 'Violence, *Volksgemeinschaft* and Empire: Interpreting the Third Reich in the Twenty-first Century', *Journal of Contemporary History* 46, no. 4 (2011), p. 922.

4    C. Kopper, 'The Breakthrough of the Package Tour in Germany after 1945', *Journal of Tourism History* 1, no. 1 (2009), pp. 67–68.

5    K. Semmens, *Seeing Hitler's Germany: Tourism in the Third Reich* (Basingstoke, 2005), pp. 16–31.

6    K. Semmens, '"Tourism and Autarky are Conceptually Incompatible": International Tourism Conferences in the Third Reich', in E. Zuelow (ed.), *Touring Beyond the Nation: A Transnational Approach to European Tourism History* (Farnham, 2011), pp. 200–201.

7    Semmens, *Seeing*, p. 10.

8    Lenkungsausschuss '1000 Jahre Heiligenkirchen', ed., 'Protokollauszüge 1882 bis 1945', 13. http://www.1000jahreheiligenkirchen.de/ Protokollauszuge_1882_bis_1945.pdf [accessed 30 September 2014].

9    Verschönerungsverein Reichenbach 1974 e.V., 'Verschönerungs- und Verkehrsverein Reichenbach (1929–1945): Historische Betrachtung' (2009), p. 26. http://www.verschoenerungsverein-reichenbach.de/vereinsgeschichte/ VVR_1929-1945.pdf [accessed 30 September 2014].

10  T. Nowack, *Rhein, Romantik, Reisen: Der Ausflugs- und Erholungsreiseverkehr im Mittelrheintal im Kontext gesellschaftlichen Wandels (1890 bis 1970)*, Ph.D. dissertation, Rheinische Friedrich-Wilhelms-Universität Bonn (2006), p. 123; Semmens, *Seeing*, pp. 10, 20.

11  Semmens, *Seeing*, p. 199, note 2.

12  S. Reichelt, *Der Erlebnisraum Lutherstadt Wittenberg: Genese, Entwicklung und Bestand eines protestantischen Erinnerungsortes* (Göttingen, 2013), p. 199.

13  Nowack, *Rhein*, p. 144; Semmens, *Seeing*, pp. 24, 38, 44–46.

14  Semmens, *Seeing*, pp. 28–31.

15  I. Kershaw, 'Consensus, Coercion and Popular Opinion in the Third Reich: Some Reflections', in P. Corner (ed.), *Popular Opinion in Totalitarian Regimes: Fascism, Nazism, Communism* (Oxford, 2009), p. 39.

16  K. Fuss, *Geschichte des Reisebüros* (Darmstadt, 1960), p. 51.

17  'Camillo Heger: Jeden Tag Zusammenstöße', Dokumentationsarchiv des österreichischen Widerstandes. http://www.doew.at/erinnern/biographien/erzaehlte-geschichte/anschluss-maerz-april-1938/camillo-heger-jeden-tag-zusammenstoesze [accessed 30 September 2014].

18  S. Appel, *Reisen im Nationalsozialismus: Eine rechtshistorische Untersuchung* (Baden-Baden, 2001), pp. 83–97.

19  Semmens, *Seeing*, pp. 33–34.

20  Ibid., p. 34.

21  Appel, *Reisen*, p. 105; Semmens, *Seeing*, pp. 136–137.

22  Semmens, *Seeing*, pp. 103–105.

23  Kopper, 'Breakthrough', p. 72.

24  J. Steinmayr, 'Vier Tage, die Österreich berauschten. Ein halbes Jahrhundert später erinnern sich Zeugen an Hitlers Triumphzug nach Wien', *Die Zeit* (11 March 1988). http://www.zeit.de/1988/11/vier-tage-die-oesterreich-berauschten/seite-3 [accessed 30 September 2014].

25  J. Sneeringer, '"Assembly Line of Joys": Touring Hamburg's Red Light District, 1949-1966', *Central European History* 42, no. 1 (2009), p. 66.

26  Nowack, *Rhein*, p. 154.

27  See Semmens, *Seeing*. Continued research supports those original findings.

28  Semmens, *Seeing*, p. 149.

29  N. Waln, *The Approaching Storm: One Woman's Story of Germany, 1934–1938* (London, 1939), p. 22.

30  A. Nagorski, *Hitlerland: American Eyewitnesses to the Nazi Rise to Power* (New York, 2012), p. 192.

31  C. Waters, 'Understanding and Misunderstanding Nazi Germany: Four Australian Visitors to Germany in 1938', *Australian Historical Studies* 41, no. 3 (2010), p. 372. See also O. Lubrich (ed.), *Travels in the Reich, 1933–1945: Foreign Authors Report from Germany* (Chicago, 2010).

32   D. Zacher, '"You Will Find Germany in Peace and Order": Edward Meeman, an American journalist who praised and condemned Nazi Germany', *Journalism Studies* 14, no. 5 (2013), p. 768.

33   'Germany: Terrorised Tourists,' *Time* 24, no. 9 (27 August 1934), p. 21.

34   J. Hagen, 'The Most German of Towns: Creating an Ideal Nazi Community in Rothenburg ob der Tauber', *Annals of the Association of American Geographers* 94, no. 1. (2004), p. 210.

35   The above comes largely from S. Baranowski, *Strength through Joy: Consumerism and Mass Tourism in the Third Reich* (Cambridge, 2004).

36   P. Fritzsche, *The Turbulent World of Franz Göll: An Ordinary Berliner Writes the Twentieth Century* (Cambridge, MA, 2011).

37   Semmens, *Seeing*, p. 117; L. Niethammer, '*Die Jahre weiss man nicht, wo man die heute hinsetzen soll'*: *Faschismuserfahrungen im Ruhrgebiet* (Bonn, 1983).

38   F. Harms, 'Wellness unterm Hakenkreuz', *SPIEGEL Online* (19 July 2007). http://www.spiegel.de/fotostrecke/nazi-propaganda-wellness-unterm-hakenkreuz-fotostrecke-108747-14.html [accessed 30 September 2014].

39   Semmens, *Seeing*, pp. 111–114. This was necessary not only in order to revitalise economically depressed regions, but also to keep commercial and KdF holidaymakers apart.

40   Harms, 'Wellness'; Baranowski, *Strength through Joy*, p. 166.

41   Sopade Reports, Central Germany, April 1939, in J. Noakes and G. Pridham (eds), *Nazism 1919–1945*, vol. 2. *State, Economy and Society 1933–1939* (Exeter, 2000), p. 158; W. Shirer, *Twentieth Century Journey*, vol. 2. *The Nightmare Years, 1930–1940* (Boston, 1984), p. 203.

42   Baranowski, *Strength through Joy*, pp. 171–174.

43   R. Evans, *The Third Reich in Power 1933–1939* (New York, 2005), p. 472.

44   U. Herbert, 'Good Times, Bad Times', *History Today* 36, no. 2 (1986), pp. 42–48.

45   Semmens, *Seeing*, p. 101; 'Historisch: Touristen-Sonderzüge nach Schongau', *Merkur-Online.de* (18 August 2011). http://www.merkur-online.de/lokales/schongau/schongau/historisch-touristen-sonderzuege-nach-schongau-1366651.html [accessed 30 September 2014].

46   Baranowski, *Strength through Joy*, p. 131.

47   Semmens, *Seeing*, p. 222, note 90; H. Waddy, *Oberammergau in the Nazi Era: The Fate of a Catholic Village in Hitler's Germany* (Oxford, 2010), p. 166.

48   K. Stankiewitz, '*Die Gegend hier ist göttlich*': *Zeitreise durch 100 Jahre Tourismus im Chiemgau* (Erfurt, 2012), p. 94.

49   'Atzinger Moorbad', Der Chiemgauer.de. http://www.derchiemgauer.de/Beitraege5/moorbad.htm [accessed 30 September 2014].

50   Nowack, *Rhein*, p. 133. See also Semmens, *Seeing*, pp. 101–102. Locals also resented having to house and feed SA and SS men for free through the 'Hitler Holiday' programme. See C. Müller, 'Auf Hitlerurlaub. Eine vergessene Variante des nationalsozialistischen Verschickungstourismus

im Licht württembergischer Quellen', *Zeitschrift für Württembergische Landesgeschichte* 72 (2013), pp. 431–445.

51 Sopade Reports, Bavaria, April 1939, in Noakes and Pridham, *Nazism*, p. 159.

52 Semmens, *Seeing*, pp. 77–81.

53 Nowack, *Rhein*, pp. 142–143.

54 Baranowski, *Strength through Joy*, pp. 146–147; Semmens, *Seeing*, p. 112.

55 Nowack, *Rhein*, p. 164.

56 Waddy, *Oberammergau*, p. 169.

57 Ibid.; Baranowski, *Strength through Joy*, pp. 167–168.

58 Baranowski, *Strength through Joy*, p. 131.

59 On Hirsch, see M. Kratz, *Jüdisches Leben im Kreis Groß-Gerau im Spiegel der Heimatpresse 1925–1933. Ein Beitrag zur Spurensuche* (Riedstadt-Erfelden, 2000).

60 'Jüdisches Leben im Kraichgau vor 1933.' http://www.juedisches-leben-kraichgau.de/page10/page36/page36.html [accessed 30 September 2014].

61 'Beständeübersicht der Abteilung "Städtisches Archiv ab 1868"'. http://www.stadtgeschichte-ffm.de/abteilungen/abteilung_2/210inhalt.html [accessed 30 September 2014].

62 Semmens, *Seeing*, p. 14.

63 'Erinnerungen an die Reichspogromnacht 1938', *Ostsee Anzeiger* (5 November 2008). http://www.ruegener-anzeiger.de/archiv/artikel/erinnerungen-an-die-reichspogromnacht-1938/ [accessed 30 September 2014]; Semmens, *Seeing*, p. 95.

64 F. Bajohr, *'Unser Hotel ist Judenfrei': Bäder-Antisemitismus im 19. und 20. Jahrhundert* (Frankfurt am Main, 2003), p. 122.

65 I. Kershaw, *Hitler, the Germans and the Final Solution* (New Haven, 2008), pp. 162, 164.

66 Nowack, *Rhein*, p. 147.

67 J. Borut, 'Antisemitism in Tourist Facilities in Weimar Germany', *Yad Vashem Studies* 28 (2000), p. 12.

68 A. Rosenbaum, 'Timeless, Modern, And German? The Re-Mapping of Bavaria through the Marketing of Tourism, 1800–1939', *Bulletin of the GHI* 52 (Spring 2013), p. 53.

69 Hagen, 'Most German', p. 214

70 Semmens, *Seeing*, pp. 60–62.

71 D. Bergen, *War and Genocide: A Concise History of the Holocaust* (Lanham, 2003), p. 75.

72 Bajohr, *'Unser Hotel'*, p. 136.

73 R. Schwoch, 'Jüdische Ärzte in der NS-Zeit: "Wir waren Ausgestssene"', *Deutsches Ärzteblatt* 103, no. 11 (2006). http://www.aerzteblatt.de/archiv/50617/Juedische-Aerzte-in-der-NS-Zeit-Wir-waren-Ausgestossene [accessed 30 September 2014].

74  I. Abella and H. Troper, 'The Line Must Be Drawn Somewhere: Canada and Jewish Refugees, 1933–39', *Canadian Historical Review* LX, no. 2 (1979), p. 178.

75  See the chapter on Schlie in T. Venus and A. Wenck, *Die Entziehung jüdischen Vermögens im Rahmen der Aktion Gildemeester: eine empirische Studie über Organisation, Form und Wandel von 'Arisierung' und jüdischer Auswanderung in Österreich 1938–1941* (Vienna, 2004).

76  G. Anderl, *9096 Leben – Der unbekannte Judenretter Berthold Storfer* (Berlin, 2012).

77  Sven Feliz Kellerhoff, 'Zwei Pfennig pro Kopf und Bahnkilometer ins KZ', *Die Welt* (3 March 2013). http://www.welt.de/geschichte/zweiter-weltkrieg/article113200916/Zwei-Pfennig-pro-Kopf-und-Bahnkilometer-ins-KZ.html [accessed 30 September 2014].

78  K. Pätzold and E. Schwarz, *'Auschwitz war für mich nur ein Bahnhof': Franz Novak – der Transportoffizier Adolf Eichmanns* (Berlin, 1994).

79  There is a poignant film about Winton's efforts, *The Power of Good* (2002).

80  M. Kent, *I Married a German* (London, 1938), pp. 327–330.

81  Lubrich, *Travels*, p. 73.

82  Bajohr, *'Unser Hotel'*, p. 137.

83  Ibid., p. 136; J. Borut, 'Struggles for Spaces: Where Could Jews Spend Free Time in Nazi Germany?', *Leo Baeck Institute Year Book* 56, no. 1 (2011), p. 326.

84  Borut, 'Struggles', p. 324.

85  P. Gay, *My German Question: Growing Up in Nazi Berlin* (New Haven, CT, 1998), pp. 76–77.

86  G. Aly et al. (eds), *Die Verfolgung und Ermordung der europäischen Juden durch das nationalsozialistische Deutschland 1933–1945*, vol. 2 (Munich, 2009), pp. 199–202.

87  Semmens, *Seeing*, pp. 147–148; Bajohr, *'Unser Hotel'*, p. 324.

88  Bajohr, *'Unser Hotel'*, p. 129.

89  Borut, 'Struggles', p. 324.

90  Bajohr, *'Unser Hotel'*, p. 123.

91  S. Friedländer, *Nazi Germany and the Jews 1933–1945: Abridged Edition* (New York, 2009), p. 38.

92  Bajohr, *'Unser Hotel'*, p. 131.

93  Borut, 'Struggles', p. 327.

94  Ibid., pp. 325, 329.

95  L. Eilitta, '"This Can Only Come to a Bad End": Annemarie Schwarzenbach's Critique of National Socialism in Her Reports and Photography from Europe', *Women in German Yearbook: Feminist Studies in German Literature & Culture* 26 (2010), p. 105.

# Select bibliography

Bajohr, F., '*Unser Hotel ist Judenfrei*': *Bäder-Antisemitismus im 19. und 20. Jahrhundert* (Frankfurt am Main, 2003).

Baranowski, S., *Strength through Joy: Consumerism and Mass Tourism in the Third Reich* (Cambridge, 2004).

Borut, J., 'Struggles for Spaces: Where Could Jews Spend Free Time in Nazi Germany?', *Leo Baeck Institute Year Book* 56, no. 1 (2011), pp. 307–350.

Herbert, U., 'Good Times, Bad Times', *History Today* 36, no. 2 (1986), pp. 42–48.

Koshar, R., *German Travel Cultures* (Oxford, 2000).

Nowack, T., *Rhein, Romantik, Reisen: Der Ausflugs- und Erholungsreiseverkehr im Mittelrheintal im Kontext gesellschaftlichen Wandels (1890 bis 1970)*, Ph.D. dissertation, Rheinische Friedrich-Wilhelms-Universität Bonn (2006).

Rosenbaum, A., 'Timeless, Modern, and German? The Re-Mapping of Bavaria through the Marketing of Tourism, 1800-1939', *Bulletin of the GHI* 52 (Spring 2013), pp. 37–54.

Semmens, K., *Seeing Hitler's Germany: Tourism in the Third Reich* (Basingstoke, 2005).

Semmens, K., '"Tourism and Autarky Are Conceptually Incompatible": International Tourism Conferences in the Third Reich', in Zuelow, E. (ed.), *Touring Beyond the Nation: A Transnational Approach to European Tourism History* (Farnham, 2011).

Walton, J., 'Welcome to the *Journal of Tourism History*', *Journal of Tourism History* 1, no. 1 (2009), pp. 1–6.

# 6

# Playing with the Third Reich: Sports, Politics and Free Time in Nazi Germany

## David Imhoof

This chapter explores the ways in which Germans used sports to participate in the Third Reich. By looking closely at sports in the mid-sized city of Göttingen, it details the various meanings of this important element of everyday life in the Third Reich. Sports demonstrate the complexity of Germans' relationship between free-time activities and the Nazi state. Germans used sports to empower and entertain themselves, and sometimes, to hide from government officials or punish others. Third Reich leaders celebrated body, health and physical activity for their racialist, eugenic vision of the world. The Nazi regime also created hierarchical organisations to direct sporting activities. The history of sports illustrates that Nazi *Gleichschaltung* (coordination) of free-time activities was a two-way street, a process by which average Germans helped to create Third Reich culture as much as they had it imposed on them.

What follows focuses on Göttingen, a city large enough (with a population of about 45,000 during this era) to experience a breadth of sporting activities, yet small enough to reveal relationships between important groups and

Parts of this chapter were originally published in 'The Game of Political Change: Sports in Göttingen during the Weimar and Nazi Eras', *German History* 27 (2009), pp. 374–394 and 'Sharpshooting in Göttingen: A Case Study of Cultural Integration in Weimar and Nazi Germany', *German History* 23, no. 4 (2005), pp. 460–493.

individuals. This analysis pays special attention to how the Third Reich grew up in Göttingen, reaching back to events before the Nazi era began in 1933.[1] It also looks closely at the years before the Second World War started, since the war eclipsed many sporting activities, and the militarisation of sports was well under way before 1939. Göttingers experienced all types of sports: football, swimming and diving, running, cycling and especially sharpshooting, a particularly 'German' sport, most popular in northern and western parts of the country. This chapter describes the experiences of sports variously as participation, spectatorship and an activity of symbolic significance for local identity, showing the links between everyday activities and Nazi ideology. Through this history in Göttingen, we see that local processes helped to determine the development of sports throughout the Third Reich.

Scholars have written a great deal on sports in the Third Reich. Lorenz Peiffer's exhaustive 2009 bibliography, for instance, lists 1,029 chiefly German-language publications on sports in the Third Reich, most appearing in the last twenty years.[2] Studies of individual sports, especially football, have illuminated the broader meaning of sports in interwar Germany.[3] Other works have analysed the role of national umbrella organisations in Germany or individual sport clubs.[4] By focusing on organisations, regulations and cultural discourses about sports in one city, this chapter illuminates some of the ways in which average Germans took part in the development of the Third Reich. Here, sport is viewed as a cultural activity, something to which participants ascribed their own meaning and which in turn shaped their worldview.[5] Such a perspective makes sport a useful vehicle for studying links between Germans' thoughts (or ideology) and actions (or practices). Sports were often rooted in older, established notions of community yet shaped by new ideas about the body, machines and 'modern' society. As such, they helped many Germans to unite potentially contradictory notions in thought and practice. The Nazis' ability to bridge these gaps explains why sports helped to bolster and even define the Third Reich.[6] In particular, the notion of sports as a vehicle for promoting a strong military and a united community reinforced Nazi racialist ideas.

What follows will, first, introduce Göttingen as the location of study and outline the importance of sports during the Weimar Republic. The next section on the period from 1927 to 1934 details the longer, gradual process of 'coordinating' sports. The third part traces the experiences of workers' clubs in Göttingen to detail the complexity of this process. The final section describes the increased militarisation of sports in the later 1930s and into the Second World War.

# The importance of sports after the Great War

An explosion of sports activities after the Great War provided Göttingers with an escape from and expression of politics. Since the turn of the twentieth century, a greater number of participants from diverse social backgrounds had been taking part in sports. Many new sport clubs moved away from the traditional gymnastics (*Turner*) activities of the nineteenth century towards competitive 'English' sports like cycling, swimming and especially football, which were changing the landscape of German sports at this time.[7] Voluntary associations served as the chief vehicle for playing and watching sports. Göttingen police registered 267 active clubs during the Weimar period.[8] Göttingers founded twenty-seven new sports clubs during the Weimar Republic (1918–1933), enlarging participation and the definition of sport.[9] Spectatorship grew even more than direct participation. Many organisations focused on football. Some clubs in Göttingen boasted over 100 members in the 1920s, and games could draw over a thousand spectators.[10] Spectator team sports required overarching organisations to coordinate competitions, and class and ideology chiefly defined the national cartels that served this purpose. As a result, the tremendous growth in participatory and spectator sports from the 1880s to the 1920s made sports an arena for ideological conflict.

Göttingen's social and political conservatism defined the landscape in which these developments occurred. Less industrialised than other parts of Germany, the city's reputation and leadership remained strongly middle class because of the many pensioners, military personnel, professors, students and bureaucrats there.[11] As a garrison and university town, important citizens cast doubt on the validity of the Republican 'system' after 1918.[12] Workers and their Social Democratic Party (SPD) comprised a vocal minority but never managed to gain control of local institutions. Göttingen's overwhelming Protestant majority (close to 90 per cent) unified conservative thought and action.[13] Many top civic offices remained in the same hands for much of the first half of the century, while the town council changed frequently and moved gradually to the right between 1919 and 1934. As in many smaller cities, local 'notables' (*Honoratioren*) simultaneously mitigated and facilitated such changes by continuing to lead civic administration and leisure organisations. Göttingen's city government exercised important control over sports through policing and taxation. The Voluntary Association Police held jurisdiction over club activities. Because many bureaucrats from the *Kaiserreich* continued to enforce laws that were especially attuned to leftist political danger, police in Göttingen scrutinised working-class clubs more than middle-class organisations. Similarly, civic government tended to follow a conservative pattern of taxation.[14] These two means of civic authority continued to shape policies and activities in the Third Reich. Indeed, Nazi policy makers used existing regulations to strengthen their ability to make sports an expression of their ideology.

The context of the liberal Weimar Republic helped to expand the significance of sports. Laws following the 1918 Revolution and in the

1919 Weimar Constitution guaranteed freedom of association and shorter workdays, prompting an explosion of cultural activities and especially voluntary associations.[15] Together with the economic and political difficulties the war had caused, restrictions placed on Germany's military by the Treaty of Versailles particularly empowered conservative discourses about sports. Conservatives in Göttingen used developments in sports to construct connections between modernisation and Nazi ideas. They also used greater participation in sports, especially by men, to update and bolster an older notion of town citizenship that ignored women's recently won full voting rights.

Political ideology shaped some basic workings of sport groups in the 1920s. Most sport clubs affiliated with national cartels, which were often defined by class and ideology, to expand competitive opportunities. The middle-class German Gymnastics (*Turner*) Association (founded in 1868) and the German Football Association (DFB, founded in 1900) proclaimed a stiff neutrality after the Great War, treating any support of the Republic negatively as 'political'. Their influence reinforced the control of sports by traditional elites, many of whom also remained sceptical, at best, about the Weimar Republic.[16] The Worker Gymnastics and Sport Association (ATSB, founded in 1893), however, embraced 'politics'. It worked directly with the SPD, promoting sports, working-class identity and the Weimar Republic. Of the many sport clubs active in Göttingen in the early 1920s, nine joined the ATSB. Football, though, remained mostly in middle-class hands. Workers played for various teams in Göttingen, yet only one working-class football club in Göttingen joined the ATSB.[17] Sports in fact both integrated and differentiated workers in Göttingen.[18] Göttingen's workers' clubs also offered women and Jews more opportunities than middle-class clubs did.[19] Although sharp differences between working-class and middle-class sport clubs had existed since the 1890s, support for the Weimar Republic particularly polarised these two groups.

Sharpshooting associations, which remained more localised and relied less on national organisations, similarly divided in the 1920s between older, politically 'neutral' and new left-leaning workers' clubs. Each summer the Sharpshooting Festival served as the most important venue for articulating the meaning of sharpshooting. It was a major event for the whole town, complete with amusement park, food stands, music and dancing into the night, as well as the competitions that determined the best shooters and crowned one man each year Sharpshooting King. Participants and media observers turned it into a venue for discussing the significance of sharpshooting and ultimately, the fate of Göttingen itself in these troubled times. Sharpshooting had begun as a predominantly middle-class activity.[20] Many shooters upheld nineteenth-century notions of unity they saw at Sharpshooting Festivals as inclusive antidotes to divisive Weimar politics. The reality was that far more people took part in festivals during the 1920s than ever before. But in the volatile Weimar era, this nostalgia helped to direct the real changes in participation and spectatorship in Göttingen sharpshooting.

In short, sports during the 1920s grew significantly in Göttingen and became vehicles for considering the role of political ideology in everyday life. The generally conservative nature of Göttingen meant that those on the right shaped public discourse about sports more than those on the left. As a result, many of the basic ideas the Nazis would use to revise sports were organically present in Göttingen before Hitler's party took power.

## A longer 'coordination', 1927–1934

In a seminal 1981 article on sports in the Third Reich, Hajo Bernett differentiated between revolutionary and evolutionary changes the Nazi regime made to German sports in the course of *Gleichschaltung* ('coordination').[21] This concept can be expanded in two ways, in order to explain changes to sports that culminated in Nazi control. First, the deep alterations in Göttingen to sports – Bernett's 'evolutionary' changes – happened over a longer period, namely, from the late 1920s to the mid-1930s. Second, Göttingers themselves – government officials, sport leaders, club members, newspaper writers and even spectators – made important changes which ultimately empowered Nazi officials. Treating the 'coordination' of sports as a longer and negotiated process in Göttingen illuminates the ways in which average Germans participated in the changes that the Nazi regime brought to sports.

In Göttingen, the 'evolutionary' alterations to sports started in 1927. In that year, city officials built two important structures that exemplified and precipitated significant changes in sports: a unique target-shooting range and the town's first outdoor swimming pool (Figures 6.1 and 6.2). Civic leaders and newspaper writers praised the modernity of both facilities and their ability to stimulate the local economy.[22] Their construction prompted public debate about health, traditions, gender relations, aesthetics and public spending, all of which could be lightning rods for social and political conflict.[23] Work on these public projects also coincided with a shift to the right in Göttingen politics, as parties like the NSDAP took votes from middle-class parties in local and national elections.[24] The construction of the swimming pool reinforced what one socialist writer called the middle-class 'frock and top-hat practice of body culture', while the new sharpshooting hall used modern technology and modernist aesthetics to shore up elite men's control of sport shooting and military sports.[25]

FIGURE 6.1 *Göttingen's first outdoor public pool, built 1927. Courtesy of City Museum of Göttingen.*

FIGURE 6.2 *The Göttingen Sharpshooting Hall, built 1927. Courtesy of City Museum of Göttingen.*

These publicly funded and managed spaces integrated the local government further in Göttingen sports. The cooperation necessary to complete these projects encouraged inclusion, discouraged party politics, promoted fiscal conservatism, treated sports as a potential economic stimulus and put middle-class leaders in charge of building facilities and defining their significance. This situation reinforced ideas many conservatives held about sports. The pool and sharpshooting hall thus lent support to Nazism in Göttingen paradoxically because of their success *and* failure. On the one hand, the facilities brought Göttingers together in an atmosphere that conservatives claimed to be free of divisive party politics and promoted a healthy *Volk* (people). Even Social Democrats agreed, although they used the term *Volk* to imply a democratic, class-free society, rather than one defined by tradition and race. On the other hand, the city government's resulting debt of 300,000 marks weakened its ability to respond to subsequent economic crises, thereby empowering those who claimed that democracy did not meet Germans' needs. And, in fact, Göttingen's financial problems helped to give a right-wing coalition an absolute majority in the November 1929 local elections, still months before Germans felt the effects of the Wall Street Crash. That coalition collapsed in 1930 and left the NSDAP in charge in Göttingen.

During the incendiary local political campaign of 1929, Göttingen's Social Democratic newspaper, the *Volksblatt*, wrote that the 'fundamental difference between worker and middle-class sport organisations' came down to support for the Republic and its democratic and socialist ideals.[26] Workers' sports clubs were on the front lines of conflict with Nazi organisations and increasingly used sports to strengthen solidarity.[27] Just a few weeks later, Göttingen's most widely-read and most conservative newspaper, the *Göttinger Tageblatt*, published a piece on the 'particular nature' of the German Gymnastics Association, the largest umbrella organisation for sports in Germany. The article stressed, in contrast, that this middle-class group attempted to overcome the 'divisions of our *Volk*' by maintaining 'a neutral basis' and promoting a *Volksgemeinschaft*.[28] These two pieces articulated the ideological poles about sports. In both cases, sports served to promote political change. At the 1929 Sharpshooting Festival, a member of Göttingen's Magistracy expressed the similar wish of many conservatives for 'apolitical' sports. About sharpshooters he claimed, 'once they were important in protecting the city, today they are important in protecting its unity'.[29] Leftist sport leaders recognised this attempt to use 'apoliticism' to bolster right-wing groups and challenge Weimar democracy.[30] Unfortunately, in a conservative town like Göttingen, the middle-class claim that 'sport has nothing to do with politics' resonated with concerns about the viability of the contentious Weimar political 'system'. Even the shared interest among shooters on the left and right in competitive shooting bolstered right-wing goals for sports as the source of 'apolitical' unity, minimising the changes necessary to 'coordinate' Göttingen sharpshooting in the Third Reich. More than simply mirroring political battles, these two different ways of politicising sports helped to shape Göttingers' ideas about politics at a critical moment in German history.

The Great Depression that began in 1929 vaulted the NSDAP to power in Germany. Financial strain unleashed by the Wall Street Crash compounded an already fragile German economy and, in turn, further undermined support for political parties endorsing the Weimar Republic. The NSDAP's disingenuous claim to be above party politics earned the backing of Germans who were frustrated by the political wrangling of the Weimar Republic. The Communist Party (KPD), also defined itself against the democratic

Weimar 'system'. In this context of anti-politics, the realm of sports and other free-time activities became important battlegrounds for the hearts of Germans. Of the various groups in Göttingen promoting sports as a model for 'apolitical' public life, the Nazis articulated this view most often and most persuasively.

Once Adolf Hitler became Chancellor and formed a government in January 1933, Nazi leaders used a suspicious fire at the Reichstag in February to enact laws that began to dismantle the Weimar Republic and eventually created the Third Reich. In 1933, the new government crafted laws that shut down many left-wing sports groups and banned Jews from participating in many sporting activities. These changes proceeded from the top-down, yet local conditions shaped their impact. The broad support in Göttingen for sports as a source of unity outside party politics empowered Nazi plans at the expense of left-wing clubs. Göttingers had also long endorsed the idea of sports as a substitute for military training, a major impetus for the Nazis' militarisation of sports.[31] Even though leftists resisted the chauvinistic implications of this idea, their own sport-oriented paramilitary organisations illustrated the appeal of militarised sports as a means for defining identity.

These developments created conditions favourable for the growth of Nazism and were the basis of the Nazis' alteration of German sports. Beginning in 1933, Third Reich ministers, police and local officials together sought to 'coordinate' all voluntary associations, to place those activities and organisations under greater state authority and to have them reflect National Socialist ideology. Viewed from the top-down, the Third Reich's official 'coordination' of sports consisted chiefly of three major actions in 1933. First, the government used the February 'Law for the Protection of *Volk* and State' to close groups associated with the Social Democratic Party and the Communist Party. In June, the Reich Ministry of the Interior outlawed national 'Marxist' sport cartels and their attending clubs and created rules by which other clubs could absorb some of those athletes. Second, the new regime required all voluntary associations to adopt the '*Führer* Principle' (for a more hierarchical organisation), to include only 'Aryan' members and to work with the SA (stormtroopers) and the Hitler Youth. Although Jewish clubs could not use public facilities or join national cartels, they could survive and even grow for a while because of an influx of members excluded from other organisations.[32] Third, Nazi leaders merged existing national groups, such as the German Gymnastics Association and the German Reich Committee for Physical Education, into new branches of the government, especially the expansive German Reich Association for Physical Education and the Reich Sport Ministry.[33] Hajo Bernett has defined this burst of activity as 'an upheaval but no break'.[34]

Local police continued to regulate voluntary associations, as they had since the turn of the century. The requirement for organised groups to register their rules, aims and membership with the police had long kept officials closely informed of associations' actions. Political conflicts in the late 1920s and early 1930s had prompted Republican officials to inspect them even more closely. Ironically, those concerns for the safety of Germany's first democracy gave Third Reich officials greater reach into the daily activities of associations after 1933.

Local leaders served important roles even in the 'revolutionary' year of 1933. For example, in December 1933, Göttingen police and Nazi Party officials forced the umbrella Burgher Sharpshooting Society to name Mayor Albert Gnade as *Führer* of the Society instead of an elected representative from one of the oldest (and most conservative) clubs.[35] A well-connected member of the political elite, SS major (*Sturmbahnführer*) and popular Nazi 'old fighter' (long-time Party member), Gnade assisted the 'coordination' of many cultural activities in Göttingen. He was essentially an old-fashioned law-and-order conservative who exploited and, to a certain extent, tempered National Socialism in Göttingen. First elected City Senator in 1929 on the Nazi ticket, he had spearheaded the pre-Depression shift to the right in Göttingen politics. From 1933, as Mayor and Police Commissioner, Gnade tried to wed both National Socialism and 'Göttingen's interests', however narrowly defined. Although he used his authority to reorganise some sport activities, especially sharpshooting, he chiefly amplified local developments in place since the late 1920s.[36]

At the 1934 Sharpshooting Festival, Gnade and other civic leaders used familiar language to describe the purpose of sharpshooting in the Third Reich.[37] New regulations from the national German Sport Shooting Association allowed only 'Aryan' Germans to join sharpshooting organisations or to participate in sharpshooting activities.[38] In Göttingen, where few Jews had been members of sharpshooting clubs, this dictate made manifest the racialist implications of terms such as *Volkssport*, *Volksfest* and *Volksgemeinschaft* that had been used since the 1920s to describe sharpshooting activities. Gradually, these changes began to make sharpshooting an official part of Third Reich sports. The Reich Sport Ministry in 1934 forced all sharpshooting organisations to focus more on sport and military sharpshooting.[39] In Göttingen, advocates of military, traditional and sport shooting had all generally cooperated in the 1920s, so once in power, Nazi officials worked with sharpshooting leaders to direct sharpshooting to the new regime's purposes.[40]

By the middle of 1934, most of the structural changes to 'coordinate' sports in Germany were in place. In many cases, events of the 'revolutionary' year 1933 had realised or radicalised ideas animating sports since the late 1920s. At a speech in the summer of 1934, Mayor Gnade articulated this perspective on the broader development of sports since the Great War by lumping together the hardships of the war, the peace treaty and the Weimar Republic. Thankfully, he said, the 'trench generation has erected the National Socialist state and thus established the preconditions for the renewed ascent of the German *Volk*'. Gnade told young athletes in the audience that 'achievement in sports' would 'set our *Volk* at its earned place at the pinnacle of peoples on earth'.[41] Gnade's own rise to power illustrated the longer *durée* of Nazi 'coordination'. And like Gnade, those others who altered sports in the Third Reich took inspiration from the early 1920s, took action in the late 1920s and took charge in 1933 and 1934.

# Sports, guns and politics: workers' clubs in the Third Reich

Scholars and supporters of associational life have frequently used stories of the experiences of sport clubs to illustrate the Nazi regime's hostility to voluntary associations and its systematic attempt to force ideological conformity on free-time activities.[42] The following four examples make clear that some clubs, especially those for workers, suffered under the Nazi regime, while others found ways to cooperate with the Third Reich to survive and even thrive. Local officials both realised and tempered national policies towards workers' associations.

The history of the working-class Water Sport Organisation illustrates the traumatic impact that 1933 had on some athletes in Germany.[43] Opening in 1924, in the 'stable' Weimar period, the club's membership grew steadily during the 1920s. It was affiliated with the ATSB and played a leading national role in the promotion of working-class swimming and diving. In the early 1930s, the club's Social Democratic identity became more and more a part of its daily activities.[44] Because the Third Reich closed the 'Marxist' ATSB cartel in the summer of 1933, local police officially shut down the Water Sport Club in October as a 'state enemy organisation'. After being pressured by police and right-wing groups for some time, other leftist organisations in Göttingen likewise closed (or were closed) by the summer of 1933. Membership in the socialist ATSB cartel thus shaped this club's identity and activities during the Weimar Republic and its fate in the Third Reich. The group's official history maintains that after 1933 leaders 'faced personal difficulties due to their activity in the club' yet continued to meet illegally during the Third Reich. The quick resumption of the club's activities after the war seems to support this claim.[45] This experience demonstrates that some groups managed to carve out spaces in which Nazi ideology played no part. Nazism, in other words, did not grow into or penetrate every organisation in Göttingen, even if the regime stopped some of them from functioning officially.

The Third Reich did not close down every working-class club, however, and some suppressed athletes managed to find opportunities to participate in sports after 1933. The 'Central' Cycling Club from the nearby village of Elliehausen made the transition more successfully.[46] Members of this working-class group, founded in 1905, walked the fine line in the Third Reich between independence and cooperation. During the Weimar Republic, this club had been affiliated with the left-wing Solidarity Worker Cycling and Riding Association. That cartel had been less politically active than the ATSB, so the history of affiliated organisations like the 'Central' Cycling Club during the Nazi era depended more on local conditions. Soon after the Nazis came to power in Germany, members of this small group re-elected almost half of their previous leaders, including the top two officers who led the club into the Second World War. In November 1933, these cyclists chose to join the new state-sanctioned German Cycling Organisation, quickly brushing away their Social Democratic past and embracing the National Socialist vision of sports. They continued to function even after the war started. Workers' clubs in other places similarly reinvented themselves in the Third Reich.[47]

The Sport Club Weende 1913 exemplifies a hybrid experience of 'coordination', in which a working-class club succeeded in the Third Reich due to its 'apolitical' cartel affiliation. Weende was one of Göttingen's largest and most industrialised suburbs. Club 1913 boasted by the mid-1920s over 100 members, most of whom were workers. They offered other sports but remained chiefly a football club. And like the Football Club 1909 from Grone (another suburb) and Göttingen's Railroad Workers Organisation, the Weende Club 1913 chose to affiliate with the middle-class DFB rather than the socialist ATSB. The ideological affiliation of cartels – not class or politics per se – thus shaped some clubs' fates in the Third Reich. Indeed, when the Nazis closed down another ATSB-affiliated sport club in the area, Club 1913 recruited its players and expanded its own scope.[48] Middle-class organisations like the old German Gymnastics Association, which quickly adopted Nazi ideas, similarly allowed its clubs to incorporate members of outlawed groups, provided they submitted written renunciation of 'Marxist' ideas and support for the new regime.[49] Weende Club 1913 assimilated itself in 1933 to the ideals and trappings of Third Reich sports, renaming its officers *Führers*, adding a military sports division and closing meetings with '*Sieg Heil*'.[50] Similarly to middle-class groups, this club retooled itself as an 'apolitical' association. In fact, one of the new members from a suppressed club, Friedel Rosenthal, managed to parlay his seemingly contradictory background as a Social Democrat, as a leading member of this successful Third Reich sport club, and as a Second World War air force officer into a regional sport leadership position after 1945.[51]

The history of Göttingen's Workers' Sharpshooting Club perhaps best illustrates the tense situation in which leftist associations found themselves after the Nazis came to power in 1933. Until the middle of the 1920s, the vast majority of shooters in Göttingen had come from the middle class, and their clubs had tended to espouse conservative politics.[52] The social and political homogeneity in Göttingen changed most obviously in 1924 when workers set up two sharpshooting clubs, the Workers' Sharpshooting Club and the Association of Proletarian Sharpshooters.[53] As vocal supporters of the Weimar Republic and the Social Democratic Party, the Workers' Sharpshooting Club members named their best shooter each year 'president'

rather than 'king', as all the other groups did.[54] Their use of the Republic's
flag in 1920s festival parades stood in marked contrast to ubiquitous
imperial symbols, paramilitary banners and even swastikas that other
organisations carried (all while claiming to be above politics).[55] Workers'
clubs offered collective means to defray the costs of weaponry, uniform and
ammunition. The Workers' Sharpshooting Club also included at least one
Jewish founding member, second-hand dealer and leftist leader, Karl Kahn.[56]

The February 1933 'Law for the Protection of *Volk* and State' seemed
to spell the demise of such clubs associated with left-wing parties or
demonstrably supportive of the Weimar Republic. Even before the Nazis
came to power, the police in Göttingen had viewed leftist sport clubs with
suspicion. The February 1933 law gave leaders the authority to close
down these voluntary associations and others like them by the autumn.
The communist Association of Proletariat Sharpshooters folded quickly.
The Workers' Sharpshooting Club, however, survived and participated in
sharpshooting activities until 1935.[57]

In March 1933, the Workers' Sharpshooting Club closed briefly because
all its members were unemployed. A month later, though, Mayor and Police
Director Gnade blessed the group's re-foundation with the same name
and under much the same leadership.[58] Police reports praised the 'patriotic
(*vaterländisch*) activity of the Workers' Sharpshooting Club'. In November
1933, the club joined with other sharpshooting associations in calling for all
Germans to vote 'yes' in the plebiscite to validate Hitler's growing authority
in Germany.[59] However, just six months later, the police noted that at recent
meetings, only 10 per cent of members joined leaders in saying '*Sieg Heil*'.
For an already suspect club under close scrutiny, this visible lack of National
Socialist zeal probably sealed its fate. Still, the State Police did not close
down the club for another year and a half. Indeed, in his speech at the 1934
Sharpshooting Festival, Gnade specifically praised the desire of this workers'
club to participate in sharpshooting activities, even with 80 per cent of its
members unemployed.[60] The club was finally outlawed in December 1935,
though police records offer no reason for the closure. Authorities did go
to great lengths to pay the leadership a fair price for its confiscated goods,
something they did not do for all suppressed clubs.[61] Former members of this
group may have either joined other sharpshooting clubs or, like a growing
number of men in town, participated as individuals at sharpshooting festivals.

Middle-class sport clubs tended to fare better in the Third Reich.
Göttingen's Football Sport Club 1905, for example, flourished during the
Third Reich, as did many 'apolitical', middle-class organisations. Riding
the wave of increased interest in football across Germany (and Europe),
the 1905ers had become one of the largest sport clubs and most successful
football teams in the region after the First World War. The 1905 Club was
affluent, well connected to local media, supported by the civic government
and boasted a large fan base.[62] It was affiliated with the DFB, which
mandated in June 1933 the incorporation of Nazi ideas such as the '*Führer*

principle' and 'Aryanisation' in club statutes.[63] The 1905ers, along with Sport Association Göttingen (the other strong football team in town) and other sport groups, elected their own *Führer* and pledged support to Nazi ideas.[64] Club 1905's established, conservative nationalism helped to legitimise Third Reich sport policies.

The various experiences of these sport clubs demonstrate that Nazi 'coordination' could result in swift change or slow fade and either crush or fulfil groups' dreams. The dramatic events of 1933 influenced the function of sport clubs in Göttingen in very different ways. In the Third Reich, clubs had to negotiate the regime's complex and sometimes contradictory relationship with voluntary associations that made their contacts with local officials even more important.[65] Clubs in Göttingen, for instance, figured out that it was important to work well with Nazi Party organisations (SA, SS, Hitler Youth and Strength Through Joy), all of which also fielded sports groups and therefore directly competed with clubs for members.[66] Even for stalwart Third Reich supporters like those in Sport Club 1905, Nazi 'coordination' was not a wholly smooth process. In March 1933, for instance, a number of younger members challenged the old leadership and selected as 'Club *Führer*' a local attorney and Nazi Party member. But other club members then replaced him at the next meeting three months later with long-time member Max Welker, sports editor of the *Göttingen Tageblatt*. At the same meeting, leaders announced that Sport Club 1905 had been officially 'coordinated'.[67] Established conservative leadership could therefore direct effective 'coordination' as well as the newly empowered National Socialists could.

# 'Coordinated' sports and the military after 1935

Although the Nazis' goal of coordinating all sport activities never fully succeeded, by 1935 most activities were nominally a part of the regime. Military and paramilitary organisations helped to reinforce these connections. Göttingen had hosted an army garrison since the *Kaiserreich*, and military leaders often held important symbolic positions in town, especially when the army itself shrank significantly during the Weimar Republic. Germany's decision to break the Treaty of Versailles in 1935 and officially rearm swelled the ranks of Göttingen's garrison. Military sports also helped to unite a wide range of sport groups in the Third Reich. Especially in 1933 and 1934, when the Treaty of Versailles still restricted Germany's armed forces, the new regime viewed sports as a means to train men to serve in the military and protect the population.[68] Many sharpshooters and supporters saw, for example, the ability to serve in the military as the final culmination of fifteen years of rhetoric about the value of sharpshooting to the city and the nation. By the same token, the existence of a real and growing military in Germany ended any illusion about sport groups serving as ersatz or paramilitary forces, relegating sharpshooting and other sports to symbolic or training functions in society. In Göttingen, leaders of sports and Nazi organisations alike appealed to these common interests. Local politicians, though, continued to mitigate the influence of the military on sport.[69]

The Nazis' attempt to militarise sharpshooting activities proceeded haltingly. Soldiers headed up both the Reich Ministry for Sport and the sub-section devoted to shooting. Since military leaders and Nazi functionaries shared the belief that sport shooting helped to train better soldiers, Third Reich officials used state authority to promote modern sport shooting as part of a more militarised society.[70] In 1934, the Reich Sport Ministry insisted that all sharpshooting organisations focus more on sport and military shooting. Unlike in Catholic regions, where some sharpshooters diverged from the regime over religion, overwhelmingly Protestant sharpshooters in Göttingen did not face such a division.[71] Sport shooting had been widely supported in Göttingen since the early 1920s, and the local army garrison had taken part in activities since the late nineteenth century. The 1935 Göttingen Sharpshooting Festival celebrated competitive sport with the motto 'In the Spirit of Sport'. That year the *Führer* of German Sharpshooting, Major van Cleve, told visitors at the Festival that competitive sport shooting united bodily strength, military training, tradition, patriotism and duty to serve the Fatherland.[72] Supporters in Göttingen rejoiced when the national German Sharpshooting Association became a part of the Reich League for Physical Education in 1936.[73]

Germany's preparation for the 1936 Olympic Games drew special attention to the importance of sport in the Third Reich.[74] By early 1935, Göttingen newspapers were regularly using coverage of the Summer Games in Berlin (and, to a lesser degree, the Winter Games in Garmisch) to comment on the function of sports in German society. Conservative leaders of the Olympic 'Movement' in Germany had quickly convinced Hitler and Goebbels of the propagandistic value of the Games.[75] Preparations for the 'national festival' of 1936 helped to direct some of the top-down changes to sports beginning in 1933.[76] The regime pointed to the need to nurture the best 'Aryan' athletes as a reason to centralise sports organisations.[77] Göttingen newspaper articles connected the Nazis' organisational and racialised control of German sports with past military might and success at the 1936 Olympics.[78] Commentators also made liberal use of the ubiquitous Olympic coverage in local papers to emphasise Germany's long history of competitive shooting, especially when German marksmen took home one-third of the medals awarded in these events.[79] Despite its brutal exclusion of Jews from public life, the Third Reich's 'Aryanisation' of sports and its wish to appear to be a 'civilised' host of the Olympics created, ironically, an inferior yet safe space for Jews to take part in sports from 1933 until 1936 and, in some cases, even until 1938. After 1938, though, that space disappeared completely.[80] As the German Olympic team won an amazing eighty-nine medals (including thirty-three gold) at the 1936 Summer Games, compared to the United States' fifty-six (twenty-four gold) and Italy's twenty-two (eight gold), Nazi officials credited their 'coordination' of sport for this success.[81]

While this nationalised direction of sports weakened some local sports in Germany, the need for superior amateur athletes also delivered resources to clubs.[82] Local clubs continued to surrender some autonomy to expanding state-sanctioned bodies in 1935 and 1936, and the number of active sport clubs declined in Germany after 1936.[83] 'Coordination' offered some Göttingen voluntary associations new opportunities. The reorganisation of football, for instance, gave Sport Association Göttingen the chance in August 1935 to play (and lose 5–1 to) the German national champions, Schalke 04. The records of smaller clubs in Göttingen reveal that many of them continued their activities much as before.[84] Similarly, the growing number of competitions organised by various Nazi and military groups further concentrated sports in the hands of the regime (and men generally) yet gave more Göttingers (and Germans) opportunities to take part in sports.[85]

Still, the actual process by which the state became integrated into daily cultural activities remained complex and was sometimes contested. At a December 1935 meeting of the Burgher Sharpshooting Society's leadership, for instance, Society members complained to local officials on the Board about insufficient municipal funding. One local official replied that 'the opposition in the Burgher Sharpshooting Society is nothing more than a reaction against the present state!' Springing to his feet, one sharpshooting leader cried, 'that is a baseless piece of impertinence!' Mayor Gnade had to step in to quell the conflict, but another sharpshooter obliquely warned local officials, 'don't wrap yourself in foreign furs'.[86] Gnade and other officials worried about the efficacy of their 'coordination' of sharpshooting. In a May 1936 report, Gnade wrote that overcoming 'resistance' from established sharpshooting associations would require 'clubs to be cleaned of members who would ruin this work because of their old social prejudices', but he had seen that such heavy-handed tactics did not work. He feared that reorganising Göttingen sharpshooting too much might undermine the Nazis' designs on sharpshooting, as happened in other places.[87]

Despite their increased power in the Third Reich, local officials in Göttingen also continued to fret about policing sport clubs. In early 1935, the Reich Sport *Führer* and local branch of the German Reich Association for Physical Education required all registered clubs to declare a 'unity statute' and to provide information about its membership and activities.[88] Yet, they still worried about the impact of 'Marxism' and 'wild' clubs.[89] Even as late as 1944, established organisations – including pro-regime groups like student fraternities – applied to change their names or statutes in order to ingratiate themselves better with the regime. The local police scrutinised these applications carefully, and sometimes it took the word of someone like an SS officer to allow any change.[90] Göttingen's Magistracy also used its financial influence over sports to garner revenue from the swimming pool and taxes on sport events.

The halting 'coordination' of sports in Germany relied upon local conditions as much as dictates from Berlin. The curious power constellation that developed in Göttingen enabled both National Socialist and local interests, sometimes at the expense of each other. At the centre stood Bruno Jung and Albert Gnade. A respected jurist and honorary professor from the moderately right-wing German People's Party, Bruno Jung, served as Lord Mayor from 1926 to 1938. He typified the interwar elite as an opportunist who quickly adapted to the Third Reich while continuing to protect some of the city's interests and traditions. Gnade became Mayor under Lord Mayor Jung and Police Commissioner in March 1933. He then succeeded Jung as Lord Mayor in 1938, serving until he surrendered Göttingen to American forces in April 1945. The regional Nazi Party had expected Gnade to help purge Göttingen's government of non-Nazis like Jung. However, the two men worked together closely.

Sometimes to the dismay of Party and military officials, Jung and Gnade emphasised law and order and placed the interests of the city – or at least their definition of those interests – above those of the Nazi Party. In fact, Gnade often clashed with Party leaders despite his own strong Nazi credentials. In 1934 and 1935, he was accused in court by the local Party leader for a lack of National Socialist zeal and had to enlist help from Berlin to overturn the guilty verdict. He argued with military officials in 1935 over their right to hold tax-discounted events. And in 1943, he was almost thrown into a concentration camp for aiding a local cinema owner who had been arrested as a 'state enemy' for listening to the BBC.[91] Gnade exercised considerable influence on sports and cultural life in Göttingen during the Nazi era. His actions in this sphere often drew from older assumptions about culture that were more common among elites during the *Kaiserreich* than the Third Reich. The impact of Jung and Gnade make plain the ways in which traditional conservatives facilitated Nazi radicalism. They helped to legitimise the Nazi regime for Göttingen citizens by anchoring it to notions of law and order, tradition and myth, civic pride and the status quo. Such continuity made discrimination against Jews, and leftists seem to grow naturally out of popular ideological positions from the Weimar era. This system engendered greater support for Hitler's regime by making its policies of discrimination, repression and eventually murder part of long-standing traditions in local public life.[92]

The experiences of an important physical education instructor at the University of Göttingen illustrate the thin line between promise and problem for those involved in sports in the Third Reich. In 1928, the University of Göttingen had become the first institution of higher education in Germany to create an Institute for Physical Education, with 42-year-old Bernhard Zimmermann as its first Director.[93] Zimmermann had been an instructor since before the war. His rigorous academic and physical requirements and close relationship with students had earned him acclaim from university colleagues and national sports educators. His wealthy uncle had even put up 100,000 marks to build the Institute. The success of this pioneering institution stemmed in part from the university requirement for physical education, which students had overwhelmingly demanded in 1920 to compensate for a restricted military. Zimmermann encouraged the growth of military sports and worked, even before 1933, with the SA to this end (Figure 6.3).

FIGURE 6.3 *Bernhard Zimmermann, founder and Director of the Institute for Physical Education at the University of Göttingen. Courtesy of City Museum of Göttingen.*

Although Zimmermann was generally liberal and somewhat sceptical about the Third Reich, he considered himself a 'practically oriented person' and wrote to a colleague in November 1933 that he was 'working well' with the new regime and its military interests. Zimmermann recognised that his Jewish wife might endanger his position. Refusing to consider a divorce, though, he continued to lead the Institute for Physical Education, even after being pressured by the Party to leave and the promulgation of the 1935 Nuremberg Laws. He worked on grand plans to host the German University Athletic Championships during the University of Göttingen's big 200-year celebration in 1937.[94] Just before the festivities, however, the University notified Zimmermann that he would have to retire immediately because he was married to a Jew. He and his family emigrated in 1939 to Great Britain, where he taught and helped to establish the Outward Bound movement.[95]

Zimmermann's case at the University of Göttingen illuminates the symbiotic relationship between sports and the Third Reich. When asked why there was no protest against the dismissal of this beloved professor, his former assistant Wilhelm Henze in 1977 recalled that Zimmermann told his epigone that demonstration would do no good, since they all 'knew the system and the power of the system'.[96] Henze recounted this story to explain their resignation to Zimmermann's firing. But Zimmermann and Henze must also have recognised the power that the Nazi 'system' had given them to expand and improve the Institute by emphasising many of the same qualities they themselves had developed during the Weimar era. The impact of various familial relations too – a munificent uncle and a Jewish wife – reminds us that personal relations shaped Germans' experience of ideological changes in the Third Reich too.

Starting in 1938, all of German society, especially sports increasingly focused on the military.[97] The tendency to combine sport, military training, entertainment and local traditions continued into the war. Local military officials and sharpshooting leaders, for instance, cooperated closely with each other. When a 1939 law restricted shooting in the Sharpshooting Festival to army teams only, the long, cordial relationship between sharpshooters and Göttingen's garrison allowed local clubs to continue to shoot. Although the war halted most sharpshooting activities, some of the older shooters and younger students managed to cobble together meetings and competitions until 1944. Generally, records indicate dwindling numbers of participants after 1942, but many sport clubs continued to meet.[98]

Although sport clubs in Göttingen carried on after fighting began, the financial and personal strain of the war immediately decreased activity from 1939 onwards.[99] In the summer of 1941, almost at the peak of the Third Reich's military efforts, Albert Gnade, now Lord Mayor, urged young athletes to keep playing sports, since 'the German *Volk* stands in a life-or-death struggle'. Drawing a clear line from the changes of 1933, through the successful 1936 Olympics, to the war, Gnade argued that sports had helped to strengthen German soldiers.[100] His speech projected a trajectory about the meaning of sports that was common throughout the interwar period. Nazi officials thus succeeded in 'coordinating' sport activities, in so far as they constructed national policies regarding sports and military training that resonated with local traditions and organisations. Of course, Germans eventually began to see through this story and would view this war, with or without sports, as even more catastrophic than the previous one.

# Conclusion

Sports blossomed after the Second World War. Almost immediately sport organisations became vehicles for reasserting local culture and restarting public life. As they had after the First World War, sports after 1945 provided Göttingers a haven from post-war difficulties. But this time, they also helped to make everyday culture a part of the process of building democracy in West Germany. This chapter has shown the ways in which sports helped turn Göttingen into a Nazi town. Playing, watching and writing about sports had given average Göttingers a way to participate in and even reinforce Nazi ideas, even while hiding behind 'Göttingen interests'. Indeed, officials' ability to blend these two approaches to power helped to make Nazi ideology an organic part of this city. After the war, though, those involved in Göttingen sports stressed their embrace of democracy, greater gender equality and broad social participation. And government policies echoed these ideals. The rebirth of old organisations (including many suppressed by the Nazis) and the explosion of new ones marked the decades after the Second World War as arguably more fecund for sports than the first three decades of the century. Furthermore, spectator sports grew as a major pastime and source of identity.

This chapter illuminates, above all, the complex process of change during the Third Reich. The individuals, institutions and ideas made developments described here unique to Göttingen, yet they demonstrate more generally that local conditions shaped Germans' experiences of change under National Socialism. The factors that integrated sports into the fabric of the Nazi regime grew from a decade-long process that began in the late 1920s. The conservatives' *völkisch* notion of participation, based on race rather democratic citizenship, helped to facilitate the National Socialist 'coordination' of sports in Göttingen. Senator Reuper's 1929 assertion about sharpshooting 'protecting [Göttingen's] unity' should perhaps be modified to state that these activities actually helped to create the *image* of unity. The Nazis' success at using sports to promote their ideology testifies as much to the importance of local conditions for national change as it does to the primacy of ideology. Alterations to sports during the Third Reich were significant and, for some, brutal. An understanding of the ways in which Germans participated in these changes shows how the Third Reich accomplished what it did and makes those accomplishments all the more disturbing.

# Notes

1    D. Imhoof, *Becoming a Nazi Town: Culture and Politics in Göttingen between the World Wars* (Ann Arbor, MI, 2013).

2    L. Peiffer, *Sport im Nationalsozialismus: Zum aktuellen Stand der sporthistorischen Forschung. Eine kommentierte Bibliographie*, 2nd ed. (Göttingen, 2009).

3    For example, C. Eisenberg (ed.), *Fußball, soccer, calico: Ein englischer Sport auf seinem Weg um die Welt* (Munich, 1997); G. Fischer et al., *Stürmer für Hitler. Vom Zusammenspiel zwischen Fußball und Nationalsozialismus* (Göttingen, 2002).

4    N. Havemann, *Fußball unterm Hakenkreuz. Der DFB zwischen Sport, Politik und Kommerz* (Frankfurt, 2005); J. Schultz, '*Sport Heil': Gründung und Etablierung eines Braunschweiger Sportvereins vor dem Hitergrund der Jahre 1933/34* (Duderstadt, 1993).

5    C. Geertz, 'Thick Description: Toward an Interpretive Theory of Culture', in *The Interpretation of Cultures* (New York, 1973), pp. 3–32.

6    C. Mack, 'The Idea of Sport in Germany, 1880–1936' (Ph.D. diss., City University of New York, 2000); J. Herf, *Reactionary Modernism: Technology, Culture, and Politics in Weimar and the Third Reich* (Cambridge, 1984).

7    C. Eisenberg, '*English Sports' und deutsche Bürger: Eine Gescellschaftsgeschichte 1800–1939* (Paderborn, 1999).

8    Stadt Archiv Göttingen (hereafter 'StadtAGö'): Pol-Dir. XXV Fach 152 Nr. 9, Ab. G, 1868–1956, pp. 146.2–153.30; AHR I B2 Fach 22 Nr. 8 Bd. 2, 30 September 1931.

9    StadtAGö: Pol.-Dir. XXV 32, 145 and 152; AHR I B3 Fach 22, Nr. 8, Bd. 2.

10   StadtAGö: Pol.-Dir. XXV Fach 147 Nr. 9 Ab. B, p. 18 and Nr. 17, pp. 6–7; H. Grüne, *Zwischen Hochburg und Provinz: 100 Jahre Fußball in Göttingen* (Göttingen, 1998), pp. 27–32, 48.

11   A. von Saldern, 'Göttingen im Kaiserreich', in R. von Thadden and G. Trittel (eds), *Göttingen: Geschichte einer Universitätsstadt, Band 3* (Göttingen, 1999), pp. 14–56.

12   H. Dahms, 'Die Universität Göttingen 1918 bis 1989', in von Thadden and Trittel (eds), *Geschichte Universitätsstadt*, pp. 395–410.

13   B. Marshall, 'The Political Development of German University Towns: Göttingen and Münster 1918–1930' (Ph.D. diss., University of London, 1972), pp. 338–355; *Göttinger Gemeindeblatt* 17, no. 5 (May 1930), p. 38.

14   Imhoof, *Becoming*, p. 19.

15   F. Kröll et al., *Vereine: Geschichte – Politik – Kultur* (Frankfurt, 1982); W. Bühler et al. (eds), *Lokale Freizeitvereine: Entwicklung, Aufgaben, Tendenzen* (St. Augustin, 1978).

16   A. Heinrich, *Der Deutsche Fußballbund: eine politische Geschichte* (Cologne, 2000), pp. 27–61; C. Eisenberg, 'Vom "Arbeiter-" zum "Angestelltenfußball"?

Zur Sozialstruktur des deutschen Fußballsports 1890–1950', *Sozial- und Zeitgeschichte des Sports* 4, no. 3 (1990), pp. 20–45.

17    Eisenberg, '"Arbeiter"', pp. 20–45; F. Filter, 'Fußballsport in der Arbeiter- Turn- und Sportbewegung', *Sozial und Zeitgeschichte des Sports* 2, no. 1 (1988), pp. 55–73.

18    J. Pieper, 'Die Zerschlagung der demokratischen Sportbewegung durch die nationalsozialistischen Machthaber ab 1933 – eine Fallstudie zu den Vorgängen in der Region Göttingen' (Unpublished Seminar Paper, University of Göttingen, 1997), p. 90.

19    StadtAGö: Pol.-Dir. XXV Fach 147, Nr. 30; W. Buss, 'Die Entwicklung der südhannoverschen Arbeitersportbewegung in d. Zeit 1920 bis 1928', in A. Krüger (ed.), *Die Entwicklung der Turn- und Sportvereine* (West Berlin, 1984), pp. 131–138.

20    StadtAGö: Pol.-Dir. XXV, F. 147, Nr. 8: Schützenverein Göttingen, Spec. 1862–1934, pp. 89–90.

21    H. Bernett, 'Der deutsche Sport im Jahre 1933', *Stadion* 7, no. 2 (1981), pp. 225–283.

22    *Göttinger Tageblatt* (hereafter '*GT*') 19 and 31 July 1927; *Göttinger Zeitung* (hereafter '*GZ*') 17 July 1927; K. Jans, 'Schießsport und Presse', *Schützenzeitung für Niedersachsen* no. 45 (April 1928).

23    D. Imhoof, 'Reflecting Pool: Sports, Politics, Hygiene, and the Construction of Göttingen's First Swimming Pool in 1927', in *Proceedings of the 11th International Congress of the European Committee for Sport History* (Vienna, 2007), pp. 540–548.

24    Imhoof, *Becoming*, pp. 11, 13–14; T. Childers, *The Nazi Voter: The Social Foundations of Fascism in Germany, 1919–1933* (Chapel Hill, NC, 1983).

25    D. Imhoof, 'Sharpshooting in Göttingen: A Case Study of Cultural Integration in Weimar and Nazi Germany', *German History* 23, no. 4 (2005), pp. 460, 473–474.

26    *Göttinger Volksblatt* (hereafter '*VB*') 6 February 1929.

27    StadtAGö: Pol. Dir. XXV Fach 147, Nrs. 18, 3 and 30; XXVII Fach 155, Nr. 11, p. 1; *VB* 27 August and 10 September 1930, 6 March 1929, 11 October 1930.

28    *GT* 31 March 1929.

29    *GZ* 30 July 1929.

30    *VB* 6 and 27 February, 17 April, 25 and 29 September 1929, 27 October 1931.

31    M. Barrett, 'Soldiers, Sportsmen, and Politicians. Military Sports in Germany, 1924–1935' (Ph.D. diss., University of Massachusetts, 1977), pp. 77–102, 170–204.

32    A. Krüger, '"Once the Olympics are Through, We'll Beat Up the Jew." German Jewish Sport 1898–1938 and the Anti-Semitic Discourse', *Journal of Sport History* 26, no. 2 (1999), pp. 354–357, 368–370.

33   A. Krüger, 'Heute gehört uns Deutschland und morgen ...? Das Ringen um den Sinn der Gleichschaltung im Sport in der ersten Jahreshälfte 1933', in W. Buss and A. Krüger (eds), *Sportgeschichte: Traditionspflege und Wertewandel* (Duderstadt, 1985), pp. 175–196.

34   Bernett, 'deutsche Sport', pp. 252, 272; Schultz, 'Sport Heil', p. 143.

35   StadtAGö: AHR I B 5,6 Nr. 16 Bd. I, 8 December 1933 and Bd. II, 22 December 1933 report.

36   StadtAGö: Pol-Dir. Fach 147, Nr. 8, pp. 93–94.

37   StadtAGö: Kl. Erwerbungen Nr. 80, 1, Gnade 1934 Speech, p. 19.

38   StadtAGö: AHR I B 5,6 Nr. 16 Bd. I, Normal-Satzung des Deutschen Schießsportverband (1933).

39   D. Sauermann, 'Studien zum Schützenwesen in den Kreisen Minden-Lübbecke und Herford', in *An Weser und Wiehen: Beiträge zur Geschichte und Kultur einer Landschaft* (Minden, 1983), p. 313.

40   This cooperation, though, did not happen everywhere: M. Schwartz, 'Schützenvereine im Dritten Reich. Etappen der Gleichschaltung traditionaler Vereinskultur am Beispiel des ländlich-katholischen Schützenverienswesens Westfalens 1933–1939', *Archiv für Kulturgeschichte* 79 (1997), pp. 454–455, 479–483.

41   StadtAGö: Kl. Erwerbungen Nr. 80 VI, 1, Gnade 1934 speech, pp. 1–2.

42   H. Best (ed.), *Vereine in Deutschland: Vom Geheimbund zur freien gesellschaftlichen Organisation* (Bonn, 1993); C. Becker, 'Zwischen (Selbst-) Gleichschaltung, kommunaler Sportpolitik und sporttreibenden NS-Gliederungen: Die bürgerlichen Turn- und Sportvereine der Stadt Hannover in der Zeit des Nationalsozialismus', *Sozial- und Zeitgeschichte des Sports* 9, no. 2 (1995), pp. 24–41; Krüger, *Entwicklung*; G. Meinhardt, *600 Jahre Göttinger Bürger-Schützen-Gesellschaft: 1392–1992* (Gudensberg-Gleichen, 1992), pp. 215–216.

43   H. Überhorst, *Frisch, frei, stark, und treu: die Arbeitersportbewegung in Deutschland 1893–1933* (Düsseldorf, 1973); K. Schönberger, *Arbeitersportbewegung in Dorf und Kleinstadt: zur Arbeiterbewegungskultur im Oberamt Marbach 1900–1933* (Tübingen, 1995).

44   A. Radtke et al., '"... wir haben uns alle verstanden, da kann man nichts sagen." Politische Erfahrungen ehemaliger Göttinger Arbeitersportler aus den Jahren 1928–1932' (Unpublished Seminar Paper, University of Göttingen, 1985, StadtAGö: E 51), p. 27.

45   Wassersportvereinigung Göttingen 1908 e.V., *75 Jahre Wassersportvereinigung Göttingen 1908 e.V.: 1908–1983* (Göttingen, 1983), pp. 19–32; StadtAGö: Pol.-Dir. XXV Fach 147, Nr. 30, p. 15; J. Bons et al., 'Im "Volksheim" war immer was los!' in K. Duwe et al. (eds), *Göttingen ohne Gänseliesel: Texte und Bilder zur Stadtgeschichte* (Gudensberg-Gleichen, 1989), pp. 68–71.

46   StadtAGö: Kl. Erwerbungen Nr. 205 Radfahrerverein 'Central' Elliehausen, pp. 50–130.

47   S. Fasbender, 'Zwischen Arbeitersport und Arbeitssport: Werksport an Rhein und Ruhr 1921–1938' (Ph.D. diss, University of Göttingen, 1997); H.

Dwertmann, "'So laßt sie auch unter sich". Ambivalente Gestaltungen und Einstellungen im hannoverschen Arbeitersport', *Sozial- und Zeitgeschichte des Sports* 7, no. 1 (1993), pp. 71–81.

48  *VB* 17 February 1931 and Sport Club Weende, *70 Jahre SC Weende 1917–1983* (Göttingen, 1983), p. 23.

49  *GT* 15–17 April, 8–9 July, 12–13 August 1933.

50  StadtAGö: Kleine Erwerbungen Nr. 113 Sport-Club Weende, Protocol Book, 1933–1940.

51  Interview with Ewald Möhle, 23 June 2001, Göttingen.

52  StadtAGö: Pol.-Dir. XXV Fach 147, Nr. 8: Schützenverein Göttingen, Spec.1862–1934, pp. 89–90; Meinhardt, *600 Jahre*, p. 104; C. Kellerman, W. Leßner, and W. Schulze, 'Vereinsgeschichte 1923–1988', in *Schützenverein Scharnhorst e.V. von 1923* (Göttingen, 1988), p. 15.

53  StadtAGö: Pol-Dir. XXV Fach 147, Nr. 21, Ab. B and StadtAGö: Pol.-Dir. XXV: Vereinpolizei Ab. B, Fach 147, Nr. 22.

54  Meinhardt, *600 Jahre*, pp. 199–200, 308.

55  *GZ* 24 June 1924.

56  StadtAGö: Pol.-Dir. XXV Fach 147, Nr. 22, Ab. B, p. 2; A. von Saldern, *Auf dem Wege Zum Arbeiter Reformismus: Parteialltag in sozialdemokratischer Provinz Göttingen (1870–1920)* (Frankfurt, 1984), p. 294. Extant records mention no other Jewish sharpshooters despite the fact that Jews in Göttingen came disproportionately from the middle class, who were otherwise heavily represented in sharpshooting organisations.

57  StadtAGö: Pol.-Dir. XXV Fach 147, Nr. 22, Ab. B, p. 2.

58  Karl Kahn left Göttingen around this time, after SA members vandalised his shop, so the police could not use his membership as an excuse to invoke the February 1933 laws: U. Schäfer-Riechter and J. Klein, *Die jüdischen Bürger im Kreis Göttingen 1933–1945: Göttingen, Hann. Münden, Duderstadt; ein Gedenkbuch* (Göttingen, 1992), p. 114.

59  *Deutsche Schützenzeitung*, 10 November 1933.

60  StadtAGö: Kl. Erwerbungen Nr. 80, 1, Gnade speech at 1934 Sharpshooting Festival, p. 12.

61  StadtAGö: Pol.-Dir. XXV Fach 147, Nr. 21, Ab. B, pp. 3–4, 7–8, 11–34; Fach 153, Nr. 21, pp. 10–23.

62  Grüne, *Zwischen*, pp. 12–48; H. Pauling, *Jubiläumsschrift des 1. Sport-Club 05 Göttingen e.V.* (Göttingen, 1955), p. 11.

63  Heinrich, *Fußballbund*, pp. 122–134; Fischer, *Stürmer*, p. 9.

64  *Göttinger Nachrichten* (hereafter 'GN') 1 and 10 June 1933; Grüne, *Zwischen*, p. 81.

65  StadtAGö: Kl. Erwerbungen Nr. 80 IV 1, 1934 Report, pp. 5–6, 11.

66  *GT* 1–2 and 17 July and 25 December 1933 and 7–8 and 29 April, 1 June, 2 August, 24 and 26 October 1934; *GN* 14 November 1934.

67  Grüne, *Zwischen*, pp. 80–81.

68    A. Krüger, 'Die Rolle des Sports bei den Kriegsvorbereitungen des nationalsozialistischen Deutschlands', in S. Güldenpfennig and H. Meyer, (eds), *Sportler für den Frieden* (Cologne, 1983), pp. 137–152; X. Bernett, 'Die "totale Mobilmachung" der deutschen Jugend: Pläne zur vormilitärischen Ertüchtigung von 1933 bis 1936', *Sportwissenschaft* 12, no. 4 (1984), pp. 345–375.

69    StadtAGö: AHR I B 6c 3 Nr.7 (Pa.Nr.341), 1929–1943 and Nr. 13 (Pa. Nr.340), 1927–1937.

70    Schwartz, 'Schützenvereine', pp. 448–450; Barrett, 'Soldiers', p. 329.

71    B. Stambolis, 'Nation und Konfession im Spannungsfeld: Aspekte historischer Vereinsforschung am Beispiel Schützenwesens', *Historisches Jahrbuch* 120 (2000), pp. 199–226.

72    *GN* 15 July 1935.

73    *GN* 20 July 1936.

74    D. Large, *Nazi Games: The Olympics of 1936* (New York, 2007); A. Krüger and W. Murray (eds), *The Nazi Olympics: Sport, Politics, and Appeasement in the 1930s* (Urbana, IL and Chicago, IL, 2003).

75    A. Krüger, 'The Ministry of Popular Enlightenment and Propaganda and the Nazi Olympics of 1936', in R. Wamsley et al. (eds), *Global and Cultural Critique: Problematizing the Olympic Games* (London, Ontario, 1998), p. 35.

76    A. Krüger, '"Dann veranstalten wir eben rein deutsche Olympische Spiele." Die Olympischen Spiele 1936 als deutsches Nationalfest', in H. Breuer and R. Naul (eds), *Schwimmsport und Sportgeschichte. Zwischen Politik und Wissenschaft* (St. Augustin, 1994), pp. 127–149.

77    *GT* 22 February 1935.

78    *GT* 15 February and 17 July 1935; *GN* 11 April 1936.

79    R. Mandell, *Nazi Olympics* (New York, 1971), p. 192; *GT* 14 and 15 July 1936.

80    Krüger, 'Once', pp. 357–362 and 'Ministry', pp. 35–37, 40–41.

81    *GT* 1 April 1938.

82    H. Teichler, *Internationale Sportpolitik im dritten Reich* (Schorndorf, 1991), pp. 367–370; *GN* 18 January 1935.

83    Teichler, *Internationale*, p. 367; H. Bernett, *Der Weg des Sports in die nationalsozialistische Diktatur* (Schorndorf, 1983), p. 52; Grüne, *Zwischen*, pp. 60–71.

84    StadtAGö: Kl. Erwerbungen Nr. 205, pp. 96–130 and Kl. Erwerbungen Nr. 113, 1935–1944.

85    *GT* 21–24 August; 2, 4–5, 7 September 1937; 5 and 14 April and 17–18 December 1938; *GN* 13 September 1937.

86    StadtAGö: AHR I B 5, 6 Nr. 16 Bd. II, 30 December 1935 meeting.

87    StadtAGö: AHR I B 5, 6 Nr. 16 Bd. II, 10 May 1936 letter; Schwartz, 'Schützenvereine'.

88  *GT* 7 and 22 February 1935; *GN* 19 February and 6 March 1935.

89  StadtAGö: Pol. Dir. XXV Fach 152, Nr. 9, pp. 218–221.

90  StadtAGö: Pol. Dir. XXV Fach 152, Nr. 7, pp. 31–45 and Nr. 8, pp. 60–144.

91  Imhoof, *Becoming*, pp. 18–19.

92  R. Gellately, *Backing Hitler: Consent and Coercion in Nazi Germany* (Oxford, 2001).

93  Unless otherwise noted, the story that follows comes from StadtAGö: Dep. 77 I Nr. 33, 4 January 1977 interview with Wilhelm Henze; W. Buss, 'Rassenideologie versus Fachkompetenz: Die erzwungene "Zur-Ruhesetzung" des ersten Göttinger IfL-Direktors Dr. Bernhard Zimmermann aus rassischen Gründen im Jahre 1937', in R. Dieckmann (ed.), *Sportpraxis und Sportwissenschaft* (Schorndorf, 1980), pp. 13–39 and 'Der allgemeine Hochschulsport und die Anfänge einer Sportwissenschaft in der Weimarer Republik und im Nationalsozialismus', in W. Buss (ed.), *Von ritterlichen Exercitien zur modernen Bewegungskultur: 250 Jahre Leibesübung und Sport an der Universität Göttingen* (Duderstadt, 1989), pp. 42–75.

94  *GT* 25 June 1937.

95  A. Krüger, 'Breeding, Rearing and Preparing the Aryan Body: Creating the Complete Superman the Nazi Way', in J. Mangan (ed.), *Shaping the Superman: Fascist Body as Political Icon – Aryan Fascism* (London, 1999), pp. 58–59; P. Carpenter, 'Die Ursprünge von Outward Bound', *Erleben und Lernen* 5, no. 4–3 (1997), pp. 7–11.

96  StadtAGö: Dep. 77 I Nr. 33, Henze interview, p. 26.

97  Krüger, 'Rolle' and 'Germany and Sport in World War II', *Canadian Journal of History of Sport* 24, no. 1 (1993), pp. 52–62.

98  Schützenverein Scharnhorst e.V Göttingen, Protokolbuch (in author's possession), 1944; StadtAGö: Kl. Erwerbungen Nr. 113, August 1940.

99  Grüne, *Zwischen*, pp. 72–73.

100 StadtAGö: Kl. Erwerbungen Nr. 80 VI, 1, pp. 2–3.

# Select bibliography

Bernett, H., *Der Weg des Sports in die nationalsozialistische Diktatur* (Schorndorf, 1983).

Crew, D. (ed.), *Nazism and German Society, 1933–1945* (London, 1994).

Denecke, V., *Die Arbeitersportgemeinschaft: Eine kulturhistorische Studie über die Braunschweiger Arbeitersportbewegung in den zwanziger Jahren* (Duderstadt, 1990).

Eisenberg, C., *'English Sports' und deutsche Bürger: Eine Gesellschaftsgeschichte 1800–1939* (Paderborn, 1999).

Hoberman, J., *Sport and Political Ideology* (London, 1984).

Imhoof, D., *Becoming a Nazi Town: Culture and Politics in Göttingen between the World Wars* (Ann Arbor, MI, 2013).

Keys, B., *Globalizing Sport: National Rivalry and International Community in the 1930s* (Cambridge, MA, 2006).

Koshar, R., *Social Life, Local Politics, and Nazism: Marburg, 1880–1935* (Chapel Hill, NC, 1986).

Large, D., *Nazi Games: The Olympics of 1936* (New York, 2007).

Peiffer, L. and Schulze-Marmeling, D. (eds), *Hakenkreuz und rundes Leder. Fußball im Nationalsozialismus* (Göttingen, 2008).

# 7

# Representing the *Volksgemeinschaft*: Art in the Third Reich

## *Joan L. Clinefelter*

The visual arts held a special place in National Socialist ideology, one that went well beyond mere propaganda designed to manipulate the masses. Art represented the *Volksgemeinschaft*, the Nazis' imagined racial community in which ethnic belonging overcame class and political divisions. For National Socialists, art was the visual manifestation of German identity, and it defined the boundaries between members of the *Volksgemeinschaft* and the 'unfit' outsiders. This chapter explores how the Nazis used art to produce the *Volksgemeinschaft*. It begins by analysing the place of the arts in society and the development of the Third Reich's cultural policies. It then argues that the Great German Art Exhibition (*Grosse Deutsche Kunstausstellung*) and the Degenerate Art (*Entartete Kunst*) show of 1937 engaged the public in ritualised performances of inclusion and exclusion that had profound effects on artists, dealers and the art market. Although in the end the Third Reich did not foster a unique, Nazi style, it effectively used the visual arts to create the illusion of a unified society grounded in the notions of racial inclusion and exclusion that lay at the heart of National Socialism.

The evolution of studies of art in the Third Reich parallels developments in the broader historiography of National Socialism. The initial focus was on the victims of the Third Reich and the role of terror implemented by the Nazi leadership from above. For the arts, this entailed discussion of the Nazis' destruction of the Weimar Republic's vibrant culture and their attacks against modernist artists. Beginning in 1949, scholars detailed the art dictatorship unleashed in 1933 and the purges of Germany's museums and art institutions.[1] By the 1970s, the focus shifted to consider the widespread support for Nazi policies and the continuities between the Third Reich and the preceding decades. Berthold Hinz, the first to treat art favoured by the Nazis as worthy of serious study, analysed the aesthetics and content of works produced by the regime's artists. He demonstrated that rather than creating a new art form, the Nazis continued traditional styles and genres popular since the nineteenth century.[2] Brandon Taylor and Wilfried van der Will pushed this strand of enquiry further, to the point that many now argue that while Nazi art rejected modernist styles, it cannot be understood as simply anti-modern.[3] The final interpretive strand interrogates the intersections between coercion and consent in the Nazi state. For example, Alan E. Steinweis unravelled the intricacies of the Reich Chamber of Culture, the Nazis' primary vehicle for controlling the arts and securing artists' support for the regime. Jonathan Petropoulos analysed Nazi policies and the impulses that drove artists towards the Third Reich.[4] Taken together, scholars have demonstrated the central role the arts played in National Socialist ideology and detailed the administrative structures that enabled Hitler's Germany to eliminate artistic modernism in favour of a supposedly pure German art.

However, the role played by the arts in the everyday lives of Germans has remained largely unexplored, in part because the fine arts have been typically regarded as a rarified realm that involved only the educated classes. Focusing on the arts as a constituent part of the *Volksgemeinschaft* offers a way to demonstrate just how seriously the Nazis sought to make culture part of daily experience and a key component of Germans' unique, racial identity. More than just a myth, the *Volksgemeinschaft* the Nazis worked to create was experienced by Germans as proof of national renewal under Hitler's leadership. Paintings, graphic works and sculptures favoured by the regime visually represented the *Volksgemeinschaft* and offered the opportunity for Germans to participate in its creation.

The idea of a *Volksgemeinschaft* had already won broad currency across the political spectrum during the Weimar Republic. The concept captured Germans' longing for a national unity that transcended the political and social differences that divided them. Hitler and the Nazis exploited Germans' hopes for a *Volksgemeinschaft* and in the process shifted its meaning. While before it had signified a community in which all Germans belonged, in the Third Reich the *Volksgemeinschaft* entailed both inclusion and exclusion.[5] Members of the 'national community' anticipated that the Nazis would bring about economic prosperity and a more egalitarian society. During the 1930s, 'a large majority of Germans really believed in a "national resurrection" and in their chances of a personal career, in a heroic future, and in a better life for themselves and future generations'.[6] As we will see, mass participation in cultural events was experienced as proof that the *Volksgemeinschaft* had been realised. However, the creation of this community also required the exclusion of internal enemies that threatened the new-found social and cultural consensus. Jews, Communists, Socialists and other Germans deemed unfit were cast as outsiders. Moreover, their outsider status was claimed to be biologically based and revealed through cultural productions. Only the racially healthy Germans willing to sacrifice their individual needs for the greater good could belong to the newly constructed community. National Socialism thus envisioned 'an ideologically homogenous, socially conformist, performance-oriented and hierarchically structured society' which could only be realised by 'educating the "well-suited" and "eradicating" the supposedly "unsuitable"'.[7]

Culture generally and the visual arts specifically formed the core of the *Volksgemeinschaft*. The public's participation in the creation and celebration of a pure German art pulled them into the 'national community' and provided them with a new, racially grounded and culturally revealed identity. Art in the Third Reich defined the borders between those who belonged to and those who were excluded from the racial community. Indeed, Adolf Hitler 'attributed deep ideological meaning to the arts'.[8] He believed that all cultural productions were expressions of race; under National Socialism, the arts diagnosed racial fitness and its opposite, degeneracy. Since the time of the ancient Greeks, who Hitler claimed were 'Aryans', the German race had consistently produced works of beauty, with classical lines, realistic imagery and styles that were clear and easy for all members of the *Volk* to comprehend.

However, according to the Nazis, the Jews had corrupted this imagined cultural unity over time. The Jews understood that the superior 'Aryan' race represented the greatest threat to their control over Germany, and that cultural modernism could erode the people's values and weaken the 'racial substance of the German people'.[9] A vast conspiracy of Jews and their supporters had thus infected culture during the Weimar Republic in an effort to alienate Germans from their artistic traditions and thus from their racial identity. Through their supposed influence in the press, museums and the art market, Jews promoted the alien avant-garde, comprised of Impressionists, Expressionists, abstract artists and practitioners of a modernist realist style (New Objectivity). Modernist artists secured teaching positions in prestigious art academies; museums and dealers purchased and exhibited their works, and critics promoted them as German innovators. The public, confused by modern art's constantly changing styles, became convinced that their lack of understanding for avant-garde art was due to their own ignorance and lack of taste, rather than their allegiance to an innate, racially determined, healthy sensibility.

Meanwhile, racially pure German artists were pushed to the periphery of the art world, derided as backward and out-of-date because they defended conservative styles. The Nazis' interpretation of the supposed Jewish control over culture resonated with contemporary artists who favoured tradition over visual experimentation. Many of these artists joined the *Kampfbund für Deutsche Kultur* (Combat League for German Culture), a National Socialist special interest group for artists established in 1928. Headed by Nazi party ideologue Alfred Rosenberg, the Combat League defended artistic tradition, now recast in racial terms. In public meetings and publications, the Combat League also claimed that the true German artists suffered economically because they remained loyal to their cultural traditions.[10] While all artists suffered from a chronically weak art market that was further devastated by the Great Depression, the stylistically conservative painters and sculptors were convinced that they suffered more than their modernist competitors.[11] The Nazis' interpretation of the Weimar Republic's culture wars between the modernists and the traditionalists legitimated the latter's suffering and gave it meaning. The Nazis promised to cure a long-standing cultural disease by eliminating the Jewish infection of the arts. Purging Jews and modernist art from German life would regenerate the nation. Once reconnected with their culture, Germans' racial identity would be awakened, and the *Volksgemeinschaft* would be achieved. Only a cultural revival, effected by a thorough cleansing campaign and state support for true German artists, could secure the Germanic renaissance that would make possible the realisation of the *Volk*'s racial mission in Europe.[12]

To effect this cultural renewal and revive the 'national community', Nazi cultural policy focused at first on regulating membership in the cultural realm. This process began early in 1933, and 'artists were among the first to be persecuted by the Nazi regime'.[13] The Prussian Academy of Art, arguably the most prestigious arts academy in Germany, was purged of Jewish and leftist members beginning in February, with leading artists such as Max Liebermann and Käthe Kollwitz expelled. The Law for the Restoration of the Professional Civil Service of April 1933 enabled the dismissal of Jewish and politically unreliable museum directors and art academy professors. Even more devastating, the Reich Chamber of Culture was created in September, under the leadership of the Minister of Public Enlightenment and Propaganda, Joseph Goebbels.

The Reich Chamber of Culture was 'the exclusive, officially recognised, compulsory professional corporation for the arts, entertainment and the media'.[14] Comprised of seven subchambers devoted to the visual arts, literature, theatre, music, press, radio and film, membership was required for anyone who sought to be active in these fields. The Chamber enacted a form of cultural eugenics. It followed a dual strategy of inclusion and exclusion that 'entailed both the "promotion of creative and productive forces" as well as the "eradication of unworthy and dangerous elements"'.[15] By 1936, the Reich Chamber of the Visual Arts claimed 42,000 members and included painters, sculptors, graphic artists, architects and dealers. Jewish artists, leftists and modernists denied membership were forbidden to exhibit and could even be served with a *Malverbot*, an order that banned them from painting at all.[16] The Chamber thus provided for the initial cleansing of the German art world.

# The Nazi debate over German art

The Reich Chamber of the Visual Arts defined who could produce, exhibit and sell art, but it was far more difficult to determine the kind of art the Third Reich should support. After all, just what did 'German' art look like? In the absence of clear guidelines, a power struggle between two rival camps developed and drew artists and the public into a cultural war over what constituted racially pure art. On the one side were defenders of non-Jewish, German modernists whose art was proclaimed as a revolutionary Nordic style. On the other, promoters of a conservative pure German art sought the wholesale elimination of cultural modernism. While nearly every leading Nazi official was involved in the struggle over the regime's cultural direction, the primary players were Joseph Goebbels and Alfred Rosenberg. As head of the Chamber of Culture and Minister of Propaganda, Goebbels sought to incorporate avant-garde artists with international reputations into the Third Reich to lend it cultural legitimacy. Rosenberg, whose Combat for League for German Culture was reorganised as the *NS-Kulturgemeinde* (NS-Culture Community), sought a racially infused, wholly German style. Hitler also granted Rosenberg an administrative office and the imposing title of the *Führer*'s Plenipotentiary for the Supervision of the Entire Intellectual and Ideological Training and Education of the Nazi Party in 1934. Both Rosenberg and Goebbels thus had significant power bases from which they could combat each other's cultural views.[17]

The rivalry quickly embroiled the art world as artists and the public joined in the battle for pure German art between 1933 and 1936. Goebbels's efforts to include some modernists won support in student circles, in particular the National Socialist German Students' League. The students promoted what they called Nordic modernism that included German Expressionists. They argued that artists such as Ernst Barlach, Erich Heckel, Emil Nolde and Karl Schmidt-Rottluff, all racially 'German', offered a contemporary aesthetic that captured the revolutionary impulses of National Socialism. They organised an exhibition, Thirty German Artists, held in Berlin's Ferdinand Möller gallery, published articles in newspapers and defended select modernists in 'highly publicised rallies'. The art journals *Kunst der Nation* and *Die Kunst für Alle* and the Reich Chamber of the Visual Arts' own publication, *Der Kunstkammer*, openly supported Expressionism as the ideal, pure German style for the new Germany.[18]

Rosenberg's supporters responded to this promotion of modernist artists with campaigns of their own. In March 1933, Bettina Feistel-Rohmeder, a member of the Combat League and head of a consortium of right-wing artist associations that comprised 250,000 members, published a call to arms.

Entitled 'What the German Artists Expect from the New Government!' it declared that artists desired clear policy directives 'drawn from a passionate national and state consciousness anchored in the realities of blood and history!' Feistel-Rohmeder demanded the dismissal of all officials 'who sinned against a needy nation...by their shameless waste of public funds' that they had spent on modern art for German museum collections. Such works needed to be purged from the museums and exhibited to the public to educate Germans about the cultural poisoning they had endured at the hands of Jews and Marxists. Next to the offending works, the names of the officials who had purchased the offending art, along with the prices paid, should be shown. And then, 'only one useful function remain[ed] for these works of nonart: namely as kindling for the heating of public buildings'.[19] Feistel-Rohmeder thus declared that modernist art and its supporters needed to be eliminated entirely.

Feistel-Rohmeder's manifesto unleashed a cultural purge at the local level, often carried out by members of the Combat League for German Culture who had secured positions of power in the Third Reich's emerging arts administration. They organised exhibits of modernist art, now derided as 'degenerate art', across Germany. Artworks were removed from local museum collections and publicly defamed. The exhibits argued that modern art served as proof of a cultural corruption at the hands of Jews and art Bolshevists who had dominated the arts during the Weimar Republic. The price of the art and the name of the director responsible for its purchase were highlighted to make the populist argument that public money had been squandered. Organisers also took it upon themselves to define pure German art, contrasting works they approved of with those pilloried in the degenerate art shows.

In his detailed reconstruction of these early degenerate art exhibitions, Christoph Zuschlag demonstrated that artists and local officials did not wait to receive orders from above. They acted on their own initiative to vilify modernist art in these exhibitions, frequently described in the press as 'chambers of horror'.[20] The first such exhibition was held in Mannheim from 4 April to 5 June 1933, and for the next four years, local degenerate art shows also opened in Karlsruhe, Nuremberg, Chemnitz, Stuttgart, Dessau, Ulm, Dresden, Breslau and Halle. They proved enormously popular with the public, visited by thousands. The Mannheim show, Images of Cultural Bolshevism, for example, recorded 20,141 visitors.[21]

The Dresden exhibition of 1933 was particularly influential; it later formed the core of the 1937 Degenerate Art show in Munich (discussed below). Held between 23 September and 18 October 1933, it was organised by three members of the Combat League for German Culture who had secured influential positions in the Third Reich: Richard Müller, director of the Dresden Art Academy, Willy Waldapfel, city councillor, and Walter Gasch, art commissioner for Dresden. The show included at least 42 paintings, 10 sculptures, 43 watercolours and 112 graphic works by artists such as Otto

Dix, Paul Klee and Kurt Schwitters, with the purchase prices displayed. It travelled to Nuremberg in 1935, where it was timed to coincide with the annual Nazi party rally and an antisemitic exhibition, The Mirror of the Jews. Hitler, Goebbels and Goering visited the exhibition. Hitler declared that 'this unique exhibition… ought to be shown in as many German cities as possible'. Between 1934 and 1936, the Dresden degenerate art exhibit was shown in various iterations in eight cities across Germany.[22] Tens of thousands of visitors streamed into these sensationalist exhibitions. Taken together, the local degenerate art exhibitions illustrated the distaste of the German public for modern art.

## The Great German Art and Degenerate Art Exhibitions

By late 1936, even Goebbels had come to embrace the rejection of modernist art, and the debate over art in the Third Reich ended. Only traditional, realistic art would be accepted as 'German'. The time had come for an official art show that would set the new direction in the arts. In January 1937, newspapers announced that the first official, national art exhibition of the Third Reich would be held in the summer and invited German artists to submit work for consideration. Hundreds of artists responded, and 15,000 submissions were accepted for review.[23] But it was not enough only to demonstrate what German art was; the Nazis also called for a final reckoning with modernist art. On 30 July 1937, barely two weeks before the official art exhibition opened, Goebbels authorised a commission 'to select and secure for an exhibition works of German degenerate art' held in Germany's museums. The decree defined 'degenerate' art as works that acted to 'insult German feeling, or destroy or confuse natural form, or simply reveal an absence of adequate manual and artistic skill'.[24] Headed by Adolf Ziegler, President of the Reich Chamber of Visual Arts and a painter himself, the commission confiscated some 700 works from thirty-two museums. The Nazis' dual policy of cultural inclusion and exclusion was about to be put on display for the German public in Munich, the capital of the Nazi movement, in two contrasting exhibitions: the Great German Art Exhibition and the Degenerate Art show.

The Great German Art Exhibition opened on 18 July 1937 with enormous pomp that capped several days of celebration. Before a crowd of Nazi dignitaries, foreign guests and the public, Hitler opened the exhibition by delivering an impassioned, ninety-minute speech in front of the House of German Art, the first public building commissioned by the Third Reich. Hitler declared that modernist art had no place in the Third Reich. Instead, he was returning art drawn from the German cultural heritage to the people. From now on, artists would create great works of art for the *Volk*, who would be able to judge for themselves the successes of the new age. Until recently, Hitler admitted,

> the people had no affinity for the so-called modern art that was placed before them. The mass of the people moved through our art exhibits in a completely uninterested fashion or stayed away altogether. The people's healthy perceptions recognised that all these smearings of canvas were really the outcome of an impudent and unashamed arrogance or a simply shocking lack of skill.[25]

But now, as they passed through the Great German Art Exhibition, Hitler was certain that Germans would 'draw a sigh of relief and joyously express agreement with this purification of art'. The exhibition represented a new beginning that would inspire a new generation of artists. It also signified 'the end of the stultification of German art and the end of the cultural destruction of our people'.[26]

Throughout his speech, Hitler demarcated the boundaries between those artists who belonged to the *Volksgemeinschaft* and those who did not by contrasting the healthy sentiments of the people with the diseased productions of modernists. Rather than celebrating the physically perfect men and women recently seen at the Berlin Olympics, Hitler declared modern artists produced works that depicted '[d]eformed cripples and cretins, women who inspire only disgust, men who are more like wild beasts, children who, if they were alive, would be regarded as God's curse!'[27] There were, he concluded, just two possibilities for such insistence upon painting diseased figures. The artists might suffer from a defect of vision, which, if found to be hereditary, 'would be a matter for the Ministry of the Interior, which would then deal with the problem of preventing the perpetuation of such horrid disorders'. Or, they did not really see this way at all and were perpetrating fraud, 'a matter for a criminal court'.[28] Racial ill-heath could thus be diagnosed through art and treated accordingly, through either the sterilisation Hitler hinted at or through imprisonment.

When the visitors streamed into the exhibition, they were treated to the first official presentation of the regime's art. Selected personally by Hitler, 884 works by 556 artists were carefully displayed in the spacious exhibition halls. Despite the heroic pronouncements, however, the paintings and sculptures did not present a new kind of art but instead replicated realistic styles and genres popular since the nineteenth century. The exhibit featured 'landscapes, nudes and pictures of farmers ... followed by portraits, still lifes, and paintings of animals and industrial subjects'.[29] Very few works had specifically Nazi themes and there was no discernible stylistic uniformity. A new Nazi style had not yet emerged.

The Great German Art Exhibition was enormously popular with the public. An impressive 554,759 visitors toured the show over its four-month run (18 July–31 October 1937). It is, however, difficult to find sources that record the public's reactions with any objectivity. Attendance was voluntary, and visitors paid to come on their own, not as part of mass tours orchestrated by Party organisations, all indications of mass support.[30] One visitor, Peter Guenther, just 17 years old at the time, later recalled his reaction. He was impressed above all 'by the silence: everybody whispered. It was obviously due to the semiecclesiastical [*sic*] atmosphere created by the size of the rooms, their decor, the impressive lighting, and the careful placement of the exhibits'.[31] Although paintings such as Richard Klein's *The Awakening* and Ziegler's *Four Elements* held little appeal for him, Guenther was aware that 'people admired works of this type because they depicted "so realistically" what was "beautiful and good"'.[32]

Indeed, the Great German Art Exhibition was much more than just an art show. Its sculptures and paintings enabled the Germans to see themselves through the lens of National Socialism and as members of the *Volksgemeinschaft*. The official Nazi art journal, *Die Kunst im Dritten Reich*, explained that the exhibit 'reflects the life of our time, it is our eyes we look into when we stand in front of these pictures'.[33] Hitler had assured visitors that their approval was a sign of their racial health and signified their place in the *Volksgemeinschaft*. Most importantly, the Nazis did all they could to make sure that the exhibit would not just be something that Germans witnessed passively. To ensure that as many Germans as possible would experience the *Volksgemeinschaft* and its cultural revival, the Great German Art Exhibition was part of a huge arts extravaganza designed to involve the public actively. The art show and the surrounding festivities combined to offer Germans the ability to become participating members in the culture-producing *Volksgemeinschaft*.

This participatory experience began months earlier with preparations for the three-day Festival of German Art that framed the exhibition. The 33,821 Germans involved provided the 690,000 work hours needed to make all of the costumes, flags, banners and other preparations. Over 4,400 'sculptors, painters, singers, actors, musicians and acrobats' found work and '[t]he labour market was virtually swept clean of skilled workers'.[34] Once the festivities began, the public was treated to free theatre performances, operas, folk dances and concerts, all designed as opportunities for the people to celebrate German culture and the arts together as equal members of the 'national community'. Those who could not attend personally were included through live radio broadcasts from Munich, as well as full coverage in newspapers and newsreels.[35] Culture and the arts were no longer the preserve of educated elites; they belonged to the *Volk*. The state encouraged the German people to become cultural consumers.

The highlight of all of this effort was the huge pageant, Two Thousand Years of German Culture, held in the afternoon after the exhibit's opening. The parade route connected the historic heart of Munich, the Königsplatz, to the House of German Art, thereby linking the Third Reich with the city's past. Lined with hundreds of flags and pylons, all topped with the eagle and swastika symbol, the route demarcated a purely German space within which the select *Volk* celebrated and experienced a profound unity and sense of purpose.[36] 'Over 3 km long, lasting two and a half hours and comprising 6,403 costumed participants, 456 horses with 420 male and 30 female riders as well as 26 floats', the parade celebrated the Great German Art Exhibition and the Third Reich as the culmination of 2,000 years of German cultural development[37] (Figure 7.1).

**FIGURE 7.1** *Parade at the opening of the Great German Art Exhibition, 1937 (WL9864). Courtesy of the Wiener Library, London.*

Beginning with Germanic warriors and a 'golden Viking ship', the parade brought German history to life, from ancient times to the contemporary era. 'What we are seeing here', enthused the *Völkischer Beobachter*,

> is another world – the images, figures and symbols of history recaptured. The language they speak is powerful and awe-inspiring. And indeed thousands upon thousands stand spellbound by this splendour, by the incredible beauty of this spectacle, a spectacle that dissolves the present day and moment, a scene that is the distillation of centuries: 'Two Thousand Years of German Culture'.[38]

At the parade's end, viewers and participants were pulled from this timeless sense of an eternal German culture and returned to the present-day. The final floats depicted buildings commissioned by the Nazis, including the House of German Art itself. At the very end, over 3,000 members of the Reich Labour Service, the army, motorised units, the SA and the SS marched in organised ranks.[39] The entire *Volksgemeinschaft* was on display, in the parade itself and in the crowds of hundreds of thousands that lined the streets. Here was the realisation of the Nazis' promise that a new, unified society would be created under their leadership.

The German 'national community', however, was shaped by both inclusionary and exclusionary practices. The *Volksgemeinschaft* was grounded not just in the belief of the purity of the 'Aryan' race, but it was also predicated upon the conviction of its superiority over the 'inferior' Jews. The experience of Germanness thus required the *Volk* to perform their racial identity both positively by accepting the values and ideas associated with it and negatively through the shared rejection of all that was alien and diseased. Thus, the very next day, 19 July 1937, the 'national community' was invited to participate in the state-sponsored rejection of 'racially inferior' art by attending the Degenerate Art exhibition.

The show opened directly opposite the Great German Art Exhibition, in rooms that had held the Archeological Institute's plaster cast collection. Ziegler explained the purpose of the show to the assembled guests:

> We now stand in an exhibition that contains only a fraction of what was bought with the hard-earned savings of the German people and exhibited as art by a large number of museums all over Germany. All around us you see the monstrous offspring of insanity, impudence, ineptitude and sheer degeneracy. What this exhibition offers inspires horror and disgust in us all.[40]

The racial content of the show was clear in the language Ziegler used, designed to elicit viewers' rejection of the art on display (Figure 7.2). Here were the results of the supposed Jewish conspiracy that had transformed the ravings of the mad and the 'racially inferior' into 'art', purchased by

FIGURE 7.2 *Hitler visiting the Degenerate Art Exhibition, 1937 (WL5097).*
*Courtesy of the Wiener Library, London.*

corrupt officials during the Weimar Republic. Over 650 paintings, prints,
sculptures and books by 112 artists were publicly pilloried in this exhibition
uniquely designed to instil revulsion in its viewers. Foreign artists like Pablo
Picasso and Marc Chagall were included but most were German modernists
associated with Weimar culture, including Max Beckmann, George Grosz,
Erich Heckel, Ernst Ludwig Kirchner, Emil Nolde and Karl Schmidt-
Rottluff.[41]

Degenerate Art was constructed to be the complete opposite of the Great
German Art Exhibition. Whereas the 'racially pure' art was displayed in
spacious rooms on gleaming white walls suffused in light, the 'degenerate'
paintings were packed tightly together in nine narrow, poorly lit rooms,
often without frames and even upside down. The celebration of pure
German art encompassed the entire city of Munich, but the Degenerate Art
show was essentially ghettoised, confined to a small space that provided
a kind of cultural quarantine. The walls were covered with burlap, and
insulting slogans were scrawled across them like graffiti. Some sculptures
were set directly on the floor rather than on any kind of stand. The chaos
of works hung so closely together and the slogans that snaked around the
walls combined with the narrowness of the rooms to create a claustrophobic
atmosphere. The labels, often inaccurate, listed the artist, the title, the date
the work had been acquired and the museum, and at times the museum
official, that had purchased it. The price paid was often cited as well. For
example, one label noted that a painting by Schmidt-Rottluff had been

purchased for 1.5 million marks; another by Heckel had cost its museum 1 million marks. Red stickers explained that such works had been 'paid for by the taxes of the German working people'.[42] Unmentioned was the fact that these purchases were made during the Great Inflation and so bore no resemblance to actual costs. The crazy prices were intended to outrage visitors and alienate them even further from the work on display.

Every effort was made to ensure that the works would be seen not as art, but as a collective indictment against modernists that justified their permanent exclusion from the *Volksgemeinschaft*. At the show's entrance, visitors were confronted by Ludwig Gies's *Crucified Christ* (*Kruzifixus*) from 1921, a large wooden sculpture of an emaciated Jesus on the Cross, with protruding ribs, knees, head and facial features rendered in sharp angles. The organisers used the work to introduce key themes that were developed throughout the exhibition: the modernists' mockery of Christian sensibilities and sacrifices born by Germans in the war; past experts' financial malfeasance; the Jewish infiltration of German culture; and the collective damage wrought as a result. The text beneath the sculpture explained that Gies had been honoured during the Weimar Republic as a professor, a clear suggestion that he had contributed to the poisoning of German youth. Even worse, the exhibit noted, the sculpture had hung in the Lübeck Cathedral as a memorial to the dead of the Great War. The large question mark superimposed over this text encouraged visitors to reject past experts' claims that this work was 'one of the richest documents of modern religious experience' and called into question its appropriateness as a commemoration of Germany's war dead.[43] This was not art but an insult to all Germans.

A whole room was dedicated to the twin themes 'An insult to German womanhood' and 'The ideal – cretin and whore'. It was filled with crude, unnaturally elongated nudes painted in vibrant colours. Prostitutes, women with whips or women displaying themselves, filled the walls. Kirchner's *Self-Portrait as a Soldier* was shown here but reinterpreted. The painting is a dramatically emotional rendering of the artist in uniform, his skin yellow, his hand amputated, as a metaphorical commentary on his inability to paint the model, who can be seen in the background. The show's organisers renamed the painting *Soldier with Whore* to make it fit in with the room's theme about women, as well as the themes related to insulting war heroes.[44] The only relief offered amid the visual onslaught was a large placard with a quote from Hitler's opening speech at the Great German Art Exhibition. In clear lettering, the words in which he attacked artists for producing works of '[d]eformed cripples and cretins, women who inspire only disgust' seemed not only to depict what was on the walls, but also to explain the works as wholly beyond the pale.

The placards with quotes from Hitler, Goebbels and Rosenberg connected Degenerate Art to the Great German Art Exhibition and underscored how each was the complete opposite of the other. Racial difference was a key component of this contrast. The show created the impression that all of the artists were Jews despite the fact that only six of the artists were Jewish. For example, paintings by Pechstein, Schmidt-Rottluff and Kirchner were featured under the heading 'German farmers – a Yiddish view', yet none of them were Jewish.[45] To the Nazi eye, all modernists painted like Jews, because modernism itself was an expression of the Jewish spirit, the values of democracy, individual expression and willingness to challenge authority. These values had no place in Nazi society; their eradication was a requirement for the realisation of the *Volksgemeinschaft*.

Germans willingly participated in this expulsion of modern art and its values, signalling their approval by attending the show in mass numbers. An astonishing 2,009,899 visitors viewed the show in Munich, so many that its planned closing date was delayed by a month, to 30 November 1937. The Nazis offered organised tours, partly to ensure participation and partly to shape it. The German Labour Front and its leisure-time organisation Strength Through Joy, Nazi party organisations and schools provided tours and promoted the show.[46] At least one source claimed that the Nazis hired actors to comment loudly and gesture wildly to encourage similar reactions, or to silence any visitor who favoured modern art.[47] Indeed, the Nazis were determined that as many Germans as possible would visit the exhibit. After closing in Munich, Degenerate Art reopened in Berlin, where 500,000 visitors endured long lines to view it. At least another half million visited the show as it toured the Reich. Leipzig, Düsseldorf, Salzburg, Hamburg, Stettin, Weimar, Vienna, Frankfurt and Chemnitz hosted the exhibit over the course of 1938–1939, and it even continued to tour in 1941.[48]

Although the few eyewitness accounts available noted that some visitors appeared to be saddened by the show's attacks, they also confirmed that the vast majority of visitors welcomed the elimination of degenerate art from Germany's cultural life. A report from Sopade, the SPD in exile, believed that 'the majority of those present came from the small business stratum, people whom one can assume do not visit art exhibitions very often'. Visitors actively evaluated the works, deriding with contempt and expressing outrage at the prices that had been paid.[49] Young Peter Guenther, who described his visit to the Great German Art Exhibition, also viewed the Degenerate Art show. He admired modernist art and was shocked by the way the show attacked works that he loved. To him, it seemed that most accepted the exhibition and its message. Visitors 'made loud, angry remarks' commenting that the so-called artists could not paint 'and that therefore there must have been a "conspiracy" of art dealers, museum directors and critics to bamboozle the public'.[50] Guenther observed on a second visit that there were a few who seemed to admire the art, but like him, they were afraid to speak up. He remembered his feelings well:

> while standing before certain works, I had wanted to say something in their defense to those who laughed and cursed and derided them, but I was too afraid to do so. I had become frightened watching the reactions

of the people around me. What would they do to me – and would they create even greater trouble for my father – if they found out that I didn't share their disgust?[51]

As he makes clear, Guenther had internalised a set of behaviours to ensure his membership in the 'national community'. Though only a teenager, he understood the danger of being cast out of the *Volksgemeinschaft*, not only for himself, but also for his family. Shared disgust for modernist art and shared support for the restoration of German art: these were the inclusionary and exclusionary processes that shaped the new 'national community'.

These processes intensified as the Third Reich continued. Just three weeks after the opening of Degenerate Art, Hitler empowered Ziegler to expand the cultural purge 'so that a total of approximately sixteen thousand paintings, sculptures, drawings and prints by fourteen hundred artists were confiscated and shipped to Berlin to await final disposal...The plundering continued until 1938'.[52] Goebbels created a commission for the disposal of 'degenerate' art to evaluate the works and select the most valuable to be auctioned off on the international art market. While debate remains of the unsold works' ultimate fate, it seems likely that 4,829 'worthless' items held in a Berlin warehouse were destroyed in 'a secret bonfire' on 20 March 1939. The remaining confiscated works, over 8,000, remained in storage, hidden away.[53]

# The effects of Nazi policy in the arts

However, it was not only art that was destroyed, but also lives and careers of those artists now cast out of the 'national community'. Many artists left Germany while others opted for 'inner emigration', retreating from the public eye and the Nazis' attention as best they could. The banned artists faced isolation and economic distress. Kirchner grew so depressed by the Nazis' removal of his works from German museums and the defamation he suffered as a 'degenerate' artist that he committed suicide in 1938. Modernist artists were consistently suspected, spied upon and forced to hide any works in progress from Gestapo agents who searched homes and studios for wet brushes or other signs of activity. Nolde resorted to 'unpainted pictures', using watercolours that left no telltale smell behind.[54] Karl Hartung, a sculptor, described his existence as 'isolated as though one were living in a catacombs'. The once-famous painter Willi Baumeister bitterly recalled that while the dismissal from his teaching post was difficult, 'the social ostracism that followed was worse'. He no longer had a public. 'No one knew that I continued to paint, in a second-storey room in utter isolation.' He kept his studio locked, and not even his children knew of his work. When an SS general moved in next door and an SS captain was 'billeted in [his] own room', he stopped painting altogether.[55]

Art dealers also suffered. Perhaps in order to prevent sudden disruptions in the art market, Jewish dealers were 'initially permitted to join the Reich Chamber of Culture, and many did so in order to continue their business'. But in the wake of the Nuremberg Laws, Jews were denied Chamber membership and proscribed from owning auction houses. In 1938, particularly after the Night of Broken Glass, the 'Aryanisation' of the economy deeply affected any Jewish dealers who had managed to hold on to their businesses, as most were forced to sell out at bargain prices. Many Jewish art dealers emigrated, often resuming their businesses in cities such as London, Paris and New York.[56] Back in Germany, the private art market was 'virtually dead'.[57]

German dealers who had supported modernist art could continue their businesses, however, and some sought to use their position from within the 'national community' to aid banned artists through covert shows and sales. For example, Karl Nierendorf held exhibits in his home and used his New York gallery to exhibit artists who could no longer show their works in Germany. Günther Franke in Munich sold Nolde watercolours to trusted clients. The Nierendorf Gallery, a long-standing supporter of modernist art, even held an evening lecture on 'the "degenerate" sculptor Gerhard Marcks. The affair was crowded and a repeat performance was scheduled, but word got out and a second lecture had to be cancelled'.[58] Modernist art had thus not entirely disappeared in the Third Reich. As these examples suggest, some Germans managed to circumnavigate Nazi censorship to support reviled artists and incorporate banned art into their daily lives. However, there were dealers who willingly cooperated with the Nazi regime. For example, Karl Haberstock, Ferdinand Möller, Karl Buchholz, Bernhard Böhmer and Hildebrand Gurlitt were selected to sell modernist works confiscated from German museums to foreign buyers for hard currency or in exchange for traditional masterpieces. Although 'certain dealers sincerely believed that they were saving modern art by exporting it', Petropoulos convincingly argues that 'the overriding factor was undoubtedly profit'.[59]

While modernist artists lived as social and cultural pariahs, artists accepted by the regime had the opportunity to prosper. This was especially true of those whose works were shown at the Great German Art exhibitions, held annually from 1937 to 1944. As the only national art shows in the Third Reich, they had an enormous impact on artists' careers, and on the art market itself, because all of the works were for sale. Indeed, 'the vast majority of contemporary works of art sold in the Third Reich' was sold at the Great German Art exhibitions.[60] In her in-depth study, Ines Schlenker convincingly demonstrates just how the Nazis' official art show shaped the entire art market. Sales at the Great German Art shows became a kind of national seal of approval that artists readily exploited. They reserved their best works for submission to the national art shows, and then used any success there to demand higher prices in galleries and at other shows. Sales to leading Nazi officials became a mark of artistic excellence and a gateway to professional success.

Goebbels, Goering and many other Nazi leaders all purchased works, but Hitler's appetite for art was voracious. At the 1937 show, he spent over 200,000 Reichsmarks on an unknown number of works. In 1938, Hitler purchased 386 items for a total of 899,780 Reichsmarks; in 1942, he bought 117 works for the fantastic sum of 1,277,025 Reichsmarks. Prices at the Great German Art shows soared from an average of 1,187 Reichsmarks in 1937 to 3,524 Reichsmarks in 1943.[61] Hitler's consumption of art sparked an increase in art prices across the entire market. Favoured artists such as Hermann Gradl, Fritz Halberg-Krauss and Hans Urban, for example, commanded far higher prices in 1944 than just a few years before due to purchases by Hitler. Such sales also led to official commissions, awards and honours that enhanced artists' reputations further, which again increased both demand and prices.[62]

Schlenker has identified a core group of 197 artists who repeatedly exhibited at the Great German Art shows. These 'court artists' in particular profited handsomely as the chosen artists for the *Volk*.[63] The sculptors Arno Breker and Josef Thorak are two very good examples of artists who benefitted from their association with the Nazis. Breker earned more than 1 million Reichsmarks annually, enjoyed tax breaks and received large donations from Hitler for properties and studios. Hitler also paid for Thorak's enormous studio, and at the 1944 Great German Art Exhibition, he purchased a sculpture for 50,000 Reichsmarks which made it 'the most expensive item purchased that year by the dictator'.[64] Although many artists continued to struggle, these select few offered hope to the thousands of artists who exhibited at the Great German Art shows that they too might prosper.

The effects of cultural inclusion and exclusion thus came into sharp relief. Artists whose works were exhibited in the Degenerate Art show were cast out of the 'national community'. Marked as inferior outsiders, they saw their careers ruined and suffered acutely from social ostracism in their daily lives. However, artists included in the Great German Art exhibitions were embraced by the *Volksgemeinschaft*, to which they belonged. As the only national art venue in Nazi Germany, the Great German Art shows signalled an artist's acceptance by the regime and provided access to sales and professional prestige. German consumers of art in turn were assured that their purchases had official approval. Their participation – as buyers of art, visitors to the shows, workers in the preparation for the surrounding events and participants in the celebrations of German culture – enabled them to experience the 'national community' as a reality and as a promise fulfilled by Hitler himself. Although the pomp surrounding the Great German Art shows was more restrained after the war started, the exhibit continued to draw crowds every summer from 1937 to 1944. Degenerate Art toured the Third Reich from 1937 to 1941. Thus both exhibitions offered multiple occasions for Germans to participate in the cultural life of the nation and to consume National Socialism as members of the 'national community'.

However, on many levels the success of both the *Volksgemeinschaft* itself and its culture proved to be more imaginary than real. For example, the inflation of art prices defeated the Nazis' desire that average Germans could incorporate fine art into their daily lives by purchasing works. Visitors did continue to attend the Great German Art Exhibition in large numbers – well over 800,000 attended in 1942 – and they purchased art, too. The *Völkischer Beobachter* reported in 1937 that over 400 works had been sold, mostly to average consumers, and some works were in such demand that the artists made copies for sale.[65] However, as prices rose, average Germans were priced out of the art market. Feistel-Rohmeder complained in her 1942 review of the official show that artists were exploiting consumers, producing poor quality works that they sold for high prices 'right off the easel' in order to make a quick profit.[66] SD (*Sicherheitsdienst*) reports also noted the mounting prices and complaints: 'People with lower incomes complained bitterly that purchasing art had once again become a privilege of the "upper ten thousand" of German society.' SD reports also observed that the average German who did purchase art tended to buy landscapes and genre scenes rather than images that promoted distinctly National Socialist themes or the war effort.[67] The equality among members of the 'national community' remained unrealised when it came to art, as in so many other areas.

## Conclusion

In the end, the Nazis failed to spark the revolution in the arts that they had predicted with such confidence in 1933. Even Hitler remained dissatisfied with the overall quality of art produced during the Third Reich and shown at the Great German Art Exhibition. In his 1939 speech, he was still waiting for a creative genius who would create a new kind of heroic art infused with National Socialist fervour.[68] But the war meant that the young generation that was supposed to provide that genius became soldiers, not artists. By 1944, cultural events were increasingly rare, and by the war's end, Germany lay in ruins. What became known as Nazi culture was thoroughly discredited. Indeed, most of the Third Reich's artists remain completely unknown today, while the so-called 'degenerate' artists are celebrated as leading examples of German culture.

However, as long as the Third Reich existed, the arts did successfully shape the *Volksgemeinschaft*. They provided visual proof of the very essence of German identity and the new society that was being created. Above all, the arts offered a sense of cultural unity and consensus that created bonds of social solidarity. The arts were no longer reserved for elites; Hitler had returned them to the *Volk* and provided repeated opportunities for the masses to celebrate both their cultural heritage and the new achievements of the era. The arts served as a mirror in which the Germans could worship themselves as the heirs to a cultural heritage that affirmed their racial superiority.[69] Art did more than simply mobilise the masses or promote Nazi ideology. It reflected the core of the German racial awakening proclaimed by the Third Reich. As such, the arts demarcated the boundaries between Germans who belonged to the new 'national community' and those who did not. Art educated Germans about the necessity of racial identity. Germans were called to witness and participate in the nation's cultural life at the Great German Art Exhibition. As the Degenerate Art show toured the Reich, the public was also encouraged to experience the nation's cultural cleansing. Both shows served as mass events within which 'national comrades' came to recognise themselves as members of the *Volksgemeinschaft*. The Great German Art and Degenerate Art exhibitions provided unifying experiences that encouraged Germans to participate in the very processes that transformed an individual into either a member of the 'national community' or one of its enemies.

# Notes

1　P. Rave, *Kunstdiktatur im Dritten Reich* (Hamburg, 1949). See also H. Lehmann-Haupt, *Art under a Dictatorship* (New York, 1954); F. Roh, *'Entartete Kunst' – Kunstbarbarei im Dritten Reich* (Hannover, 1962); H. Brenner, *Die Kunstpolitik des Nationalsozialismus* (Reinbek bei Hamburg, 1963); J. Wulf (ed.), *Die bildenden Künste im Dritten Reich: Eine Dokumentation* (Reinbek bei Hamburg, 1966); O. Thomae, *Die Propaganda-Maschinerie: Bildende Kunst und Öffentlichkeitsarbeit in Dritten Reich* (Berlin, 1978); S. Barron (ed.), *'Degenerate Art': The Fate of the Avant-Garde in Nazi Germany* (New York, 1991).

2　B. Hinz, *Art in the Third Reich*, trans. R. and R. Kimber (New York, 1979), first published as *Die Malerei im Deutschen Faschismus: Kunst und Konterrevolution* (Munich, 1974). See also R. Müller-Mehlis, *Die Kunst im Dritten Reich* (Munich, 1976); R. Merker, *Die bildenden Künste im Nationalsozialismus: Kulturideologie, Kulturpolitik, Kulturproduktion* (Cologne, 1983); J. Clinefelter, *Artists for the Reich: Culture and Race from Weimar to Nazi Germany* (Oxford, 2005).

3　B. Taylor and W. van der Will (eds), *The Nazification of Art: Art Design, Music, Architecture, and Film in the Third Reich* (Winchester, 1990). Also important on the modernity issue is J. Herf, *Reactionary Modernism: Technology, Culture, and Politics in Weimar and the Third Reich* (Cambridge, 1984).

4　A. Steinweis, *Art, Ideology and Economics in Nazi Germany: The Reich Chambers of Music, Theater, and the Visual Arts* (Chapel Hill, NC, 1993); J. Petropoulos, *Art as Politics in the Third Reich* (Chapel Hill, NC, 1996); J. Petropoulos, *The Faustian Bargain: The Art World in Nazi Germany* (New York, 2000).

5　M. Wildt, *Hitler's Volksgemeinschaft and the Dynamics of Racial Exclusion: Violence Against Jews in Provincial Germany, 1919–1939,* trans. B. Heise (New York, 2012); M. Wildt, 'Die Ungleichheit des Volkes: "Volksgemeinschaft" in der politischen Kommunikation der Weimarer Republik', in F. Bajohr and M. Wildt (eds), *Volksgemeinschaft: Neue Forschungen zur Gesellschaft des Nationalsozialismus* (Frankfurt am Main, 2009), pp. 24–40; N. Frei, 'People's Community and War: Hitler's Popular Support', in H. Mommsen (ed.), *The Third Reich between Vision and Reality: New Perspectives on German History 1918–1945* (Oxford, 2001), pp. 59–77.

6    Frei, 'People's Community and War', p. 64.

7    D. Peukert, *Volksgenossen und Gemeinschaftsfremde: Anpassung, Ausmerze und Aufbegehren unter dem Nationalsozialismus* (Cologne, 1982), p. 295, cited in Wildt, *Hitler's Volksgemeinschaft*, p. 3.

8    P. Paret, *An Artist against the Third Reich: Ernst Barlach, 1933–1938* (Cambridge, 2003), p. 6.

9    Ibid.

10   A. Steinweis, 'Weimar Culture and the Rise of National Socialism: The *Kampfbund für deutsche Kultur*', *Central European History* 24 (1991), pp. 402–423.

11   Clinefelter, *Artists for the Reich*.

12   Steinweis, 'Weimar Culture and the Rise of National Socialism'; D. Dennis, *Inhumanities: Nazi Interpretations of Western Culture* (Cambridge, 2012).

13   Petropoulos, *The Faustian Bargain*, p. 217.

14   A. Steinweis, 'Cultural Eugenics: Social Policy, Economic Reform, and the Purge of Jews from German Cultural Life', in G. Cuomo (ed.), *National Socialist Cultural Policy* (New York, 1995), p. 23.

15   Ibid., p. 24.

16   Petropoulos, *Art as Politics in the Third Reich*, pp. 28, 95.

17   The rivalry between Goebbels and Rosenberg has been treated extensively. For a good overview, see ibid., ch 1, and Paret, *An Artist against the Third Reich*, pp. 51–76.

18   Petropoulos, *Art as Politics in the Third Reich*, p. 24; see also H. Brenner, 'Die Kunst im politischen Machtkampf, 1933-1934', *Vierteljahrshefte für Zeitgeschichte* 10 (1962), pp. 17–42; B. Werner, 'Der grosse Pendelschlag: Zur Frage "Was ist deutsche Kunst?"', *Die Kunst für Alle* 49 (1933), pp. 12–15; U. Christoffel, 'Wo stehen wir heute in der Kunst?', *Die Kunst für Alle* 49 (1934), pp. 229–238.

19   'Was die Deutschen Künstler von der neuen Regierung erwarten!', *Deutscher Kunstbericht*, March 1933, reproduced in B. Feistel-Rohmeder, *Im Terror des Kunstbolschewismus: Urkundensammlung des 'Deutschen Kunstberichtes' aus den Jahren 1927–1933* (Karlsruhe, 1938), pp. 181–182.

20   For example, 'Schreckenskammer', *Kölnische Illustrierte Zeitung*, 17 August 1937.

21   C. Zuschlag, 'An "Educational Exhibition": The Precursors of *Entartete Kunst* and Its Individual Venues', in Barron (ed.), '*Degenerate Art*', pp. 83–103, and Zuschlag's Table 1: Exhibitions of 'Degenerate' Art Preceding the 1937 'Entartete Kunst' Exhibition in Munich, in ibid., pp. 98–101.

22  The quote is from the *Kölnische Illustrierte Zeitung*, 17 August 1935, cited in Zuschlag, 'An "Educational Exhibition"', p. 85. The Dresden details are from Zuschlag's Table 1, pp. 100–101.

23  I. Schlenker, *Hitler's Salon: The Grosse Deutsche Kunstausstellung at the Haus der Deutschen Kunst in Munich 1937–1944* (Bern, 2007), pp. 76, 78.

24  S. Barron, '1937: Modern Art and Politics in Prewar Germany', in Barron (ed.), *'Degenerate Art'*, p. 19.

25  'Hitler's Speech Dedicating the House of German Art', in B. Sax and D. Kuntz (eds), *Inside Hitler's Germany: A Documentary History of Life in the Third Reich* (Lexington, 1992), p. 231.

26  Both quotes from ibid., pp. 231, 232.

27  Ibid., p. 230.

28  Ibid.

29  Hinz, *Art in the Third Reich*, p. 17; see also Brenner, *Die Kunstpolitik des Nationalsozialismus*, pp. 112–113.

30  Schlenker, *Hitler's Salon*, p. 80.

31  P. Guenther, 'Three Days in Munich, July 1937', in Barron (ed.), *'Degenerate Art'*, p. 34.

32  Ibid., p. 35. Positive memories of the 1939 exhibit and its surrounding celebrations are remembered by Germans in the film *Good Morning, Mr. Hitler* (dir. L. Holland and P. Yule; Chicago, IL: International Historic Films, 1994); see also R. Wistrich, *Weekend in Munich: Art, Propaganda and Terror in the Third Reich* (London, 1995), pp. 92–96.

33  Cited in Schlenker, *Hitler's Salon*, p. 145.

34  Schlenker, *Hitler's Salon*, p. 64.

35  Ibid., p. 71.

36  Guenther, 'Three Days in Munich', p. 34; Wistrich, *Weekend in Munich*, pp. 68–69.

37  Schlenker, *Hitler's Salon*, p. 67, and see her full description, pp. 65–71.

38  *Völkischer Beobachter*, 19 July 1937, reproduced in Hinz, *Art in the Third Reich*, p. 2.

39  Schlenker, *Hitler's Salon*, p. 69; Hinz, *Art in the Third Reich*, p. 5.

40  Adolf Ziegler, speech from the opening of the Degenerate Art exhibition, 19 July 1937, cited M. von Lüttichau, *'Entartete Kunst*, Munich 1937: A Reconstruction', in Barron (ed.), *'Degenerate Art'*, p. 45.

41  'The Works of Art in *Entartete Kunst*, Munich 1937', in Barron (ed.), *'Degenerate Art'*, pp. 193–355.

42  The overview is from von Lüttichau, *'Entartete Kunst*, Munich 1937', pp. 45–46; the quote is from p. 45; the prices are from his note 8, p. 81. His reconstruction of the exhibition is the most detailed to date. Also useful is Hinz, *Art in the Third Reich*, pp. 23–44, and Rave, *Kunstdiktatur in Dritten Reich*, pp. 145–146.

43  Text from placard, reproduced in von Lüttichau, *'Entartete Kunst*, Munich 1937', p. 51.

44 Von Lüttichau, 'Entartete Kunst, Munich 1937', p. 54.

45 Ibid.

46 Brenner, Die Kunstpolitik des Nationalsozialismus, p. 109; 'Augenzeugenbericht zur Ausstellung "Entartete Kunst", 1937', in Deutschlandberichte der Sozialdemokratichen Partei Deutschlands (Sopade), vierte Jahrgang (1937) (Salzhausen/Frankfurt am Main, 1989), p. 1534.

47 Zuschlag, 'An "Educational Exhibition"', p. 89.

48 See ibid., pp. 90–95, and his Table 2: Venues of the 'Entartete Kunst' Exhibition, 1937–1941, pp. 102–103.

49 'Augenzeugenbericht zur Ausstellung "Entartete Kunst", 1937', pp. 1534–1535.

50 Guenther, 'Three Days in Munich', p. 38.

51 Ibid., p. 43.

52 Barron, '1937', p. 19.

53 Petropoulos, Art as Politics in the Third Reich, p. 82, and note 50, p. 338; see also his ch 3.

54 E. Nolde and W. Haftmann, Emil Nolde: Unpainted Pictures, revised edition (New York, 1972).

55 All quotes are from Lehmann-Haupt, Art under a Dictatorship, pp. 84–87. For more on exiled artists see J. Jackman and C. Borden (eds), The Muses Flee Hitler: Cultural Transfer and Adaptation, 1930–1945 (Washington, DC, 1983); J. Hermand, Culture in Dark Times: Nazi Fascism, Inner Emigration, and Exile (New York, 2013).

56 Petropoulos, The Faustian Bargain, pp. 65–67; the quote is on p. 65.

57 O. Tolischus, 'Nine Muses Regimented to Serve Nazi Kultur', New York Times, 22 August 1937, p. SM4.

58 Lehmann-Haupt, Art under a Dictatorship, pp. 84–85.

59 Petropoulos, The Faustian Bargain, p. 68.

60 Schlenker, Hitler's Salon, p. 193.

61 Ibid., pp. 199–201.

62 Ibid., pp. 199–200, 206–208.

63 Ibid., pp. 206–220.

64 Ibid., p. 209. The quote is from Petropoulos, The Faustian Bargain, p. 266; see also his discussion of both Breker and Thorak, pp. 223–239.

65 Schlenker, Hitler's Salon, p. 195.

66 Feistel-Rohmeder, 'München 1942', Das Bild, July/August 1942, p. 117; see also Steinweis, Art, Ideology and Economics in Nazi Germany, pp. 150–151.

67 Chef der Sicherheitspolizei und des SD, Amt III, Berlin, Meldungen aus dem Reich, 15 February 1943, Bundesarchiv Berlin, R58/180-2, Nr. 359, frames 9–11; Chef der Sicherheitspolizei und des SD, Amt III, Berlin, Meldungen aus dem Reich, 22 February 1943, Nr. 361, frames 67–72; Schlenker, Hitler's Salon, pp. 195–197; Steinweis, Art, Ideology and Economics in Nazi Germany, p. 151.

68  Brenner, *Die Kunstpolitik des Nationalsozialismus*, pp. 116–118; 'Die Rede des Führers zur Eröffnung der "Grossen Deutschen Kunstausstellung 1939" im Haus der Deutschen Kunst in München', *Die Kunst im Dritten Reich*, August 1939, pp. 347–381; see also Schlenker, *Hitler's Salon*, pp. 123–127.

69  E. Michaud, *The Cult of Art in Nazi Germany*, trans. J. Lloyd (Stanford, 2004), p. 29.

# Select bibliography

Barron, S. (ed.), '*Degenerate Art': The Fate of the Avant-Garde in Nazi Germany* (New York, 1991).

Brenner, H., *Die Kunstpolitik des Nationalsozialismus* (Reinbek bei Hamburg, 1963).

Clinefelter, J., *Artists for the Reich: Culture and Race from Weimar to Nazi Germany* (Oxford, 2005).

Hinz, B., *Art in the Third Reich*. Trans. Robert and R. Kimber (New York, 1979).

Lehmann-Haupt, H., *Art under a Dictatorship* (New York, 1954).

Petropoulos, J., *Art as Politics in the Third Reich* (Chapel Hill, NC, 1996).

Petropoulos, J., *The Faustian Bargain: The Art World in Nazi Germany* (New York, 2000).

Rave, P., *Kunstdiktatur im Dritten Reich* (Hamburg, 1949).

Schlenker, I., *Hitler's Salon: The Grosse Deutsche Kunstausstellung at the Haus der Deutschen Kunst in Munich 1937–1944* (Bern, 2007).

Steinweis, A., *Art, Ideology and Economics in Nazi Germany: The Reich Chambers of Music, Theater, and the Visual Arts* (Chapel Hill, NC, 1993).

# PART THREE

# Religion

# 8

# Protestantism in Nazi Germany: A View from the Margins

## *Christopher J. Probst*

In a work titled *Kirche und Volkstum* (Church and Nationality, 1928), the moderate and affable Protestant theologian Paul Althaus brooded over '[t]he foreign invasion of our literature, the theatre, the arts, fashion and parties, the [political] party system...the surrender to *Volk*-less financial powers [which] agonisingly came to consciousness'.[1] In a three-volume work published between *Kristallnacht* and the start of the Second World War titled *Luther und die Juden* (Luther and the Jews), the lesser-known professor of Protestant religious studies and Nazi sympathiser Theodor Pauls bellowed, 'God's judgement is spoken about Judaism .... [The church has to] avoid any Judaising in doctrine and church tradition'.[2] Shortly after the end of the war, Heidelberg pastor Hermann Maas, who was an outspoken member of the Confessing Church during the Third Reich, lamented to the Rabbi of Frankfurt:

> How terrible is the burden of guilt that weighs so heavily on the conscience of the non-Jewish German people – strictly speaking, on every single individual and also on myself. We share in the guilt, even if we have sincerely loved Israel and have fought against those evil forces, as I have tried .... I cannot expiate this guilt only before God .... I must

also atone to you, the faithful protector and spokesman of the Jewish community in Germany.[3]

Research on the German Protestant Church in Nazi Germany has demonstrated that, where care and concern for their fellow Jewish citizens was concerned, Hermann Maas represents the attitudes of a miniscule proportion of his Protestant cohort. Many, perhaps most, German Protestant ministers and theologians had decidedly deprecating views of Jews and Judaism. Furthermore, most were deeply nationalistic. Even so, these three comments demonstrate that a range of views existed regarding church, state, race and *Volk*.

Protestants represented a significant demographic during the Third Reich, making up approximately 60 per cent of the German population. Their ministerial rolls numbered some 18,000. This chapter seeks to answer a number of questions about German Protestant experiences and views during Hitler's Third Reich. What tack did Protestant pastors and theologians take towards the Nazi regime? How did the pressures and strictures of living in the Nazi state help to fracture the Protestant church into competing factions with distinct views on myriad issues? How did Protestant clergy and theologians confront the so-called 'Jewish Question'?

In the process of finding answers to these questions, a deeper understanding of the social and cultural life of a significant segment of the German population living under the Nazi regime will be gained. While a very small number of Protestants actively resisted the efforts of the Nazi regime to 'coordinate' their church, most supported the state – some did so wholeheartedly, while others did so with reservations. Even prior to the Nazi rise to power, antisemitism and anti-Judaism permeated the German Protestant scene. In this respect, Protestants needed little incentive to support at least certain aspects of Nazi anti-Jewish policy. This chapter will illuminate these important facets of life in Nazi Germany.

The views of pastors and theologians will be in focus here. It is assumed by many historians, and argued by some, that laity generally supported most of the positions taken by their pastors in the *Kirchenkampf* (Church Struggle). Manfred Gailus argued that what pastors had to say in this regard often had a 'decisive influence' on their congregants' points of view. Yet, much more research is needed to demonstrate conclusively the views of the average person in the pews of German Protestant churches.[4] In the second part of the chapter, the outlooks on Jews and Judaism of two figures from opposite ends of the Protestant ideological spectrum will be examined. But first, a broader survey of the German Protestant scene will serve to address the cultural and ideational context in which these individuals expressed themselves (Figure 8.1).

FIGURE 8.1 *Street scene outside the Potsdamer Garnisonkirche (WL14389).*
*Courtesy of the Wiener Library, London.*

# The German Protestant Church during the Third Reich

During the Third Reich, Protestants generally fell into three groups: the *Bekennende Kirche* (Confessing Church), the *Deutschen Christen* (German Christians) and those who chose not to affiliate with either of these groups, which will be called here the Protestant 'middle'.[5] This unaffiliated 'middle' grouping is often referred to as 'neutrals' in the literature on German Protestantism during the Third Reich. While they generally chose neutrality in their church politics, their theological ideas often could resemble those in either the Confessing Church or the German Christian wings of the German Protestant Church. Thus, the terms middle and unaffiliated, rather than neutral, will be used here.[6]

The German Christians espoused both ardent German nationalism and vituperative antisemitic sentiment. Far from being a marginal German Protestant group, as argued by some, they in fact were quite influential. The German Christians had the backing of the Nazis in the 1933 church elections for representatives to local church councils of the German Protestant Church (*Deutsche Evangelische Kirche*), which is one reason why they won a resounding victory.[7] The German Christians remained generally enthusiastic backers of the Nazi regime, but this support increasingly went unrequited.[8] Though they comprised only a small minority of German Protestants (representing a mere 2 per cent of the Protestant population), the German Christians made their influence fully felt throughout Germany.[9] At arguably their weakest point, there were 600,000 in their ranks. In 1937, they held twelve of the seventeen deanships in Protestant theology in German universities, along with more than a third of the total number of posts in the theology faculties.[10]

By contrast, members of the Confessing Church exhibited varying degrees of opposition to Nazi encroachment on church sovereignty, but only scattered opposition to measures against Jews. Almost from the outset of Nazi rule, the Confessing Church opposed Nazi attempts to form a 'Reich Church' based on a nebulous and variously defined 'positive Christianity'. Point twenty-four of the Nazi party programme called for a 'positive Christianity' that crossed confessional boundaries, as long as it did not 'endanger' the state or 'conflict with the customs and moral sentiments of the Germanic race'.[11] The key issue for many in the Confessing Church was not the antisemitism of the Nazis, but the efforts on their part to control the churches, something that could not be countenanced by a church grounded in scriptural and confessional unity. The language of the Barmen Declaration of 1934, the founding document and clarion call of the movement, makes this point abundantly clear.[12] While it opposed emphatically both the German Christians and so-called 'Aryan' Christianity, the increasingly precarious predicament of German Jews did not appear in the declaration, foreshadowing the reality that many in the Confessing Church would show themselves to be either apathetic to their plight or antisemitic themselves.[13]

Clashes between the Confessing Church and the German Christians generally centred on theological and church-political concerns. This *Kirchenkampf*, as it came to be called, was very real for its participants, particularly as it concerned the theological ideas at stake. Yet, these divisions often masked an underlying consensus on what to do with or about the German Jewish community.

The majority of Protestants attempted to stay neutral in the *Kirchenkampf* – that is, they chose not to affiliate formally with either the German Christian or Confessing Church wings – but most held views of the *Volk* (people) as an 'order of creation'. Systematic theologian, Paul Althaus, of Erlangen University, was one of the most influential figures of the unaffiliated Protestant middle and was the leading proponent of a theology shaped by *Schöpfungsordnungen* (orders of creation). Althaus defined the orders (*Ordnungen*) as the (God-given) 'forms of human beings living together, which are essential conditions of the historical life of mankind'. They included family, governmental authorities and – crucially during the latter years of the Weimar Republic and the Third Reich – the *Volk*.[14] Thus, the German *Volk* effectively gained a semi-divine status.

The doctrine of the orders of creation represented one side of the coin of Protestant sentiment in Nazi Germany, while more direct antisemitic views and pronouncements represented the other. This doctrine was married to an all-too-prevalent German nationalism. Steeped in the bitterness felt by many Germans towards the harsh terms inflicted upon the fatherland by the Treaty of Versailles and the perceived malaise of the Weimar era, this theological outlook provided fertile ground for both latent and overt antisemitism.[15]

As there has been much discussion about the definition of the terms anti-Judaism and antisemitism among historians and others, a word about terminology is in order. The term anti-Judaism will be used here to refer to hostility towards Jews that is expressed in nonrational, or symbolic, language, the kind of language found in art and affirmations of belief. The term 'antisemitism' will be used to refer to animosity against Jews that is expressed in irrational language, language that is in conflict with rational empirical observation. Readers need not regard the nonrational/irrational distinction as critical to the argument of this chapter to comprehend the historical phenomenon of hatred of Jews described here.[16]

The German Protestant legend of the *Kirchenkampf* as a valiant fight against Nazism, which was propagated after the war mainly by pastors and theologians bent on painting their actions and that of their churches in the most sympathetic light, has been demythologised. Many of the churches in fact cooperated with Hitler, in effect (and in many cases in actuality) promulgating Nazi ideology, including antisemitism.[17] Pro-Nazi and anti-Jewish sentiment within the German Protestant Church during the Third Reich was abetted by an anti-democratic outlook and theological reappraisal spurred on by a decade-old Luther Renaissance, as well as by the now ready availability of a variety of editions of Martin Luther's works.[18] A sizeable, vocal minority avidly and openly supported the Nazis in their nefarious goals concerning the 'Jewish Question'.

It must also be recognised that overt resistance to Nazism and covert assistance for Jews living under Nazi oppression and the threat of murder did exist in small corners of the German Protestant scene. The *Büro Grüber* (Grüber Office), based in Berlin, provided Jews (including Jews who converted to Christianity) who were under grave threat in the Third Reich with advice about emigration, finding employment abroad, social assistance, legal matters and educational support.[19] In Württemberg (in southwest Germany), a group of pastors and parishioners sheltered at least seventeen Jewish refugees in sixty church parsonages in a so-called 'Rectory Chain'.[20]

On 7 April 1933, the Nazi regime introduced its first wave of sweeping repressive legislation, beginning with the Law for the Restoration of the Professional Civil Service. Paragraph 3 (which came to be known as the 'Aryan' Paragraph), coupled with subsequently enacted decrees, effectively excluded Jews from employment as civil servants.[21] The introduction of the 'Aryan' Paragraph into the German Protestant Church in September 1933 may be regarded as a seminal event in the *Kirchenkampf*. Subsequently reintroduced and repealed several times, it became a flashpoint for divisions among German Protestants and led eventually to the formation of the Confessing Church. Again, it was primarily the issue of church autonomy, theologically considered, that coloured the debates about the 'Aryan' Paragraph, rather than the rights of 'Jewish Christian' pastors (those who had converted from Judaism to Christianity), who constituted a miniscule percentage of the German Protestant clergy.[22]

## *Heimat* and the orders of creation

Protestants did not, of course, live their lives in a vacuum. Regional ties and modes of thinking were especially important to Germans living in the first half of the twentieth century. The malleable and untranslatable German term *Heimat* (home, homeland) conveys the sense of how, collectively, Germans living in provinces across the nation felt about their home, their land and their people. The concept developed after the unification of Germany in 1871 (and especially from the 1880s to the early 1900s). Alon Confino argues that, while *Heimat* was promulgated primarily by members of the middle and upper classes through books, school curricula and museums, it was an idea that cut across social, economic, political and religious lines. As its symbols and expressions could change from one epoch to the next, the concept was supple. Yet its characteristic elements – history, nature and folklore – remained constant. It is important for our understanding of how the individuals described in this chapter saw themselves, not only as Christians but also as Germans. Celia Applegate rightly contends that, while educated twenty-first-century cosmopolitans might associate *Heimat* with a narrow-minded 'provincialism', it did not clash so dramatically with nationalism. In a sense, it defined the kind of nation Germany was, or at least the kind of nation that Germans aspired for it to be.[23]

This sense of *Heimat* suited quite nicely the doctrine of the orders of creation. This is not to suggest that Althaus consciously patterned this doctrine after *Heimat*; rather, that the elevation of the *Volk* to such a high plane that was so prominent in his thinking would have resonated very closely with the concept of *Heimat*. The elevation of the *Volk* to semi-divine status in Althaus's theology served a crucial role in justifying antisemitic attitudes among Protestants in Nazi Germany.

Despite the fact that German Protestant clergy and theologians generally utilised the technical language of theology, rather than everyday speech, to describe their views on church, state, nation and *Volk*, still they inhabited the same world as did their fellow countrymen. Certainly, they studied theology in the hallowed halls of respected universities such as Tübingen and Erlangen and devoted their Sundays to teaching and preaching about God in church. But they also frequented the same shops, read the same newspapers, listened to the same radio broadcasts and breathed the same air. Their home province was their *Heimat* as much as it was their neighbours'. Their cultural sensibilities were, in varying degrees, shaped by the same outside influences.

Thus, it was not only nationalism and racism that fed the anti-Judaic and antisemitic pronouncements of German Protestants, but it was also the cultural expressions of *Heimat* – its history, nature and folklore – which they believed German Jews did not or could not imbibe. This notion of *Heimat* pointedly did not include Jews or Judaism. For many German Protestant pastors and theologians, as for the Nazis, expressions of anti-Judaism and antisemitism were expressions of a desire for a new Germany, a 'world without Jews'.[24]

The broader context in which the Protestant church operated from 1933 to 1945 included, of course, the ascent to power of Hitler and the Nazis, the ruthless consolidation of their power in the early years of the Third Reich (including their brutal oppression of Jews, Communists, gays and lesbians, Roma and Sinti, Jehovah's Witnesses, Afro-Germans, and the physically and mentally handicapped), Hitler's aggressive moves in the arena of foreign policy between 1936 and 1939, the Second World War and the Holocaust. These were heady and frightening times for Germans and Europeans (especially Jews, Roma and Sinti, who were singled out for genocide). How did German Protestants regard their Jewish neighbours – and, for many, only 'Jews' who existed as 'others' or chimeras in their minds – during such times?

Most German Protestant pastors and theologians demonstrated consistently anti-Judaic and antisemitic attitudes during the Third Reich. These perspectives were expressions – whether couched in racial, religious, economic or political terms – of a deeper and broader cultural sensibility in which Jews were regarded as obstacles to a new German civilisation devoid of any Jewish taint. While a small number of German Protestants spoke out publicly on behalf of Jews, others demonstrated a perplexing mix of antisemitism and love of neighbour while rescuing Jews in the face of great peril to themselves and their families.[25] Antisemitic and anti-Judaic views that already prevailed among German Protestants during the Weimar era were abetted by the thoroughly 'coordinated' racial state erected by Hitler and the Nazi regime.

Having established the societal and ecclesiastical contexts in which German Protestants operated during the Third Reich, the next sections of this chapter will examine the attitudes of two German Protestants towards Jews and Judaism (and, in this context, towards church, state, nation and *Volk*). The first, Theodor Pauls, worked on the margins of Protestant theology for much of his career, first as a secondary school teacher and administrator and later as a professor of religious studies at a college for teacher education. Despite his otherwise low profile on the Protestant scene, Pauls gained a measure of notoriety during the Nazi era for his publication of a three-volume selection of German Protestant reformer Martin Luther's works about Jews and Judaism. The second figure, Hermann Maas, was a pastor in Heidelberg whose affinity for Jews and Judaism led him to risk his safety by helping endangered Jews to emigrate. Pauls was sympathetic to the German Christian cause; his evaluation of Jews and Judaism was baldly antisemitic. Maas exhibited generally philosemitic views while being actively involved in the Confessing Church. Thus, these two individuals come from opposite poles of the German Protestant scene. In this sense, they are not 'representative' of German Protestants' views of Jews and Judaism during the Third Reich. Though most Protestants held views that resembled and were influenced by those of Althaus and Tübingen Professor of New Testament Gerhard Kittel,[26] some reached for less sophisticated approaches, which they found in the works of Pauls and Jena Professor of Practical Theology Wolf Meyer-Erlach,[27] while others (a tiny minority) embraced the more humane and sometimes philosemitic works of Dietrich Bonhoeffer and the lesser-known Maas. The disparate outlooks of Pauls and Maas demonstrate that, while the overwhelming majority of Protestants were nationalistic, *völkisch* and often antisemitic, a wide range of views existed on the margins of the German Protestant Church about the roles of church, state, nation and *Volk*.

# Hirschberg professor of Protestant religious studies Theodor Pauls

The son of a Lutheran pastor, Theodor Pauls was born in 1885 in Großefehn (in northern Germany, east of Emden). His university studies included philosophy, Protestant theology, geography and history at Halle-Wittenberg, Heidelberg, Göttingen and Berlin. He received his PhD at Berlin in 1908; his dissertation dealt with the regional history of East Frisia during medieval times. Shortly thereafter, he became certified to teach history, geography, and Protestant religion at the secondary school level. In 1912, he became the head teacher at a secondary school in Wilhelmshaven. After serving as a reserve lieutenant during the First World War, he returned to his teaching post at Wilhelmshaven. Then, from 1921 to 1929, he taught at a Pietist secondary school in Halle on the Saale. He then became a professor of religious studies at a pedagogical academy in Erfurt until it closed in 1932. At this point, he became Director of Studies and Head of a secondary school in Senftenberg, where he remained until 1938, when he became professor of Protestant religious doctrine and methodology at the College for Teacher Education in Hirschberg-Riesengebirge (Lower Silesia; present-day Jelenia Góra, Poland).[28]

Pauls was a signatory of the Godesberg Declaration of 26 March 1939. The declaration described Christianity as the 'unbridgeable religious contradiction to Judaism' and called for the 'establishment of an institute for research and removal of the Jewish influence on the church life of the German people'.[29] The antisemitic and purportedly academic Institute for Research into and Elimination of Jewish Influence in German Church Life, which was dominated by members of the German Christians and commonly called the 'Eisenach Institute', was founded shortly thereafter.[30] Pauls had a running engagement with Protestant theology via the German Christians, most notably by his publication of a three-volume work titled *Luther und die Juden* (Luther and the Jews), which was part of a long series of ostensibly scholarly works about positive Christianity. He also co-authored a volume on the 'de-Judaising' of Luther research with Dr Werner Petersmann, a Breslau pastor and regional chairman of the German Christians in Silesia.[31] Pauls offered *Luther und die Juden* as a 'gift' to the Eisenach Institute. In these volumes, Pauls weaved together Martin Luther's two-kingdoms doctrine[32] with ardent nationalism and antisemitism, lifting the most incendiary passages from Luther's anti-Judaic and antisemitic works and infusing them with Nazi racial conceptions.

The book appeared on a short list of texts recommended by Dr Friedrich Werner, director of the main office of the German Protestant Church in Berlin, in an April 1939 memorandum to the leaders of all the regional Protestant churches. At the suggestion of the Reich Minister for Church Affairs, Hanns Kerrl, Werner asked these church authorities to 'motivate the ministers' in their area of supervision 'in an appropriate way to an engagement with the position of Luther on the Jews'.[33] Pauls's interaction with the Eisenach Institute was not limited solely to publications. In June 1942, he held the closing lecture of the annual meeting of Institute collaborators. The lecture was titled 'Die Ursprünglichkeit des Gotteslobes bei Luther' (The Indigenousness of the Praise of God in Luther). The Institute's reviewer noted that Pauls's lecture showed the importance of recognising not only a 'possible Jewish influence over Pauline theology', but also the 'clear view of the German Luther in contrast to the ways of thinking of Paul'.[34]

In a 1941 *Völkischer Beobachter* article titled 'Jews Falsify Luther', a 'Schmidt-Clausing' (probably Fritz Schmidt-Clausing, at that time a doctoral student of Meyer-Erlach at Jena)[35] complained that until 1933 the German *Volk* had heard nothing of the reformer's position towards the Jews. Even

Protestant theology students were kept in the dark about Luther's 'great *Judenschriften* [writings about Jews and Judaism]'. Pauls, however, in his three-volume work, supposedly showed that Luther was the first to destroy the 'delusion of [the Jews as] the "chosen *Volk*"'.[36]

Volume 1 is subtitled *In the Dawn of the Reformation, 1513–1524*. Here Pauls put forth his most fundamental argument – that Luther's position towards the Jews was singularly negative, or at least sceptical. *That Jesus Christ was Born a Jew* (1523) 'is no mission sermon for Jews'. Pauls made this claim despite the fact that one of Luther's two stated goals in writing the treatise was that he 'might perhaps also win some Jews to the Christian faith'.[37] According to Pauls, the work instead served Luther's 'self-defence and the pastoral care of his own church'.[38] Cutting against the grain of the Luther scholarship of his day, Pauls contended that the reformer's approach to Judaism was consistently 'severe'. Yet, he complained that, despite Luther's 'German understanding of Christ', the 1523 treatise offered no treatment of the 'question of the Aryan Christ'.[39] Despite the pretence of scholarship, Pauls did not even engage the second stated goal of Luther's writing – his affirmation of the virgin birth of Jesus to parents of Jewish descent.[40]

Affirming Luther's *Zwei-Reiche-Lehre* (two-kingdoms doctrine), Pauls argued that the reformer's distinction between 'worldly' and 'spiritual' governance was '*unjüdisch und unalttestamentlich*' ('un-Jewish and un-Old Testament'). Luther taught the existence of two kingdoms, one spiritual and the other temporal.[41] In this schema, ordinary Christian citizens were expected to obey authority. Yet, it is doubtful that Luther encouraged the radical quiescence that has been assumed by many historians.[42] In any case, most German Protestants believed that they were commanded by God to obey the Nazi authorities despite the nefarious nature of the regime.[43]

Pauls regarded Jews as being under God's judgement. Yet, in his mind, they were also an imminent threat to the church. Thus, the church should 'fashion its own life under the omnipresent Lord' in a *German* way and 'avoid any Judaising (*Verjudung*) in doctrine and church tradition'.[44] Pauls managed to paint a singularly negative portrait of Luther's view of Jews and Judaism even in the reformer's least combative, and arguably philosemitic, phase. At the same time, here as elsewhere he stressed Luther's Germanness.

The dates in the subtitle of the second volume, *The Struggle, 1524–1526*, are misleading as the volume actually includes summaries and sparse analysis of Luther's later writings about Jews and Judaism, including *Von den Juden und ihren Lügen* (On the Jews and Their Lies, 1543) and *Vom Schem Hamphoras und vom Geschlecht Christi* (On the Ineffable Name and on the Lineage of Christ, 1543). In a brief discussion of *Wider die Sabbather* (Against the Sabbatarians, 1538), Pauls reiterated a point made in the first volume, that Luther did not express hope for conversion of Jews. Luther supposedly left the question open, but did not really expect it to happen.[45]

In *On the Jews and Their Lies*, the 'storm' was now appointed against the 'total front of Judaism'; it represented a return to 'old realisations and decisions' about them – including the 'Jewish world danger' and their usury. Here, Pauls mingled typical Nazi language ('storm' and 'total front') with an affirmation of medieval antisemitism. He concluded with a summary of the contents of the polemical works of 1543 and a brief recounting of Luther's retrospective view of his fight against the Jews.[46] Here as elsewhere, Pauls's account is hardly objective.

The approach of the third volume, subtitled *From Luther's Polemics Against the Jews*, was really quite simple. It was a topical compendium of quotes about the 'Jewish Question', all taken from Luther's *Judenschriften* from 1538 to 1543. Each long quote or series of quotes received a heading from Pauls. The language of the headings is quite revealing. The works covered are *Against the Sabbatarians, On the Jews and Their Lies, On the Ineffable Name and on the Lineage of Christ, Von den letzten Worten Davids* (On the Last Words of David, 1543) and *Vermahnung wider die Juden* (Admonition against the Jews, 1546). Theological themes drawn from Luther appear in Pauls's subheadings. The Jews falsely boast in the Law, the Temple and circumcision. They reject the Messiah, who has already come. The Messiah that the Jews expect is of a 'different nature' (*wesensverschieden*) from Christ. They boast of being of 'Abraham's seed'. Such argumentation is clearly representative of Luther's views.

Yet Pauls included emphases and inflammatory Nazi language that either did not fit with Luther's intentions or were an exaggeration of the same; that is, they were meant to serve Pauls's purposes rather than Luther's. In the first section of his outline of *On the Jews and Their Lies*, titled 'On the False Glory and Pride of the Jews', Pauls dealt with the issue of 'blood'. He called the Jews' reliance upon blood Luther's 'most distinguished and strongest argument'.[47] While there is no question that Luther decried what he saw as Jewish dependence upon their pedigree, it is debatable whether this argument was for Luther his 'strongest' or 'most distinguished'. Furthermore, the term 'blood' had racial overtones for Pauls, which for Luther it clearly did not carry. The typical Nazi conception of blood emphasised the superiority of 'Aryan' blood over non-'Aryan' and especially Jewish blood.[48] Pauls endorsed this conception of Jewish blood elsewhere when he referred to the Jews' 'unnatural bloodstream'.[49] When Luther spoke of 'blood', he was decrying what he perceived as Jewish reliance upon their lineage for their chosen-ness. This is obvious from the context of many of the quotes which Pauls included, beginning with the very first one, which is taken from the Gospel of Matthew.

The Jews, according to Luther, gloat in the fact that they were born 'of the highest people on earth, from Abraham, Sarah, Isaac, Rebecca, Jacob, and the Twelve Patriarchs'.[50] It is not the racial purity of their blood with which he was concerned, but their supposed appeal to their nobility. Luther declared here that Jews rely upon such nobility to their detriment. Soon after, Luther appealed to Jesus' contention that God can 'raise up children of Abraham from these stones', a view that countered his Jewish opponents' assertion that they are of 'Abraham's seed'. Luther's message was not about 'blood' in the racial-biological sense embraced by Pauls; instead, Luther was highlighting Jesus' claim that the 'children of Abraham' are those who believe his message and do not rely on their lineage for salvation.[51] Despite the confrontational language, there is no hint of a racialised, Nazi conception of blood here. Where Luther spoke of the priority of being circumcised over and above the nobility of birth, Pauls gave the section the title 'God Commands more than mere Blood'.[52] Pauls again injected the spectre of blood into his topical subheadings even when Luther's complaint had more to do with purported Jewish boasting or pride of ancestry.

In the end, Pauls simply lifted the most incendiary passages from only Luther's anti-Jewish works and infused them with racialised conceptions of which Luther knew nothing. In Pauls's treatment, there is no discussion of the biblical passages to which Luther appealed time and again. Nor is there serious contemplation of the theological reasoning behind Luther's (often anti-Judaic) censure. Though he did not ignore theological argumentation altogether, clearly it is racially based antisemitism that dominated his treatment of Luther's anti-Jewish works.

Pauls's intent was clear. He sought to utilise the antisemitism of Luther to win support for Nazi anti-Jewish policy. In the Eisenach Institute, which received his volumes as a 'gift', he had a receptive audience. When the weekly German Christian paper *Positives Christentum* (Positive Christianity) carried an editorial on the subject and a discussion of Pauls's volumes over a number of editions in the summer of 1939 (just a half year after the terror of *Kristallnacht*),[53] he had a broader audience to influence. In contrast to, for example, Erich Vogelsang's *Luthers Kampf Gegen die Juden* (Luther's Fight against the Jews, 1933), which encompassed a much more subtle approach to the topic of Luther and the Jews, Pauls's *Luther and the Jews* entailed bald antisemitic propaganda dressed in theological language. Rather than merely highlight the many negative things which Luther declared about Jews, Vogelsang, at the time a young but well-regarded Protestant theologian, contextualised the reformer's views towards them with a taste of the historical and theological development since the Protestant Reformation. Vogelsang shared a similarly dim view of the Jewish people, but his more nuanced analysis was in fact more effective with a more theologically sophisticated audience.[54]

Pauls's tack was, of course, unsophisticated. Yet, as evidenced by its appeal to certain authorities within the German Protestant Church, it gained wide attention. While part of Luther's stated purpose in writing *That Jesus Christ was Born a Jew* was that he might 'win some Jews to the Christian faith', Pauls brushed this aside in volume 1, averring that it was 'no mission sermon for Jews'. Moreover, in volume 3, there is very little reflection, only a series of damning quotations demarcated by section headings in bold type which sometimes reflect Luther's meaning fairly and sometimes not. Pauls also made very little effort to include counterclaims regarding Judaism from Luther's writings. Clearly, Pauls found what he wanted to find in Luther. The picture that emerged was solely that of the 'older'[55] Luther, the Luther that could serve as a powerful tool of Nazi propaganda both inside and outside the Protestant Church.

Vogelsang, too, championed the 'German' Luther. Yet Vogelsang's Luther – even in his 'German-ness' – was first and foremost the 'Christian' Luther. He approached Luther in a much more sophisticated manner than did Pauls. His argumentation was primarily anti-Judaic but contained occasional glimpses of irrational antisemitism. Vogelsang and Pauls, despite their differences in approach and personal notoriety, supported at least the irrational antisemitism of the Nazis, and perhaps the anti-Jewish policies of the regime.

# Heidelberg pastor Hermann Maas, the Confessing Church and the 'Jewish Question'

Hermann Maas was born in 1877 and grew up as the son of a pastor in Gernsbach, near Baden-Baden. He studied theology from 1896 to 1900 in Halle, Straßburg and Heidelberg. After his ordination in Freiburg in 1900, he went on to become first a vicar, later a parish administrator and finally a pastor in Laufen/Sulzburg in the Black Forest (1903–1915). In 1903, he took part in the sixth Zionist Congress in Basel. This began what would become a lifelong engagement with issues surrounding Christianity, the Jewish people and Palestine/Israel. Maas's ministry was characterised by both political and theological liberalism, which were expressed in his active participation in the German Democratic Party (DDP) beginning in 1918, and his involvement in various ecumenical activities, including his participation in the 'World Alliance for International Friendship Work of the Churches' conference in Stockholm in 1925 and his work for *Die Christliche Welt* (The Christian World), an influential liberal Christian periodical edited by Marburg theologian Martin Rade.[56] He also became well-known across Germany for his participation in the funeral of Reich President Friedrich Ebert (SPD), a lapsed Catholic, in 1925. His address at the funeral caused uproar within Protestant circles. Maas was accused of blasphemy and disobeying church authorities; yet, the conservative, nationalistic politics of the church leadership likely played a part in the acrimony.[57]

Maas joined the *Verein zur Abwehr des Antisemitismus* (Society for Protection against Antisemitism) in 1932. One year later, he spent several months studying in Palestine. In the first year that the Nazis were in power, he became a member of the Pastor's Emergency League (a precursor of the Confessing Church) and, later, the Confession Community of Baden. In

August 1935, he spoke about 'The Question of the Christian Non-Aryans' at the preliminary session of the World Alliance's meeting in Chamby. He proposed offering concrete help to affected 'non-Aryan' Christians in the areas of education, employment and land for housing but cautioned that the Gospel – not political animosities – had to motivate the church's work.[58]

Maas was a co-founder of the Grüber Office with Heinrich Grüber in 1938. Maas was responsible for the organisation's work in Baden, while Grüber worked from Berlin. Through this work and his ecumenical contacts abroad, including George Bell, Bishop of Chichester, he assisted in the emigration of many persecuted Jews.[59] He accomplished all of this while serving as pastor of the *Heiliggeistkirche* (Holy Spirit Church) in Heidelberg from 1915 to 1943. Because of such daring activities, he was harassed by the Gestapo and eventually had speaking, writing and professional prohibitions levelled against him. In 1943, he was forced by the high church council, under pressure from the Nazi authorities, to resign his position at Heidelberg, and later that year was transferred to France to endure work in a hard labour camp. He returned to ministerial employment in Heidelberg after the war. Shortly after his retirement in 1966, he received a Yad Vashem Medal from the State of Israel. Maas died in Heidelberg in 1970.[60]

During Maas's tenure as pastor in Heidelberg, the *Vorläufige Kirchenleitung* (VKL or Provisional Church Administration of the German Protestant Church) appointed a 'Theological Committee for the Study of the Jewish Question'. The VKL was the 'Confessing Church government established … as a counterpart to the Church Consistory and Chancellery in Berlin, which were headed by German Christians or "neutral" leaders'.[61] It was a quasi-national group in the sense that Confessing Church pastors in the regional churches viewed it as a sort of 'spiritual' leadership for the Confessing Church, but these pastors still fell under the leadership of their respective regional church governments.[62] In any case, the VKL-appointed committee was charged with creating a 'memorandum and a synod declaration on the Jewish question' that was to serve as a model for a Reich Confessing Synod (which never came to fruition). The committee met in Berlin-Dahlem on 22 February 1937. The VKL chose as members of the committee, among others, Franz Hildebrandt (Berlin-Dahlem) and Maas. Each of the participants, including Maas, had engaged themselves previously with the topic of the 'Jewish question' from a theological standpoint.[63]

Three months earlier, Maas had written some theses on the topic 'The *Volk* and the *Völker*'. According to Maas, Israel's vocation, as God's chosen people, was 'to be a blessing for all of the nations'.[64] Because of their 'unfaithfulness' and their rejection of Jesus, 'the crucified one', they experienced God's wrath. Despite all of this, God still held to his 'plan of salvation', which entailed His breaking off of the 'disobedient branches' from Israel, the 'olive tree' and grafting in of new (gentile) branches. Continuing his explication of the argument of Paul in Romans 9–11, Maas maintained that the 'community of the New Covenant' (i.e. the Christian

Church) was comprised of both gentile believers and 'Jewish Christians'. From all of this, Maas concluded that gentile Christians had a special responsibility towards Jews, who he called (again following Paul) 'Israel according to the flesh'.[65]

Despite Maas's calls for Jews to convert to Christianity, which were, then as now, regarded by many Jews as either antisemitic or at the very least impolitic, several of the Heidelberg pastor's recommendations for Christian treatment of Jews were remarkably sympathetic, especially when one considers that the overwhelming majority of German Protestant pastors and theologians regarded Jews and Judaism with suspicion at best and virulent disdain at worst. The Christian community, Maas averred, should renounce all traces of arrogance and 'blind hatred' towards the Chosen People and repent for both the sins that they had committed against the Jewish people and their failure to act on their behalf in their time of suffering. Christians should actively demonstrate faith, hope and love towards their Jewish neighbours. Uniquely, he regarded Zionism as a 'sign of the times', explicitly referring to it as an 'end-time movement' of world-historical importance.[66]

Fellow committee member Franz Hildebrandt responded to Maas's piece with a detailed memorandum. Hildebrandt's mother was of Jewish descent; as a 'half-Jew' who did not practice Judaism, he was thus, in Nazi parlance, a '*Mischling* of the first degree'. A close friend of Dietrich Bonhoeffer, a relationship which influenced Bonhoeffer's response to the 'Jewish Question',[67] Hildebrandt was also an assistant to Martin Niemöller in Berlin-Dahlem. However, after Niemöller's arrest in summer 1937 (just a few months after Hildebrandt's participation on the VKL committee on the 'Jewish Question'), Hildebrandt fled Germany and ended up in London as a guest of the German congregation there.[68] The issues discussed in the exchange between Hildebrandt and Maas, while considered in terms that might be regarded as esoteric outside of the theological discipline, quite obviously had very weighty real-world implications.

Despite some important points of disagreement with his Heidelberg colleague, Hildebrandt, like Maas, rued Christian treatment of German Jews in their time of dire need. Among other things, Hildebrandt scolded Christians for offering no comfort to Jews in their distress and, furthermore – by their strict adherence to the Lutheran doctrine of obedience to authority – giving the impression of their 'joyful' approval of the state's handling of the 'Jewish Question'. Still worse, by supplying baptismal certificates as proof of 'Aryan' descent to Nazi authorities, the church had supported the Nuremberg Laws. The church needed to repent of its espousal of 'false doctrines' relating to race, nationality and '*völkisch* movements'. Significantly, Hildebrandt targeted the prevailing Protestant doctrine of the orders of creation. Rather than seeing the division of humankind into distinct peoples and languages as an indicator of divine wrath for human sin, Protestants celebrated race and *Volkstum* as divine orders of creation.[69]

Hildebrandt's sharpest criticism of Maas is significant, even if implicit (he did not name Maas) and not ultimately decisive. The view that '*völkisch* movements such as antisemitism and Zionism could be interpreted as a sign of salvation and eschatological history' was also to be regarded as false doctrine. Hildebrandt thus rejected both antisemitism and Zionism as false, while Maas embraced the latter. They were false 'because the New Testament reveals only the Church as the *Volk* of God and conceals the future of Israel under the secret of the election (Rom 11:25)'.[70] For Hildebrandt, Israel's future was much more ambiguous than it was in Maas's more sanguine interpretation. Yet, not least because of his own predicament, he called for the church to reject the formation of separate Jewish–Christian churches, to continue to perform marriages between Jews and Christians, to protect *Mischlinge* children from the 'hate of the world' and to practise *Nächstenliebe* (love of neighbour) towards all, including their Jewish neighbours.[71]

Maas responded in kind to Hildebrandt with a document titled 'The Confessing Church and the Jewish Question. Passing Remarks on the Memorandum of Lic. Hildebrandt'.[72] As Maas and Hildebrandt both were members of the Confessing Church's only committee dedicated to studying the 'Jewish Question', Maas's reply demonstrates that even the very few German Protestants who agreed to help endangered Jews did not do so from precisely the same motivations.

A few passages highlight some of the conceptual differences Maas had with Hildebrandt. Demonstrating an aversion to describing animosity towards Jews as *antisemitic*, Maas argued that those who speak and act from a 'political worldview' do so in a manner that is 'not anti*semitic* but anti-*Jewish*'. Furthermore, he posited that the church must 'stand completely on God's Word and preferably avoid political terms'. He included both 'swastika' and 'guest *Volk*' among the terms to be shunned. 'Yes, I think that the church must also be careful with its comments on the present racial ideology!'[73] Maas was cognisant of the danger of the situation in which the Confessing Church found itself and of the oppressive nature of the Nazi regime. Two examples of such oppression – the Röhm purge, including the 'Night of the Long Knives' (30 June 1934) in which Ernst Röhm, the combative leader of the *Sturmabteilung* (SA), and hundreds, perhaps thousands of political opponents were murdered by Himmler's *Schutzstaffel* (SS), together with the arrest and brief imprisonment of hundreds of Confessing Church leaders in March 1935 for their opposition to aspects of Nazism that clashed with their religious views – make the point all too clearly.[74] Yet, Maas's desire to shirk direct commentary on 'the present racial ideology' was also consistent with his stated desire for a purely theological answer to the 'Jewish Question'. Later, he claimed that Hildebrandt 'pushes the Jewish Question to the side' when he argued that many of the non-'Aryan' Christians had not been conscious of their 'connection with Judaism'. Maas asked pointedly whether this fact would relieve affected non-Aryan Christians of their suffering.[75]

He supported his position with repeated appeals to the Bible and to biblical concepts. Using I Corinthians 12 as his basis, Maas argued that the church's Jewish Christians were both 'neighbours' and 'members of the body of Christ'. The non-Jewish members of the church must not 'merely hear' the words of the passage, which says in part 'as one member suffers, so all members suffer', but they must recognise the worth of those members who are 'sons and daughters of Israel' and incorporated into the body of Christ by baptism.[76] Like many in the Confessing Church, Maas rejected the creation of separate Jewish–Christian congregations within the German Protestant Church, an idea which was supported by many German Christians and even some in the unaffiliated Protestant middle. Yet, it is noteworthy that Maas did not share the same sorts of antisemitic views espoused by many of his Confessing Church brethren.[77]

At the heart of Maas's argument was a bibliocentric and theocentric approach that attempted to sidestep political debates altogether. As such, his definition of the term 'Jew' was determined by a biblical-theological construct, rather than by a culturally accepted conception. Being part of the 'Volk of God' was not contingent on race. Being a 'Jew' was a 'unique concept', which 'fits into no scheme'. One was a 'son of Israel' because 'God, not an earthly father or an earthly mother, conferred the name "Israel" on the patriarch Jacob'.[78] For Maas, being a Jew was divine, not political (or even cultural) in nature. One unspoken implication here was that the Nazi state had no right to define Jews in purely racial terms. Maas's strict exclusion of political and cultural ways of thinking from the arena of theology was unusual for a German Protestant in this era. Yet, it was his dogged belief that God had chosen the Jewish people as His Volk that motivated his efforts to offer assistance to both Jews who embraced Christianity (who were few in number) and those who did not, efforts that he undertook at great risk to himself and his family.

In a manner more in keeping with contemporary dispensationalist evangelicalism than with either Lutheran or Reformed German Protestantism, Maas argued that Christians should help the Zionists, despite their 'thousand erring ways'. For Maas, their 'homecoming' (i.e. to the land of Israel) was prophesied in the Bible. 'A loving church can preach, plead [with], and threaten' the Zionists, so that they 'purify themselves therewith before God of all nationalistic pride, and will open [their] ear and heart for the Christ, who is [their] salvation for time and eternity'.[79] Maas's address to the 'Jewish Question' encompassed a unique brand of Christian Zionism informed by a stubbornly biblical ecclesiology, which he refused to define in relation to political or cultural norms. Hermann Maas demonstrated sympathy with the Jewish victims of Nazism, whether they were converts to Christianity or not.

On the other hand, the Stuttgart Declaration of Guilt (October 1945) – which confessed vaguely that German Protestants had not witnessed, prayed, believed or loved vigorously enough, and made equivocating allusions to both German suffering and supposedly widespread Protestant resistance to Nazism, while making no direct mention of Jews – was more representative of how German Protestants dealt with their Nazi past in the early post-war years. Even this was highly controversial for what it did confess and was probably influenced by international and ecumenical ecclesiastical pressure that was brought to bear on the German participants.[80] Maas's posture in the wake of the war and the Holocaust contrasts starkly with that of the German Protestant Church as a whole.

# Conclusion

Elevating the *Volk* – the people of the German nation – to quasi-divine status via the doctrine of the orders of creation while imbibing the spirit of *Heimat* shared by fellow Germans, many Protestants could not countenance Jewish participation in German cultural or ecclesiastical life. The effects of this combination of *Schöpfungsordnungen* and *Heimat* became toxic for many German Protestants and included the justification of anti-Judaism and antisemitism in their ranks. Many of them could now envision a Germany without Jews, even if most did not call actively for the physical destruction of their Jewish neighbours. A tiny minority, like Hermann Maas and Dietrich Bonhoeffer, thought and acted courageously on the behalf of German Jews, at great risk to their own safety. Such a stance was exceptionally rare in Nazi Germany.

Maas's address on the 'Jewish Question' represents an approach to the issue that was unique within German Protestant circles (and, even within the Confessing Church). While his adherence to biblical ecclesiology was in keeping with that of his pastoral colleagues, his Christian Zionism was shared by very few. Maas demonstrated overt sympathy with Jewish victims of Nazism, both within the church and without. This view, too, was in short supply within German Protestantism during the Third Reich. Most theologians from the Confessing Church camp sought to rescue Christianity – but not their Jewish neighbours – from the Nazis.[81] Many German Protestant theologians and pastors who addressed issues of church, state, nation, *Volk* and race coupled often careful scholarship with anti-Judaic and antisemitic sentiments, lending such nefarious views an air of almost genteel respectability. Yet Theodor Pauls, and others like him, took a less sophisticated approach, seeking overtly to move their readers' views of Jews closer to that of Hitler and the Nazis.

This view from the margins of German Protestant theology has shown that the Nazi regime's attempts at permeating all areas of German society were appreciably aided by a readiness on the part of Protestants to 'self-coordinate'.[82] In the German Protestant Church, the interplay between Nazi ideology and Christian theology was significant. Especially where notions about race and *Volk* were concerned, many Protestants employed both technical theological language and Nazi jargon. Even many of those who might have been uncomfortable with Nazi attempts to control the churches could be moved closer to Nazi ideology via the potent orders of creation doctrine. If their *Heimat* was threatened by a 'foreign invasion' in all areas of life, including economics, the arts and politics, a 'world without Jews' might have seemed an attractive cultural imagining. In these respects, the differences between the Protestant church and the German culture as a whole were negligible.

# Notes

1    P. Althaus, *Kirche und Volkstum: Der völkische Wille im Lichte des Evangeliums* (Gütersloh, 1928), p. 9.

2    T. Pauls, *Luther und die Juden: In der Frühzeit der Reformation, 1513–1524* (Bonn, 1939), p. 137. Hereafter, *Luther und die Juden* 1.

3    H. Maas, *Public Opinion and Relations to the Jews in Nazi Europe*, vol. 5 of *The Nazi Holocaust*, ed. M. Marrus (Westport, 1989), pp. 30–32, here p. 31.

4    M. Gailus, 'Overwhelmed by Their Own Fascination with the "Ideas of 1933": Berlin's Protestant Social Milieu in the Third Reich', trans. P. Selwyn, *German History* 20, no. 4 (2002), pp. 462–493, here p. 482. On the Church Struggle, see below.

5    The material in this section is reproduced, with minimal alteration, from C. Probst, *Demonizing the Jews: Luther and the Protestant Church in Nazi Germany* (Bloomington, IN, 2012), pp. 8–11. Courtesy of Indiana University Press. All rights reserved.

6    See, for example, D. Bergen, 'Storm Troopers of Christ: The German Christian Movement and the Ecclesiastical Final Solution', in R. Ericksen and S. Heschel (eds), *Betrayal: German Churches and the Holocaust* (Minneapolis, MN, 1999), pp. 40–67, here p. 46; M. Hockenos, *A Church Divided: German Protestants Confront the Nazi Past* (Bloomington, IN, 2004), p. 4.

7    Throughout this chapter, the German term *evangelisch* is translated as 'Protestant'. While some translate it as 'Evangelical', this might be misleading because *evangelisch* has a specifically confessional association with the three main Protestant traditions in Germany (Lutheran, Reformed and United), whereas to most Americans 'Evangelical' generally connotes conservative, mainly Protestant, Christian churches that promote active proclamation of the Christian Gospel to those who do not share their faith.

8    S. Baranowski, *The Confessing Church, Conservative Elites, and the Nazi State* (Lewiston, 1986), pp. 45–46; D. Bergen, *Twisted Cross: The German Christian Movement in the Third Reich* (Chapel Hill, NC, 1996), pp. 7, 178.

9    Bergen, *Twisted Cross*, p. 229; S. Heschel, 'Nazifying Christian Theology: Walter Grundmann and the Institute for the Study and Eradication of Jewish Influence on German Church Life', *Church History* 63, no. 4 (1994), pp. 587–605.

10   Bergen, *Twisted Cross*, pp. 7 and 176–178.

11   A. Rosenberg, *Das Parteiprogramm: Wesen, Grundsätze und Ziele der NSDAP* (Munich: Zentralverlag der NSDAP, 1922), pp. 15ff., 57ff.

12   Baranowski, *Confessing Church*, pp. 56ff.

13   The term 'Aryan', borrowed by Hitler and the Nazis from eighteenth- and nineteenth-century racial theorists, was a fiction that described the supposedly 'pure' German *Herrenvolk* (master race). While it originally referred to a group of people in ancient India, in Nazi Germany it came to mean the opposite of Jew. See D. Bergen, *War and Genocide: A Concise History of the Holocaust* (Lanham, MD, 2009), pp. 36–37; on the Confessing Church, Barmen, and the Jewish people, see, for example, W. Gerlach, *And the Witnesses Were Silent: The Confessing Church and the Persecution of the Jews*, trans. V. Barnett (Lincoln, 2000); V. Barnett, *For the Soul of the People: Protestant Protest against Hitler* (New York, 1992), p. 54.

14   Probst, *Demonizing the Jews*, pp. 27–37, here pp. 33–37.

15   M. Fulbrook, *History of Germany, 1918–2000: The Divided Nation*, 2nd ed. (Oxford, 2002), pp. 15–36; R. Ericksen, *Theologians under Hitler: Gerhard Kittel, Paul Althaus, and Emanuel Hirsch* (New Haven, CT, 1985), p. 26.

16   See G. Langmuir, *History, Religion, and Antisemitism* (Berkeley, CA, 1990) and G. Langmuir, *Toward a Definition of Antisemitism* (Berkeley, CA, 1990); see also Probst, *Demonizing the Jews*, pp. 3–6, 17–19.

17   R. Ericksen and S. Heschel, 'The German Churches and the Holocaust', in D. Stone (ed.), *The Historiography of the Holocaust* (New York, 2004), pp. 296–318.

18   Probst, *Demonizing the Jews*, pp. 25–27.

19   Gerlach, *Witnesses*, pp. 154–160.

20   E. Röhm and J. Thierfelder, *Vernichtet, 1941–1945*, vol. 4/I of *Juden-Christen-Deutsche, 1933–1945* (Stuttgart, 2004), pp. 182ff., 198–199; M. Richarz (ed.), *Jewish Life in Germany: Memoirs from Three Centuries*, trans. S. Rosenfeld and S. Rosenfeld (Bloomington, IN, 1991), pp. 448–460.

21   S. Friedländer, *The Years of Persecution, 1933–1939*, vol. 1 of *Nazi Germany and the Jews* (London, 1997), pp. 27–28.

22   Gerlach, *Witnesses*, pp. 24, 64ff.; Barnett, *For the Soul of the People*, pp. 34–35, 128–133.

23   A. Confino, *Germany as a Culture of Remembrance: Promises and Limits of Writing History* (Chapel Hill, NC, 2006), pp. 34–35, 61–65, 81ff.; C. Applegate, *A Nation of Provincials: The German Idea of Heimat* (Berkeley, CA, 1990), pp. 3, 8ff.

24   See A. Confino's provocative history of the Holocaust, *A World Without Jews: The Nazi Imagination from Persecution to Genocide* (New Haven, CT, 2014).

25   See the example of Confessing Church pastor Heinrich Fausel, in Probst, *Demonizing the Jews*, pp. 1–2, 94–99, 170–172.

26   On Kittel, see especially Ericksen, *Theologians under Hitler*, pp. 28–78.

27 On Meyer-Erlach, see Probst, *Demonizing the Jews*, pp. 8–75.

28 M. Tielke (ed.), *Biographisches Lexikon für Ostfriesland* (Aurich, 2001), pp. 337–338; P. von der Osten-Sacken, 'Der Nationalsozialistische Lutherforscher Theodor Pauls: Vervollständigung eines Fragmentarischen Bildes', in P. von der Osten-Sacken (ed.), *Das Mißbrauchte Evangelium: Studien zu Theologie und Praxis der Thüringer Deutsche Christen* (Berlin, 2002), pp. 136–166.

29 K. Meier, *Der Evangelische Kirchenkampf*, 3 vols. (Göttingen, 1976–1984), vol. 3, pp. 76–77; Probst, *Demonizing the Jews*, p. 128.

30 Von der Osten-Sacken, 'Der Nationalsozialistische Lutherforscher Theodor Pauls', pp. 136–137. On the Eisenach Institute, see especially S. Heschel, *The Aryan Jesus: Christian Theologians and the Bible in Nazi Germany* (Princeton, NJ, 2008).

31 W. Petersmann and T. Pauls, *'Entjudung' selbst der Luther-Forschung in der Frage der Stellung Luthers zu den Juden!*, 3rd ed. (Bonn, 1940).

32 See below.

33 *Evangelisches Zentralarchiv*, Berlin (hereafter, EZA), 7/3688. Kerrl had also lent financial assistance for the publication of the volumes. P. von der Osten-Sacken, *Martin Luther und die Juden: Neu untersucht anhand von Anton Margarithas 'Der gantz Jüdisch glaub' (1530/31)* (Stuttgart, 2002), p. 277.

34 *Landeskirchenarchiv der Ev.-Lutherischen Kirche in Thüringen* (hereafter, LKA Eisenach), DC III 2a, 'Gesamtmitarbeitersitzung des Institutes zur Erforschung des jüdischen Einflusses auf das deutsche kirchliche Leben 1942', p. 6. This lecture also appeared with the same title in the printed version of the conference proceedings. W. Grundmann (ed.), *Germanentum, Christentum und Judentum* (Leipzig, 1943), vol. 3, pp. 137–192.

35 UJ, Bestand J, Nr. 92 'Promotionsakten der Theologischen Fakultät, 1941-1947'.

36 EZA, 7/3688, Schmidt-Clausing, 'Juden fälschen Luther!', *Völkischer Beobachter*, 18 March 1941.

37 M. Luther, *Daß Jesus Christus ein geborener Jude sei*, in M. Luther (ed.), *D. Martin Luthers Werke: Kritische Gesamtausgabe*, 120 vols. (Weimar, 1883–2009), vol. 11, pp. 307–336, here p. 314. This work appeared in the so-called *'Weimarer Ausgabe'* or Weimar Edition of Luther's works. Hereafter, WA.

38 Pauls, *Luther und die Juden* 1, p. 119.

39 Ibid., p. 128. On contemporary approaches to the issue of continuity and discontinuity in Luther's position towards the Jewish people from the 1520s to the 1540s, see, for example, R. Lewin, *Luthers Stellung zu den Juden: Ein Beitrag zur Geschichte der Juden in Deutschland während des Reformationzeitalters* (Berlin, 1911) and W. Holsten, *Christentum und nichtchristliche Religion nach der Auffassung Luthers* (Gütersloh, 1932), pp. 106ff.

40 See, for example, E. Gritsch, *Martin Luther's Anti-Semitism: Against His Better Judgement* (Grand Rapids, MI, 2012), pp. 63–65.

41 P. Althaus, *The Ethics of Martin Luther*, trans. Robert C. Schultz (Philadelphia, PA, 1972), pp. 43–82.

42   And indeed by historical actors such as Karl Barth, Reinhold Niebuhr and Thomas Mann. See especially the essays by Tracy, Brady and Gritsch in J. Tracy (ed.), *Luther and the Modern State in Germany*, vol. 7 of *Sixteenth Century Essays and Studies* (Kirksville, MO, 1986); T. Brady, Jr., 'Luther's Social Teaching and the Social Order of His Age', in G. Dünnhaupt (ed.), *The Martin Luther Quincentennial* (Detroit, 1985), pp. 270–290.

43   See, for example, Ericksen, *Theologians under Hitler*, pp. 25, 84, 115, 178; U. Tal, *Christians and Jews in Germany: Religion, Politics, and Ideology in the Second Reich, 1871–1914*, trans. Noah Jonathan Jacobs (Ithaca, NY, 1975), pp. 292, 305.

44   Pauls, *Luther und die Juden* 1, p. 137.

45   T. Pauls, *Luther und die Juden: Der Kampf, 1524–1526* (Bonn, 1939), p. 75. Hereafter, *Luther und die Juden* 2.

46   Ibid., pp. 96ff.

47   T. Pauls, *Luther und die Juden: Aus Luthers Kampfschriften gegen die Juden* (Bonn, 1939), p. 26. Hereafter, *Luther und die Juden* 3.

48   See, for example, C. Hutton, *Race and the Third Reich: Linguistics, Racial Anthropology and Genetics in the Dialectic of Volk* (Cambridge, 2005), pp. 91–92.

49   T. Pauls, 'Die Ursprünglichkeit des Gotteslobes', in Walter Grundmann (ed.), *Germanentum, Christentum und Judentum* (Leipzig, 1943), vol. 3, pp. 137–192, here p. 174.

50   Pauls, *Luther und die Juden* 3, p. 26; M. Luther, 'Von den Juden und ihren Lügen', in M. Luther, *D. Martin Luthers Werke: Kritische Gesamtausgabe*, 120 vols. (Weimar, 1883–2009), 53: pp. 417–552, here p. 419.

51   Pauls, *Luther und die Juden* 3, p. 26; Luther, *Von den Juden*, p. 420; Matthew 3:9.

52   Pauls, *Luther und die Juden* 3, p. 28.

53   Von der Osten-Sacken, 'Der Nationalsozialistische Lutherforscher Theodor Pauls', pp. 136–137.

54   E. Vogelsang, *Luthers Kampf Gegen die Juden* (Tübingen, 1933); on Vogelsang, see Probst, *Demonizing the Jews*, pp. 63–68.

55   There is a great deal of discussion about applying such terminology to Luther's views on Jews and Judaism later in his life. The term is used hesitantly, given its potential for being misunderstood. There is no doubt, however, that it is the 'older' Luther that wrote more directly and more harshly about the Jews. See Probst, *Demonizing the Jews*, pp. 39–58.

56   P. Noss, 'Maas, Hermann', in *Biographisch-Bibliographisches Kirchenlexikon*, 28 vols. (Herzberg: Verlag Traugott Bautz, 1990–), vol. 5, pp. 505–510; E. Röhm and J. Thierfelder, 'Hermann Maas – der stadtbekannte "Judenpfarrer"', in *Entrechtet, 1935–1938*, vol. 2/I of *Juden-Christen-Deutsche, 1933–1945* (Stuttgart, 1992), pp. 127–135; K. Barnes, *Nazism, Liberalism, and Christianity: Protestant Social Thought in Germany and Great Britain, 1925–1937* (Lexington, 1990), pp. 29, 35.

57  J. Thierfelder, 'Hermann Maas: Retter und Brückenbauer', http://www. maasfoundation.com/ger/thierfelder.html (accessed 11 November 2014); Noss, 'Maas, Hermann', pp. 505–510.

58  Noss, 'Maas, Hermann', pp. 505–510; Gerlach, *Witnesses*, pp. 130–131.

59  R. Webster, 'Archives and Sources for Religious History: German "Non-Aryan" Clergymen and the Anguish of Exile after 1933', *The Journal of Religious History* 22, no. 1 (1998), pp. 83–103. See also Thierfelder, 'Herman Maas – Retter und Brückenbauer'.

60  Noss, 'Maas, Hermann', pp. 505–510; Grüber was arrested on 19 December 1940 and taken to Sachsenhausen. His colleague, Werner Sylten, continued running the office but was arrested and taken to Dachau on 27 February 1941, where he was killed a year-and-a-half later. Grüber was also later moved to Dachau but released after a total of two-and-a-half years in concentration camps. Just a few of the fifty-five workers in the office survived the end of the war, with many probably dying in the gas chambers. Gerlach, *Witnesses*, pp. 154–160.

61  Gerlach, *Witnesses*, p. 288.

62  Barnett, *For the Soul of the People*, pp. 69–70.

63  Röhm and Thierfelder, *Entrechtet, 1935–1938*, pp. 289–291.

64  Maas likely has in mind here Genesis 12:1–3, where God blesses Abraham and promises to make a great nation from his descendants. See also Genesis 18, especially vv. 17–19.

65  Maas, in Röhm and Thierfelder, *Entrechtet, 1935–1938*, p. 291.

66  Ibid., pp. 291–292.

67  F. Schlingensiepen, *Dietrich Bonhoeffer 1906-1945: Martyr, Thinker, Man of Resistance* (New York, 2010), pp. 124, 127; R. Hilberg, *The Destruction of the European Jews*, 3rd ed. (New Haven, 2003), vol. 2, p. 434; Gerlach, *Witnesses*, pp. 25ff.; on Bonhoeffer's stance towards Jews and Judaism, see K. Barnes, 'Dietrich Bonhoeffer and Hitler's Persecution of the Jews', in Ericksen and Heschel (eds), *Betrayal*, pp. 110–128; E. Bethge, 'Dietrich Bonhoeffer und die Juden', in H. Kremers (ed.), *Die Juden und Martin Luther – Martin Luther und die Juden: Geschichte, Wirkungsgeschichte, Herausforderung* (Dusseldorf, 1985), pp. 211–249.

68  Gerlach, *Witnesses*, pp. 153, 288.

69  Hildebrandt, quoted in Röhm and Thierfelder, *Entrechtet, 1935–1938*, pp. 294–295.

70  Ibid.

71  Ibid., pp. 297–298.

72  EZA 50/207, H. Maas, 'Die Bekennende Kirche und die Judenfrage: Randbemerkungen zu dem Memorandum von Lic. Hildebrandt', 22 February 1937, pp. 22–32.

73  Maas, 'Die Bekennende Kirche und die Judenfrage', p. 22.

74  On the Röhm purge, see, for example, R. Evans, *The Third Reich in Power: How the Nazis Won Over the Hearts and Minds of a Nation* (London, 2006),

pp. 31–41. On the arrest of the Confessing Church leaders, see President of the Confessing Synod of the German Protestant Church, 'Kundgebung der Bekenntnissynode der evangelischen Kirche der altpreußischen Union: 500 Pfarrer verhaftet', *Der Präses der Bekenntnissynode der Deutschen Evangelischen Kirche: Bad Oeynhausen*, 28 March 1935, p. 2. According to this article, approximately 500 pastors were arrested and briefly detained in March 1935 for planning to read a statement critical of the religious aspects of Nazism from their pulpits. Other documents put the number of arrested pastors at 715. See Gerlach, *Witnesses*, p. 80.

75  Maas, 'Die Bekennende Kirche und die Judenfrage', p. 23.

76  Ibid., pp. 22–23. The pertinent passage is I Corinthians 12:12–26, which says in part: 'The body is a unit, though it is made up of many parts; and though all its parts are many, they form one body. So it is with Christ. For we were all baptised by one Spirit into one body – whether Jews or Greeks, slave or free ... If one part suffers, every part suffers with it; if one part is honoured, every part rejoices with it.'

77  See, for example, Gerlach, *Witnesses*. Particular examples of Confessing Church antisemitism include United States Holocaust Memorial Museum Fausel Collection, 42, Unpublished Lecture Manuscript, H. Fausel, 'Die Judenfrage', 10 January 1934, pp. 14–15; H. Schroth, *Luthers christlicher Antisemitismus Heute* (Wittenberg, 1937).

78  Maas, 'Die Bekennende Kirche und die Judenfrage', pp. 22–23.

79  Ibid., p. 32.

80  Hockenos, *A Church Divided*, pp. 75–100.

81  Gerlach, *Witnesses*.

82  See, for example, Ericksen's discussion of the 'self-coordination' of churches and universities in Nazi Germany in R. Ericksen, *Complicity in the Holocaust: Churches and Universities in Nazi Germany* (Cambridge, 2012), pp. 143ff.

# Select bibliography

Applegate, C., *A Nation of Provincials: The German Idea of Heimat* (Berkeley, CA, 1990).

Bergen, D., *Twisted Cross: The German Christian Movement in the Third Reich* (Chapel Hill, NC, 1996).

Confino, A., *Germany as a Culture of Remembrance: Promises and Limits of Writing History* (Chapel Hill, NC, 2006).

Confino, A., *A World Without Jews: The Nazi Imagination from Persecution to Genocide* (New Haven, CT, 2014).

Ericksen, R., *Theologians under Hitler: Gerhard Kittel, Paul Althaus, and Emanuel Hirsch* (New Haven, CT, 1985).

Ericksen, R. and Heschel, S. (eds), *Betrayal: German Churches and the Holocaust* (Minneapolis, MN, 1999).

Gerlach, W., *And the Witnesses Were Silent: The Confessing Church and the Persecution of the Jews*, trans. Victoria J. Barnett (Lincoln, 2000).

Hockenos, M., *A Church Divided: German Protestants Confront the Nazi Past* (Bloomington, IN, 2004).

Probst, C., *Demonizing the Jews: Luther and the Protestant Church in Nazi Germany* (Bloomington, IN, 2012).

Stone, D., *Histories of the Holocaust* (Oxford, 2010).

# 9

# Catholic Life under Hitler

## *Kevin P. Spicer*

In October 1936, the Gestapo undertook an investigation of Father Anton Kehl, associate pastor in Wülfershausen, a rural farming community in the diocese of Würzburg. It initiated this enquiry after receiving complaints that Kehl had founded Youths for Christ (*Christus-Jugend*), an illegal youth group, and had also spoken negatively about the government in a homily. Alois Stahl, the Mayor of the neighbouring town of Eichsenhausen, described Father Kehl as 'not political' but cautioned that he was still 'not completely in unison with today's state'. When interrogated, Kehl admitted:

> I absolutely deny making attacks on the state in my sermons. If I say anything in this respect, it is only a defensive measure against an attack on the Church. I am completely aware that the state has a right to exist, but the Church also desires to live. I repeat once more that I have no intention to make hidden attacks against the state; on the contrary, I want to work with the state so state and Church can prosper for the benefit of the entire *Volk*. On the other hand, however, as a priest I am also obligated to protect the Church against unfounded attacks.[1]

Fortunately for the priest, the Gestapo was unable to round up sufficient evidence to charge him with any criminal offence. Though he escaped imprisonment, it would not be the last time that Kehl tangled with state authorities.[2]

The case of Father Kehl was not a particularly unusual one in Hitler's Germany. In fact, between 1933 and 1945, one-third of Germany's diocesan priests came into conflict with the Gestapo or other police agencies.[3] Yet the majority of these clergymen refused to be labelled antagonists who purposely bucked state authority. Like Father Kehl, they instead viewed themselves as pastoral ministers, churchmen called to fulfil their priestly duty by defending their Church against any hostility facing it.[4] Protests arose from a desire to practise their faith without restrictions. This encompassed providing the faithful with the sacraments and perpetuating Catholicism through religious education and associational life.

Under National Socialist rule in Germany, traditional practice of the Catholic faith became, at times, a challenge, as the state gradually encroached on the Church's freedom to operate in the public sphere. Both National Socialism and Roman Catholicism contained all-encompassing worldviews. While these competing worldviews intersected on points such as condemnation of Bolshevism and vice-related moral issues, generally there was a vast divide between them. Still, as in any human condition, not everyone who professed either or both of these worldviews upheld every aspect of them. Similarly, as an institution, the Catholic Church's position towards and view of National Socialism also changed over the course of time: (1) 1930–1933, when German bishops publicly opposed National Socialism; (2) 1933–1934, when the German bishops jointly reversed their stance towards National Socialism, while holding on to the delusion that they could work with the state; (3) 1934–1939, when the state directly attacked the Church's value system and worked to remove it from the life of the *Volksgemeinschaft* ('national community'); (4) 1939–1945, when the state, while threatening to blot out the Church as a matter of policy, engaged in an annihilative war that simultaneously carried out the murder of thousands of physically handicapped and mentally ill people, as well as the deportation and murder of millions of European Jews.[5] These four phases provide a framework with which to examine the interaction of Catholics and their Church with National Socialism and, in particular, a construct to study how on a daily basis, German Catholics negotiated the practice of the faith while living under Hitler's rule.

# 1930–1933

In 1933, of the nearly 66 million people living in Germany, almost 41 million (62.7 per cent) were Protestant, just over 21 million (32.5 per cent) were Catholic and fewer than 500,000 (0.8 per cent) were Jewish. Another 2.6 million (4 per cent) individuals did not identify with any of these religious traditions.[6] Those who did identify themselves as Protestants or Catholics were officially registered as members of their respective tradition. In turn, such registration obligated an individual annually to pay *Kirchensteuer* (church tax) that financed the Church.[7] Individuals could avoid such taxation by legally unregistering from the Church and declaring themselves as unaffiliated. Though movements existed prior to Hitler's rule to encourage withdrawal, few individuals took such drastic steps, even if they did not regularly attend weekly services, since this ultimately meant no access to any sacramental care. Under National Socialism, this situation changed as the government pressured civil servants and Party members to withdraw from the churches. Despite such coercion under Hitler, the German state continued both the Church taxation system and its annual subsidies as compensation for the appropriation and secularisation of former ecclesiastical properties. Yet, it did eventually introduce limitations on the Church's tax exemptions and, after 1943, refused assistance in overseeing the collection of Church taxes in certain German states.[8]

Though there were nearly twice as many Protestants in Germany as Catholics before the 1938 *Anschluss* with Austria, the Catholic Church still had a significant presence in Germany. In the Old Reich – Germany until 1938 – there were six archdioceses, eighteen dioceses and one prelature *nullius* (Schneidemühl), the latter the result of territorial changes with Poland following the First World War.[9] Though Catholics could be found throughout Germany, with many living in diaspora communities, there were particularly large concentrations in Bavaria, Baden, Rhineland, Westphalia and Upper Silesia.[10] More than half those registered as Catholics fulfilled their Easter duty and weekly Sunday obligation.[11] Such weekly practice of the Catholic faith generally remained constant over the course of Hitler's rule and only noticeably declined during the war.[12] Of those who were Catholic and had entered into marriage with a spouse of the same faith, more than 97 per cent married in a Catholic church. This number dropped considerably to 35 per cent with mixed marriages, making it no surprise when the editors of the 1939 *Catholic Church Handbook* cautioned: 'Religious mixed marriage therefore remains a most serious worry for the Church, to which the greatest attention must be given in the religious education of children unless the strength that it has gathered elsewhere through great difficulty and prayers pour out of its continually bleeding wound.'[13] In such situations, practice of the faith, especially the baptism of children, remained a central concern.

The German Catholic Church was neither 'a monolithic whole' nor an ecclesial entity insularly overcome by an Ultramontanist outlook, which gave excessive emphasis to the Pope's authority.[14] Rather, its diversity of religious practice reflected the country's regional history prior to its 1871 unification. Recollections of the Reformation also affected it, especially when recalling the laws of the 1870s *Kulturkampf*, which denigrated Catholics as alien, dishonourable and traitorous in a botched effort to force Catholics' allegiance to a unified Germany.[15] Such a destructive campaign, however, was hardly necessary since German Catholics longed for inclusion in the new German state.[16] Many Catholics, too, eagerly engaged in legislative government through their own political party, the Centre Party, and, in Bavaria after late 1918, the more conservative and provincial Bavarian People's Party. At first, the Centre Party advocated primarily for Catholic interests; but over time, it began to represent a wider spectrum of concerns.

In fact, in 1930, the Berlin Centre Party added Georg Kareski, the chair of Berlin's Jewish Community, to its list of candidates for the 14 September 1930 Reichstag election.[17]

The Centre Party's decision to include a prominent Jew among its Reichstag candidates was not a completely magnanimous one. In fact, Heinrich Krone, a leading Centre Party member, explained that the 'leadership of the Greater Berlin Centre Party supports the view that the nomination of a Jewish candidate will be an incentive for orthodox Jews in Berlin to vote for the Centre Party'.[18] Ultimately, this action reflected the essence of Catholicism of the 1930s: professing practical altruism towards its 'neighbour' while, in reality, essentially concerning itself with its own existence and perpetuating its moral milieu.

At first, National Socialism did not seem a significant concern of the German bishops until the Nazi Party rose from 12 seats (2.6 per cent of the vote) to 107 seats (18.3 per cent) in the September 1930 Reichstag election.[19] Prior to this, the German bishops had issued joint statements in 1921 and, again in 1924, warning Catholics of the dangers that certain nationalistic and patriotic associations, such as the Young German Order and the Stahlhelm, could pose to their faith. Clergy were encouraged to withhold the sacraments from anyone who blatantly supported such groups though they were cautioned never to enquire about an individual's voting record during the sacrament of confession. Neither directive, however, mentioned the National Socialist German Workers' Party (NSDAP) by name.[20] Despite such warnings, the bishops were not in agreement about how to deal specifically with Catholic participation in nationalistic associations.[21]

By the summer of 1929, agitation against the Church by Hitler supporters had reached a boiling point, yet the bishops still had not yet made any statements against National Socialism. The case of Father Johannes Rachor, pastor of Bechtheim in the diocese of Mainz, illustrates this. On the morning of 17 June 1929, three Nazi Party members approached Father Rachor and asked him to preside at the funeral of a 23-year-old Party member. Unsure how to respond, yet convinced that the Hitler movement was 'hostile to the Church', Rachor wrote to his diocesan superiors to ask how he should handle the situation. He specifically wanted the diocese to make a pronouncement, since he found the 'opinion of an individual pastor ... now worthless'.[22] Father Philipp Mayer, the vicar general of the diocese of Mainz, promptly replied that as a Catholic, the individual was entitled to a funeral. However, this fact did not give his colleagues the right to attend it, wearing Party uniforms or marching with flags in closed rank.[23] Father Rachor was not alone. Other pastors were writing to Mayer seeking assistance. While he answered them privately, Mayer also took a further step by publicly addressing the issue of Catholicism and National Socialism in an article, which the *Mainzer Journal* carried on 25 August 1930. In it, Mayer singled out point 24 of the Nazi Party's platform, which provided 'freedom for all religious denominations provided they do not threaten the state's existence nor offend the ethical feelings of the German race', calling it a threat to Catholicism and its pastoral freedom. Similarly, he condemned the National Socialists' 'blind adoration of their own race and ... hatred toward all alien races' as 'unchristian and un-Catholic'.[24] In Mainz, a battle between the two conflicting worldviews had begun.

Over the summer, with the support of his bishop, Ludwig Maria Hugo, Mayer hardened his position against National Socialism and began advising diocesan clergy to do the same. This unflinching stance sufficiently fortified Father Heinrich Weber, the Catholic pastor of Kirschhausen, to ascend the pulpit during Sunday Mass and expressly forbid his parishioners to join the NSDAP or risk separation from the sacraments. Weber's pronouncement rapidly became national news.[25] Some Catholics, primarily those who were NSDAP members or sympathisers, wrote to their respective diocesan chanceries protesting this development.[26] A number even appealed directly to Pope Pius XI to weigh in on the issue.[27]

The stance of the Mainz diocese towards National Socialism forced all the other German dioceses to address the issue. In December 1930, Cardinal Adolf Bertram, the prince archbishop of Breslau and head of the German Bishop's Conference, saw the need for the bishops to issue a joint statement and thus prepared a draft, but was unable to obtain consensus on the wording.[28] In particular, not all bishops agreed that the sacraments should be withheld from Catholic NSDAP members.[29] In the end, each of the six church provinces issued individual statements on National Socialism. All stressed that their statements addressed only spiritual concerns and were in no way politically motivated. Thus while none condemned Nazi antisemitism directly, they did critique Nazi racial teaching, especially when it contradicted the efficacy of the sacrament of baptism.[30] Despite such limitations, by mid-1931, anyone living in Germany knew that Catholics should not be card-carrying members of the NSDAP.[31]

# 1933–1934

When President Paul von Hindenburg appointed Hitler Chancellor of Germany on 30 January 1933, the German Catholic Bishops' ban on membership in the NSDAP was still in effect. In 1933, the NSDAP counted only 850,000 members.[32] An analysis of the 5 March 1933 Reichstag election reveals that the Centre Party and the Bavarian People's Party drew votes from half of Germany's Catholic population.[33] Registered Catholics also cast a fourth of the national total of 43.9 per cent votes for the NSDAP. One political analyst surmised that if all the voters had been Catholic, the NSDAP would never have been able to overcome its minority party status to gain control of the Reichstag.[34] Still, such numbers and statements are deceptive. For example, Catholic support for National Socialism throughout Germany varied by district, with some areas offering particularly strong support for it.[35] Similarly, the German bishops' backing of the Centre Party, even as it worked in coalition with the Social Democratic Party (SPD) during much of the Weimar Republic, drove extremely nationalistic and politically conservative Catholics to look towards alternatives such as the German National People's Party (DNVP) or the NSDAP.[36] A select group of Catholic clergymen also shared this anti-Centre, nationalistic outlook and openly cast their support for National Socialism.[37] Finally, it is important to note that over the course of the Third Reich, even those Catholics who chose not to consistently support the NSDAP often continued to stand by Hitler, placing him above his party and thus sparing him any blame for unpopular decisions[38] (Figure 9.1).

Hitler's actions did not always please German Catholics. Following the March 1933 elections, the Reich Chancellor, though a registered Catholic, refused an invitation to attend a Mass in St. Peter and Paul Church in Potsdam, celebrating the opening of the Reichstag. He publicly attributed the bishops' ban on his party as his motive. Instead, he travelled to Berlin's Luisenstadt Cemetery to visit the graves of fallen SA men. This clever move quickly reawakened in Catholics feelings of exclusion dating back to the 1870s *Kulturkampf*.[39] Catholics feared being alienated from the German *Volksgemeinschaft* that National Socialism promised. In turn, the bishops felt considerable pressure from their 'flocks' to reverse their stance. On 23

FIGURE 9.1 *Arrival of Bishop Nicolaus Bares of Berlin for Confirmation at Christ the King parish in Schönow in Pomerania on 2 July 1934. Also pictured are Father Anton Majewski (left) and Father Franz Ritter (left) and two parishioners (names unknown). Courtesy of Diözesanarchiv Berlin.*

March, while addressing the Reichstag, Hitler provided the perfect olive branch by publicly declaring that his government 'sees Christianity as the unshakeable foundation of the moral and ethical life of the *Volk*, attaches the utmost importance to friendly relations with the Holy See, and seeks to develop this relationship'.[40] Following the speech, the Catholic Centre Party delegates, led by their chairman, Monsignor Ludwig Kaas, joined the National Socialist delegates to pass an Enabling Act, which placed legislative power in the hands of Hitler's Cabinet, thus hammering the final nail in the coffin of Weimar democracy.[41] A few days later, on 28 March, the German bishops lifted their ban against National Socialism, though they still maintained their previous 'condemnation of definite religious-ethical errors' found within the movement's ideology.[42]

Though most Catholics welcomed the bishops' reversal, not all were pleased by it. Among the latter was Father Franziskus Stratmann, a Dominican priest and prominent member of the German Catholic Peace Movement, who on 10 April wrote to Cardinal Michael von Faulhaber, the Archbishop of Munich and Freising, to alert him of his dissatisfaction and that of a sizeable group of Catholics.[43] The bishops' statement was not the sole impetus motivating Stratmann, but rather he was deeply troubled by two additional events: the 1 April government-sponsored national boycott of Jewish owned businesses and the 7 April Civil Service 'Reform' Law that dismissed or forcibly retired Jews and anyone deemed politically unreliable, including Catholics.

In his letter, Stratmann reminded Cardinal Faulhaber that violence against Jews was 'a blasphemy if one remembers that Christ eternally belongs to this race and that Christianity would never have come into being without Judaism'.[44] Faulhaber did not respond to Stratmann, but in correspondence with another clergyman he acknowledged: 'This action against the Jews is so unchristian that every Christian, not just every priest, must stand up against it.' Despite such a statement, Faulhaber admitted that Church authorities had 'far more important urgent questions' facing them. Among these, he included the future of Catholic schools, the continued existence of Catholic associations and the debate over legalisation of forced sterilisation. The Cardinal concluded, 'we may assume, or have already partly experienced that the Jews can help themselves, so, therefore we have no reason to give the government a reason to turn attacks on the Jews into an attack on Jesuits'.[45]

As their words reveal, both Faulhaber and Stratmann found the state's early persecution of Jews problematic. However, they were worlds apart on how the Church should respond. Stratmann had already moved to a place of solidarity with persecuted Jews. He paid for his stance by eventually having to flee Germany.[46] Few Catholics embraced Stratmann's point of view[47] and, even fewer, were willing to risk their lives to directly assist Jews.[48] Like most Catholics, Faulhaber viewed Jews as outsiders, beyond the Church's and his direct sphere of concern. Their plight did not motivate him to action. Nor was he willing to place the Church and its institutions in jeopardy to intercede for them.[49] The majority of Catholics chose a similar path as their Jewish neighbours were persecuted, robbed, deported and murdered. Still this does not mean that Catholics were not to be found among the perpetrators and enablers of the Holocaust, indirectly or directly, or among those who tolerated the mechanisms of death.[50] Centuries of antisemitism grounded on the original deicide charge against Jews affected the worldview of most Christians and easily led to contemporary prejudice and discrimination.[51] Most Catholics did not embody such a bias to the extent that they were led to commit horrific crimes of genocide. However, such negative portrayals of Jews emboldened Catholics to tolerate or even support the gradual ostracisation and persecution of Jews in German society.[52]

While Catholics said and did little to respond to the plight of their Jewish neighbours, they certainly reacted to state infringements on their Church and the practice of their faith. After Hitler's March 1933 pronouncement on the Christian churches, the German bishops eagerly hoped that such words would lead to a positive working relationship between church and state. A Concordat between the Holy See and the German government in July 1933 strengthened such hope and enabled Catholics to believe that the state would allow the Church and its institutions to operate freely in the National Socialist state without interference.[53] On the local parish level, such hopes were quickly dampened by impromptu searches of church properties by SA men and by the disruption of Catholic parish meetings by state authorities.[54] Such acts were often random by nature and varied by district and region, often depending on the zealousness of local Nazi Party leaders and pre-existing church–state relations. The event that significantly changed church–state relations was the murder of Erich Klausener, the former head of the police division of the Prussian Interior Ministry and the Berlin director of Catholic Action, an organisation that promoted lay participation in the Church's mission. Klausener was among the nearly 200 individuals who lost their lives on 30 June 1934 during the Night of the Long Knives, when the SS, with Hitler's permission, murdered those deemed to be prominent political opponents. To destroy any evidence of foul play, Reinhard Heydrich, the head of the *Sicherheitsdienst* (SD), the SS's intelligence division, had Klausener's death ruled a suicide and his body cremated. Despite the ruling, Bishop Nicholas Bares of Berlin, Klausener's ordinary, celebrated a memorial Mass for Klausener and also accompanied the family to the parish cemetery to bury Klausener's ashes. Canon law prohibited Catholic burial for suicide victims, so Bares's action sent a clear message to Germany's Catholics.[55] Even more so, Catholic leaders were now aware that they were living in a murderous state that expected radical loyalty from its citizens. At the same time, they knew their Church was a public institution that had to exist in such an oppressive state.

# 1935–1939

The murder of Erich Klausener was only the beginning of increased tensions between church and state. As the gatherings of National Socialist organisations such as the Hitler Youth impinged upon Sunday worship and threatened the future existence of the Catholic youth organisations, clergymen pushed back in their sermons and public statements. On 16 July 1935, Prussian Minister President Hermann Goering had his fill of such resistance and ordered that the leaders of the German states no longer tolerate any political dissent from the Catholic Church. In particular, Goering lamented, 'It has gone so far that faithful Catholics leave Mass with the impression that the Catholic Church' rejected all possible 'manifestations of the National Socialist state because political questions and daily events are alluded to in polemical ways in sermons'.[56] The National Socialist worldview was all-encompassing and Goering was determined to ensure its ideological absorption by the Catholic church-going populace.

A week later, Goering issued an additional decree forbidding the continuance of all non-religious-based youth groups that were not solely spiritual by nature. At the same time, he also prohibited the members of the permitted associations from publicly wearing any type of uniform or identifiable badge and from gathering in groups for activities such as hiking or camping.[57] Goering's action was a blatant offence against article 31 of the Concordat between the Nazi government and the Vatican, which was meant to protect Church associations. In the view of Church leaders, all Catholic associations contributed to perpetuating the Church's spiritual mission by supporting Catholics as they lived out their faith. The state disagreed with this interpretation completely and pushed to dissolve any organisations that were not strictly spiritual in nature, considering them to be politically motivated and therefore not protected by the Concordat.

The restrictions did not end with Goering's two decrees. On 1 December 1936, at the request of Baldur von Schirach, the Nazi youth leader, Hitler moved the Hitler Youth from the Ministry of the Interior to the Reich Chancellery declaring it a 'Supreme Governmental Agency', a stand-alone entity. At the same time, Hitler placed the Hitler Youth on the same level as school and home, making all equally responsible for educating Germany's youth 'physically, intellectually, and morally in the spirit of National Socialism to serve the nation and the community'.[58] Six months later, Schirach banned simultaneous membership in the Hitler Youth and Catholic youth organisations.[59] Finally, on 6 February 1939, Goering ordered all remaining Catholic youth groups to be dissolved and on 29 March 1939, Hitler decreed membership in the Hitler Youth compulsory for all German youth.[60]

The German bishops did not take such restrictions lightly. In their pastoral letters and sermons, they regularly protested encroachments on the practice of the Catholic faith, especially any limitations on instructing and forming Catholic youth. On 1 April 1936, they also jointly issued Guidelines for Pastoral Care of the Catholic Youth, which encouraged priests to use every opportunity possible to educate the youth in the Catholic faith.[61] Many Catholic clergy and laity took this call seriously. Gestapo records are filled with cases of priests arrested for illegally establishing youth groups and instituting unauthorised after-school religious education programmes.[62] Similarly, there were significant cases of Catholic laity who also ran into problems with the Gestapo for illegal religious instruction and youth work. For example, the Gestapo interrogated Catholic teachers Margaret Barnikel of Stephanskirchen, Alfons Achatz of Schönbrun bei Landshut and Hildegard Wankel of Neumarkt-Sankt Veit. All three were from towns located in Bavaria. They were questioned for offering religious instruction and for overemphasising the practice of Catholicism for German youths at the expense of cultivating support for National Socialist ideology. Primarily, these individuals were ensuring the continuance of their Catholic faith rather than engaging in bold acts of political resistance. Still the specific impetus for such actions is challenging, especially regarding the Gestapo's report on Achatz. In its report on Achatz, the Gestapo accused him not only of offering religious instruction, but also of actively encouraging the young men of his town to resist joining the SA.[63]

Given the fact that such resistance existed among Catholics, state authorities were not content to repress Catholic youth groups alone to limit religious influence over Germany's youth. In September 1935, motivated by Goering's decree, the Reich Ministry of Education began a campaign against church-affiliated schools. Using the overarching concept of *Volksgemeinschaft*, state authorities and the state-controlled press repeatedly and forcefully advocated for interconfessional community schools. Priests took to the pulpit in an effort to sway the vote in favour of Catholic schools. Region by region, parents participated in referenda to decide whether or not to support such schools. In many areas across Germany, the Church lost this battle as the government convinced Catholic parents that community schools would better serve the interests of both society and families. State authorities noted those religious schools that first escaped transformation and gradually dealt with them over time until few denominational schools existed in Germany.[64] At the same time, in the newly established interconfessional community schools, state officials endeavoured to remove priests from authority positions and from teaching religion. Such actions were often unsystematic and took place sporadically throughout Germany. Yet, in March 1940, the state did succeed in abolishing religious instruction in secondary schools and a year later limited it solely to the first eight years of education.[65]

In a few regions in Germany, the community school issue was interpreted even more narrowly to mean the removal of all religious symbols from schools. This was the case in Oldenburg (Münster diocese), in early November 1936, when Julius Pauly, the local state administrator in charge of churches and schools, issued a decree forbidding religious consecration of school buildings and, in turn, called for the removal of any religious symbols. This included the removal of crucifixes from the classrooms. Although Oldenburg was an overwhelmingly Protestant region, two of its districts, Cloppenburg and Vechta, were piously Catholic and predominantly rural farming communities. Accustomed to asserting their faith, the inhabitants of both Catholic districts publicly resisted the decree through a variety of means, such as attending special Masses at places of pilgrimages; composing, signing and personally delivering protest letters and petitions; and adorning public and private buildings with crucifixes. The resistance was unlike anything local state authorities had ever previously encountered. In the end, the combined resistance of the 'social and ideological' homogeneous districts was too great, forcing the local government to withdraw its decree.[66] Such a change of direction on the part of the Nazi state reveals that popular resistance to policies, which were not central to National Socialist ideology, could be undertaken with success and without serious repercussions, chiefly when communities acted as a whole and in complete solidarity with one another.

German Catholics were not alone as they endeavoured to practice their faith under National Socialism. Pope Pius XI and his secretary of state, Eugenio Pacelli, former nuncio to Germany, also kept careful vigil over German church–state relations. Since September 1933, the Vatican had dealt with the Church question in Germany by sending 'thirty-four notes to the Berlin government, five *promemoriae*, three *aide-mémoires*, six letters containing proposals and outlines for discussion and six other letters, in all covering some three-hundred and sixty pages'.[67] However, such correspondence was private and its contents known only among diplomats and government officials. In March 1937, this diplomatic path changed when Pope Pius XI issued the encyclical, *Mit brennender Sorge* ('With Burning Concern'), which used the tenets of the Reich Concordat to detail the Reich government's offences against the Church. Robert d'Harcourt, a foreign observer in Berlin, described its reading during Palm Sunday Mass in churches throughout Germany as striking 'like a bomb'.[68] Agreeing with d'Harcourt's observation, the Gestapo immediately set out to contain the collateral damage it incurred by shutting down printing presses that reproduced it, confiscating copies and arresting clergy who distributed it. Hanns Kerrl, the Reich Minister of Church Affairs, warned the German bishops that it was 'a serious breach' against the Reich Concordat, especially with its 'attacks against the welfare and interest of the German state'.[69]

To counter the negative publicity, especially internationally, to the publication of *Mit brennender Sorge*, the Reich government heightened its attack on the Church by resuming 'morality trials' against Catholic clergymen, which had been halted shortly before the 1936 Olympics. The initial trials had come about in May 1936 after legitimate arrests took place for sexual assaults by fifty-four brothers of the St. Francis Waldbreitbach religious community, which staffed an orphanage for boys in Ebernach, near Cochem, in the Rhineland. The German bishops responded by issuing frank pastoral letters that forthrightly addressed the crimes. Josef Goebbels and his staff at the Ministry of Propaganda and Popular Enlightenment, recognising its inherent anti-Church value, seized upon the situation. Yet, instead of focusing on the religious brothers who were arrested and convicted, Goebbels launched a media campaign against clergy as a whole, promising the German public thousands of trials. The German bishops countered the accusations by issuing further pastoral letters and conducting their own countrywide survey to discover the true extent of recorded abuse.[70] In the end, the bishops learned that of the 25,635 priests in Germany, less than 0.25 per cent had been accused of sexual abuse, though like the state's propaganda ministry, the bishops did not target the considerable number of religious brothers involved in such immoral and criminal activity.[71]

German Catholics regularly encountered salacious coverage of the trials in the state-controlled media. The bishops countered such reporting through their pastoral letters and the parish clergy through their sermons. On the whole, the sexual abuse scandal did not shake the Church significantly enough to cause its leaders to lose their moral authority over the Catholic laity. Nevertheless, the years 1937, 1938 and 1939 experienced a significant number of withdrawals from the Church: in 1937, 108,054 or more than double the 1936 figure of 46,000; in 1938, 88,715; and in 1939, 88,335. In 1940, however, the number of withdrawals declined, returning to figures in line with those of the latter years of the Weimar Republic.[72] Although such figures alarmed the bishops and parish clergy, in reality the numbers were not exceedingly troubling when compared to the total number (22.7 million) of Catholics living in Germany in 1939.[73] Such a short-lived increase in departures may be attributed in large part to the 'morality trials', but several additional factors must also be considered. In 1936, the government made it possible for individuals who withdrew from either the Catholic Church or the Protestant Church to identify as *Gottgläubig* (believer-in-God) and thus avoid being labelled atheists. In February 1937, the state also made it illegal for churches to publicly announce the names of anyone who withdrew. Even more importantly during these years was the increased pressure senior state officials were placing on civil servants to withdraw from the churches.[74]

Despite such obstacles facing the Church as its ministers attempted to provide pastoral care to the Catholic faithful, the Church was still able to continue its mission to German Catholics (Figure 9.2). Moreover, the system of church taxation continued, thus enabling the Catholic Church to meet its financial obligations. Any limitations that German Catholics experienced with regard to their freedom to practice their faith was in no way comparable to the persecution experienced by German Jews during the same period. In September 1935, the Nuremberg Laws deprived German Jews of their citizenship, while German Catholics had the 'privilege' of continuing their membership in the German *Volksgemeinschaft*, even if they did not agree with all the tenets of National Socialism.[75]

FIGURE 9.2 *Twentieth anniversary celebration of the Congregation of the Virgin Mary on the grounds of St. Joseph's home in Birkenwerder (Berlin diocese) in May 1937. Courtesy of Diözesanarchiv Berlin.*

# 1939–1945

On the evening of 9 November 1938, members of the SA and SS, together with ordinary Germans, launched a pogrom of terror against Germany's Jews by specifically targeting the destruction of synagogues and Jewish-owned businesses. Before the violence ended, more than 91 Jews had been murdered and 191 synagogues had been either partially or completely destroyed, and these were only the estimates reported by the SD. An additional 30,000 Jewish men were rounded up and imprisoned in Dachau, Buchenwald and Sachsenhausen concentration camps. Afterwards, Hermann Goering, Prussian Minister President and the director of the government's Four Year Plan, devised a law to make German Jews financially responsible for the damage.[76]

Despite the countrywide violence, both state and church archives are disturbingly silent about how Catholics responded to *Kristallnacht*.[77] The German bishops issued no public statement or condemnation. Neither did the Holy See. Shortly after the pogrom, Monsignor Bernhard Lichtenberg, the rector of St. Hedwig, shared his solidarity with Jews by proclaiming from the pulpit, 'We know what happened yesterday. We do not know what tomorrow holds. However, we have experienced what happened today. Outside, the synagogue burns. That is also a house of God.' Lichtenberg continued to publicly pray for both Jews and Christians of Jewish heritage during the cathedral's services until his arrest in 1941.[78] Since the cathedral was located in the middle of the Reich capital, the congregation would regularly have included visitors. Yet no Catholic who attended Mass or evening prayer during this time denounced Lichtenberg for his intercessions on behalf of the Jews. However, on 29 August 1941, two Protestant students, Ilse Herbell and Lieselotte Schmachtenberg, were troubled when they heard Lichtenberg praying for Jews during evening prayer while visiting the cathedral for a school assignment on architecture. Perplexed by what they heard, a few days later the students shared their experience with a classmate, Jutta Hanke, who, in turn, told her father, a member of the SS. An intense investigation ensued that included the interrogation of Herbell and Schmachtenberg. By the end of October, Lichtenberg was in Gestapo custody, never to experience freedom again.[79] Two years later, on 5 November 1943, Lichtenberg died in a hospital in Hof, a town on the border of Thuringia and Bavaria, while awaiting transportation to Dachau.[80] Few Catholics followed the path chosen by Monsignor Lichtenberg to speak out for persecuted Jews.

While Catholics rarely interceded for their Jewish neighbours, they were concerned with injustices being perpetrated against Catholic members of the *Volksgemeinschaft*. The clearest and most well-known case took place in the summer of 1941 in Münster. Following two strongly worded sermons that rebuked the state authorities, especially the Gestapo, for their encroachment on the rights of the Church and their arbitrary persecution of individual Catholics, on Sunday 3 August 1941, Clemens von Galen, the Bishop of Münster, condemned the state's secret euthanasia policy in his sermon in Münster's St. Lambert's Church. Implemented with Hitler's approval in the autumn of 1939, the T4 programme targeted those deemed as having 'life unworthy of life', such as the physically and mentally handicapped, primarily housed in state-run facilities.[81]

Bishop von Galen's protest against the 'euthanasia' programme infuriated Nazi leaders. Some, such as Martin Bormann, chief of staff for Deputy *Führer* Rudolf Hess, advocated the bishop's arrest and execution, though others such as Goebbels cautioned against any radical measures for fear of public unrest.[82] Hitler agreed with Goebbels, though he promised to 'exact retribution' against the bishop after the war ended.[83] Bishop von Galen was able to remain in his diocese, unlike Johannes Baptista Sproll, the Bishop of Rottenburg, who had to flee his home in August 1938 after church–state tensions in his region threatened to become deadly.[84]

What impact did von Galen's sermons have on Catholics and on the T4 programme? Primarily, the bishop's sermons ensured that rumours about a state-approved yet secret T4 euthanasia programme became a hard cold fact, out in the public arena for all to discuss. The sermons became *the* central topic of discussion among the Catholics of Münster and far beyond as news about their content quickly spread. From person to person, Catholics passed mimeographed copies of von Galen's summer sermons. Copies made their way over the German border to foreign countries and soon became world news.[85] Even more important, not long after von Galen's third sermon, the state abandoned its T4 programme. Some scholars believe such developments had been predetermined before von Galen's sermons, especially since T4 had fulfilled its killing goals and euthanasia personnel were needed further east to work in the Holocaust death machinery.[86] Unofficially, the euthanasia programme actually continued uninterrupted as it transitioned from centralised killing centres with gas chambers to 'hygienic' killing policies of forced starvation and lethal injections in institutions throughout Germany.[87] At most, such protests drove Catholics to mistrust state authorities even more; but as Germany was in the midst of war, it was challenging, if not unworkable, for anything more significant to happen. The Gestapo also acted swiftly and mercilessly against any form of resistance. Moreover, most Germans in no way wished to appear to be endangering the unity of the *Volksgemeinschaft*, especially during the war, as soldiers – their sons, brothers, fathers and husbands – were losing their lives fighting for the fatherland.[88]

Bishop von Galen's protest against euthanasia, however, was quite remarkable. In the midst of a 'total war' that tolerated almost no dissent, his stance was truly heroic and reveals how it was possible for Catholic leaders to challenge the state. At the same time, von Galen's protest must also be viewed alongside the many letters written by Germany's Catholic bishops to state authorities protesting policies that had encroached on the Church's sphere of influence. However bold von Galen's protest was, it was against acts that directly affected Catholics and contradicted Church teaching and practice. Though German Jews died in T4's gas chambers, the primary victims were Christian. In the 1930s and 1940s, the spiritual and moral priority of Catholics was the preservation of their own belief system and the security of their own baptised members (Figure 9.3).

FIGURE 9.3 *Father Karl Willimsky presides at a Mass during which children of the parish are making their First Communion in St. Bonifatius Church in Bergen (Berlin diocese) on 27 October 1940. Courtesy of Diözesanarchiv Berlin.*

# Conclusion

Overall, this chapter has shown that in their daily lives, Catholics, especially the Church's clergy, primarily 'resisted' the state when it encroached on the traditional religious freedoms the Church normally experienced in Germany. Though clearly such pastoral-motivated 'resistance' was the norm, an event that took place in May 1942 in the rural agricultural communities of Wiesenfeld and Halsbach (Würzburg diocese) offers an insight into the variety of motivational factors at play as Catholics attempted daily to negotiate their practice of their faith under National Socialism.

On Sunday 10 May 1942, Michael W., a farmer and a NSDAP member, told his pastor, Father Felix Dürr, that he and the beadle, Klara S., had organised a group of parishioners to make a *Bittage* (days leading up to the Feast of the Ascension) pilgrimage from the church in Halsbach to the church in the neighbouring town of Wiesenfeld. Halsbach was the filial parish of Wiesenfeld and Dürr was pastor of both. According to Michael W., Father Dürr replied, 'I know nothing about a pilgrimage, only that Mass will be at 7 o'clock'. When later questioned by the Gestapo, Dürr stated that he had said, 'You are not allowed to do that. Pilgrimages are prohibited and I am not taking on any responsibility.' Since 1935, the Gestapo had required the registration of church processions and pilgrimages and, since 1941, had placed serious restrictions on them, though enforcement varied from region to region.[89]

The pilgrimage took place on that Monday, and neither Father Dürr nor Father Michael Meyer,[90] the parochial vicar, was present. A few days later, the local police received word that an 'illegal' pilgrimage had taken place and summoned Klara S., Michael W. and Father Dürr for questioning. Separately, both Klara and Michael gave similar testimony, with Michael stating:

> Until now, a pilgrimage to Wiesenfeld has taken place every year during the *Bittage*. This year, during the time of the *Bittage*, a great drought held sway and the crops were very poor, so I said to myself, we have to organise a procession and call upon God's blessing so that He will allow rain and the crops will be all right, so that there will be grain to provide nourishment for the *Volk*.

Michael continued, 'In his speeches, the *Führer* very often has said everyone can live his faith and if we have called upon God's blessings that He allows the crops to prosper, I do not believe that I have done anything wrong, since we have brought the necessary rain so the crops can grow.' Michael's explanation did not impress the police, who fined him 150 Reichsmarks for leading a prohibited pilgrimage. Neither Father Dürr nor Father Meyer was held accountable.[91]

The case of the Wiesenfeld pilgrimage is fascinating for it reveals the mindset of ordinary Catholics living in a rural farming community. Amid the persecution and deportation of Jews, the oppression of practice of the

Catholic faith and the world war, the main concern for these Catholic farmers was the successful growing of crops. The farmers' solution to the drought was a pilgrimage; by performing a religious act, a pilgrimage, God would bestow a blessing on the crops and a rich harvest would follow. The Catholic farmers' mentality was not very different from that of Catholics who lived in Europe more than 300 years earlier.[92] Though clearly not all Catholics operated within such a mindset, such evidence provides caution as we search to understand the daily interaction of German Catholics with the National Socialist state. As long as the state did not interfere with these farmers' hold on the Almighty (by way of pilgrimage), the boundary between the two – citizens and state – remained intact. All else – from mass deportations to mass murders – remained inconsequential. All that counted was the reconciliatory action – a pilgrimage, in this case – between the believer and God to keep things right in the world. The inseparability of God from neighbour, from any human being, whether the person was Catholic or non-Catholic, had yet to startle these farmers' insular Catholic piety.

Generally, Catholics' response to National Socialism did not stray very far from that of the Wiesenfeld farmers. The majority of Catholics viewed themselves as loyal, patriotic Germans who supported their country, especially the economic and global revitalisation that they believed Adolf Hitler was offering to their country. Catholics were boldly willing to support National Socialism, at least in the beginning, as if it were the greatest asset a government could provide. There were few who questioned its racial policy. Nevertheless, Catholic support of the National Socialist state had its limits evidenced often when the state encroached in an area that was traditionally occupied by the Church. In such cases where specific Church interests were at stake, Catholics, both lay and clergy, could forcefully raise their voices in opposition. Rarely, however, were such voices raised against any state measure or action that did not directly affect Catholics and their religious ethos. At this point, the Catholic Church's sphere of concern was quite narrowly focused on the parochial. Anyone or anything outside of its canonical domain could easily be overlooked or ignored. It had not yet become a Church that completely embraced the gospel command to love one's neighbour, whoever that might be or however much despised.

# Notes

1   Bad Neustadt Gestapoamt to Bezirksamt Königshoffen, 7 January 1937, Staatsarchiv Würzburg (StAW), Gestapoakte (GSW) Nr. 3336, n.f.

2   See the correspondence in StAW GSW Nr. 3336 and U. von Hehl, C. Kösters, P. Stenz-Maur and E. Zimmermann (eds), *Priester unter Hitlers Terror. Eine Biographische und Statistische Erhebung*, fourth revised edition (Paderborn, vol. II, 1998), pp. 1579–1580.

3   Von Hehl et al., *Priester unter Hitlers Terror*, I, p. 73.

4   On priests and resistance, see K. Spicer, *Resisting the Third Reich: The Catholic Clergy in Hitler's Berlin* (DeKalb, IL, 2004).

5   See K. Gotto, H. Hockerts and K. Repgen, 'Nationalsozialistische Herausforderung und kirchliche Antwort. Ein Bilanz', in K. Gott and K. Repgen (eds), *Die Katholiken und das Dritte Reich*, third revised edition (Mainz, 1990), pp. 178–179.

6   H. Hürten, *Deutsche Katholiken 1918 bis 1945* (Paderborn, 1992), p. 559.

7   On *Kirchensteuer*, see H. Marré, 'Die Kirchenfinanzierung durch Kirchensteuern', in *Geschichte des Kirchlichen Lebens in den deutschsprachigen Ländern seit dem Ende des 18. Jahrhunderts, vol.* VI: *Die Kirchenfinanzen* (Freiburg im Breisgau, 2000), pp. 213–227, especially pp. 224–227.

8   E. Gatz, 'Die Zeit der nationalsozialistischen Herrschaft in Deutschland und in den annektierten Gebieten', in *Geschichte des Kirchlichen Lebens in den deutschsprachigen Ländern seit dem Ende des 18. Jahrhunderts, vol. VI: Die Kirchenfinanzen* (Freiburg im Breisgau, 2000), pp. 273–227; G. Hartmann, 'Kirchensteuer', *Historisches Lexikon Bayerns* (18 August 2010). http://www.historisches-lexikon-bayerns.de/artikel/artikel_44744 [accessed 11 September 2014]. I would like to thank Elias Füllenbach, O.P., Gotthard Klein and Christoph Kösters for sharing their insights on Germany's complex system of *Kirchensteuer*.

9   E. Gatz (ed.), *Die Bistümer der deutschsprachigen Länder. Von der Säkularisation bis zur Gegenwart. Ein historisches Lexikon* (Freiburg im Breisgau, 2005), pp. 682–687.

10  'Anteil der katholischen Bevölkerung in Deutschland', in K. Hummel and M. Kißener (eds), *Die Katholiken und das Dritte Reich: Kontroversen und Debatten* (Paderborn, 2009), pp. 312–313.

11  Zentrale für katholische Statistik des katholischen Deutschlands (eds), *Kirchliches Handbuch für das katholische Deutschland*, 21: 1939–1940 (Cologne, 1939), foldout 1936 statistical sheet.

12  P. Müller, 'Seelsorge unter dem Hakenkreuz', in P. Thull (ed.), *Christen im Dritten Reich* (Darmstadt, 2014), p. 127.

13  Zentrale für katholische Statistik (eds), *Kirchliches Handbuch*, 21, p. 283.

14  C. Kösters, 'Katholisches Milieu und Nationalsozialismus', in *Die Katholiken und das Dritte Reich: Kontroversen*, p. 150.

15  On the meaning of *Kulturkampf* under Hitler, see C. Kösters, '"Kulturkampf" im Dritten Reich – Zur Deutung der Konflikte zwischen NS-Regime und katholische Kirche im deutschen Episkopat', in T. Brechenmacher and H. Oelke (eds), *Die Kirchen und die Verbrechen im nationalsozialistischen Staat* (Göttingen, 2011), pp. 67–112.

16  See R. Bennette, *Fighting for the Soul of Germany: The Catholic Struggle for Inclusion after Unification* (Cambridge, MA, 2012).

17  R. Lill, 'German Catholicism's Attitude towards the Jews in the Weimar Republic', in O. Kulka and P. Mendes-Flohr (eds), *Judaism and Christianity under the Impact of National Socialism* (Jerusalem, 1987), p. 154.

**18** Quoted in U. Mazura, *Zentrumspartei und Judenfrage 1870/71-1933. Verfassungsstaat und Minderheitenschutz* (Mainz, 1994), pp. 186–187. Kareski was a controversial figure among German Jews, and his future choices under National Socialism were quite problematic. On the latter, see H. Levine, 'A Jewish Collaborator in Nazi Germany: The Strange Career of Georg Kareski, 1933-37', *Central European History* 8 (1975), pp. 251–281 and F. Nicosia, *Zionism and Anti-Semitism in Nazi Germany* (Cambridge, 2008), pp. 190–206.

**19** J. Falter, T. Lindenberger and S. Schumann, *Wahlen und Abstimmungen in der Weimarer Republik: Materialien zum Wahlverhalten 1919–1933* (Munich, 1986), p. 41.

**20** Winke betr., 'Aufgaben der Seelsorger gegenüber glaubensfeindlichen Vereinigungen', in W. Corsten (ed.), *Sammlung kirchlicher Erlasse Verordnungen und Bekanntmachungen für die Erzdiözese Köln* (Cologne, 1929), pp. 619–624 and Protokoll der Fuldaer Bischofskonferenz, 18–20 August 1924, Point 14, in H. Hürten (ed.), *Akten deutscher Bischöfe über die Lager der Kirche 1918–1933*, I: 1918–1925 (Paderborn, 2007), p. 589.

**21** For the lack of accord among the bishops, see Bertram to Members of the Fulda Bishops' Conference, 3 March 1924, in Hürten (ed.), *Akten deutscher Bischöfe*, I, 560–561. Also see the discussion in U. Ehret, *Church, Nation and Race: Catholics and Antisemitism in Germany and England, 1918–1945* (Manchester, 2012), pp. 138–139. Although on 15 September 1924 Bertram did reinforce the ban, the bishops did not as Ehret argues stand 'firmly by their condemnation of patriotic associations… until 1933'. Further evidence of this may be found in the correspondence in Erzbistumsarchiv Paderborn, Generalvikariat XVIII, 23. For a detailed discussion of the bishops and the patriotic associations, see W. Vogel, *Katholische Kirche und Nationale Kampfverbände in der Weimarer Republic* (Mainz, 1989), chapters III and IV.

**22** Rachor to Mayer, 17 June 1929, in S. Durchhardt-Bösken (ed.), *Das Bischöfliche Ordinariat Mainz und der Nationalsozialismus bis 1933. Eine Dokumentation* (Mainz, 1983), p. 13.

**23** Mayer to Rachor, 18 June 1929, in Durchhardt-Bösken (ed.), *Das Bischöfliche Ordinariat Mainz*, p. 14.

**24** 'Katholik und Nationalsozialismus. Von einem katholischen Geistlichen', *Mainzer Journal*, 25 August 1930, in Durchhardt-Bösken (ed.), *Das Bischöfliche Ordinariat Mainz*, pp. 24–28.

**25** Weber to Ordinariat Mainz, 25 August 1930; Ordinariat Mainz to Weber, 1 September 1930; Gauleitung Hessen to Ordinariat Mainz, 27 September 1930; Ordinariat Mainz to Gauleitung Hessen, 30 September 1930, in Durchhardt-Bösken (ed.), *Das Bischöfliche Ordinariat Mainz*, pp. 28–30.

**26** For example, see the letters in Dom- und Diözesanarchiv Mainz, Abteilung 52–54.9b and Bistumsarchiv Osnabrück, Verhältnis von Kirche und Staat 04-61-00.

**27** See the correspondence in United States Holocaust Memorial Museum, RG 76.001M, Reel 10/Vatican Secret Archives, Secretariat of State, Pos 606 Fasc. 117.

28   Entwurf, 2 December 1930, in Stasiewski (ed.), *Akten deutscher Bischöfe*, I, pp. 787–789 and Faulhaber to Bertram, 18 December 1930, in Stasiewski (ed.), *Akten deutscher Bischöfe*, I, pp. 798–799.

29   For example, see Faulhaber to Bavarian Episcopate, 6 December 1930 in Stasiewski (ed.), *Akten deutscher Bischöfe*, I, pp. 789–791.

30   See the documents in Stasiewski (ed.), *Akten deutscher Bischöfe*, I, pp. 800–843.

31   Confirmed in Protokoll der Fuldaer Bischofskonferenz, 17–19 August 1932, Point 3, in H. Hürten (ed.), *Akten deutscher Bischöfe über die Lager der Kirche 1918–1933*, II: 1926–1933 (Paderborn, 2007), p. 1206.

32   M. Kater, *The Nazi Party: A Social Profile of Members and Leader, 1919–1945* (Oxford, 1985), p. 263.

33   O. Blaschke, *Die Kirchen und der Nationalsozialismus* (Stuttgart, 2014), p. 70.

34   J. Falter, *Hitlers Wähler* (Munich, 1991), p. 179.

35   O. Heilbronner and D. Mühlberger, 'The Achilles' Heel of German Catholicism: "Who Voted for Hitler?" Revisited', *European History Quarterly* 27 (1997), pp. 221–249, especially pp. 230–231.

36   L. Jones, 'Catholics on the Right. The Reich Catholic Committee of the German National People's Party, 1920-33', *Historisches Jahrbuch* 126 (2006), pp. 221–267. Also see D. Hastings, *Catholicism and the Roots of Nazism: Religious Identity and National Socialism* (New York, 2010).

37   K. Spicer, *Hitler's Priests: Catholic Clergy and National Socialism* (DeKalb, IL, 2008).

38   See I. Kershaw, 'The "Everyday" and the "Exceptional": The Shaping of Popular Opinion, 1933–1939', in *Hitler, the Germans and the Final Solution* (New Haven, CT, 2008), pp. 119–138.

39   *Germania*, 22 March 1933.

40   M. Domarus, *Hitler Reden und Proklamationen, 1932–1945: Kommentiert von einem deutsche Zeitgenossen*, vol. Ia. (Munich, 1965), pp. 232–236.

41   R. Morsey, *Der Untergang des politischen Katholizismus. Die Zentrumspartei zwischen christlichem Selbstverständnis und 'Nationaler Erhebung' 1932/33* (Stuttgart, 1977), pp. 142–147.

42   Kundgebung der deutschen Bischöfe, 28 March 1933, in Stasiewski (ed.), *Akten deutscher Bischöfe*, I, pp. 30–32.

43   On Stratmann, see A. Timmermann and D. Steubl, *Pater Franziskus Maria Stratmann O.P.. Die Biographie eines unermüdlichen Friedenskämpfers* (Munich, 2009).

44   Stratmann to Faulhaber, 10 April 1933, in L. Volk (ed.), *Akten Kardinal Michael von Faulhabers 1917–1945*, I: 1917–1934 (Matthias Grünewald, 1975), p. 711.

45   Faulhaber an Wurm, 8 April 1933, in Volk (ed.), *Akten Kardinal Michael von Faulhaber*, I, p. 705.

46   See F. Stratmann, *In der Verbannung. Tagebuchblätter 1940 bis 1947* (Frankfurt am Main, 1962).

47 On those who did share Stratmann's view, see J. Connelly, *From Enemy to Brother: The Revolution in Catholic Teaching on the Jews 1933–1965* (Cambridge, MA, 2012).

48 For a general discussion, see M. Paldiel, *Churches and the Holocaust: Unholy Teaching, Good Samaritans and Reconciliation* (Jersey City, NJ, 2006), especially pp. 24–68.

49 On Cardinal Faulhaber and Jews, see H. Hürten, 'Kardinal Faulhaber und die Juden. Eine frühe Stellungnahme der katholischen Kirche zum Nationalsozialismus', *Zeitschrift für bayerische Landesgeschichte* 68 (2005), pp. 1029–1034 and S. Kornacker, 'Faulhaber und die Juden', in *Kardinal Michael von Faulhaber. 1869 bis 1952. Eine Ausstellung des Archivs des Erzbistums München und Freising, des Bayerischen Hauptstaatsarchivs und des Stadtarchivs München zum 50. Todestag* (Neuburg, 2002), pp. 321–344.

50 More work needs to be done on the question of perpetrators and religion. For preliminary analysis regarding Catholics, see A. Lasik, 'Historical-Sociological Profile of the Auschwitz SS', in Y. Gutman and M. Berenbaum (eds), *Anatomy of the Auschwitz Death Camp* (Bloomington, IN, 1994), pp. 271–287 and M. Mann, 'Were the Perpetrators of Genocide "Ordinary Men" or "Real Nazis"? Results from Fifteen Hundred Biographies', *Holocaust and Genocide Studies* 14 (2000), pp. 331–366, especially pp. 347–349. Both articles are discussed in S. Brown-Fleming, 'Recent Historiographical Contributions to the History of the Churches and the Holocaust: The Catholic Case', in D. Herzog (ed.), *Lessons and Legacies. XII: The Holocaust in International Perspective* (Evanston, IL, 2006), pp. 303–313.

51 On antisemitism and its link to Christianity, see R. Michael, *A History of Catholic Antisemitism: The Dark Side of the Church* (New York, 2006) and K. Spicer (ed.), *Antisemitism, Christian Ambivalence, and the Holocaust* (Bloomington, IN, 2007).

52 Recently, scholars have focused primarily on the question of the Vatican and the Holocaust. Further research needs to be conducted on German Catholics and the persecution of Jews. For now, see I. Kershaw, *Popular Opinion and Political Dissent in the Third Reich: Bavaria 1933–1945*, 2nd ed. (Oxford, 2005), especially pp. 224–277, 358–372.

53 On the Reich Concordat, see T. Brechenmacher (ed.), *Das Reichskonkordat 1933. Forschungsstand, Kontroversen, Dokumente* (Paderborn, 2007).

54 For example, in June and July 1933, the Eichstätt diocesan priests, Ferdinand Freiherr von Papius and Franz Sand were harassed by SA men because of their previous participation in the BVP and 'political statements', respectively. See Papius to Eichstätt Generalvikariat, 30 June 1933 and Sand to Eichstätt Generalvikariat, 14 July 1933, in Diözesanarchiv Eichstätt, Kreuz und Hakenkreuz 2.

55 On Klausener, see Spicer, *Resisting the Third Reich*, pp. 38–42.

56 Goering Runderlass, 16 July 1935, Brandenburgisches Landeshauptarchiv Pr. Rep. 2A Regierung Potsdam I Pol. 3034, ff. 242–254.

57 Verordnung Goering über die Betätigung katholischer Jugendverbände, 23 July 1935, in H. Gruber (ed.), *Katholische Kirche und Nationalsozialismus 1930–1945. Ein Bericht in Quellen*, (Paderborn, 2006), pp. 233–234.

58   Law on the Hitler Youth, 1 December 1936, in J. Noakes and G. Pridham (eds), *Nazism 1919–1945, II: State, Economy and Society 1933–1939* (Exeter, 2003), p. 225.

59   Hitler-Jugend und konfessionelle Verbände, 18 June 1937, in W. Corsten (ed.), *Kölner Aktenstücke zur Lage der katholischen Kirche in Deutschland 1933–1945* (Cologne, 1949), pp. 217–218.

60   Goering Erlass, 6 February 1939, in H. Roth (ed.), *Katholische Jugend in der NS-Zeit unter besonderer Berücksichtigung des Katholischen Jungmännerverbandes. Daten und Dokumente*, (Düsseldorf, 1959) and Noakes and Pridham (eds), *Nazism 1919–1945*, II, p. 226.

61   Richtlinien für die katholische Jugendseelsorge, 1 April 1936, in L. Volk (ed.), *Akten deutscher Bischöfe über die Lage der Kirche 1933–1945*, IV: 1936–1939 (Mainz, 1981), pp. 761–764. On the guidelines, see B. Schellenberger, *Katholische Jugend und Drittes Reich* (Mainz, 1975), pp. 163–169.

62   For example, see T. Haaf, *Von volksverhetzenden Pfaffen und falschen Propheten. Klerus und Kirchenvolk im Bistum Würzburg in der Auseinandersetzung mit dem Nationalsozialismus* (Würzburg, 2005), pp. 40–130. The Gestapo and other state authorities investigated at least 2,700 cases in which clergy broke laws regarding illegal pastoral care to youth groups and other Church associations. See the statistical information and corresponding biographical capsules in von Hehl et al., *Priester unter Hitlers Terror*, especially I, p. 128.

63   B. Höpfl, *Katholische Laien im nationalsozialistischen Bayern: Verweigerung und Widerstand zwischen 1933 und 1945* (Paderborn, 1997), pp. 290–314, here pp. 295–296.

64   See W. Damberg, *Der Kampf um die Schulen in Westfalen 1933–1945* (Mainz, 1986).

65   E. Helmreich, *The German Churches under Hitler. Background, Struggle, and Epilogue* (Detroit, 1980), p. 320.

66   J. Noakes, 'The Oldenburg Crucifix Struggle of November 1936: A Case Study of Opposition in the Third Reich', in P. Stachura (ed.), *The Shaping of the Nazi State* (New York, 1978), pp. 210–223. Also see M. Zumholz (ed.), *Katholisches Milieu und Widerstand: Der Kreuzkampf im Oldenburger Land im Kontext des nationalsozialistischen Herrschaftsgefüges* (Berlin, 2012).

67   W. Harrigan, 'Nazi Germany and the Holy See, 1933-1936: The Historical Background of *Mit brennender Sorge*', *Catholic Historical Review* 47 (1961), p. 195.

68   Quotation from Robert d'Harcourt, member of the Académe Française and visitor to Germany, who heard the encyclical read aloud during Palm Sunday Mass. See R. Leiber, 'Mit brennender Sorge: März 1937-März 1962', *Stimmen der Zeit* 87 (1961/1962), p. 418.

69   Kerrl to German Bishops, 23 March 1937, in *Kardinal Preysing und zwei Diktaturen: Sein Widerstand gegen die totalitäre Macht* (Berlin, 1971), p. 81.

70   H. Hockerts, *Die Sittlichkeitsprozesse gegen katholische Ordensangehörige und Priester, 1936/1937: Eine Studie zur nationalsozialistischen Herrschaftstechnik und zum Kirchenkampf* (Mainz, 1971).

71  Preysing to Ordinarien Deutschlands, 27 May 1937, in Bistumsarchiv Fulda Generalvikariat 270–12 Fasz. 64, n.f.

72  Zentrale für katholische Statistik (eds), *Kirchliches Handbuch*, 22 (1943), p. 289.

73  Ibid., p. 404.

74  Hockerts, *Die Sittlichkeitsprozesse*, pp. 185–188. Also see C. Kösters, 'Katholisches Kirchenvolk 1933-1945', in C. Kösters and M. Ruff (eds), *Die katholische Kirche im Dritten Reich: Eine Einführung* (Freiburg im Breisgau, 2011), p. 101.

75  Law for the Protection of German Blood and German Honour, 15 September 1935; Reich Citizenship Law, 15 September 1935; Supplementary Decree, 14 November 1935, in Noakes and Pridham (eds), *Nazism 1919–1945*, II, pp. 341–346.

76  M. Kaplan, *Between Dignity and Despair: Jewish Life in Nazi Germany* (New York, 1998), pp. 121–125 and Noakes and Pridham (eds), *Nazism 1919–1945*, II, pp. 359–368.

77  See K. Repgen, 'Judenpogrom, Rassenideologie und katholische Kirche im Jahre 1938', in R. Bendel (ed.), *Die katholische Schuld? Katholizismus im Dritten Reich – Zwischen Arrangement und Widerstand* (Berlin, 2002), pp. 56–91.

78  H. G. Mann, *Prozeß Bernhard Lichtenberg: Ein Leben in Dokumenten* (Berlin, 1977), p. 9.

79  Protokoll, 29 September 1941, in Mann, *Prozeß Bernhard Lichtenberg*, pp. 44–45 and G. Klein, *Berolinen Canonizationis Servi Dei Bernardi Lichtenberg: Sacerdotis Saecularis in Odium Fidei, Uti Fertur, Interfecti (1875–1943). I: Informatio* (Rome, 1992), p. 83, n. 6.

80  On Lichtenberg's life and resistance to National Socialism, see Spicer, *Resisting the Third Reich*, pp. 160–182.

81  On the euthanasia programme, see E. Klee, *'Euthanasie' im NS-Staat. Die 'Vernichtung lebensunwerten Lebens'* (Frankfurt am Main, 1994).

82  M. Burleigh, *Death and Deliverance: 'Euthanasia' in Germany 1900–1945* (Cambridge, 1995), p. 178.

83  H. Trevor-Roper (ed.), *Hitler's Table Talk 1941–1944. His Private Conversations*, trans. Norman Cameron and R. H. Stevens (New York, 2000), p. 555.

84  On Sproll, see D. Burkhard, *Johannes Baptista Sproll: Bischof im Widerstand* (Stuttgart, 2013); S. Sproll, *'Ich bin der Bischof von Rottenburg und bleibe der Bischof von Rottenburg'. Das Leben von Johannes Baptista Sproll* (Ostfildern, 2009).

85  W. Süss, 'Ein Skandal im Sommer 1941. Reaktionen auf den "Euthanasie" – Protest des Bischofs von Münster', in H. Wolf, T. Flammer and B. Schüler (eds), *Clemens August von Galen. Ein Kirchenfürst im Nationalsozialismus* (Darmstadt, 2007), pp. 181–198.

86  Burleigh, *Death and Deliverance*, p. 180.

87   G. Aly, *Die Belasteten: 'Euthanasie' 1939–1945. Eine Gesellschaftsgeschichte* (Frankfurt am Main, 2013), pp. 193–290.

88   C. Kösters, 'Kirche und Glaube an der "Heimatfront". Katholische Lebenswelt und Kriegserfahrungen 1939-1945', in K. Hummel and C. Kösters (eds), *Kirchen im Krieg. Europa 1939–1945* (Paderborn, 2007), pp. 263–398. Also see M. Steinert, *Hitler's War and the Germans: Public Mood and Attitude during the Second World War*, ed. and trans. Thomas E. J. De Witt (Athens, OH, 1977).

89   'Kirchliche Prozessionen und Wallfahrten', *Würzburger Diözesanblatt*, 10 May 1939 and 'Verordnung über die Handhabung des Feiertagsrecht während des Krieges vom 27. Oktober 1941', *Reichsgesetzblatt*, no. 122, 28 October 1941, p. 662.

90   Father Meyer was a Benedictine monk (Pater Marold) of Münsterschwarzach abbey that the Gestapo dissolved and confiscated in May 1941. See von Hehl et al., *Priester unter Hitlers Terror*, II, p. 1611. Also see, J. Düring, *Wir Weichen nur der Gewalt. Die Mönche von Münsterschwarzach*, vol. II (Münsterschwarzach, 1997), p. 304.

91   Gendarmerie Wiesenfeld to Landrat Lohr am Main, 15 May 1942, StAW GSW 16917.

92   For example, see the cases presented in W. Christian, Jr., *Local Religion in Sixteenth-Century Spain* (Princeton, NJ, 1989).

# Select bibliography

Bennette, R., *Fighting for the Soul of Germany: The Catholic Struggle for Inclusion after Unification* (Cambridge, MA, 2012).

Blaschke, O., *Die Kirchen und der Nationalsozialismus* (Stuttgart, 2014).

Brechenmacher, T. and Oelke, H. (eds), *Die Kirchen und die Verbrechen im nationalsozialistischen Staat* (Göttingen, 2011).

Connelly, J., *From Enemy to Brother: The Revolution in Catholic Teaching on the Jews 1933–1965* (Cambridge, MA, 2012).

Hastings, D., *Catholicism and the Roots of Nazism: Religious Identity and National Socialism* (Oxford and New York, 2010).

Hürten, H., *Deutsche Katholiken 1918 bis 1945* (Paderborn, 1992).

Kösters, C. and Ruff, M. (eds), *Die katholische Kirche im Dritten Reich: Eine Einführung* (Freiburg im Breisgau, 2011).

Spicer, K., *Resisting the Third Reich: The Catholic Clergy in Hitler's Berlin* (DeKalb, IL, 2004).

Spicer, K. (ed.), *Antisemitism, Christian Ambivalence, and the Holocaust* (Bloomington, IN, 2007).

Spicer, K., *Hitler's Priests: Catholic Clergy and National Socialism* (DeKalb, IL, 2008).

# 10

# Christmas as Nazi Holiday: Colonising the Christmas Mood

## *Joe Perry*

For the 4,000 celebrants who attended the 'German Christmas Party' thrown by the NSDAP to commemorate the 1921 holiday season, the highpoint may have been the rather un-Christmas-like 'Yule Speech' delivered by Adolf Hitler, the recently appointed Party leader. Undercover police spies, on hand to monitor the threat posed by these right-wing extremists, noted the crowd's applause when the *Führer* swore 'not to rest [until] the Jews, Ebert, and the Scheide-men…lay shattered on the ground' (Ebert and Scheidemann were prominent Social Democratic politicians). Voicing the Nazis' hardline antisemitism, Hitler condemned the 'cowardly Jews for beating the world-liberator on the cross'. Flyers and posters for the event that stated 'Entry of Jews Strictly Forbidden' underscored the favoured racial status of attendees. On some level, so did the very German entertainment, which included group singing of classic German carols and performances of Beethoven and Schubert, Bavarian folk songs, Handel's *Largo* and Wagner's *Entry of the Gods into Valhalla*. According to the Nazi Party newspaper *Völkischer Beobachter*, decorations included a 'tree of light [*Lichterbaum*] that towered to the ceiling'; poorer attendees received charity gifts of toys, baked goods and children's clothes. The evening concluded with a group rendition of 'O Highly Esteemed Germany', an 1859 nationalist hymn 'sung with such fire and powerful belief and faith' that the result, wrote the Nazi reporter, was emotional overload: 'Many eyes were moist and cheeks were pale…because in their hearts the serious, difficult, terrible oath, to sacrifice everything, everything was renewed, in order to save our homeland from decadence and collapse.'[1]

Did the attendees really weep at the end of the 1921 'German Christmas Party', as the *Völkischer Beobachter* asserted? We will never know for certain, but the question is a good one, because it highlights the role of the emotions in shaping popular support for National Socialism. For the committed National Socialist supporters who wished to turn Christmas into a celebration of the Nazi *Volksgemeinschaft* ('national community'), the holiday represented a treasure trove of emotional expression, open to colonisation for Nazi ideological goals. Celebrations of German Christmas had long been said to evoke a 'Christmas mood', which turned on moving feelings of *Gemütlichkeit* (comfort, cosiness), *Innerlichkeit* (inner warmth, soulfulness), family love and deeply felt spirituality. Now, a group that might be called the Nazi 'intelligentsia' – ethnographers, historians, poets, school teachers and regime functionaries, and most obviously politicians and propagandists – undertook a determined attempt to channel these emotions into support for the racial state, to lend a patina of depth and normalcy to what was in fact a radical programme of sociopolitical national transformation. As one poet-propagandist wrote: 'The significance of holidays and rituals...lies in the spiritual or emotional deepening of the experience of community. [Christmas] should appeal not to the knowledge of the few, but to the spirit, the life feeling, of the many...to make people aware of their responsibility for the nation's fate.'[2]

Scholars working on the history of emotions have established three key concepts that can help us to understand Nazi emotional engineering. First, recent studies assert that although feelings are grounded in human physiology, the ways they are expressed, repressed and valued are social-historical constructs, shaped by specific human needs and interests in specific historical periods. Second, at a given moment in time, a society accepts a bounded set of emotions as normal and appropriate and so establishes a dominant 'emotional regime' enforced primarily by cultural means. Third, when people talk about or share emotions, they engage in a discursive practice that helps to construct community identification. These historically grounded 'emotional communities' intersect with other markers of identity such as social status, religion or ethnicity, and they may reinforce or contradict other allegiances and identities, including the predominant emotional regime.[3] Following these ideas, this chapter uses the history of Nazi Christmas to explore the emotional appeal of Nazism and the power of the Nazi intelligentsia to impose its vision of a National Socialist 'emotional regime' on society by making inner worlds of feeling conform to Nazi ideology. If Nazi authorities and supporters could harness the power of German Christmas and the elusive 'Christmas mood' evoked by the holiday's observance to their political agenda, this process of 'affective integration'[4] would help to normalise and legitimise the racial policies at the core of the Nazi state.

The Nazi attempt to colonise the Christmas mood was a subtle process of emotional and cultural appropriation and transformation that drew on existing traditions and observances. In many respects, for example, the 1921 German Christmas Party appeared quite normal. The 'potpourri' of holiday entertainment enjoyed by the attendees (e.g. singing, feasting, gifting and carousing) faithfully mirrored the activities on offer at a lower middle-class office party, a 'Christmas Ball' in a dance club or cabaret, or, indeed, in a private family celebration.[5] Yet, in Nazi celebration, familiar symbols and rituals were tweaked to carry an ideological charge. Communal feasting and drinking, renditions of familiar and 'revised' holiday carols, Christmas trees and candlelight were all twisted to evoke and naturalise support for regime goals: popular appreciation of the deep 'Germanic' roots of Christmas that supposedly exemplified and brought to life the deep historic and racial bonds of the *Volksgemeinschaft*. The potentially awkward juxtapositions of Christian and pagan themes already in place in 1921 would thus become a common feature of Nazi observance. Hitler's evocation of Jesus as the 'world liberator' rather than Christian Saviour, the 'tree of light' (rather than 'Christmas tree'), described in the Party newspaper, and the casual use of 'Yule' alongside or instead of 'Christmas' de-emphasised the Christian aspects of the holiday and played up the putatively ancient 'Germanic' solstice customs that defined a 'racially correct' nationalist holiday. The Nazi intelligentsia would return again and again to supposedly Nordic-pagan symbols and observances in order to 'dechristianise' Christmas and turn the holiday into a celebration of a German racial community rooted in *Blut und Boden* (blood and soil). As Propaganda Minister Joseph Goebbels mused in 1935, Christmas was certainly 'the most German of all holidays. It is a Christian celebration', he continued, 'but insofar as we give it an intensely deep and inward meaning, it is also in the truest sense of the words a National Socialist holiday. Because, when we consider the great ideals of community that bind together the entire German *Volk*, the commandment "love thy neighbour" has gained a new and surprising significance for us all.'[6]

If we took such comments – and the full range of other Nazi Christmas publications and practices – at face value, we might conclude that Germans readily accepted the transformation of Germany's favourite holiday during the Third Reich. Yet a thoroughly Nazified emotional community remained elusive: Nazi ideologues never turned Christmas into a celebration of widely shared social/political meaning, and the 'Christmas mood' could in the end not only support but also challenge and undermine National Socialist agendas. This process of negotiation is difficult to track, but it left traces in the documents recorded by the Nazis themselves, especially the 'mood and opinion' reports gathered for the Nazi elite by the internal Security Service (SD) and the activity records complied by other Nazi institutions. Testimony by the underground agents of the Social Democratic Party in Exile (Sopade), who wrote extensive reports on the popular mood, offers further insight, as do personal records such as diaries and letters.

To 'decode' Nazi efforts to colonise the Christmas mood takes us into the field of everyday life history, opening access to a cultural arena in which ordinary Germans might embrace, ignore and/or reject Nazi ideologies.[7] To access this arena, this chapter begins with a consideration of the basic ideological framework of Nazi Christmas. It then examines the way this ideological apparatus was put into play in public holiday observances and then in private family celebrations in the Third Reich. The chapter ends with an analysis of *Kriegsweihnachten* ('War Christmas') during the Second World War, the apotheosis not only of Nazi Christmas in the hands of radical Nazis but also of the contradictions and ultimate failure of the colonising project. This history suggests that Nazi attempts to colonise Christmas generated conflict as well as consensus, fragmentation as well as cohesion and distrust as well as loyalty. Here, Nazi Christmas and the Christmas mood become a test case of fascist legitimacy – an interpretative approach that views popular culture and the emotions as constantly shifting sites of the struggle for power and hegemony, of vital importance for understanding how and why Germans became Nazis.[8]

# Pagans, Christians, Germans: rewriting Christmas in the Third Reich

National Socialist attempts to colonise the 'Christmas mood' by casting the pre-Christian roots of the holiday as evidence of the deep history of the German *Volk* were not entirely new. Beginning in the mid-nineteenth century ethnographers, historians and theologians had begun writing a history of the holiday that emphasised the close connections between solstice worship and the Christian holiday, 'the intimate connection of Germandom and Christendom' in the word of one churchman.[9] The notion that the links between ancient 'Nordic' observances and Christian piety made the German version of Christmas uniquely special was popularised in middle-class illustrated magazines, the mass press and the colourful pages of numerous family 'Christmas Books', prescriptive texts published for the holiday season. The classic example is Hugh Elm's elegant *Golden Christmas Book* (1878), which included a proudly nationalist survey of the holiday's history based on descriptions of the Roman Saturnalia, 'Teutonic' solstice worship, Norse myths and Richard Wagner's *Tannhaüser*.[10] The radical-nationalist *völkisch* movement that emerged in the late-nineteenth century likewise championed the 'pagan' roots of the German holiday, as did the German Socialist Party (SPD) in the late *Kaiserreich* and the Weimar Republic. SPD propagandists repeatedly described Christmas as an example of bourgeois exploitation and used the winter solstice as a metaphor for the 'new life…and new being' that would follow the socialist revolution.[11] Beginning in the early 1920s, the Nazi intelligentsia 'rewrote' these pre-existing ideas to conform to the ideologies of National Socialism. In short, they added racial ideology to the mix, generating an available arsenal of ideas and practices targeted on the feelings generated by holiday customs.

It hardly mattered that the 'invented traditions' popularised by Nazi writers had little grounding in empirical research and were, for the most part, pseudo-scientific inventions.[12] Rather, the imaginary qualities of an *'artgerechte'* ('true to type' or 'racially correct') German Christmas opened space for creativity and improvisation. Nazi authors followed several tracks in their efforts to turn Christmas into a dechristianised celebration of the German *Volk* (even though its origins were so patently Christian). In the early 1920s, many commentators followed their nineteenth-century predecessors, claiming that the holiday originated as a solstice celebration among 'our primitive ancestors', but that only the arrival of Christianisation had lent 'the German soul [the] deeper inwardness that we now cherish'.[13] Others simply omitted mention of Christianity altogether and described supposedly pagan customs in glowing tones, explaining, for example, that holiday candlelight was a holdover from 'the deepest longings of our ancestors for light, the sun, the living fire [when] the illuminated tree was a symbol of the newborn sun and nature's power at Christmastime'.[14] The panoply of appropriations ranged from tinkering to radical revision, underscoring the overall fluidity of National Socialist attempts to rewrite the relationship among Christian traditions, 'pagan' rituals and German identities.

In the 1920s, Nazi holiday rhetoric often had an ugly edge that reflected general feelings of anger and cultural despair evoked by defeat in the First World War, the punitive aspects of the Treaty of Versailles and the crises of the Weimar Republic. Like SPD propagandists before them, Nazi writers claimed the winter solstice as a metaphor for the *Schicksalswende* ('turn of fate') that would follow the NSDAP's rise to power and cast Jesus as a revolutionary fighter who 'turned his sword' against 'false prophets'.[15] Articles, stories, songs and poems in the Nazi press reminded readers about 'front Christmas' in the First World War and the post-war betrayal of honoured veterans or condemned the Weimar Republic and the contemporary sociopolitical situation. A bitter 1925 'Christmas Letter' by Joseph Goebbels, for just one example, explained that 'for us [Nazis], Christmas 1925 is a celebration of sorrow and desperation' that meant 'unrelenting struggle' until the coming of the 'world transformation'.[16] Antisemitic ranting filled the pages of the Nazi press during the holiday season. Inflammatory attacks claimed that 'for Jews the most inward celebration of Christendom is only an opportunity for a great cheat' and compared Jewish-owned department stores to 'oriental bazaars' that exploited 'poor German *Volksgenossen* (people's comrades)'.[17] Jews were blamed for the over-commercialisation of the holiday, symbolised by the 'electrically illuminated Christmas trees in the shops'. 'Jewish big-capital' was condemned 'for taking over and corrupting the most noble German holiday'.[18] After the Nazis took power in 1933, however, most holiday propaganda dropped the messages of 'Christmas Hate' against Jews and Socialists. The Nazi press now preferred to emphasise the new feelings of collective solidarity supposedly expressed in the holiday season; such community togetherness demonstrated that the Party had resolved the class and political conflicts of the Weimar years.

Nazi intellectuals tolerated and even embraced slippage among Christian and pagan traditions, hate-filled political propaganda and antisemitic themes – but how far would committed Nazis go in their efforts to remake Christmas? One limit is represented by the *Deutschen Christen* (German Christians), a reformist splinter group founded in 1932 by far-right nationalists who wished to combine Christian theology with Nazi ideology and build an official state religion that would openly embrace Nazi racial goals. Though the German Christians were never quite accepted by the Nazi leadership, the holiday traditions they invented clearly influenced broader Nazi revisions. The group also did very well in its initial attempts to take over administrative positions in the existing Protestant Church hierarchy; its success led more progressive Protestants to form the *Bekennende Kirche* (Confessing Church) in opposition. Though their efforts encompassed a range of approaches, in general the *Deutschen Christen* sought to purge Christian belief of supposedly 'foreign' Jewish influences, incorporate 'racially correct' *völkisch* beliefs into Christian observance and shape new texts and rituals that would express and popularise these ideas – all while remaining within the formal boundaries of Protestant Christianity.[19]

Christmas, given its obvious importance to the Christian calendar, received special attention from German Christians in 'dejudaised' bibles, hymnals and sermons. According to the editor of *Das Volkstestament* (*The People's Testament*), a version of the Gospels prepared in accordance with German Christian ideas, the Christmas story of the birth of Jesus 'could not be omitted' because of its popularity among the German *Volk*. It nonetheless should be 'freed ... of Jewish-Christian accretions'.[20] German Christian Pastor Wilhelm Bauer's *Celebrations for German Christians* (1935) showed how. Bauer's script for a 'Germanised' Advent celebration described a 'morning star' that rose out of the darkness on 25 December but omitted reference to Bethlehem and Joseph, Mary or even Jesus. Jerusalem, Bauer suggested, should be renamed 'the heavenly abode' in order to purge Judaism from Protestant scriptures. The author, who also co-edited the journal *Christenkreuz und Hakenkreuz* (*Christian Cross and Swastika*) was quite frank about the way the holiday's appeal to the senses might generate an emotional charge harnessed to the movement's doctrines: 'The spoken word, music, and readings come together, then the visual image that is awakened in us through the word and reading moves us further, and rhythm and sound open the soul to the reception of God's truth.'[21]

The tenets promoted by German Christians may seem on the radical fringe, but similar *völkisch* ideas permeated the entire range of

National Socialist Christmas texts. By the mid-1930s, the fragmented and piecemeal invention that dominated holiday propaganda in the early 1920s had coalesced into a more coherent set of ideas focused on 'racially correct' celebratory forms rooted in dechristianised 'Germanic' solstice symbols and rituals. On the internal level, the central offices of Nazi mass organisations, such as the Propaganda Ministry, the German Labour Front (DAF) and the National Socialist Teachers' League (NSLB), issued instructions on how to observe a 'correct' Nazi holiday to local officials; the most prominent was the Propaganda Ministry journal *The New Community: Party-Archive for the Organisation of National Socialist Celebrations and Leisure Time.*[22] A vast array of Nazi-approved Christmas books, articles and pamphlets supplemented these internal materials. A small selection of exemplary titles, available in bookshops and by mail order, included *The Christmas Book for the Hitler Youth* (guidelines for internal celebration, circa 1930), *German Christmas: The Role of the German Poets* (a compendium of 'contemporary' holiday poems to be read aloud, 1934), *Christmas Primer for the German Home* (on gifts, decorations and rituals, 1935) and *We Maidens Sing* (songbook for the League of German Girls, 1936) – there were many others. During the Nazi era, a vast state apparatus wielded this dense net of rewritten holiday texts as emotional scripts for the colonisation of both public and private holiday observances.

## The colonisation of public celebration

Though the nominal highpoint of German Christmas was and is the private family celebration on Christmas Eve, in Nazi Germany (and today) the holiday season included an array of public and semi-public observances and festivities. The weeks around Christmas brought media campaigns that carried the Nazi message, group parties sponsored by Nazi mass organisations and the imposing Christmas charity drive of the *Winterhilfswerk* (WHW), which culminated in public celebrations of *Volksweihnachten* (People's Christmas) on or around 21 December, the day of the winter solstice. Such activities represented attempts to colonise familiar holiday customs and the emotional intensity they evoked. So abundant were public festivities that some Nazi writers worried they might encroach upon the intimacy of the family holiday; as one put it, 'indecent customs' threatened to destroy the 'National Socialist spirit of Christmas' and the 'original purpose' of the holiday, defined as the feelings of national or *völkisch* sense of belonging supposedly engendered in family homes on Christmas Eve.[23] Nazi intellectuals worried much less about the impact of public celebration on the Christian aspects of Christmas. In fact, many of their efforts were designed to appropriate or displace traditional forms of Christian observance.

Well before the Nazi takeover of power in 1933, Germans had been entertained by descriptions of Christmas traditions and events in the annual holiday issues of newspapers and family magazines, newsreels and holiday radio programmes. Once in power, and given the regime's control of the mass media, the Nazi intelligentsia readily used these forms to popularise their version of the holiday. Newspaper and magazine articles repeatedly described local group celebrations, reported on the holiday speeches of Party leaders and the charity work of Nazi mass organisations and explained 'the meaning and customs of the ancient Germanic Sacred Nights' – there are countless examples.[24] Beyond print media, state propagandists were uniquely positioned to take advantage of the growing popularity of film and radio. As Michael Geyer writes, Nazi functionaries used the modern mass media to create a 'national audiovisual space' that encouraged Germans to develop 'an awareness of the nation as an audiovisual unity' through a National Socialist lens.[25] Radio was central to this process. Well before 1933, Christmas-themed radio shows had been an integral part of the holiday season, at least for those who could afford what was still a costly appliance. Nazi leaders famously made radio more accessible by encouraging production of the relatively inexpensive Volksempfänger VE-301 ('People's Receiver') released in 1933 and nicknamed the 'Goebbels Snout' for the Propaganda Minister's inescapable on-air presence. The combination of entertainment and propaganda that dominated Nazi airwaves could reach ever-larger numbers of Germans – the number of registered listeners grew from about 4.3 million in 1933 to about 9 million in 1938 and then 16 million in 1943 – and Christmas boosted audience numbers.[26] Holiday broadcasts began in late November, increased tempo during December and ended in a crescendo on Christmas Eve, always mingling special shows for children and women, scholarly explanations of 'Germanic' traditions and recordings of popular holiday music with upbeat reports on the WHW or the activities of leading politicians. The official Christmas Eve show from 1937, for example, included Rudolf Hess's annual 'Christmas Address' to the 'German peoples' living outside Germany's borders, carols sung by a children's choir, a report on Christmas in the German military and recordings of church bells ringing in famous German cathedrals – a common feature of Nazi Christmas media productions.[27]

The newsreels Germans saw as preludes to feature films similarly inextricably bound together entertainment and propaganda. A typical 1935 newsreel included footage of Reich Minister and Nazi potentate Hermann Goering and Goebbels playing Father Christmas for groups of indigent children. Clips from Goebbels's speech about the 5,200,000 needy Germans helped by the WHW were followed by images of swastika banners and Christmas trees. This example concluded, again, with shots of church bells ringing in Germany's most famous churches.[28] Another newsreel bracketed stories about policemen collecting for the WHW and the successful hunting party of 'Reich Hunt-Master' Goering ('sixty-seven game animals were killed here and put at the disposal of the WHW') with scenes of the Christmas guests of US President Roosevelt and his wife, as well as traditional caroling in a village church, mixing the familiar with the political.[29] The repetitive representations of local church bells or children's choirs singing religious carols show that propagandists aggressively appropriated the sense of emotional depth associated with familiar religious themes and imagery. Yet in context, shots of ringing bells in famous local steeples demonstrated the strength of the German *Volksgemeinschaft* as much as or more than the depths of Christian piety. The 'normalcy' of what was in fact a propaganda piece was aided by the context of apparently non-political Christian material. Few official media productions, however, went beyond such surface pastiche to expound upon the Christian aspects of the holiday.

State control of the mass media ensured that millions of Germans were exposed to Nazi ideology, and the account above may reinforce the image of a 'top down' behemoth state apparatus enforcing its vision on an unwitting or captive audience. Studies of audience reception, however, suggest that the process is much more subtle.[30] When individuals respond to media products, they actively engage and parse messages, 'decoding' content to meet their own interests – even in a media dictatorship. Following this line, listening to a Christmas radio show or watching a holiday newsreel was a participatory process that allowed audience members to negotiate cultural meaning and accept, neglect or perhaps reject the intended message. Was the emotional engineering undertaken in Nazi media effective? Though SD reports repeatedly commented on the popularity of holiday entertainment, particularly the annual speeches by Party leaders, we can only begin to gauge the response of millions of Germans who made up the audience.[31] Even if they disliked heavy-handed propaganda, listening to a Christmas radio show or watching a holiday newsreel in the Nazi years surely encouraged numerous ordinary Germans to feel that they belonged to the 'audiovisual' *Volksgemeinschaft* described by Geyer.

Beyond the mass media, Nazi functionaries reached Germans through a range of public activities, including parties sponsored by Nazi mass organisations, schoolroom lessons and annual WHW charity drives. Group parties with colleagues or co-workers were a familiar holiday practice, and here, again, the National Socialists readily colonised existing popular customs. Nazi mass organisations all sponsored holiday parties for their members, as did civic groups and employers. In general, these festivities resembled the 1921 NSDAP celebration described above: they fused ideology and traditional observances. These public festivities animated the cultural 'web' of symbolic practices, feelings and material rewards that brought Germans together in what would have been a familiar sense of emotional community generated by familiar traditions, now centred on celebrating the *Volksgemeinschaft*. The 1936 'grand party' of the Wilhelm Limpert publishing company (Dresden) organised by the German Labour Front (the regime-controlled workers' organisation that replaced independent unions after 1933) was typical of many others. Some 400 workers and their families enjoyed a workplace celebration complete with theatrical performances and collective caroling, angels who greeted participants 'in the name of the Christ Child', a visit from Father Christmas and gift packages. A local scholar explained the meaning of 'German' Christmas traditions, and fifty workers received cash to support a 'Strength Through Joy' trip. Music played by an SA band included the 'O How Joyfully', 'Silent Night' and 'Oh Christmas Tree'. The extravagant entertainment and gifts were coupled with ceremonies of loyalty that embedded ideological notions of workplace paternalism and class 'alliance' in familiar holiday customs. A speech from the manager, laced with quotations from Goebbels, called on each worker to 'fulfill their duty to the company' and to show their gratitude. The workers, in response, pronounced that they 'happily [recognised] the alliance of the worker and the workplace'. Photographs of the event show happy children, a stage surrounded by tables with dinner settings and gift packages, the 'chief' delivering his speech and company wives who made 'authentic Dresden Christmas Stollen with tender hands'.[32] Thus familiar emotional bonds among families, co-workers and employers were both 'Nazified' and cemented by the performance of Christian and sentimental workplace holiday practices.

Primary and secondary schools were another important point of contact between ordinary Germans and Nazi intellectuals interested in remaking the holiday, especially given the 300,000 politically committed teachers who joined the National Socialist Teachers' League (NSLB), an organisation dedicated to disseminating ideology in the classroom. The December issues of the NSLB journal were filled with proud explanations of 'blood and soil' Christmas customs and curriculum guidelines for introducing this material into the classroom. Recommendations for organising school Christmas celebrations encouraged teachers to shape events around the supposed customs of pre-Christian Germanics, 'the primordial and eternally new beliefs in light among our *Volk*'. Capitalising on the Christian vision of Mary and Jesus, but omitting mention of their names, guidelines encouraged teachers to emphasise that 'mid-winter-night is also mother-night' and to pay homage to mothers as 'givers of fertility' by decorating the room with a horn of plenty.[33] In practice, teachers sometimes combined Christian and 'Nordic' rituals. A Christmas play performed at one girls' school included scenes of Jesus in the manger, but the main content took the form of a 'Germanic Yule Celebration' (complete with an appearance by the 'earth spirits' and Wotan with his 'wild army'); this was meant to demonstrate that 'our Christmas observances and customs are rooted in Germanic traditions'.[34] Once again, it is impossible to know exactly how many teachers organised holiday classroom time around such activities, which were clearly intended to appropriate the religious sentiment associated with the holiday for ideological purposes. Enough did, however, to cause concern among the leading church officials. Members of the Protestant Upper Consistory (EOK), the highest authority in the Prussian Protestant Church, received letters from pastors worried about the emphasis on 'Germanic' customs and non-Christian carols in local schools and kept track of reports about the 'transformation of the Christian content of Christmas'.[35]

Perhaps the most visible public aspect of Nazi Christmas was the annual WHW holiday drive, organised by the central office of the National Socialist People's Welfare (NSV) in Berlin and carried out by local members of mass organisations, especially the Hitler Youth (HJ). The annual Christmas campaign – labelled *Volksweihnachten* ('People's Christmas') – was the centrepiece of the WHW, which lasted from October to March each year. The NSV used a variety of means to encourage ordinary Germans to contribute, including advertising campaigns, aggressive and extensive public collection drives and 'voluntary' salary deductions. The regime banned all but a handful of other charities and thus directly appropriated long-familiar forms of Christmas caritas – and the positive feelings of caring and gratitude that presumably went along with doing a good deed or receiving a 'gift'. If the appeal was familiar, the ideological goals directly challenged justifications for charity rooted in Christian mercy or liberal humanism. 'We do not start with the individual, we do not represent the view that one must feed the hungry, give drink to the thirsty, and clothe the naked', explained Goebbels at a 1938 NSV meeting. 'Our motives are of an entirely different type. They can be simply stated in one sentence: we must possess a healthy *Volk* so that we can assert ourselves in the world.'[36]

A 'Reich Command' sent from the central WHW office to regional offices in 1936 (along with other materials) allows us to reconstruct a typical Christmas drive. The central directive ordered HJ members to join the 'action' under the slogans 'Youth in the Fight against Need! Youth to the Front!' After a week-long propaganda blitz – including a newsreel feature with Goebbels, Goering and Hess collecting WHW donations at the Brandenburg Gate – uniformed Hitler Youth members began street collections on 18 December.[37] At a 'roll call' on 19 December, they received the 'order of the day' from Reich Youth Leader Baldur von Schirach. The main collection on Sunday 20 December (to coincide with the solstice) required 'the deployment of all powers'. The militarised language of this 'Reich Command' may seem odd for a charity programme undertaken in the Christmas season, but it helped to socialise youths in the 'military heroism' at the base of the Nazi worldview – always 'closely tied up with the exaltation of the Teutons as a chosen race' in the words of the Jewish philologist Victor Klemperer, who lived in Dresden during the Nazi years.[38]

To bring such ideals to life, the Hitler Youth marched in parades, banged drums, sang songs and performed short 'impromptu' skits, all meant to pressure passersby to give to the cause. Those who did received that year's WHW badge (made of paste or wood, typically shaped like a Christmas ornament with the year's date) as proof of their generosity. In one skit, HJ members dressed up as shirkers who used various means to avoid making a donation. The cast of characters included a 'bourgeois' (*Spiesser*) who pretended his pockets were empty; a man who wore an oversize WHW badge from 1934, according to the guidelines 'electrically illuminated if possible'; a heavy-set man who ordered an expensive dinner with sparkling wine but when asked for a donation 'complains about the bad times and has no money'; two 'coffee-klatsch type women' who 'knit wool socks for negro children and get upset about the eternal collections'; and finally a 'grumbler' who drank round after round of beer, claimed that things were better under the Kaiser and refused to contribute. Angered by such evident examples of transgression, the Hitler Youth 'teach them all'. In the denouement, notable for its release of pent-up tension, the HJ members brought out a giant collection tin to contain the eager and ample donations of the newly converted.[39]

In the event, millions of Germans participated in the 1936 'People's Christmas' campaign, as organisers, givers or charity recipients. Numerous lower-class Germans received holiday 'gift packages' of cash, food or coal. Some even received a Christmas tree, carried to their front door by HJ and SA men, a much-publicised symbol of the willingness of the *Volksgemeinschaft* to care for its members. According to internal records, the 1936 Christmas campaign collected over 3.2 million Reichsmarks, handed out almost 18 million badges and gave away about 700,000 Christmas trees.[40] Such campaigns generated not only tangible popular support, because of their practical benefits, but also the emotional appeal of social solidarity – at a time of year when charity was nominally expected and publicly lauded (Figure 10.1). As Herbert Vorländer concludes, WHW was 'the human face of an inhuman regime'; internal NSV reports and SD agents recorded general approval.[41] Underground Sopade agents similarly commented on WHW's popular appeal; an extensive report on the 1934–1935 campaign quoted a Bavarian worker who remarked that: 'By and large one must say that for us the Winter Aid was very generous. Above all, it is worth noting the brilliant organisation [of the campaign].' Yet, the same report noted cases of discontent with the distribution, quality and quantity of the 'gifts' – WHW generated tension as well as satisfaction.[42] In 1937, internal NSV reports noted that some Germans refused to donate or gave to 'illegal' charity drives, especially in rural regions, where Catholic clergy encouraged them to support the Church rather than the State.[43] Malcontents subjected the earnestness of WHW 'actions' to mocking underground humour. WHW stood for '*wir hungern weiter*' ('we're still hungry'), they whispered, or rephrased the slogan 'no one will go hungry, no one will freeze' into 'no one will go hungry without freezing'.[44]

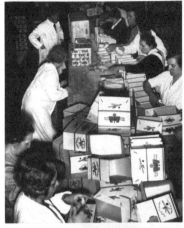

WEIHNACHTEN
IM WINTERHILFSWERK

FIGURE 10.1 'Christmas in the WHW'. The Volksgemeinschaft in action during the 1936 WHW Christmas campaign, clockwise from top right: NSV volunteers pack WHW gift packages; an elderly woman receives a WHW tree and gifts; 'the anonymous helpers' stand in line to empty their collection buckets at a regional WHW office; 'happy children with their gift bags'; sorting Christmas Stollen for later distribution; NSV 'sisters' hand out gifts to children at a state-sponsored holiday party (Leipziger Illustrierte, 10 December 1936). Private collection of the author.

# A 'racially correct' family Christmas

In 1935, a prominent professor of German literature argued that Christmas had to be celebrated at home, preferably with pre-Christian 'Nordic' customs, because 'during this celebration [the Aryan man] retreats inward, the boundary between present and past disappears, ancestors blessedly approach the circles of kin and holy peace fills mankind with new power'.[45] The author of a 1936 Nazi pamphlet dedicated to the 'protection' of the holiday agreed. 'Christmas Eve is the single, *decisive* highpoint of the holiday season ... Our celebrations should serve to deepen and activate the entire joy, the entire openness of the soul, and the entire inner homewardness of all the weeks before Christmas.'[46] Such comments suggest that the Nazi intelligentsia recognised that the emotional impact of Christmas Eve evoked the normative values and feelings they now sought to enlist in the construction of the racial state – family togetherness and love, spiritual depth and community cohesion, all bound together by putatively 'natural' feelings of connectedness to German 'blood and soil'.

Though functionaries working for the Ministry of Propaganda tended to leave the family holiday alone until after the start of the Second World War, private celebration in the 1930s was nevertheless surrounded by a racialised holiday discourse dedicated to these ideals. As we have seen, propagandists, party functionaries, schoolteachers and 'Germanophile' groups within the NSDAP (such as the SS and the Amt Rosenberg) paid close attention to the family holiday, as did the *NS-Frauenschaft* (NSF or National Socialist Women's League). These *völkisch*-minded authors produced an array of prescriptive texts. Family and women's magazines, Christmas Books, newsreels and newspaper articles instructed German families – and especially German mothers – about the 'Germanic' customs that supposedly made up an authentic German Christmas. Nazi culture makers thus colonised existing family observances and used persuasion and rewards – symbolic, material, but also emotional – to push the point. After 1933, for example, the Nazis cast the holiday as a celebration of inclusion and prosperity and rarely used Christmas propaganda to attack German Jews, as they had in the 1920s. Yet continual references to notions of 'primordial' Germandom and the cheery colour pictures of blond-haired men and women with many healthy children gathered around the Christmas tree that graced the covers of family magazines suggested that only those with the 'correct' racial features would share the private, family joys of the holiday. Victor Klemperer well understood the regime's intentions. In December 1938, he wrote in his diary that Christmas had been 'completely dechristianised. Greater German Christmas – the rebirth of light of the German soul, signifying the resurrection of the German Reich. The Jew Jesus and everything relating to the spirit and humanity in general excluded.'[47]

Nazi writers placed special emphasis on the role of German women in family celebration. As pedagogue and family author Elisabeth Schnidtmann-Leffler put it, women were 'undoubtedly more deeply anchored in the native soil of authentic *Volk* culture' than men, so they could infuse private festivities with the Nordic-Germanic traditions that defined a 'racially correct' holiday.[48] The array of Nazi prescriptive texts that promoted such ideas looked familiar – after all, books and articles about holiday customs had been around since the mid-nineteenth century – but now they were subtly dechristianised, permeated with discussions of 'Germanic' customs, descriptions of the love between mother and child that omitted mention of Jesus or Mary and evocations of the deep feelings of *völkisch* belonging supposedly engendered by the holiday. A typical 1938 book on 'Pre-Christmas Celebrations' (*Vorweihnachtliche Feier*) (a term often substituted for 'Advent' in Nazi publications) encouraged families to make homemade gifts and decorations as a way to create an 'authentic' sense of togetherness, free from the 'haste and alarm' of everyday life. Parents should decorate the tree with apples and nuts, and hand-made stars, stallions and stags, because 'these are all primordial (*uralt*) – often older than the tree itself'. Singing 'the good old Christmas songs' was also important, since they spoke 'about the holiness of life, about mother and child, about light and tree and fruit and bear witness, that for the Germanic peoples ideals of motherhood and the transformation of life and the year belong together'. Illustrations in the book included wooden Christmas tree stands carved with Norse runes and a Christmas plate bearing the 'tree of light' inside a border of linked swastikas. No custom, it seemed, was too small to overlook in the pursuit of re-enchanting family life with putatively 'pagan' customs.[49]

Nazi intellectuals strove to colonise one of the most familiar holiday customs, the Christmas carol, which had a deep and profoundly national history. Cherished German-language songs dated back to the medieval and Reformation eras, as well as the nineteenth-century bourgeois family 'house music' movement, which generated what later became international classics including 'Silent Night' (1818) and 'O Christmas Tree' (1824). Though carols may appear static and timeless, Christmas songs attracted Nazi intellectuals because music was a cultural form that was in fact always open to revision. In addition, carolling traversed the public/private divide. Germans sang at home, of course, but also during religious services, at parties with friends, at group celebrations and in newsreels and on radio broadcasts. The Nazis also appreciated the emotional impact of carols. Communal singing or listening to songs or classical music evoked deep feelings associated with the birth of Christ, the tender relationship among loving family members, the awesome beauty of the decorated family room or the more joyous, raucous visit of Father Christmas. At least since the late nineteenth century, singing or hearing classic carols had contributed to the construction of a very German emotional community.

From the 1920s to 1945, committed Nazis wrote a number of new carols and rewrote the words to many more to mobilise ordinary Germans around National Socialist ideals. Again, the focus was on replacing Christian with pagan or *völkisch*-racial content. The most famous Nazi carol, 'Glorious Night of Shining Stars', by HJ poet Hans Baumann, was only one of many. The song, one Nazi reviewer bragged, 'rings with the recuperated and liberated life-rules of our type'.[50] Baumann's melody mimicked traditional Christmas music; his lyrics cited winter fires lit 'on mountains mile by mile', the mother as the 'heart of the wide world' and the earth's renewal 'like a newborn radiant child'. With its vague solstice references and evocations of a non-Christian mother and 'radiant child', the carol was regularly printed in Nazi Christmas publications and repeatedly sung at group parties, in newsreels and on the radio. 'Glorious Night' survived the war and was sung in family celebrations and sometimes publicly (and mistakenly) cast as a 'traditional' German carol.[51]

Other Nazi songs – by committed German Christians, 'blood and soil' ideologues and propagandists – went further. A 'Germanised' version of 'O How Joyfully' replaced the chorus line 'Rejoice, Rejoice, O Christianity' with 'Rejoice, rejoice to be the German Type'. The lyrics to the German Christian hymn 'Weihenacht' included the lines 'Christmas! Blood and soil awake! *Volk*, from God's light and power; your honour and heroism come.' Such revisions troubled religious authorities and ordinary Germans alike. An anonymous writer in a Catholic weekly angrily concluded that Nazi substitutions were 'in fact an outrage!'[52] Yet carols offered a means to challenge regime colonisation. The Bishop of Würzburg noted that the 'beauty and power of attraction' in religious carols could help to preserve a Christian '*Volk* culture' in the face of Nazi encroachment. The authorities at the EOK took note of dechristianised songs and the events where they were sung, and Church leaders of both faiths asked local ministers to ensure that their services included traditional choral performances.[53] Churchmen, like their counterparts in the propaganda ministry, utilised the emotional pull of Christmas carols in everyday life situations to enlist Germans in their respective and at times competing ideological/emotional communities.

How successful were National Socialist attempts to penetrate the family Christmas? The answer points to a grey area that ranged from embrace to rejection of Nazi forms, with some confusion over the proliferation of redefined or new symbols and rituals. One way to evaluate the ability of the state to remake private celebration is to examine the activity reports of the National Socialist Women's League (NSF) and its affiliated organisations, which by the mid-1930s had over 10 million members.[54] During the holiday season, NSF directives encouraged members to work with WHW campaigns and organise Christmas markets and craft exhibitions, but not to forget their primary 'duties' as housewives and mothers: to observe a National Socialist Christmas at home. An NSF activity report from 1936 captures the way the church–state conflict penetrated everyday activities and raised the level of emotional intensity, noting that: 'Advent and the Christmas season have naturally raised much doubt and anxiety about whether convinced National Socialists can still celebrate a Christian Christmas, if nativity plays are allowed and whether Christian carols can still be sung.' Anger over the 'tasteless revision of old German carols' undermined attempts to create a religion-free, National Socialist holiday culture. The conflict raised 'intense anxiety' among women who were still religiously observant but 'were still for the most part positive National Socialists'. In addition, clergymen were using holiday activities such as house visits, coffee evenings and choral rehearsals to remind parishioners of the Christian aspects of the holiday and even to engage in 'open opposition to National Socialism'. As a result, the *Volksgemeinschaft* was falling into 'camps', with opposing groups of women who either embraced the Nazi holiday or threatened to boycott group celebrations and WHW collections. The best that could be said, the report concluded, was 'Now we have at least arrived at clear positions: each woman must personally decide if she wants to join the great community of women (*Frauengemeinschaft*) or not.'[55]

# Nazi 'War Christmas'

Christmas celebrations during the Second World War exacerbated the tensions and ambiguities that already shadowed the holiday in the Nazi years, not least those between Church and State. Once the war began, Nazi propagandists eagerly dusted off the familiar tropes of what Germans called *Kriegsweihnachten* ('War Christmas'), in place at least since the Franco–Prussian War and the First World War. Both at home and at the front, the Christmas 'cult of death' familiar from the First World War reappeared, the language of Wilhelmine Protestant nationalism replaced by the rhetoric of the *Volksgemeinschaft*. On the home front, though civilians were bombarded with War Christmas propaganda and readily participated in WHW campaigns to support the troops at the front, families struggled with the practical and emotional costs of the wartime holiday. For enlisted men, the patriotic speeches, drinking bouts and amateur performances that had long been a staple of soldiers' barracks celebration were now framed by Nazi propaganda focused on 'blood and soil' ideologies and loyalty to the state.

Intense propaganda efforts reached soldiers and civilians alike during the holiday season. The 'golden bridge' that supposedly united front and home during the holiday season was the subject of countless media stories (Figure 10.2). War Christmas Newsreels typically included generic content: cheerful WHW workers packing gifts for soldiers at the front, Joseph Goebbels at yet another charity party, solemn soldiers celebrating around modest Christmas trees – one example from 1940 showed soldiers at a Berlin flak battery receiving Christmas gifts from Goebbels (a package of cookies with a picture of the Propaganda Minister himself), German ships delivering

WHW presents to soldiers stationed in Norway, attractive women reporters in uniform at a party in France and Hitler's 'surprise visit' to troops stationed on the English Channel.[56] Christmas issues of military newspapers, special holiday booklets and full-length books distributed to enlisted men promoted ideological messages in the guise of holiday escapism. In occupied Norway, soldiers read Norwegian sagas and Knut Hamsen stories; local customs were described as remnants of the ancient 'Nordic' Christmas shared by 'Germanic peoples'. On the eastern front, they read about 'Bolshevik' attempts to prohibit the holiday altogether.[57]

War Christmas underscored the tensions between ideology and politics, and tradition and popular piety, and military and state leaders recognised that the emotional costs of the war might undermine whatever success functionaries might have had in turning the holiday into a celebration of the *Volksgemeinschaft*. A remarkable order issued in December 1939 by General Wilhelm Keitel, Chief of the Supreme High Command of the German Armed Forces, and Martin Bormann, Head of the Party Chancellery, addressed such concerns, noting that 'the Christmas holidays present troop leaders with a task that can only be resolved with the greatest tact'. The 'guidelines' reserved 24 December – Christmas Eve, the key moment of family celebration – for official military festivities of 'German Christmas'; the centre-point was the Christmas tree, presented as a 'primordial Germanic symbol of the Life Tree'. On 25 or 26 December, however, soldiers should be given the opportunity to attend a Christian service, or at least listen to one on a radio broadcast. Chaplains might attend official festivities on Christmas Eve, but because of the 'non-denominational (*überkonfessionellen*) character of the ceremonies they [could] neither take up the word nor otherwise actively participate'.[58]

Church leaders, for their part, continued to work behind the scenes to protect the religious aspects of Christmas from overt dechristianisation and nationalisation, again hoping that ordinary parishioners would still feel the pull of the emotional community supposedly evoked by Christian observance. As an extensive EOK report from 1939 put it, the holiday's 'ancient customs' and 'the personal character' of a Christian mass best confirmed 'the soulful connection between *Volk* and Church' and preserved the 'popular spiritual dynamic of the Protestant message' from 'anti-Christian propagandists'.[59] In public, however, clergymen of both faiths supported the war effort. In their sermons and texts, clergymen typically expressed sympathy for private suffering, noted that the deceased were in God's hands, condemned the 'Bolshevik' threat and wished the best for the state leadership.

Cheerful propaganda from the first years of the war masked a grittier reality. According to US correspondent William Shirer, stationed in Berlin for the 1939 holiday season, 'The first war Christmas somehow has brought the war home to the people more than anything else .... This year it's a bleak Christmas', he wrote in his diary, 'with few presents, Spartan food, the men folk away, the streets blacked out, the shutters and curtains drawn tight in accordance with police regulations.'[60] In the Nazi press, upbeat

FIGURE 10.2 *Standing in front of a giant Christmas tree decorated with silver tinsel, Dr Joseph Goebbels delivers a holiday speech at a Christmas celebration in the working-class district of Friedrichshain, Berlin, in 1936; the propaganda minister later handed out the toys on the stage to children attending the party. Such events, designed to harness familiar observances and the emotions they evoked to Nazi visions of National Community, were widely publicised in the press, on the radio and in holiday newsreels. Courtesy of Art Resource/Pruessischer-Kulturbesitz.*

War Christmas stories soon gave way to more sober if not sombre pleas for loyalty and support, embodied in the massive 1941 WHW campaign to support German troops in the failed assault on Moscow. Ordinary Germans readily donated winter clothes and other materials to the poorly prepared *Wehrmacht*. In December 1942, the looming defeat of the German Sixth Army at Stalingrad cast an inescapable pall on the holiday season. Despite the infamous Stalingrad 'Ring Broadcast', which included soldiers' reports and Christmas greetings supposedly broadcast directly from the Stalingrad 'front', and the apparent appeal of Goebbels's annual holiday speech, the SD reported that the 1942 holiday season failed to generate 'the otherwise normal Christmas mood'.[61]

Shortages of basic goods were particularly galling during the holiday season. In December 1942, according to SD agents, the lack of toiletries, Christmas candles, leather goods, stationary, holiday comestibles and other essentials encouraged widespread 'shopping madness' that state attempts to provide special distributions of rations failed to alleviate; at least, the agents noted, unhappiness with shortages and other everyday cares offered a distraction from the bad news from the eastern front and other negative political concerns.[62] The situation worsened in 1943 and 1944, when endemic shortages, missing and dead family members, ruined urban landscapes and continual allied bombing raids made celebration fleeting at best.

As this overview suggests, War Christmas set the stage for disappointment and conflict. Popular expectations for a 'traditional' holiday placed constraints on the regime's ability to use the holiday to reconfirm a sense of Nazi community, and attempts to do so created a *'Teufelskreis'* (devil's or vicious circle) that ultimately undermined Nazi intentions. Three new family rituals, meant to replace Christian observance with 'blood and soil' themes that encouraged loyalty and 'holding out', exemplify the trend. Such efforts represented the increasing radicalism of the Nazi leadership during the war and its growing willingness to colonise the private family emotions associated with the holiday.[63] The first new ritual, the heavily publicised *Lichtersprüche* ('Light Oaths'), instructed Germans to recite short slogans as they placed lit candles on the family Christmas tree. The content varied, but the oaths were typically dedicated to solstice sun and light, mother love, Hitler, the army and the fatherland. Propagandists promoted a second ceremony titled *Heimholung des Feuers* ('Bringing Home the Fire'). The language reflected traditional notions of bringing the deceased 'home' to God, in which children were supposed to bring a burning candle on a pine branch, lit by a Party leader in a public celebration, into the family home. This ceremony embodied the ties between public, Nazi-sponsored solstice celebrations and private family festivities but was quickly discarded because of war-related blackout regulations.

The third and most prevalent War Christmas ritual promoted by the state in the later years of the war was the *Heldengedenken* ('Heroes' Remembrance'), invented for grieving families by NSDAP functionary and author-poet Thilo Scheller. A prominent feature of the series of War Christmas books and other propaganda materials published from 1942 to 1944, the ceremony drew on popular stories about holiday visits from the ghosts of dead soldiers; it most certainly had roots in Walter Flex's First World War 'fairy tale' about the same, written in 1914 and reprinted many times in the Nazi years. On Christmas Eve, according to Scheller's instructions, the bereaved family should decorate a table with a lit candle, and food and drink, to welcome the ghost soldier, and then retire to bed. A macabre poem meant to frame the ceremony described the dead man's visit. After sampling the refreshments and reliving cherished memories, according to the poem, 'The dead soldier lays his earth-encrusted hand/ Lightly on each of the children's young heads.' He then intones: 'We died for you, because we believed in Germany.'[64]

The effectiveness of such last ditch efforts to insert dechristianised Nazi values into private moments of intense grief and thereby preserve morale by promoting new holiday rituals remain questionable. A cynical joke that made the rounds in Berlin in the last years of the war captures one response: '*Praktisch denken, Sarge schenken*' ('think practically, give coffins'). For many families, however, things were probably more nuanced. Placing lit candles on family graves on Christmas Eve was an observance dating at least from the First World War, and some Germans might have 'updated' such practices along the lines suggested by the authorities. In one case, as rare as it is revealing, an extant copy of the 'Light Oaths' published by the Propaganda Ministry in a 1942 'Christmas Calendar' bears the pencilled-in revisions made by an anonymous German mother. The opening 'oaths' about the winter solstice remain unchanged, but the final lines were changed from 'My light oath is dedicated to the *Führer*/Who always thinks of us and of Germany' to 'My light oath is dedicated to God/Who always thinks of mankind'.[65] This anonymous revision suggests that at least one family accepted the connections between Christmas and the solstice and even performed a Nazi ceremony but preferred familiar family and Christian comforts over radicalised Nazi inventions.

Another way to understand the contradictory effects of Nazi War Christmas is to examine closely the Christmas festivities of Klaus Granzow, an officer-in-training who celebrated Christmas at a military school in Ponikau, Saxony, in 1944. His experiences were typical, at least for units behind the front lines that could observe the holiday in relative peace. In his diary, Granzow recorded his loneliness and efforts to find some Christmas cheer with comrades, undermined by the political appropriation of the holiday in the highly charged ideological atmosphere of the last years of the war. Even as the men in his class used the first weeks of December to rehearse the 'silly skits and jokes', they would perform during their party, Granzow fretted that the 'serious content' of the holiday would 'degenerate into a comradeship night with Christmas tree'. The clash between colonisation and Granzow's longing for the appropriate emotional mood dominated the celebration itself, which took place on 23 December. The school commander's opening speech annoyed Granzow because it had what he called a 'new order' character – focused on the 'veneration of light, [the speech had] nothing to do with Christmas'. In a clear reference to competing Nazi and Christian observances, Granzow noted with some pride that only the younger men 'who were now supposed to believe solely in the "light" and not in the Jesus-child' knew the words to traditional carols; the older men and the teachers did not. Singing traditional carols, for Granzow, was a self-conscious act of nonconformist behaviour that expressed an allegiance to a set of Christian ideals and familiar emotions that moved beyond (or behind) official rituals.

The mood lightened during the second half of the evening. Drunk on punch, Granzow and his fellow officers-in-training performed their Christmas show. A Berliner sang a song called 'Krumme Lanke' (named after a lake in a Berlin park) and an infantryman, dressed in drag, parodied film star Zarah Leander. The soldiers read aloud from the holiday issue of the school 'beer magazine', which poked fun at the absurdities of army life. All in all, though, Granzow was disappointed: this was 'no Christmas celebration'. On Christmas Eve, Granzow and several fellow students went to a Christmas mass (whoever wanted to 'was allowed to go', Granzow noted). Though his mother had asked him to 'keep the word of God in his heart' during the holidays, here too he felt let down. The preacher was unconvincing, the music somehow false. Only back in his quarters, singing 'Silent Night' and 'Oh Christmas Tree' with the soldiers in his class, did Granzow finally realise the 'Christmas mood'. The hybrid celebrations of the ordinary soldier, which included not only barracks rowdiness but also more intimate observances, were probably more effective in creating bonds of emotional community than Nazi propaganda, though in the end the result was similar. 'And now it is really Christmas', Granzow mused. 'A wonderful feeling, when one senses that only now do the comrades also experience what "Christmas" is. It creates such deep contact, when one knows that we are all brothers and all there for each other.'[66]

# Conclusion

Starting in the 1920s, the Nazi intelligentsia undertook determined efforts to turn Christmas into a celebration of the much-vaunted *Volksgemeinschaft*. Drawing on already existing notions about the holiday's connections to pre-Christian, pagan solstice worship, they promoted a number of dechristianised Christmas symbols and rituals that supposedly testified to the deep historic roots of the German 'Aryan' race. With the support of an extensive cultural apparatus that ranged from state-controlled mass media to Nazi-sponsored group festivities, these remade holiday observances reached millions of Germans. The family Christmas was also permeable to Nazi penetration; numerous publications as well as outreach efforts by organisations such as the National Socialist Women's League surrounded private celebration with putatively 'Germanic' observances intended to 'bring to life' the deep racial connections that bound together the German *Volk*. Such efforts reached a crescendo in the Second World War, which heightened the tensions between popular celebration and politicisation already present during the 1930s. The emotions evoked by the holiday were central to this process. Nazi functionaries eagerly worked to colonise the Christmas mood, because the feelings of communal solidarity and family togetherness supposedly engendered during holiday celebrations might be used to strengthen the social bonds at the heart of the *Volksgemeinschaft*.

In the end, National Socialist attempts to colonise Christmas and the Christmas mood turned the holiday into a site of cultural-political conflict. The decision to sing a certain song, attend a holiday party, or donate to WHW opened up a realm of quotidian activity in which such relatively modest acts could demonstrate acceptance of the regime or avoidance, rejection or resistance. We cannot quantify the number of times people did these things, but we can use the records we have to identify patterns of everyday life that help us to understand the ways the emotions evoked by holiday observances contributed to the appeal of Nazi ideology. As Geoff Eley writes, it is 'in the micro-political contexts of everydayness that the spread of Nazi ideology [will] ultimately be found having – or not having – its effect'.[67] Such conclusions challenge a perhaps reassuring sense that the Nazi dictatorship used propaganda spectacles and overt ideological messages to impose National Socialism on a captive population; rather, the material presented above reveals a nuanced and interactive web of ideological penetration and colonisation, in which small acts took on freighted political meaning. A study focused on Christmas can only go so far in identifying this process, because, after all, it is perforce limited to the weeks of the holiday season. Yet, it reveals dense networks of state institutions, everyday life behaviour and emotional conditioning, involving regime functionaries and ordinary citizens, which were in place throughout the year, albeit under different circumstances. The history of Christmas in the Third Reich suggests that emotional engineering evoked powerful feelings of community integration as well as discontent with the politicisation of everyday life and especially cherished holiday observances. Many Germans were no doubt left in something of an in-between situation, in which they accepted the outward trappings of Nazi celebration but at the same time searched for their own meaning in familiar holiday customs; the Christmas mood both lent itself to Nazi colonisation but also resisted the same.

# Notes

1    The police files of the Staatsarchiv-Munich include a flyer, the report, and 'Die Weihnachtsfeier der Nationalsozialistischen Deutschen Arbeiterpartei München', *Völkischer Beobachter*, 11 January 1922. Staatsarchiv-München,

Polizeidirektion/NS Zeit, 6700 NSDAP 1920–1923. The party was held on 9 January 1922.

2   H. Kremer, 'Neuwertung "überlieferter" Brauchformen?', *Die Neue Gemeinschaft* 3 (1937), p. 3005.

3   For an overview of this newly emerging field and these key concepts, see S. Matt, 'Current Emotion Research in History: Or, Doing History from the Inside Out', *Emotion Review* 3 (January 2011), pp. 117–124. For discussions of emotions in German history, see F. Biess (ed.), 'Forum: History of Emotions', *German History* 28 (March 2010), pp. 67–80; P. Eitler, B. Hitzer and M. Scheer, 'Special Issue: Feeling and Faith – Religious Emotions in German History', *German History* 32 (September 2014), pp. 343–430.

4   I. Kershaw quoted in G. Eley, *Nazism as Fascism: Violence, Ideology, and the Ground of Consent in Germany 1930–1945* (New York, 2013), p. 62.

5   D. Foitzik, *Rote Sterne, braune Runen: Politische Weihnachten zwischen 1879 und 1970* (Münster, 1997), p. 88. On German Christmas in general see J. Perry, *Christmas in Germany: A Cultural History* (Chapel Hill, NC, 2010); on Nazification see J. Perry, 'The Nazification of Christmas: Politics and Popular Celebration in the Third Reich', *Central European History* 38 (December 2005), pp. 572–605.

6   J. Goebbels, 'Bekenntnis zur Kraft, Sinnbild des Glaubens', *NSK (Nationalsozialistische Parteikorrespondenz/Pressedienst der NSDAP)*, 27 December 1935.

7   See D. Bergerson, P. Steege, M. Healy and P. Swett, 'The History of Everyday Life: A Second Chapter', *Journal of Modern History* 27 (June 2008), pp. 358–378.

8   See P. Fritzsche, *Life and Death in the Third Reich* (Cambridge, 2009).

9   J. Marbach, *Die heilige Weihnachtszeit nach Bedeutung, Geschichte, Sitten und Symbolen* (Frankfurt, 1865), p. 123.

10   H. Elm, *Das Goldene Weihnachtsbuch* (Halle, 1878). This impressive book can be downloaded at the website of the Digitale Bibliothek Braunschweig. http://digisrv-1.biblio.etc.tu-bs.de:8080/docportal/receive/DocPortal_document_00000332 [accessed 16 September 2014].

11   'Weihnachtsbetrachtungen', *Vorwärts*, 25 December 1909.

12   See E. Gajek, 'Nationalsozialistische Weihnacht: Die Ideologisierung eines Familienfestes durch Volkskundler', in R. Faber and E. Gajek (eds), *Politische Weihnacht in Antike und Moderne: Zur ideologischen Durchdringung des Fests der Feste* (Würzburg, 1997), pp. 183–215.

13   'Wider das undeutsche Festefeiern', *Völkischer Beobachter*, 24 December 1927.

14   F. Schulze-Langendorff, 'Weihnachtsfeuer Weihnachtsfreude', *Völkischer Beobachter*, 24 December 1927.

15   'Wintersonnenwende – Schicksalwende', *Völkischer Beobachter*, 24 December 1925; 'Weihnacht 1926', *Völkischer Beobachter*, 25/26/27 December 1926.

16   J. Goebbels, 'Weihnachtsbrief 1925', *Völkischer Beobachter*, 25 December 1925.

17 'Sie machen in Weihnachten', *Illustrierter Beobachter*, 7 December 1929, p. 655; 'Weihnachten und Warenhaus-"Zauber"', *Illustrierter Beobachter*, 24 December 1932, pp. 1268–1269.

18 'Wider das undeutsche Festefeiern', *Völkischer Beobachter*, 24 December 1927.

19 See D. Bergen, *The Twisted Cross: The German Christian Movement in the Third Reich* (Chapel Hill, NC, 1996).

20 Quoted in Bergen, *Twisted Cross*, p. 163.

21 W. Bauer, *Feierstunden Deutsche Christen* (Weimar, 1935), pp. 44–48, 200.

22 For an in-depth account of these institutions, see Foitzik, *Rote Sterne*, pp. 92–104.

23 'Weihnachten gehört in die Familie. Weihnachtssinn im nationalsozialistischen Geiste. Gegen die Unsitte vorweihnachtlicher Vereinsfeier', *Völkischer Beobachter*, 24 November 1933.

24 R. von Elmayer-Vestenbrugg, 'Wintersonenwende! Sinn und Brautthum der altgermanischen Weihe-Nacht', *Illustrierter Beobachter*, 17 December 1936, pp. 2138–2140. The briefest review of any mass publication in the Nazi period will turn up many other examples.

25 M. Geyer, 'Germany, or, The Twentieth Century as History', *South Atlantic Quarterly* 96 (Fall 1997), p. 679.

26 Statistics in K. Lacey, *Feminine Frequencies: Gender, German Radio, and the Public Sphere, 1923–1945* (Ann Arbor, MI, 1999), p. 2.

27 Schedule in *Sieben Tage: Funkblätter mit Program*, 19 December 1937.

28 'Weihnachtssbescherung für Berliner Kinder', Deulig – Tonwoche Nr. 209, 30 December 1935, Federal Film Archive (BA-FA) Wochenschauen DTW 209/1935.

29 'Weihachtsvorbereitungen', Ufa – Tonwoche Nr. 224, 19 December 1934, BA-FA Wochenschauen UTW 224/1934.

30 See S. Hall, 'Encoding/Decoding', in T. Corrigan et al. (eds), *Critical Visions in Film Theory* (Boston, MA, 2011), pp. 77–87.

31 Perry, *Christmas*, p. 213.

32 'Das große Weihnachtserlebnis der Limpert-Gefolgschaft Dresden', *Arbeit ist Leben*, 22 January 1937, pp. 9–11, in Federal Archive-Berlin (BAB), NS 5 VI (DAF Clipping file)/17393.

33 O. Zacharias, 'Gestaltungsfragen der Schulweihnachtsfeiern', *Aus der Städtischen Arbeit*, circa December 1938, pp. 895–896, in Central Evangelical Archive (EZA), 7/3199.

34 F. W., 'Elsen und Wichte unter dem Tannenbaum: Eine Mädchen Schule rüstet sich zur Weihnachtsfeier', *Völkischer Beobachter*, 13 December 1936.

35 Examples in EZA 7/2772; 7/3199.

36 Quoted in H. Vorländer, *Die NSV. Darstellung und Dokumentation einer nationalsozialistischen Organisation* (Boppard am Rhein, 1988), p. 369.

37 'Echo der Heimat, Folge 5', 1937, BA-FA Dokumentarfilme 620.

38   V. Klemperer, *The Language of the Third Reich LTI – Lingua Tertii Imperii: A Philologist's Notebook*, trans. Martin Brady (London, 2000), p. 8.

39   *Reichsbefehl der Reichsjugendführung der NSDAP*, 27 November 1936, 'Sonderdruck: Einsatz der Hitler-Jugend für das Winterhilfswerk des Deutschen Volkes 1936/37', BAB, NS 37/1017.

40   'Lage- und Stimmungsbericht des Hauptamtes für Volkswohlfahrt', December 1936 BAB, NS 22/845; 'Rechnenschafts-Bericht, Winterhilfswerk 1935/1936', BAB, NS 22/843.

41   Vorländer, *Die NSV*, p. 186.

42   K. Behnken (ed.), *Deutschland-Berichte der Sozialdemokratischen Partei Deutschlands (Spoade) 1934–1940* (Frankfurt: Petra Nettelbeck Zweitausendeins, vol. 2, 1980), pp. 168–175; quote on p. 168.

43   'Lage- und Stimmungsbericht des Hauptamtes für Volkswohlfahrt', December 1937, BAB, NS 22/845.

44   K. Hirche, *Der 'braune' und der 'rote' Witz* (Düsseldorf, 1964), p. 125.

45   'Germanisches Jul und christliche Weihnachten', *Völkischer Beobachter*, 20 December 1935.

46   'Deutsche Geselligkeit. Vorschläge und Anregungen für die Pflege gutter Gegselligkeit. Weihnacht' (Abteilung Volkstumpflege im Reichsamt für Schulung im Deutschen Handlungsghilfen-Verband, circa 1936).

47   V. Klemperer, *I Will Bear Witness: A Diary of the Nazi Years 1933–1941*, trans. Martin Chalmers (New York, 1998), p. 284.

48   E. Schnidtmann-Leffler, 'Frau und Volkstum, Brauch und Sitte/Eine weihnachtliche Betrachtung', *Deutsche Frauen-Kultur*, December 1934, p. 227.

49   *Vorweihnachtliche Feier* (Amt 'Feierabend' der NS-Gemeinschaft 'Kraft Durch Freude', 1938), pp. 52–53.

50   W. Pudelko, 'Zur Frage des Weihnachtliedes', *Die Musik. Monatschrift*, December 1938, p. 157.

51   I. Weber-Kellermann, *Das Buch der Weihnachtslieder* (Mainz, 1994), pp. 308–310.

52   Quoted in 'Neue Weihnachtslieder?' *Katholisches Wochenblatt*, 10 January 1937.

53   Perry, *Christmas*, pp. 221–224.

54   C. Koonz, *Mothers in the Fatherland: Women, the Family, and Nazi Politics* (New York, 1987), p. 183.

55   'Monatsbericht der Reichsleitung der NSDAP, Reichsfrauenführung/NS.-Frauenschaft', November/December 1936, pp. 2–3, BAB NS 22/924.

56   'Kriegsweihnacht', *Deutsche Wochenschau* no. 539, 2, 1941; 1 January 1941, BA-FA Wochenschauen, DW 539.

57   For holiday publications for soldiers, see Federal Military Archive (BA-MA) RWD 26/1; RHD 53/60.

58   'Richtlinien für die Gestaltung der -sfeiern in der Wehrmacht', 14 December 1939. BAB, NS6/329, pp. 155–157.

59 'Gutachtung über Verantwortung und Möglichkeiten der Kirche für Kriegsweihnachten', 15 October 1939, EZA 7/3199.

60 W. Shirer, *Berlin Diary: The Journal of a Foreign Correspondent 1934–1941* (New York, 1941), p. 263.

61 H. Boberach (ed.), *Meldungen aus dem Reich: Die geheimen Lageberichte des Sicherheitsdienstes der SS, 1933–1944* (Hersching, 1984), p. 4577.

62 Ibid., pp. 4504, 4577.

63 Foitzik, *Rote Sterne*, pp. 124–131.

64 The poem was repeatedly reprinted in War Christmas publications, including the pamphlet H. Liese (ed.), *Licht muß wieder werden* (Munich, circa 1943).

65 Reprinted in J. Breuer and R. Breuer, *Von wegen Heilige Nacht! Das Weihnachtsfest in der politischen Propaganda* (Mülheim an der Ruhr, 2000), p. 74.

66 K. Granzow, *Tagebuch eines Hitlerjungen, 1943–1945* (Bremen, 1965), pp. 139–145.

67 Eley, *Nazism*, p. 66.

# Select bibliography

Bergen, D., *The Twisted Cross: The German Christian Movement in the Third Reich* (Chapel Hill, NC, 1996).

Bergerson, D., Steege, P., Healy, M. and Swett, P., 'The History of Everyday Life: A Second Chapter', *Journal of Modern History* 27 (2008), pp. 358–378.

Eley, G., *Nazism as Fascism: Violence, Ideology and the Ground of Consent in Germany 1930–1945* (New York, 2013).

Faber, R. and Gajek, E. (eds), *Politische Weihnacht in Antike und Moderne: Zue ideologischen Durchdringung des Fests der Feste* (Würzburg, 1997).

Foitzik, D., *Rote Sterne, braune Runen: Politische Weihnachten zwischen 1879 und 1970* (Münster, 1997).

Fritzsche, P., *Life and Death in the Third Reich* (Cambridge, 2009).

Hall, S., 'Encoding/Decoding', in Corrigan, T. et al. (eds), *Critical Visions in Film Theory* (Boston, MA, 2011).

Matt, S., 'Current Emotion Research in History: or, Doing History from the Inside Out', *Emotion Review* 3 (2011), pp. 117–124.

Perry, J., *Christmas in Germany: A Cultural History* (Chapel Hill, NC, 2010).

# INDEX

Note: Locators with 'f' and 'n' denote figures and note numbers.